WITHDRAWN

HARVARD LIBRARY

WITHDRAWN

JEWISH LITERATURES AND CULTURES

Program in Judaic Studies
Brown University
Box 1826
Providence, RI 02912

BROWN JUDAIC STUDIES

Edited by

David C. Jacobson
Ross S. Kraemer
Saul M. Olyan
Michael L. Satlow

Number 349

JEWISH LITERATURES AND CULTURES
Context and Intertext

edited by
Anita Norich and Yaron Z. Eliav

JEWISH LITERATURES AND CULTURES

CONTEXT AND INTERTEXT

Edited by

Anita Norich and Yaron Z. Eliav

Brown Judaic Studies
Providence, Rhode Island

© 2008 Brown University. All rights reserved.

No part of this work may be reproduced or transmitted in any form or by any means, electronic or mechanical, including photocopying and recording, or by means of any information storage or retrieval system, except as may be expressly permitted by the 1976 Copyright Act or in writing from the publisher. Requests for permission should be addressed in writing to the Rights and Permissions Office, Program in Judaic Studies, Brown University, Box 1826, Providence, RI 02912, USA.

Library of Congress Cataloging-in-Publication Data

Jewish literatures and cultures : context and intertext / edited by Anita Norich and Yaron Z. Eliav.
     p. cm.—(Brown Judaic studies ; no. 349)
  "Most of the essays . . . emerged from a conference held at the University of Michigan's Frankel Center for Judaic Studies"—Introduction.
  Includes bibliographical references and index.
  ISBN 978-1-930675-55-1 (cloth : alk. paper)
  1. Judaism—20th century—Congresses. 2. Judaism and culture—Congresses. 3. Religion and culture—Congresses. 4. Judaism—History—Modern period, 1750—Congresses. 5. Secularism—Congresses. 6. Jews—Identity—Congresses. 7. Jewish literature—History and criticism—Congresses. I. Norich, Anita, 1952- II. Eliav, Yaron Z. III. Title. IV. Series.

BM565.J49 2008
296.09—dc22

                                                                  2008016542

Printed in the United States of America
on acid-free paper

This book is dedicated to the Frankel family
whose generosity and passion make it possible for their
descendants and ours to flourish
in all the languages, cultures, and histories
of the Jews.

בינו שנות דור ודור (דברים לב, ז)

Contemplate the Wisdom of the Generations

Contents

Acknowledgments ix

Abbreviations xi

Introduction
- Jewish Literatures and Cultures: Context and Intertext
  Anita Norich 1

Opening Essay
- From Continuity to Contiguity: Thoughts on the Theory of Jewish Literature
  Dan Miron 9

Articles

1 • Beyond Influence: Toward a New Historiographic Paradigm
   Michael L. Satlow 37

2 • Hellenistic Judaism: Myth or Reality?
   Gabriele Boccaccini 55

3 • "He Was Renowned to the Ends of the Earth"
   (1 Maccabees 3:9): Judaism and Hellenism in 1 Maccabees
   Martha Himmelfarb 77

4 • Roman Statues, Rabbis, and Greco-Roman Culture
   Yaron Z. Eliav 99

5 • The Ghetto and Jewish Cultural Formation in Early Modern Europe: Towards a New Interpretation
   David B. Ruderman 117

6 • Hybrid with What? The Variable Contexts of Polish Jewish
Culture: Their Implications for Jewish Cultural History
and Jewish Studies
Moshe Rosman 129

7 • Idols of the Cave and Theater: A Verbal or Visual Judaism?
Kalman P. Bland 155

8 • "Reverse Marranism," Translatability, and the Theory and
Practice of Secular Jewish Culture in Russian
Gabriella Safran 177

9 • Intertextuality, Rabbinic Literature, and
the Making of Hebrew Modernism
Shachar Pinsker 201

10 • Brooklyn Am Rhein?: The German Sources of
Jewish American Literature
Julian Levinson 229

11 • Diaspora and Translation: The Migrations of
Jewish Meaning
Naomi Seidman 245

Authors' Biographical Information 259

Acknowledgments

We wish to express our gratitude to the Jean and Samuel Frankel Center for Judaic Studies at the University of Michigan. The Frankel Center sponsored a conference entitled "Jewish Literatures and Cultures: Context and Intertext," and then helped bring this volume to completion. We are honored to express our debt to the Frankel family, whose vision, friendship, and support have allowed us to carry out our work for so many years. This book represents the fruits of their labor as much as of ours.

We thank all the participants who attended the conference and also those who submitted essays based on the papers they presented, as well as those who did not speak at the conference but who have contributed articles to this volume. In preparing the book for publication, we benefited from the editorial assistance of David Lobenstine and Jason Von Ehrenkrook. Matt Weingarden's invaluable assistance and expertise shepherded this book through its final stages. We thank Brown Judaic Studies and the anonymous readers whose insightful comments helped shape the final version of this book.

Yaron Eliav
Anita Norich
Ann Arbor, October 3, 2006

Abbreviations

AB	Anchor Bible
ABD	*Anchor Bible Dictionary*, ed. David Noel Freedman. 6 vols. New York: Doubleday, 1992.
AHR	*American Historical Review*
AJS Review	*Association for Jewish Studies Review*
ANF	*Ante-Nicene Fathers*
ANRW	*Aufstieg und Niedergang der römischen Welt: Geschichte und Kultur Roms im Spiegel der neueren Forschung*, ed. H. Temporini and W. Haase. Berlin: de Gruyter, 1972–.
BO	*Bibliotheca orientalis*
BJS	Brown Judaic Studies
CII	*Corpus inscriptionum iudaicarum*, ed. J. B. Frey. 2 vols. Rome: Pontificio istituto di archeologia christiana, 1936–52.
CP	*Classical Philology*
DOP	*Dumbarton Oaks Papers*
HTR	*Harvard Theological Review*
JJS	*Journal of Jewish Studies*
JQR	*Jewish Quarterly Review*
JR	*Journal of Religion*
JRS	*Journal of Roman Studies*
JSJ	*Journal for the Study of Judaism*
JSOTSup	Journal for the Study of the Old Testament Supplement Series
JTS	*Journal of Theological Studies*
LCL	Loeb Classical Library
PW	A. F. Pauly, *Paulys Realencyclopädie der classischen Altertumswissenschaft*. New Edition G. Wissowa. 49 vols. Munich: A. Druckenmüller, 1980.
OTP	*Old Testament Pseudepigrapha*, ed. James H. Charlesworth. 2 vols. New York: Doubleday, 1983.
SBLDS	Society of Biblical Literature Dissertation Series
SUNT	Studien zur Umwelt des Neuen Testaments
TWNT	*Theologische Wörterbuch zum Neuen Testament*, ed. G. Kittel and G. Friedrich. Stuttgart: Kohlhammer, 1932–79.

Introduction

Jewish Literatures and Cultures

Context and Intertext

ANITA NORICH
University of Michigan

The essays in this volume enter into current scholarly conversations in Judaic studies that view it as an interdisciplinary, multilingual, transhistorical field. In varying ways, the authors argue that Jewish culture has always developed alongside *and* inside a wider, non-Jewish world and that, nonetheless, for all the diversity within and among Jewish communities, there is such a thing as Jewish culture and Jewish particularity. In broad methodological considerations and in specific case studies, the authors examine the ways in which Jewish culture has always taken place in a mutually enriching, if sometimes problematic, relationship with surrounding non-Jewish cultures.

Most of the essays that follow emerged from a conference held at the University of Michigan's Frankel Center for Judaic Studies. Organized by Todd Endelman, Yaron Eliav, and Anita Norich, the conference bore the title of this volume. In our invitations to speakers, we wrote the following guiding principle:

> One of the hallmarks of contemporary Judaica scholarship is its insistence on the close links between Jewish cultural life—at all times and in all places—and the larger world in which Jews lived. Whereas earlier generations of Jewish scholars often assumed that 'traditional' Jews lived in cultural isolation from the Gentile world and that Jewish culture was autonomous, recent scholarship has emphasized the contrary—its embeddedness in and indebtedness to surrounding cultures. At the same time, different linguistic expressions of Jewish culture (most famously, Hebrew and Yiddish) have related to, borrowed from, and reinterpreted each other.

The conference was dedicated to exploring these currents in Jewish scholarship, as do the multiple examples contained in these essays.

Some readers may seek a more decisive answer to the question of what unites the Jews rather than what differentiates them from one another. This volume, indeed, does not offer a definitive response to that question. Instead, it offers nuanced examinations of particular historical periods, places, languages, and beliefs that have shaped Jewish culture—whether understood in the singular or the plural—through the millennia. It neither adjudicates among the various contenders for what is essential to Jewish culture—for example, religious practice or belief, a canon of texts, land, language—nor does it seek to deny that such contenders matter deeply. It takes seriously Judaism's endless debates over how to define the essence of its culture and seeks to clarify the ramifications of claiming one element rather than another. Primarily, these essays situate the "essences" of Jewishness in the contexts from which they have emerged.

Judaic studies, Jewish *Wissenschaft*, as a mode of study is a modern phenomenon, although the study of Judaism certainly is not. Rather than declaring independence from earlier Jewish scholarship, many of the essays in this volume embrace the methodologies, conclusions, and questions that have preceded them, while bringing to the fore more recent scholarly trends. In doing so, this book addresses those already in the burgeoning field of Judaic studies and those—scholars and other readers—to whom the languages and histories of the Jews may be less familiar. Its essays are paradigmatic of the kinds of connections and exchanges that have always been the mark of Jewish culture: using the vocabulary and conceptual frameworks of the present, considering the languages, texts, and histories of the Jewish past, and relying on both Jewish and non-Jewish sources. Through this amalgam, Jewish culture exemplifies the study of "thick culture," of how and where Jews have lived, how they have conceived of their culture, what they have thought and produced at particular times and in particular places.

These essays underscore both the contexts in which Jewish culture has been produced and the texts with which it has been in dialogue. This volume also urges readers to consider "text" in broader terms, to include not only written materials but also other works of art, other material and spiritual creations produced over millennia. In short, these essays attest to the need for a more finely textured view of Jewish culture, one in which "text" is returned to its etymological roots, linked not only to writing but also to texture and textile, to something that is woven.

The mistaken belief that there is some monolithic entity we may call "traditional" Judaism or "traditional" Jewish society is surprisingly tenacious, despite the abundance of scholarly material challenging it. The mythic view of traditional Judaism—mythic in the sense that it is a long-lasting, powerful story of origins rather than a historical account—clings to the idea that Jews in some premodern periods were more unified and similar than they have become. It imagines a world in which Jews were ghettoized—literally or figuratively—but were also more autonomous, somehow purer, less tainted by the assimilation and acculturation that are often believed to have begun with the Enlightenment and culminated in American suburbs. This volume counters that idea. *Jewish Literatures and Cultures* forces us to question, yet again, what we can mean by the notion of a "normative Judaism." It does not, for the most part, focus on populations generally considered liminal—conversos, Falashas, the Jews of Kochin, B'ney Yisrael, modern or ancient Canaanites, and so on—all of them, to be sure, significant for a more nuanced understanding of Judaism. Instead it ranges in time and place to consider those whose Jewish identities are undisputed, but who nonetheless differ from one another in noteworthy ways. In doing so, this volume does not purport to adjudicate among them, but it does argue that all have made vital, if not always recognized, contributions to the rich spectrum of Jewish culture.

Reflections about what constitutes Jewish identity and Jewish culture are often mapped onto a series of Venn diagrams where hyphens meet or opposites are presumed to be clearly visible. Jewish-American or German-Jewish (note the different order of words) may suggest the possibilities of integration, of making a new identity out of two different ones. Hebraism and Hellenism are usually understood (and not just by Matthew Arnold) as coterminous but opposite. There are, of course, Jewish versions of the more general tensions understood in the dialectics between the universal and the particular; influence and originality; the collective or the individual; secular or religious. The Jews are often considered to have a particular relationship to time, but not to place, a belief that Zionism in particular has vigorously countered. Moreover, increasingly, concepts and terminology that have long been part of the study of Jews—exile/Diaspora vs. home/Zion, for example—have permeated intellectual and cultural discussions more widely. To consider culture in these or similar dialectical terms is to strive for some kind of unified, and therefore reductive, synthesis; the result, almost invariably, is to flatten and simplify the incredible complexities of reality. The authors of this volume all demonstrate that the creation of culture has always been more dynamic and multidimensional than such oppositions would suggest.

We have all become better attuned to the oftentimes anachronistic uses of such terms as "assimilation" and "acculturation," as well as equally problematic understandings of secularism, the family, the self, and, in particular, identity, the most contemporary term of them all. The significance of such foundational terms changes over time and across cultures. As a result, the ultimate meaning of "Jewish culture" grows more complex and seems more fragmented the more one explores it. This makes the search for Jewish continuity through the ages all the more urgent. And it helps explain the earnest yearning for a more-or-less linear, organic wholeness connecting Jews not only to their surroundings synchronically but to one another diachronically

Many have found that continuity not in place or language or even practices and beliefs, but rather in the famous textuality of the Jews, in their readings of the Bible and, even more, in the wranglings of the Talmud(s) and in the hermeneutic tradition they instantiated. Even here, of course, we encounter the inevitability of the plural in our discussions of Jews and Judaism. Just as we must take into account the existence of two Talmuds, so must we acknowledge the multiplicity of cultural and historical forms that Jews have always lived and created. There is one written law, but two so-called oral traditions—the Bavli (Babylonian) and Yerushalmi (Palestinian) Talmuds—developed in different places and subject to different influences. Yet no one denies the legitimacy of each or each one's significance for the development of Judaism. And they are only two prime examples out of many. To them we may add the literature lost and then found in Qumran; and perhaps the Hellenistic Jewish tradition embedded in what later became Christianity; and any number of other ancient texts and traditions. Nor, of course, is the rabbinic tradition the only one followed by Jews. It is, in any case, worth recalling that many, even most, Jews in premodern times as in modern times have had very little serious engagement with the texts of Judaism and that this has never been a necessary or defining feature of Jewish engagement.

The beginnings of the twenty-first century have been marked by the ascendance of two prefixes: the first is "multi" (as in multiculturalism and multilingualism); the second is the much-used and much-derided "post" (as in post-modernism, post-Zionism, post-structuralism, post-capitalism, and so on). We are not yet at the "post-multi" era, but that cannot be too far away. Between multiculturalism and post-modernism or post-traditionalism, is there any room for a discussion of Jewish cultures? This volume asserts that there is, that Jewish cultures are not only part of this discussion, but may illuminate it. If by multiculturalism we mean the relationships among a wide range of diverse, distinct cultural influences in which something new is created, then Jews may well offer a paradigmatic example of this process. Jews have always been part of a multilinguistic universe, always lived among others, always interacted with other religions and other peoples. The cumulative evidence of these essays suggests that Jewish culture may offer us the strongest proof of the viability and comparative strength of multiculturalism—not only in the postmodern era, but throughout time.

With the exception of Dan Miron's opening essay, which invokes many of the authors, texts, and concerns in the pages that follow, the essays in the book develop chronologically. There are, to be sure, enormous gaps in that chronology; there has been no attempt to be all-inclusive either geographically or historically, but rather to highlight new insights into recurring tropes and particular conditions of production, reception, and imagination. The focus in these essays is primarily European and American, with the exception of the essays dealing with the ancient world, which naturally focus on Palestine and other places in the Near East (such as Egypt and Persia). Within those confines, a number of terms and concepts reappear in many of these essays, underscoring the scholarly interest in certain contemporary methodologies and topics. "Diversity" and "complexity" are certainly two of those, along with "translation," "textuality," and "intertextuality." For Michael Satlow and David Ruderman "syncretism" is central. Finding his object of study in Jews rather than Judaism, Michael Satlow underscores the fluidity of Jewish identity even in (or perhaps we should say "especially in") antiquity. David Ruderman examines Venice and the transnational Jewish culture that was prevalent in early modern Europe. His work expands our understanding of the medieval Italian ghetto, putting to rest the belief that it was isolated or effectively severed from the rest of the world.

Martha Himmelfarb and Gabrielle Boccaccini turn to Hellenism and to texts that show other ancient and very fluid Jewish cultural formations. Martha Himmelfarb offers a reading of 1 Maccabees that rejects the view of that text as a battle between Greek and Jewish values and sees it, instead, as illustrating precisely the opposite: the cultural synthesis that the Hasmoneans achieved. Gabrielle Boccaccini examines the figure of Wisdom in Hellenic and various forms of Jewish thought in order to illustrate the ways in which such figures could be adapted, and new cultures thus produced.

Objecting to the "textification of Judaism"—the view that the written texts of the Jews take precedence over all other cultural expressions—Kalman Bland refocuses the discussion on the visual arts and Jewish artists. He reminds us that the second commandment (against making graven images) is not a Jewish injunction against the visual but rather a warning against idolatry. Yaron Eliav also turns our gaze to the visual as well as material culture by examining ancient statuary. In doing so, he considers the ways in which the rabbis distinguished between statues that might be regarded as graven images, meant to be worshiped, and those that lacked the ritual aspect and functioned on many other levels of ancient society (e.g., as displays of historical heritage, political power, and social hierarchy).

All of these essays show the intimate connections between the Jewish world and the non-Jewish world in the ancient and the early modern periods. Examining such connections is, of course, a staple of scholarship concerning modern, post-Enlightenment Jews. And this connective impulse is at the very core of postmodern scholarship, with its resistance to hegemony, unitary cultures, and the notion of organic, linear development. The messiness—another word for fluidity and complexity—of Jewish culture and identity in every period is a cause for celebration in many of these essays. Dan Miron's opening essay offers a different way of framing the discussion. Whether considering Hebrew, or Hebrew and Yiddish, or other languages in which Jews have written, he urges us to shift away from a model that sees Jewish culture in terms of continuity and to understand it in terms of contiguity instead. While acknowledging many points of contact between Jewish and non-Jewish cultures and, in particular, within Jewish literatures, Dan Miron refuses any attempt to establish hierarchies among them. Taking up the problem of hierarchies from a different perspective, Moshe Rosman examines Polish-Jewish history and historiography and concludes with a critique of hybridity, showing how it fails as a useful theoretical term when applied to the Jews. The alternative to hybridity theories is not an insistence on Jewish cultural autonomy, he reminds us, but rather a consideration of both Polish and Jewish cultures as polysystems, dynamic and heterogeneous. Furthermore, his essay challenges scholars to look not only at the interdependent paradigms of cultures in contact, but also at their independent structures, their autonomy from one another and the different internal dynamics they each may follow.

Intertextuality is another central theme in several of these essays, asking us to look beyond questions of influence and derivation to a more dynamic understanding of cultural contacts. Shachar Pinsker returns us to midrashic and rabbinic texts, and identifies within this religious canon the intertextual sources of modernist Hebrew writing. Julian Levinson proposes yet another intertext: that of German Jewish sources. Tracing the influence of German culture, he challenges the central role of Yiddish as the authentic precursor of modern Jewish American literature.

The question of translation remains inescapable to a robust understanding of Jewish culture. In considering the complicated compositional history and reception of Sh. An-sky's play *Der dybbuk*, Gabriella Safran analyzes the possibilities of cultural translatability—among Russian, Yiddish, Hebrew, and other languages, between Jews and non-Jews. Translation—as the act of carrying one culture over and into another—is an impossible task, and yet it is precisely the task scholars set for themselves. In that sense, every one of these essays may be considered an act of translation, raising a similar set of concerns. In thus translating, what is lost along the way? What is deliberately dropped because it will be of no use in the new context? What is carried from one circumstance to another, from one century to another, and how? When and where does the comforting shock of recognition, of similarity, of familiarity, occur? In retelling a story about her father's canny use of Yiddish in France, Naomi Seidman shows us not only the cultural gap between Yiddish and French but also her father's ability to use both effectively, to say what each listener needed to hear and could understand.

The story attests to a particular kind of intimacy with the subtleties of different languages and cultures. All the essays in *Jewish Literatures and Cultures* spring from this intimate engagement with culture, from a devotion to its subtleties. And so, these essays rely on a deep knowledge and sympathy with the sometimes parallel, sometimes interweaving forms integral to each culture, and they understand the ways in which something new is produced as a result. That, indeed, is an excellent model for students, teachers, and scholars alike to emulate.

Opening Essay

From Continuity to Contiguity

*Thoughts on the Theory of Jewish Literature**

DAN MIRON

I

For almost forty years now, since the advent of the so-called Tel Aviv School of structuralist poetics as a dominant force in Hebrew literary studies, we have come to view all earlier study of Jewish (and particularly Hebrew) literature as devoid of a theoretical component. While ancient and medieval Hebrew literature, we believe, was thought about mainly on a philological level, the so-called modern or new literature of the last two centuries was studied either by impressionist critics or by bio-bibliographical scholars. At best, we think, it was studied not as literature but rather historically, as sets of documents illustrating the development of social and political movements such as the Jewish Enlightenment or Zionism.

This view, both patronizing and uninformed, is not borne out by the historical facts. Modern Jewish literature in general and Hebrew literature in particular had been studied with seriousness and significance since the emergence of this field in the 1890s. This scholarship continued, unabated, throughout the first half of the twentieth century. These studies, anchored at first in late-nineteenth-century positivistic concepts of literary development and influence, eventually absorbed characteristic twentieth-century approaches, such as Wilhelm Dilthey's poetics of *Erlebnis*, or the *Gehalt und Gestalt* approach of Oskar Walzel. The influence of other influential

---

* This essay offers a broad view of its subject, based on understanding culled from hundreds of texts. It cannot support the weight of the abundance of footnotes that it might normally have called for and I have therefore chosen to present it to the informed reader as is.

German scholars of the Weimar Republic decade can be detected in Hebrew criticism and literary scholarship of the 1930s and 1940s. Marxist dialectics as it was applied to the study of literature both inside and outside of the Soviet Union was introduced to Hebrew literary studies at the same time, as was the Freudian interpretive methodology based on the understanding of art as sublimated psychic conflicts.

It is true that these literary scholars usually avoided focusing on a general theoretical or methodological issue, and they often shunned—both in their theoretical thinking and as interpreters or historians of literature—formalist tendencies. However, this avoidance was not due to a resistance to theory in the name of either historical factuality or textual specificity. Nor was it due to sheer lack of theoretical acumen and subtlety. Scholars such as Dov Sadan, Meir Viner or Hayim Nahman Shapiro, to name but a few, were as theoretically savvy as any latter-day structuralist. Rather, this partial evasion of abstract, conceptualized theoretical argument in general and a formalist one in particular resulted from the pre–World War II cultural situation (and in the case of Hebrew scholarship, the pre-Israeli one). This cultural atmosphere so radically changed during the second half of the twentieth century that it is barely understandable to us at the beginning of the twenty-first century.

The cultural situation—or perhaps more aptly, condition— of the early twentieth century possessed at least three dimensions that we, for better or worse, have all but lost sight of:

1. All Jewish literary scholars during the first half of the twentieth century, as well as most of those who read and used their works, were not only multilingual but also multicultural. Not only could they speak, read, and write in at least two or three European languages (most prominently Russian and German); they were also fully acquainted with the respective cultures and literatures that had been created by the people who spoke these languages. Indeed, in many cases they related to these literatures and cultures with the intimacy of native sons, feeling at home in them as much and perhaps more than they felt with regard to their own. Thus, these scholars and many of their readers, fully or at least partly abreast of current trends in European literary scholarship, felt no need to reproduce in Hebrew or Yiddish the theoretical and methodological arguments that were easily accessible in their original Russian or German formulations.

2. As much as Jewish literature itself evolved at the time as part of a national cultural revolution—which set for itself no lesser aim than to replace the religious-rabbinical Jewish cultural

tradition with a new, secular Jewish culture—literary scholarship was also informed and guided by the precepts of the new Jewish nationhood. It therefore tended to focus theoretically, as well as practically, on issues pertaining to the national aspects of literature and to the specifics of the Jewish literary situation. This rendered generalized theoretical discussion relatively uninteresting, and as a matter of course, made any theoretical concept that predicated the separation of literature from societal and national concerns all but untenable. Thus, scholars who, as avid readers of Russian literature and literary criticism, were aware of formalism and its basic theoretical concepts had limited, if any, use for it either as practicing critics or as literary historians.

3. During the time under discussion, the new Jewish culture was created against a background rife with ideological rivalries and stormy polemics. This new culture was thus forced not only to choose its specific linguistic matrix—Hebrew, Yiddish, and any of the European languages Jews employed for the purposes of enhancing their cultural identity, such as Russian, German and English—but also to further choose from among the ideologies embedded within each language. For instance, those who believed that modern Jewish culture and literature should be developed in Yiddish, had to align themselves either with the belief that Yiddish was the core of a secular-national culture (which transcended class struggle), or as inherently tied to the struggle of the Jewish proletariat (and therefore a part of the supra-national culture of international socialism). The choice of Hebrew, although it more or less aligned itself with the Zionist project, nevertheless necessitated a further choice among any number of Zionist cultural options: from the religious Zionism of Rabbi Abraham Isaac Kook to the blatant atheism of Hashomer Hatsair, or from the proto-fascism of Uri Zvi Greenberg to the communism of Alexander Pen.

Against this background of fiercely competitive ideological options literary scholars could hardly go about their business in the calm mood of disinterested observers and commentators. Often they were called upon to tell not only what literature was like but also what it should be. For such scholarly figures as Yosef Klausner, Max Weinreich, Shmuel Niger and Dov Sadan, cultural prognosis was every bit as important as critical and historical analysis. While all literary scholarship is ideologically conditioned—and theory perhaps reveals ideological biases most clearly—the kind of ideological warfare Jewish literary scholars waged throughout the first half of the twentieth century left little, if any, room for rarified theoretical arguments.

Thus, we can argue that Jewish literary scholarship of the first half of the twentieth century evaded one type of literary theory in order to indulge in another. Its chief proponents did not question the nature of the literary text or inquire after the universal dynamics of literary development. Their scholarly practice was, of course, based on assumptions and presuppositions about these issues, but they focused on a theoretical area that seemed more relevant and pressing in light of the substantial cultural pressures surrounding them. They felt they had to focus not on the theory of literature per se, but rather on a theory of Jewish literature, on a conceptual system that would delineate and elucidate the specific nature of the Jewish literary complex and its cultural-national ramifications. Over time, this meta-criticism or theory of Jewish literature gradually evolved in seminal essays written by at least a dozen of the more prominent critics and literary historians of the era.

These efforts at theory began sporadically in the 1880s and 1890s, exemplified by Ahad Ha'am's seminal essay *Halashon vesifruta* (Language and Its Literature), or Sholem Aleichem's theories of the Jewish novel. The work took roots in the decade before Word War I, in Haim Nahman Bialik's essay *Shiratenu hatseira* (Our Young Poetry) and his 1914 lectures on the nature and development of Hebrew poetry, in David Frishman's *Mikhtavim al devar hasifrut* (Letters Dealing with Literature), or in the well-known essay by the Yiddish-Hebrew critic Isidor Elyashiv (known by the penname *Bal Makhshoves*) on the unity of a Jewish literature written in both Hebrew and Yiddish. The theoretical argument became more complex and polemical during the 1920s and the 1930s, as it evolved in different and contradictory directions through the work of critics and scholars such as Shmuel Niger, Max Erik, Meir Viner, Fishl Lakhover, Kh. N. Shapiro, Yaakov Rabinovitsh, and Eliezer Shteynman. These ideas culminated in two extensive essays: one by Dov Sadan (*Al sifrutenu: masat mavo*—On Our Literature: An Introductory Essay) and another by Baruch Kurzweil (*Beayot yesod shel sifrutenu*—Fundamental Problems of Our Literature), both published around 1950, against the significant backdrop of a nascent Israel.

Then this kind of meta-literary discourse all but disappeared. Changing cultural circumstances seemed to render it and the issues it addressed irrelevant; and eventually the scholarship became incomprehensible to a new literary intelligentsia, whose background and concerns were very different from those we have just described. Most members of this new intelligentsia (mainly its Israeli contingent) were monolingual and fed up with nationalistic ideologies. Many felt that the crisis of Jewish secular identity was over, because of the elimination of European Jewry by the Holocaust, on the one hand, and the foundation of the state of Israel, on the other.

Issues such as the possible unity of a literature written in several languages were all but meaningless to these scholars, since they did not—indeed, could not—read the works of Jewish writers written in "foreign" languages.

Thus, the stage was set for the emergence of a new kind of literary theory. It would not be a theory of what was different in Jewish literature, but rather a general literary theory illustrated by Hebrew texts simply because they were relatively known and could be directly experienced as literary constructions. The concerns and achievements of an erstwhile theory of Jewish literature were buried under a new theory of literature—which took for granted or was indifferent to the Jewish origin and character of the textual corpus on which it based itself.

I believe the time has come for a reversal of this "progress." The need for such a reversal has been with us for quite a long period, perhaps a full decade or even two. The circumstances that in the 1960s rendered inevitable the shift from a theory of Jewish literature to a general literary theory have long disappeared. On the one hand, the intellectual and theoretical climate that necessitated the adoption of structuralism, with its universally applicable rules, has drastically changed. On the other hand, and perhaps most importantly, Jewish self-awareness has outgrown the illusion of normalcy that the foundation of the state of Israel and its astounding military and social achievements during the 1950s and 1960s inculcated both inside Israel and, to a considerable degree, beyond.

Unlike structuralism, the complex of current poststructuralist literary-theoretical approaches seems widely open to issues arising from historical, cultural, and ideological differentiations. Indeed, such differentiations are at the very center of today's minority discourse, postcolonial and gender-related theories. The conceptual framework, terminology, and philosophical origins of these theories are, of course, entirely different from those that informed the work of scholars sixty or seventy years ago. Nevertheless, the questions asked decades ago, by everyone from Shapiro to Sadan, strike me as very contemporary. These include: What kind of literature could Jews as a political and cultural minority create? How could Hebrew, as a de-territorialized, anagogic language, function as the vehicle for a secular, modern literature? What could have been the dynamics of the relationships between Hebrew literature and the literatures of other Jewish languages, from Aramaic to Ladino to Judeo Persian? What could a modern literature, propelled by ideological fiat and written without a living, spoken idiom, accomplish?

We know now that a normalized secular Jewish identity has never been anything but an illusion. Of all the promises Zionism made, this one—the promise to free modern, posttraditional Jewry from the burden of that haunting question, what is a Jew?—was the one least kept. Now that the euphoria of the first decades following Jewish political independence has all but dissipated, we know that the identification of nationhood with statehood was untenable, a cultural impasse. The existence of Israel, essential as it is, does not solve the existential—let alone the cultural—problems Jews as a stateless collective had faced. Anti-Semitism has not disappeared as the founding fathers of Zionism predicted, but rather changed foci and rephrased its rationalizations. Similarly, the fractured identity of modern Jews, both inside and outside of Israel, did not heal and become the unproblematic, intuitively experienced state of mental well-being it was supposed to become. (Indeed, we doubt now that this romantic ideal of organic collectivism is even possible.)

The existence of the Jewish state, instead of lessening tensions between the various brands of Judaism, traditional and modern alike, has exacerbated them, triggering crises within Israel as well as between Israel and the Diaspora. These conflicts have already given rise to a renewed quest for a deeper, more intellectually convincing sense of collective identity on the part of, as Alain Finkielkraut put it, imaginary Jews (*juifes imaginaries*)—that is, Jews who seek a Judaism that has yet to become an authentic and truly experienced reality. In this quest, the concept of a Jewish literature must be reproblematized (as current theoretical jargon would have it)—and so we need a new, or renewed, theory of Jewish literature.

To fill this need, we should, I think, return to the all-but-forgotten theory of Jewish literature of the first half of the twentieth century. We must ask ourselves what it ultimately was about and uncover what the needs were that propelled it, and the import of the questions that obsessed its creators. We will then know which, if any, of these needs and questions still concern us today; and which, if any, of the solutions our forefathers found for (still pressing) problems can help us in our ongoing search.

II

We should start by reemphasizing a point that has already been made. The old theory, like much of the literature out of which it grew, was the product of a revolutionary crisis. Modern Jews might have left behind traditional Jewish society with its religious ethos, but they would not part with their sense of collective separateness and cultural cohesion; they forged new concepts of Jewishness, and strove to realize these ideals in new brands of Jewish culture distinct from that of their parents and traditional Jewish communities. We should by no means simplify, and thus falsify, the traditional world these new Jews had left: that world was neither monolithic nor undifferentiated. The best modern Jewish historians have shown us how complex, sometimes self-contradictory, and open to destabilizing currents many traditional Jewish societies have been. Nevertheless, to those who left them, the chasm between themselves and these societies seemed not only wider than the divisions between the warring factions within the community (the tensions between the Mitnagdim and Hasidim is one among many examples), but also of a different order. The individualistic Jews who had forsaken communal Jewish life represented something new, and the culture and literature they created were new Jewish cultures and literatures, differing from everything that had preceded them.

We cannot address here the interesting questions of when this sense of radical newness found its first expressions, and in what terms it was defined by its early exponents. But what is more important for our purposes is the effect of this development. These new Jewish cultures, and new literatures, initiated a self-awareness that would eventually develop into a full-fledged conceptualization of the self as different, as an other. What we have described as the theory of Jewish literature was a direct, albeit not immediate, product of this notion of the self as an *alter ego*.

Emerging from a deep sense of difference and cleavage with the past, the theory of Jewish literature was obsessed with the concepts of continuity and integrity. The theorists conceived of both continuity and integrity in terms of time and space, or rather in terms both vertical and horizontal. To scholars who focused on modern Hebrew literature, such as Yosef Klausner, Fishl Lakhover, Hayim Nahman Shapiro, and particularly Baruch Kurzweil, the problems of continuity and integrity presented themselves mainly in their vertical dimension. For critics and scholars who were mainly interested in Yiddish literature, such as Bal Makhshoves and Shmuel Niger, the horizontal dimension seemed of paramount significance. Dov Sadan, whose scholarly interest was divided (albeit unequally) between the two literatures, and whose erudition encompassed both in their historical totality, conceived of the theory of Jewish literature in terms both vertical and horizontal. This is one among many justifications for viewing his theoretical work as the very apex of the meta-literature under discussion here.

Considered vertically, or across the span of time, the problem of continuity in Jewish literature led critics to ask questions such as the following: Could the rich but often interrupted flow of Jewish writing since biblical times be viewed as one continuous literature unified by any inherent common denominator? Could even the Hebrew component in this bewildering literary complex be regarded as continuous and unified? Is there, in fact, one Hebrew literature? If what we call Hebrew poetry encompasses the Psalms, the Song of Solomon, the Palestinian Piyut of Yosey and Hakilir, the wine and love poetry of Moshe Ben Ezra and Yehuda Halevi, the sonnets of Immanuel of Rome, the poetic dramas of Moshe Luzzatto, the didactic and satirical poems of the exponents of the Hebrew Enlightenment such as Yehuda Leyb Gordon, and the personal and nationalistic lyrical poetry of Bialik, Tshernihovsky and the other bards of the Zionist Renaissance—if all these go under the title Hebrew poetry does that title retain the sense we can ascribe to English poetry as it has evolved from Chaucer to the present or to the continuity of French poetry from the Middle Ages to the Symbolists? Clearly, some parts of this alleged continuum have nothing to do with the others. The Piyut, for example, seems to belong in a linguistic sphere all by itself and is essentially not related either to biblical or to modern Hebrew poetry. And Jewish poetry, if such a thing exists, was written not only in Hebrew but also in Aramaic (by the Kabbalists), Judeo Arabic, Judeo Persian, Ladino, Italian, German, Russian, English and French and, of course, Yiddish. Would it then not be more true to the historical reality to assume that the complex of Jewish writing in fact produced not a literature but rather several literatures separated from each other by both time and place? Would it not be more honest to relate to biblical literature, for instance, as a totally separate and autonomous literary complex that flourished, developed, went into decline, and finally petered out rather like its ancient Greek counterpart? Does biblical literature belong with the later literary developments it nourished—both Jewish and non-Jewish—no less but also no more than the Homeric epics belong with their many imitations in all European languages, including modern Greek?

Such questions could be asked with regard to all eras and areas of Jewish literary creativity: the Bible, the Mishnah, the Talmud, the Kabbalah, medieval and renaissance Jewish writing in a host of languages, rabbinic and Hasidic literatures, and so on. But of course they emanated primarily from the dynamics of Jewish modernism, which paradoxically emphasized newness and at the same time engendered the anxiety of discontinuity.

Dissociating themselves and their literature from the so-called old or traditional literary culture (which sometimes, as in the case of Hasidism, was as young and innovative as modernism itself), the moderns also anxiously insisted that they were a new branch growing from the old trunk. Rejecting one past, they were quick to ground themselves in another. The search for vertical continuity was therefore informed by both the verve and the nervousness of the revolutionary who at one and the same time proclaimed his independence of the past but also his legitimacy as the heir of that past. The bravura was fraught from the start with the angst of illegitimacy.

The horizontal aspect of the problem of continuity was equally deeply imbued with the hopes and fears inherent in the revolutionary modern Jewish condition. These concerns could, of course, be projected onto the past. It is difficult to find any unifying principle in Jewish literary products of any given epoch within the last millennium. It is easy to doubt the coherence of a literature that encompassed the following: Maimonides' philosophical-rationalist masterpiece *The Guide to the Perplexed*, written in the highly conceptualized language of the Arabic Aristotelian philosophers; Moshe de Leon's *Sefer hazohar* (The Book of Splendor), the quintessential Jewish mystical midrash, written in the fourteenth century in a fabricated Aramaic and presented as the creation of the second century C.E. *tanna* Shimon Bar-Yohai; Al-Harizi's *Sefer takhkemoni* (Book of the Wise One), the collection of mundane and sensual novellas written in rhyming prose; Moshe Ibn Ezra's florid homosexual love poetry, written in medieval Spanish Hebrew but based on Arabic court poetry

Not only were these written in five different languages and within unrelated intellectual frames of reference, but each of these works was also distanced from some of the others by deep ideational rifts. To the followers of Maimonides, de Leon's mysticism was nonsensical and subversive, characterized by gross, all but pagan mythologization and sexualization of the Jewish deity. The Kabbalists viewed Maimonides' rationalism as heretical, or at least as deaf to the inner significance of the Torah. Both rationalists and Kabbalists vehemently disapproved of the witty hedonism of Al-Harizi and Ibn Ezra. All of them would seem foreign and quite irrelevant to the Ashkenazi writers of the era of the Crusades. If there was one Jewish literature of the High Middle Ages, it was not only multilingual and multifarious but also characterized by its intrinsic unrelatedness; by lacunae, gaps, differences of mentality, terminology, and intellectual commitment that a common religious tradition could not unify.

This lack of coherence and unity, however, hardly compares with the radical fragmentation of Jewish writing in modern times. During the nineteenth and early twentieth centuries Jewish writing was conducted in any number of languages—a host of Jewish ones, of which Hebrew, Yiddish, and Ladino were only the most prominent, and more then a dozen non-Jewish ones, including German, Russian, Polish, French, Spanish, English, and Arabic. Within this vortex of languages, each carrying a legacy of literary traditions and conventions, Jewish writing occurred within at least three different—and mostly antagonistic—ideological matrices: that of the so-called religious tradition; that of secular, particularist Jewish nationalism; and that of a non-particularist, but not necessarily assimilationist, ethos of Jewish participation in non-Jewish cultures and literatures. Within each of these groups different, often fiercely competitive trends vied with each other for ascendancy and hegemony. In the traditionalist matrix, various brands of Hasidic writers waged literary battles with their rabbinical Mitnagdic counterparts, as well as with each other. Within the secular nationalist fold Hebraism struggled with Yiddishism, and Zionism opposed Bundism, Folkism, Autonomism and Territorialism, and even Zionism and Hebraism were often at odds with one another.

As for Jewish writing in non-Jewish languages, its complexity made clear delineations impossible. The central problem was how to distinguish between what was truly Jewish writing and what was merely writing by Jews. Dov Sadan's well-known definition of Jewish writing in non-Jewish languages—writing done by Jews for Jews—was generally felt to be too narrow. Such writing was done by writers of very limited talent during the short, mostly one-generational span in which semitraditional Jewish communities in Germany and Russia already spoke and read the language of their respective countries but still were not truly acculturated. Even in these periods, writers of talent, such as Auerbach, Heine, and Boerne in Germany, appealed to the general readership, and their works would therefore not fit Sadan's definition and not be included in his concept of Jewish literature. Whether they do or do not fit this or that definition, writers such as Heine or Kafka or Isaac Rosenberg or Henry Roth and Joseph Roth and Philip Roth or Saul Bellow or Paul Celan or Primo Levi or Cynthia Ozick, who certainly did not target their writing at exclusively Jewish readerships, gave direct or indirect (but always meaningful) expression to what we may call the Jewish (or at least a Jewish) experience and should belong within a map of modern Jewish writing, no matter how fuzzily drawn. On the other hand, many of the writers included in Sadan's definition—the Phillipsohns, Lehmans, and Levandas—might best be left altogether out of our consideration of the modern Jewish literary complex and relegated to the domain of cultural or social history.

III

Viewing these variegated literary vistas, the theorists of Jewish literature in the first half of the twentieth century, with very few exceptions, sought out both overt and covert patterns of continuity. Their search for both vertical-historical and horizontal-contemporary unifying characteristics was dictated by their various brands of Jewish nationalism; while opposing each other, these ideologies still defined themselves as inclusive, as able to draw on whatever was creative and authentic, both in the past and in the present. Only those of them who were ideologically committed to a total breach with the past and to the most radical abrogation of the Jewish continuum in the present eschewed this attempt at reaching common ground.

At the extreme right wing of the Zionist camp, for instance, emerged in the late 1930s the so-called Canaanite group headed by the poet-ideologue Yonatan Ratosh. He deemed "young Hebrews"—Jews born and/or raised in Israel—the constituents of a new nation; they were unconnected to the Jewish people of the past or the present (who formed not a nation but rather a religious community). Ratosh and his followers regarded themselves as the harbingers of a new, native Hebrew culture and literature, inspired by the pre-monotheistic pagan culture of Canaan rather than by any part of the Jewish tradition. To them the problem of continuity just obfuscated the real issues that the new Hebrew nation had to face if it was to thrive politically and culturally.

However, the majority of literary scholars—within both the Hebraist and the Yiddishist camps—were undeterred in their ongoing search for Jewish literary continuity. The one Hebrew critic-theorist who did not believe in the existence of this sort of continuity, Baruch Kurzweil, was the exception that confirms the rule. While Kurzweil rejected the commonplace notion that modern secular Hebrew culture formed a new but connected link in a long cultural-historical chain, he did so on grounds diametrically opposed to those of the Canaanites or the so-called vulgar Marxists who would do away with continuity as chains fettering a new and vibrant culture to an irrelevant, decrepit past. To Kurzweil, continuity was everything, and the ultimate tragedy was what he saw as modern Hebrew culture's fatal breach with the past. Kurzweil unhistorically idealized the traditional past and vehemently objected to whoever—the great scholar Gershom Scholem, for instance—undermined this monolithic, and harmonious image.

Despite his visibility and influence, Kurzweil's view of modern Hebrew culture's breach with the past was unacceptable to most Zionist and Hebraist cultural theorists; for them, the notion that the new culture they represented was also a continuation became a foregone conclusion. All of them shared with the ideologues of the Hebrew Enlightenment the belief that modern Hebraism was, among other things, a renaissance-like reversion to the pristine source of Hebraity, that is, to the Bible. This faith manifested itself in many of the main characteristics of Hebrew literature throughout the nineteenth century and, to some extent, even the beginning of the twentieth. We can see a widespread adoption of a pseudo-biblical style that would years later be laboriously peeled off, first from nonfiction, then from prose fiction and only very late—already after Bialik, Tshernihovsky, and their disciples—from the diction of poetry. There were innumerable attempts to revive distinctly biblical genres, from biblical narrative to Psalms, and from Proverbs to the prophetic burden, the *masa* (which Bialik made popular and Uri Zvi Greenberg merged with the twentieth-century genre of the political exhortative poem). The Bible, these critics argued, had been created within a politically independent Hebrew commonwealth, and by a Hebrew society that was monolingual and centered on agriculture. The renewal of Jewish political independence, they believed, along with the reconstitution of a Hebrew-speaking society that would replace Jewish commerce with agriculture and counteract urban alienation through a new intimacy with nature, would make the Bible culturally accessible as it had not been for millennia. Very few doubted the tenability of a new Hebrew biblicalism under modern, secular circumstances.

These beliefs about continuity were extended to postbiblical Jewish culture as well. From at least the last third of the nineteenth century, writers and thinkers tried hard to find viable connections with various postbiblical traditions and modalities. This went hand in hand with the reintroduction of postbiblical Mishnaic Hebrew and even Talmudic Aramaic as legitimate and, in fact, dominant components of modern Hebrew prose; and with the reappraisal and recanonization of the talmudic and midrashic Aggada, and of such formerly despised genres as the esoteric Piyut. Different writers and thinkers espoused different trends in postbiblical Judaic culture. Ahad Ha'am, the major Zionist philosopher, identified most easily with the legacy of Maimonides and the other medieval and renaissance exponents of philosophical rationalism. Berdichevsky, Ahad Ha'am's opponent, scoured the Talmud, the midrash, and the medieval Jewish novella and folktale for an echo, be it ever so faint, of a defiant Jewish individualism and physicality, a visceral Judaism of the body, the senses, the passions. Bialik, Ahad Ha'am's disciple, identified with the Talmudic Aggada and with the medieval poets-masters, just as others turned to the messianic traditions. Uri Zvi Greenberg sometimes represented himself as a reincarnation of Shlomo Molkho, the sixteenth-century Marrano who, after returning to his Jewish faith, was executed as a messianic martyr. Finally, Hasidism, the energetic opponent of the Jewish Enlightenment, was rehabilitated, popularized, and modernized by such luminaries as Y. L. Peretz, Berdichevsky, Martin Buber, and Sh. Y. Agnon.

The fact that modern thinking could be inspired by these myriad, divergent sources proves that traditional Judaism was not monolithic. The traditional sphere contained different and antagonistic components and often became an arena for clashes between different interpretations of Jewishness. Thus, modernists could be revolutionaries and yet attach themselves to whatever part of the Judaic legacy fit their views and needs; with this approach, cultural and literary historians found abundant evidence of their sought-after continuity. A case in point is that of the early-eighteenth-century Jewish-Italian poet and mystic Moshe Hayim Luzzatto. Better known by the acronym Ramhal, he was respected and imitated by writers of the Hebrew Enlightenment as the author of neoclassical allegorical dramas and as a felicitous stylist who both implemented and encoded the rhetorical conventions of biblical, poetic Hebrew. Nevertheless, very few of the Hebrew Enlighteners would have crowned him as the founding father of modern Hebrew literature, which, many believed, was initiated by the Mendelssohnian circle at the dawn of the Haskalah in the second half of the eighteenth century.

In a fascinating example of how literary traditions are created, or recreated, Jewish theorists at the beginning of the twentieth century suddenly declared that modern Hebrew poetry was somehow launched by Ramhal. Nahum Slouschz's book on the history of the new Hebrew literature (*Korot hasifrut ha'ivrit hahadashah*, 1906) initiated the idea. Immediately, Bialik bestowed his enormous prestige upon this unorthodox innovation and made it the center of his famous 1914 series of lectures on the history of Hebrew poetry. At this point the alleged modernity of Ramhal was explained mainly in stylistic and metrical terms, his hidden Sabbatianism being glossed over as an unfortunate aberration. However, it soon became apparent that this Sabbatianism formed the ideational core of Ramhal's plays. Critics from Eliezer Shteynman to Fishl Lakhover began to argue that the essence of his modernity came in his coupling of aesthetic innovation and messianic mysticism, rather than in his elegant pseudobiblical style and neoclassical form. Thus, the roots of modern Hebrew literature were plucked out of the ground of the Enlightenment and stretched back into the beginning of the eighteenth century and into a border zone where rationalism and messianic mysticism intermingled.

Of course, this attempt to present modern Hebrew literature as akin to mystical tradition was not acceptable to all. But as evidence of its surprising acceptance by some, even the astute historian Hayim Nahman Shapiro maintained that modernity itself was a direct, albeit modified, continuation of what he called the terrestrial or earthly component in the Jewish character and cultural legacy, as opposed to its spiritual-unearthly counterpart. Using Gershom Scholem's hypothesis—which predicated a link between Sabbatianism and the advent of the Jewish Enlightenment—Shapiro created an extensive history of modern Hebrew literature, in which its earthly Jewish continuity was highlighted as much as its ties with European humanism. Tragically, this ten-volume *opus magnum* was destroyed, together with its author, in the Holocaust. Only the first volume, which was published in Lithuania on the eve of World War II, survived. In another remarkable scholarly turn, Shapiro's legacy was taken up by the poet-scholar Shimon Halkin, who inculcated it in generations of students of Hebrew literature at the Hebrew University of Jerusalem. Thus, the vertical continuity of Hebrew literature was confirmed by some of the most prominent Hebrew writers and literary scholars of the first half of the twentieth century.

Yiddishist writers and literary scholars in interbellum Poland and North America were also committed to the search for literary continuity. The novelist Yoysef Opatoshu brought to life the figure of the renaissance Yiddish *shpilman* (the Yiddish troubadour). Yeshaye Trunk resurrected the figure of the late-fifteenth/early-sixteenth-century Italian Hebrew philologist and Yiddish poet Elijah Levita (better known as Elye Bokher) by beautifully adapting and modernizing his Yiddish epic poem *Bovo dAntona* (which had enjoyed vast popularity throughout the eighteenth and nineteenth centuries in folksy prose adaptations going under the title *Bove mayse*). Max Weinreich, the dean of Yiddish scholarship, published a variety of scholarly books that traced the development of Yiddish literature since its inception in the Middle Ages without laying much emphasis on the breach separating the new literature from the old one. As the title of one of his books (*Shtaplen—fir etyudn tsu der yidisher shprakhvisnshaft un literaturgeshikhte* [1923]) proclaimed, he conceived of Yiddish literature as a continuous progress moving in *shtaplen*, step by step. Another book, *Bilder fun der yidisher literatur* (1928), which focused mainly on old Yiddish writing, characteristically ended with chapters dealing with the nineteenth-century writers Ayzik Meir Dik and Sh.Y. Abramovitsh. Dik, a moderate *maskil* whose novellas were written in a format that was very similar to that of the folksy didactic chapbook, and whose much diluted *maskilic* messages could often be read as those of a traditional moralist preaching sane religion, good manners, and common sense, also became the literary hero of Shmuel Niger. Indeed, he had to be the favorite of whoever needed to point to a connective link between traditional and modern Yiddish writing, predicating an evolutionary and gradual passage from the former to the latter. Scholars like Niger also developed the notion popularized by Y. L. Peretz— that modern Yiddish fiction was rooted in the fertile ground of the Jewish homiletic folktale and the Hasidic novella.

As we have noted, it was mainly the Yiddishists who worried about the horizontal integrity of Jewish literature. To them this meant mainly the affirmation of Hebrew/Yiddish bilingualism as an essential feature of modern Jewish literary creativity. Since the proclamation of Yiddish as a national language in the famous gathering in Tshernovits in 1908, and the subsequent publication of Bal Makhshoves' essay *"Tsvey shprakhn— eynuneyntsike literatur"* (Two Languages—Only One Literature) the bilingual character of modern Jewish literature was assumed by most Yiddishist scholars. In the late 1930s, Shmuel Niger extended this assumption onto the Jewish literary past, offering the hypothesis that postbiblical Jewish literature was *always* bilingual, matching the Hebrew, or the holy tongue (*loshn koydesh*), with a non-Hebraic language—Aramaic, Greek, Arabic, and then the Jewish languages Yiddish and Ladino—and employing both for different literary purposes. Even the Bible, Niger argued, contained non-Hebraic, Aramaic sections; and as Aramaic became the spoken Jewish language in the later part of the second commonwealth era, as well as the main language in which the halachic traditions evolved, bilingualism became the foundational characteristic of Jewish literary activity. It directly flowed from the duality of a culture that, on the one hand, was anchored in its sacrosanct origins but, on the other hand, was flexible, alive, and very much in touch with its non-Jewish linguistic and cultural environment.

With Jews living for more than two millennia in a series of linguistically and culturally diglottic situations, bilingual literary creativity was inevitable. Indeed, it became the salient and universal characteristic of Jewish literature, enabling it to change, evolve, adapt new forms and process new contents, and yet remain loyal to itself, tightly wrapped around its historical core. The ones who threatened the continuity and integrity of Jewish literature—the fanatic Hebraists in Zion and the Soviet cultural commissars who banned Hebrew altogether—Niger argued, were those determined to abrogate Jewish literary bilingualism and replace it with an arbitrary monolingualism.

The vitality of Jewish bilingualism, according to the Yiddishists, could be found in the work of some of the greatest Jewish writers throughout the ages who employed more than one language. Yehuda Halevi, for example, wrote his poems in Hebrew and his philosophical masterpiece *Hakuzari* in Arabic. Maimonides wrote *Guide to the Perplexed* in Arabic and his extensive halachic compendium *Mishne Torah* in Hebrew. In the eighteenth and early nineteenth centuries, Hasidic literature employed both Yiddish and Hebrew. And closer to the present, the bilingualism of literary pillars like Sh. Y. Abramovitsh and Y. L. Peretz confirmed what some theorists believed was an irrefutable historical truth.

In the late 1940s, already in the wake of the Holocaust and the founding of the Jewish state, Dov Sadan took up where Niger had left off, using his ideas as the basis for an altogether new theory of Jewish literary continuity and integrity. In its conceptual subtlety and visionary scope, Sadan's work would far surpass everything that had preceded it. Sadan did not gloss over the bewildering fragmentation of modern Jewish writing; neither did he minimize the dimensions of the chasm separating Jewish modernity from a persistent traditional Jewish mainstream. Far from a thing of the past, Sadan identified this mainstream as an ongoing, self-renewing cultural tradition, which evolved alongside and in opposition to the newer secular-nationalist trend and responded in its own way to the crisis of modernity. Thus, Sadan charted the two intersecting triads that crisscrossed the map of modern Jewish literature. The first was a linguistic triad: Hebrew, Jewish languages (mainly Yiddish) and non-Jewish languages employed by Jews for the benefit of a Jewish readership. The second was an ideological triad: secular nationalism; Hasidism; and anti-Hasidic, rabbinical orthodoxy. Between these two triangles, Sadan argued, modern Jewish writing was evolving in different and seemingly irreconcilable directions.

The unity and continuity of this literature inhered, however, not in any kind of overt evolutionary linkage but rather in its seemingly centrifugal dynamics, which Sadan interpreted in dialectical terms that were simultaneously Hegelian and Freudian. According to the Hegelian formula, Jewish culture reacted to the challenges of modern times by developing a set of sharply etched thesis/antithesis dichotomies. Each of the culture's traditional components, with the addition of newly acquired ones, seemed to turn against all the others. However, such extreme polarization promised an eventual reunification, since the sweeping centrifugal pull was bound to trigger a centripetal reaction. A strong thesis/antithesis polarity invited an equally strong synthesis. Thus, modernity, which drove Jewish culture to either/or positions, would necessarily be followed by what we may today call postmodernity, which would surmount these oppositions and allow for a culture in which tradition and modernity would commingle and coalesce into a new compound.

According to the Freudian formula, adaptation to modernism came at the cost of a cultural repression that caused a whole series of schizophrenic manifestations. Modern Jewish culture exhibited all kinds of splits and reaction formations. However, the collective Jewish cultural personality was not sick. Its schizophrenic symptoms emanated from the present historical crisis rather than from an inherent imbalance, Sadan argued, and in the future this cultural personality would regain balance and harmonize its conflicting aspects. Modern Judaism was on its way toward *kuliyut*, an abstract noun coined by Sadan, which means something like "all-inclusiveness"; in fact, it calls to mind the concept of catholicity (from the Greek *kata*—completely; and *holon*—whole). One can justifiably describe Sadan as the theorist of a catholic Jewish culture. The term is particularly apt because it points to the religious-mystical notion that is at the core of this scholar's *Weltanschauung*—a notion without which he could not have harbored his surprisingly optimistic faith in the Jewish future. In the late 1940s, however, Sadan found it difficult to identify many precursors of the hoped-for *kuliyut*. If they could be sought anywhere, it would be in the works of the greatest Jewish writers, such as Agnon and Bialik, which he analyzed with much critical acumen. In a few literary epiphanies, where a superb aesthetic balance harmonized otherwise deeply conflicted views of the human condition in general, and of the Jewish condition in particular, Sadan argued that one could glimpse the future of Jewish culture.

IV

In Sadan's work, half a century of important conceptual search peaked but also, as noted earlier, reached its abrupt end. If we are now to take up this search and attempt once again a theory of Jewish literature, we should ask ourselves what, if anything, in the work done by the scholars and thinkers of the first half of the twentieth century can still be of use to us. We must begin by asking why this arduous work, in which critics and scholars invested so much, was suddenly terminated about fifty years ago? What rendered it irrelevant to the three or four generations of scholars who came after Sadan, Kurzweil, Shapiro, and Halkin?

Some, but not all, of the changing cultural circumstances that can explain this cessation have already been touched upon in the first part of this essay. Now we must consider the cataclysmic shift in the Jewish world at mid-century: the destruction of European Jewish cultural centers in the Holocaust; Stalin's final attempt at uprooting Jewish cultural autonomy throughout his communist empire; and the sharp decline in the fortunes of both Hebrew and Yiddish cultural creativity in the West. As a result, Israel's literary culture, as well as an upsurge of Jewish cultural and literary activity conducted in non-Jewish languages in various Western countries and particularly in North America, became of paramount significance in any consideration of the future prospects of Jewish culture and literatures. However, the theorists we discussed and the concepts they developed offer little, if any, help in understanding Israeli culture and literature or the post–World War II Jewish creativity emerging outside of Israel.

As for developments outside of Israel, we have already seen how Sadan's very narrow definition of a Jewish literature written in non-Jewish languages left every vital manifestation of Jewish literary creativity outside his field of vision. To this we can add Shimon Halkin's doctrinaire view of the future of Jewish culture in North America. Himself an American Hebraist, he could see only doom and gloom following the demise of both traditional and modern national Hebrew/Yiddish cultures. To him North American Jewry was as good as culturally lost. With Bellow, the Roths, Primo Levi, Ozick, and Paul Celan excluded from both Sadan's and Hakin's maps of modern Jewish literature, no wonder their outlooks were so bleak. All that remained outside of Israel, in their view, were a few wilting remnants of Hebrew and Yiddish writing.

More importantly, the theorists' concepts of cultural and literary continuity rendered them insensitive to almost all authentic and significant developments inside Israel. To Kurzweil, with his sense of Jewish culture as a grand opera approaching its tragic denouement, Israeli culture and literature signaled the bitter end. Thus, he waged unending battles against everything that was alive in Israeli literature: S. Yizhar, Amos Oz, Nathan Zach, and countless others. In the final analysis, what he said about Israeli literature—even when it deserved his acrimony because of its poor quality—was devoid of real insight and interest.

Despite Sadan's harmonious personality and charming sense of humor, which allowed him to develop a pleasant enough rapport with the Israeli literary republic, his all-inclusive theory also had very little to contribute to the understanding and evaluation of Israeli writing. Waiting for Israeli culture to evince a need for *kuliyut*, Sadan in the meantime hardly listened to what it had to say. When he made choices, pointing to one or another literary phenomenon in which he detected an increased Jewish awareness, he usually made the wrong choices, either in terms of literary quality and taste, or in his actual understanding of the texts involved. Halkin, willing enough to assume the role of a mentor for the younger literary generation of Israel, revealed in his single extensive article on young Israeli poetry a surprisingly unfocused view of the topic. His comments lacked real insight and a clear sense of the needs Israeli young writers were responding to in the wake of the War of Independence. In short, the theorists were more or less deaf to the music that Israeli literature was trying to make. Not surprisingly, Israeli literature became quite indifferent to theories that seemed to account only for the past or the ideologically imagined future and did not know how to look at the realities of the present, which, of course, constituted the real future in the making.

As we examine these theorists more closely, we realize that it was not only the literary present that evaded their grasp. Propelled by their overriding literary-ideological agendas, they often turned a myopic eye to large portions of the cultural and literary past, with which, as scholars, they were fully acquainted. Sadan could not find a niche within his complex system of multilingual and multi-ideological Jewish literature for Heine's *Rabbi of Bachrach* or Leon Feuchtwanger's *Jud Süss* or Gershonzon's metaphysical poem about the meaning of Jewish history or Abe Cahan's *Rise of David Levinsky* or Henry Roth's *Call It Sleep*. Kurzweil was unable to accept any scholarly discovery, no matter how meticulously substantiated, that undermined his idealized and simplistic view of the world of traditional Jewry; his vision could never have harbored the multitude of antinomian, libidinal, and subversive forces that Scholem had discovered and amply illustrated.

There were other cases of glossing over or misconstruing significant phenomena in the cultural past. I want to call attention to one of them here, since the error it involved was not only telling but also bore directly on the question that is at the center of our discussion: is there or isn't there a unified and continual Jewish literature that encompasses all historical epochs, all languages Jewish authors employed, and all religious or ideological persuasions they swore by. The issue I want to address here is that of the continuity of Jewish bilingualism. We have seen that Jewish writing since postbiblical times has been often bilingual and sometimes multilingual; but has Jewish writing always exhibited similar kinds of bi- and multilingualism, caused by similar diglottic situations and with similar literary ramifications? We may discover that we face totally different kinds of bilingualisms that had very different sources and altogether dissimilar literary consequences, and that therefore do not predicate a substantive continuity. It is useful in this context to differentiate between at least two kinds of literary bilingualism (although there exist more than two): what I shall call differential and nondifferential bilingualisms.

Differential bilingualism was the norm in medieval Jewish literature, particularly the major part created in Spain and other Mediterranean countries. This bilingualism was differential because it strictly regulated how the two languages were used according to differences between genres and targeted readerships. Thus, poetry was written only in Hebrew and for a Hebrew reading elite. Some poems were allowed to include macaronic sections, where the Hebrew could be dexterously commingled with other languages in a virtuoso bilingual performance. However, the brilliance and wit of such poems would be completely incomprehensible to readers who could not appreciate the relationships between their various linguistic components; that is, they were also targeted at a sophisticated Hebrew readership that could savor a highly literary, florid, and colorful Hebrew. Nobody without thorough knowledge of the language and its biblical and postbiblical sources could read or enjoy it.

Nonfiction of the philosophical or moralistic kind or systematic disquisitions on topics such as poetics, rhetoric, or grammar—in short, all nonfiction that necessitated abstractions, conceptualizations, and the use of professional jargon—would in most cases be written in Arabic (Halevi's *Kuzari*, Maimonides' *Moreh nevukhim*, Bakhya Iben Pakuda's *Hovot halevavot*, Moshe Ibn Ezra's *Shirat yisra'el*, Yona Ibn Janakh's *Sefer hadikduk* to name just a few). This was so not only because, as the writers themselves often said, Hebrew lacked the terminology upon which such discourse depended, but also because the works under discussion were targeted at a select readership already well versed in Arabic Aristotelian philosophy and grammatology. It was regarded as religiously appropriate and safe to put these works in the hands of these experienced and sophisticated readers who might use them with caution and discretion. The language was supposed to function as a barrier as much as it was as a means of communication. In contrast, nonfiction genres aimed for large-scale consumption both inside and outside of the Jewish-Spanish Mediterranean region, such as halachic compendia or popular interpretations of the Bible, would be written in a Hebrew that was lucid, syntactically simple, and lexically familiar enough to render it accessible to anyone with an elementary Jewish education. Thus, while in his *Moreh nevukhim* Maimonides sported a densely conceptual discourse which demanded studying rather than reading, in his *Mishneh torah* he created a Hebrew style that was so lucid, well balanced, and classical that it made the reading of this fourteen-volume compendium not only easy but also pleasurable. To our own day this medieval classic can be easily perused by all readers familiar with elementary literary Hebrew.

One more rule regulating this clearly defined literary-linguistic system needs to be mentioned here: under no circumstances would an author, no matter how accomplished a bilingual stylist he was, write the same work in both of the languages he employed. That would be not only unnecessary but also a nuisance undermining the entire system of logical and consequential differentiation between languages and stylistic levels. A single text could fit one and only one linguistic-stylistic modality. Works written in Arabic would be translated into difficult, artificial, and infelicitous Hebrew (such as that of the Ibn Tibbon translators) after the author's death and only in areas, such as Provence, where Arabic was unknown and where an interest in such works would begin to emerge.

Could this brand of differential bilingualism or even multilingualism support a unified literature? Could it achieve a continuity, both vertical and horizontal, surmounting linguistic and other differences? All other things being equal, the answer is yes; but more interesting is that historically there was nothing particularly Jewish about such a differential bilingualism. Most European literatures of the time were bilingual, as Latin and a given vernacular were employed side by side in a similar differential manner. For all practical literary purposes, we may view all the components of such a compound as belonging to one language, which literature uses in a differential manner, allocating to each genre, topic, and intended group of readers the appropriate linguistic-stylistic vehicle.

In the Jewish modern literary complex we find a very different reality: differential bilingualism is so rare that it is almost insignificant. Even where such bilingualism seems to emerge, it is, in comparison with that of the medieval masters, of such a different nature, flowing from such different sources and having such different consequences that it scarcely seems a continuation of medieval and renaissance bilingualism. An interesting case in point is that of that trailblazing modernist Micha Yosef Berdichevsky, who at the turn of the nineteenth century revolutionized both the art of Hebrew fiction and Hebrew nationalist thinking.

Berdichevsky was trilingual, writing mainly in Hebrew but also in German and Yiddish. His trilingualism was differential in the sense that he never wrote the same work in more than one language and his literary corpus in each of the three languages has a distinct tonality. But this is as far as we can go in comparing Berdichevsky's trilingualism to the bilingualism of the old masters. In every other way the two phenomena do not lend themselves to a meaningful comparison. For one thing, the ideological-poetic source of Berdichevsky's differential poetics is diametrically opposed to that of Halevi or Maimonides. While they shared a classical poetics, which demanded a parallel differentiation and matching between topic and genre, on the one hand, and their linguistic-stylistic renderings, on the other hand, Berdichevsky followed a romantic poetics or even a Crocean-expressionistic one requiring total unity of specific *erlebnis*—

experience—with its verbal externalization. Since a specific experience could have one and only one authentic expressive verbalization, the notion that a poem or a story or even a piece of emotive nonfiction could have two or more original versions amounted to a poetic heresy. An authentic experience could have only one such version; all others would be mere translations, which, by definition, could present only a partial aspect of the original if they did not altogether subvert it. That was why Berdichevsky would not follow what was at the time a norm acceptable to almost all Hebrew as well as many Yiddish writers: that of writing the same work in more than one language. In all other ways, however, Berdichevsky's trilingualism was nondifferential; that is, he saw no connection between topic or genre and the specific language employed. He wrote novellas as well as topical and philosophical articles and literary reviews and criticism in all three languages.

More importantly, Berdichevsky's semi- or quasi-differential trilingualism was not only rare but actually provocative, one manifestation of the all-out literary war the author declared on what he branded as the erasure of boundaries in contemporary Jewish writing. (He meant by this the already mentioned norm of presenting the same literary work in two original versions, a Hebrew and a Yiddish one.) Berdichevsky even threatened to boycott those publications and literary magazines that would support such literary bastardy. Of course, his protest was of no avail. The norm was at the time so entrenched that even masters who were not accomplished stylists in both languages made the pretension of following it. Thus, Sholem Aleichem, whose talent as a Hebrew writer was miniscule in comparison with his amazing brilliance in Yiddish nevertheless wrote a series of Hebrew short stories and feuilletons, and then persuaded his son-in-law, the bilingual writer Y. D. Berkovitsh, to eliminate his name as the translator of *Tevye der milkhiker*, and to authorize the publication in 1910 of the Yiddish masterpiece in his Hebrew translation as if the Hebrew version had been penned by the author himself, even buttressing this untruth in a special Hebrew introduction he wrote.

This phenomenon—the simultaneous writing of the same work in more than one language—is not entirely unknown in the annals of Jewish literature. One recalls, for instance, *Megiles vints,* an early-seventeenth-century poem commemorating the delivery of a German Jewish community from the grave danger caused by a popular rebellion that had anti-Semitic, pogromist traits. The poem was written in the current western Yiddish as well as in a peculiar, singularly inarticulate and ungrammatical Ashkenazi Hebrew. We do not know what triggered this ineffectual bilingual production. Probably the leaders of the community thought that while the Yiddish version would be read and savored, the Hebrew one would somehow leave a more enduring memorial to this characteristic episode of last-moment deliverance. However, the bilingualism of *Megiles vints* is a relatively rare phenomenon.

Literary work in two languages became more common in the latter part of the eighteenth century and the early decades of the nineteenth, as the Hasidic and Jewish Enlightenment movements fought each other for the hearts and minds of Eastern European Jews. Unwilling to lose either the more learned men or the uneducated artisans and women, the founding fathers of Hasidism published more popular hagiographic and narrative works in both Hebrew and Yiddish versions. (The more theoretical and contemplative theses were written either in Hebrew or in pseudo-Zoharic Aramaic). Proponents of the Enlightenment, in spite of their loathing for Yiddish and all it stood for, could not but imitate their rivals in the most literal sense of the term: they wrote anti-Hasidic parodies, such as Yosef Perl's brilliant *Megale temirin*, in both Hebrew and Yiddish versions. The former aimed—through its grossly ungrammatical language—to debunk the Hebrew of the Hasidic authors and expose them for the ignoramuses they allegedly were; the latter were meant to reach a wide readership, making the simple men and women realize what charlatans and con men their Hasidic leaders were. Being the consummate artist that he was, Perl succeeded in elevating his polemic parodies in both versions to great carnival-like masterpieces; he endowed each of the versions with unique and untranslatable stylistic vivacity, making them equally original but subtly different works of art.

In the latter part of the nineteenth century, against the backdrop of the nascent Jewish nationalism, Sh. Y. Abramovitsh, originally a writer of Yiddish fiction and Hebrew social and cultural criticism as well as scientific textbooks, improved on this strategy as he continuously and tirelessly expanded and recast his Yiddish stories, fleshing them out as both Yiddish and Hebrew gems. His great prestige and influence as the founding father of both Yiddish and Hebrew modern prose fiction popularized this kind of bilingualism.

Simultaneously, the rapidly growing Yiddish and Hebrew press, which demanded a constant flow of publishable literary works, was the perfect home for bilingual publication. Thus a special method evolved of recasting works written in one language in a form that would make use of the unique resources of another language. This has been described as "compensatory translation," since the translator, not finding in the language into which he translated good equivalents for the staple linguistic characteristics of the original, would compensate for this deficit by adding to the translated version elements available in the language of translation but missing in that of the original. Thus, for instance, he would replace the wealth of Yiddish's idiomatic expressions with the textual allusions and subversions abundant in Hebrew.

These were not translations in any meaningful sense of the term. To begin with, there was no real need for translation, at least not from Yiddish into Hebrew, since all readers of Hebrew were at the time fully conversant in Yiddish and read the famous Yiddish works in their Yiddish originals. The so-called translator (who in most cases was the author of the original) had no need to compensate for anything. What he needed was to entertain a public already familiar with the work in one version by informing its other version with an altogether new and exhilarating stylistic verve. He was ultimately creating a new original, to be enjoyed within literary and stylistic traditions essentially unrelated to those of his (other) original.

Thus, this modern Jewish bilingualism lent Bal Makhshove's proclamation, *tsvey shprakhn—eynuneyintsike literatur*, an aura of truth. It was responsible for the creation of two different original versions of the same text and thus was essentially nondifferential—it did not allocate to either of the two languages a different function within a clearly defined literary system. On the contrary, it blurred distinctions, as Berdichevsky complained, but at the same time it offered the possibility of simultaneous literary creativity within two unrelated systems. This paved the way for a simultaneous development of two alternative literary systems that could supplant and eventually supersede each other. And this was exactly how both Yiddish and Hebrew literatures progressed in the twentieth century, with high velocities and heated ideological rivalries.

In their mutual urge to replace each other, the two Jewish literatures were asserting their quintessential dynamics. Rather than amity and mutual supplementation, they drove incessantly toward confrontation and mutual displacement and replacement. Modern Hebrew and Yiddish literatures were not and could not be, even in the golden age of the great bilingual masters, *an eynuneyntsike literatur*—(solely one literature). The sheer logic of nondifferential bilingualism undermined and eliminated such a possibility. When bilingualism is nondifferential there can be no one literary system that holds together its different components, counterbalancing the centrifugal and divisive potential that any linguistic duality must contain. The so-called golden age of Abramovitsh, Peretz, and so many other nondifferential bilingual writers was no more than a phase in the progress that inexorably propelled both Yiddish and Hebrew literatures toward total separation.

In fact, it was during that phase that both literatures equipped themselves with the necessary resources for their independent and mutually exclusive existences. Nondifferential bilingualism was one of the chief tools used for the purposes of this self-equipping. Yiddish literature used it to achieve the status of an artistic literature by transcending its linguistic and stylistic primitive beginnings, which either reduced it to a series of colloquial dialogues bound by a local dialect or undermined it artistically through the use of an artificially Germanized style of questionable elegance. Hebrew literature used it in its effort to transcend the so-called *melitsa*, the florid, bombastic, cliché-ridden and imprecise pseudo-biblical style it had evolved. Although shuttling between the two languages seemed natural enough to the literary masters (Abramovitsh compared it to breathing through both nostrils), these writers were actually straddling two horses who were galloping in different directions. Inevitably, their stunt became increasingly more difficult. Peretz found it quite exasperating. Much of the Hebrew works written in the last fifteen years of his life were actually translated from the Yiddish by others, with Peretz merely adding his own finishing touches. Sholem Aleichem, as we have seen, only went through the motions of practicing the art that his mentor, Abramovitsh, so brilliantly controlled.

The new Hebrew and Yiddish literatures, despite sharing the common denominators of secularism and (to a lesser extent) modern Jewish nationalism, did not by any means form a unified literature. This was precisely because their respective versions of Jewish modernism, secularism, and nationalism were sufficiently divergent and mutually exclusive enough to justify the employment of two totally different—indeed, diametrically opposed—languages with utterly dissimilar historical and literary traditions. They had to evolve as two literary systems that were distant enough to render them completely independent of each other and yet also close enough for rivalry and confrontation. Needless to say, if these two sibling rivals could not be squeezed into one unifying entity, no matter how flexible its definition, literary works written by Jews either for Jewish or for non-Jewish readers certainly could not be made to fit into any meaningful concept of a unified modern Jewish literature.

There is simply no such thing as one modern Jewish literature. There are multiple Jewish literatures and a rich plethora of Jewish literary works written in non-Jewish languages and belonging within their respective non-Jewish literary milieus. Yet by the sheer fact that these works were formed and informed by Jewish experience—no matter of what nature and whether it was directly or indirectly articulated—they also belong, together with the literatures clearly defined as Jewish, within a large and fluid complex that evades simple definitions and demarcations. We can compare this complex to a galaxy: though parts of it constantly move away from each other, they also form one spatial configuration.

In fact, modern Jewish culture as a whole can be compared to such a galaxy, in spite of the fact that it was not born in a Big Bang explosion out of one monolithic particle. Jewish culture, we must insist once again, has been dichotomous and often schizophrenic even when all of it was still grounded in religious faith and halachic practice. One can argue that even before modernity there existed several Jewish cultures, each with its respective and unrelated literature. However, there can be little doubt that any unity and continuity that traditional Jewish culture possessed were crushed and splintered in the collision with the modern condition. This is the reality of the modern Jewish condition, which we must not blur or obfuscate.

V

Despite the difficulty, we need a theory of Jewish literature that allows for a conceptualization of the Jewish literary complex past, present, and future. Indeed, such a theory is required in order to hone a sharper, more pointed concept of literature per se, general and universal, with its dynamics of change and evolution. We need this theory not only because literature per se is an abstraction, based on a conglomerate of national literatures, but also because the distinctive characteristics—or what some may call the abnormalities—of the Jewish literary complex, resulting from its unique cultural history, can help us consider the problematic nature of literary normalcy itself.

What we should part with—indeed, what we must exorcise from our cognitive system—is the obsessive theoretical craving for all-encompassing unities and continuities. Though we can understand the deep cultural insecurities that give rise to such cravings, and even aesthetically relish the beautifully arranged projections by which such insecurities are kept at bay, we cannot afford to let them replace historical realities. This is not a call for the banishing of ideological considerations from historical and literary thinking. Such banishment is both impossible and unwarranted. All history is informed by ideological considerations. However, ideological projection and wishful thinking are not one and the same. An authentic, scholarly historical narrative can balance such inevitable projections with a genuine interest in the ever so complex and multifarious facets of historical reality. The more we study the realities of the Jewish literary complex the less we feel the need to superimpose upon them a symbolic order (in the Lacanian sense of the term), to organize them hierarchically under an overarching principle. We should remind ourselves that the hierarchically tiered systems we are often offered by cultural theorists are at best no more than temporary and fluid constructions. Almost all can be differently arranged with lower, recessive, and conditioned tiers replacing the upper, dominant, and conditioning ones. The hierarchy is often only in the eye of the ideological beholder. That is an important lesson we can and should learn from observing closely the Jewish literary complex, and especially its modern evolution since the second half of the eighteenth century. Modern Jewish history, with its wildly colliding crosscurrents, did not allow for the emergence of one unified modern Jewish culture or for an integral, albeit multilingual, modern Jewish literature. It rather forces upon the scholarly observer the realization that Jewish culture and literature were fragmented beyond repair.

It was this realization that sent the early Zionist and Yiddishist theorists on their wild-goose chase after ideologically wished-for but historically impossible unities and continuities. Without necessarily adopting post-Zionist attitudes, I believe we can reverse this process. Zionist theorists, we know, sought a new, or revived, Jewish normalcy: this normalcy would entail a reunification of an exiled and scattered people, as well as a reorganization and streamlining of this people's abnormal, fractured, and scattered cultural legacy. If we accept the so-called *abnormality* of modern Jewish culture, or even assert its essential normality, we can shed new light on the so-called normal literatures which are, in fact, not that much different from the aggregate of Jewish literatures. For these literatures—particularly the richer and more extensive and expansive ones—are ultimately no more than aggregates of their own, governed by projected hierarchies and imagined common denominators.

As the scholarship triggered by the theories of minority discourse and minor literatures demonstrate, these hierarchies reflect the relative stability of the social and political power structures that approve of a culture and a literature of a certain tenor. They purport to express and define the universal human ethical identity while, in fact, they assert and define the identity of the sociocultural powers that be. At the same time, they eliminate other identities, through preferences, canonization, marginalization, and exclusion.

Jewish culture, lacking the organized socioeconomic and political basis that supported the hierarchical structures of other cultures, could not achieve such impositions—no matter how much Jewish ideologues craved them. It was therefore unable to develop a modern Jewish canon. (This very concept is necessarily self-contradictory; Ruth Wisse's recent treatise, *The Modern Jewish Canon*, for example, unwittingly demonstrates this by excluding most of the important modern Jewish fiction writers and by disregarding modern Jewish poetry altogether.) As a result of these weaknesses, however, modern Jewish culture and literature only made clear what all modern cultures harbored in the depths of their complex and repressive bulks. What has surfaced throughout the second half of the twentieth century is that cultures and literatures that were supposedly national and monolingual have actually been created, in part, by a host of foreigners and neophytes, whose language of writing was not their mother tongue. We have seen members of repressed and peripheral societies— colonial and otherwise—who have deterritorialized and denationalized languages such as English or French. In fact what we see in the last fifty years can be called the Judaization of modern Western civilization, in the sense that what was once regarded as a peculiar and unfortunate Jewish cultural condition has become quite the normal cultural condition of the West as a whole.

Yes, the modern Jewish cultural and literary complex failed to establish agreed-upon supremacies and uniformities. It gave rise to a host of rival or unrelated systems which themselves proved short-lived. That, however, did not diminish its vitality. On the contrary, these myriad systems, with their endless disagreements, only enhanced Jewish creativity, allowing it to energize not only two national Jewish literatures but also other, sometimes great and powerful, literatures. Rather than ruing the nonunified and disorganized condition of the Jewish literary complex, perhaps we should rejoice in it. In any case, ruing or rejoicing, we have to learn to live with it and make the most of it. Among other benefits we can draw from it is a fuller exposure of the vitiating influence of ideologically oriented attempts at streamlining literature and charting a culture's literary maps by unifying theorems.

As our examination of the old theorists of Jewish literature has shown, the more sophisticated and complex the concept, the clearer the colonizing intentions they projected. Thus, Sadan's subtleties projected nothing less than an imperial urge to pronounce a neoreligious Zionism as the final victor in the race for Jewish cultural hegemony. The victory Sadan envisioned was so great and decisive that the neoreligious Hebraic nationalism he championed could afford to be magnanimous, even to its erstwhile rivals and enemies: secularism, orthodoxy, Yiddishism, and even, up to a point, acculturation into non-Jewish cultures. Instead of fighting and eliminating them, Sadan suggested that they could be swallowed and internalized within a new hierarchy, in which they would form the recessive and conditioned lower tiers. As he used to say, he was ready to offer them a humble niche in the wall of the new Jerusalem. The faith in this victory based itself on nothing that actually existed and on everything that should have existed. Sadan's theory did not contain a grain of existentialist humility, only essentialist eschatology. In spite of Sadan's low-keyed and humorous mien, his vision was the epitome of Zionist hubris.

Needless to say, none of Sadan's expectations have or could have been realized. More importantly, the concepts they shaped and informed have only blocked our progress toward new concepts that may better serve us in our search for a more realistic, more humble, but no less fruitful, theoretical understanding of the Jewish literary complex. Chief among these new articulations, I think, should be the concept of contiguity, which should replace that of continuity. This concept suggests relatedness, fluid and unregulated contacts, even moments of close adjacency, but not containment of one entity by another, not superimposition or *Gleichschaltung*.

Contiguity, once we start investigating its dynamics, will emerge as not altogether arbitrary or accidental series of contacts and semi-contacts caused by a general, vague relatedness. While it will never exhibit the neat order, or causal-temporal linearity, of unity and continuity, it might reveal some rules of its own that will be subtle and perhaps not uniformly applied, but therefore more intriguing and certainly in need of further research. It is my contention that a new theory of Jewish literature, if it ever takes off, would focus among other things on the ways—sometimes underground and secret ways—of literary contiguity, its high tides and low ebbs, its attractions and repulsions, its centripetal and centrifugal energies. We may discover that what was unconvincingly explained in terms of continuity—such as the stylistic resemblances Bialik detected between Ramhal's poetry and his own, or the moments that Gershom Scholem highlighted of cultural and literary overlapping between the Jewish Enlightenment and the legacy of Sabbatianism and Frankism—can be better explained by contiguity. Cultural and literary histories consist of many dialogues, colored by diverse tonalities, rather than of one continuous monological soliloquy delivered by a unified national-cultural personality. Theories of history and literature should also strive toward a dialogical rather than monological status. Preliminary insights and differentiations pertaining to the nature and workings of Jewish literary contiguity may be offered within the framework of such a dialogical exchange.

1

Beyond Influence

Toward a New Historiographic Paradigm

MICHAEL L. SATLOW

Writing the history of the Jews in antiquity used to be a much easier business. From the Hellenistic to the Roman periods, the story was one of religious and cultural conflict. Against the great colonial powers of Seleucid Syria, republican and then imperial Rome, and the "evil empire" of the Christian East, Jews struggled to defend their ancestral faith from interfering outsiders and even those other Jews seduced by alien cultures. This is not entirely a "lachrymose" vision of Jewish history; the historiography is rich with accounts of Judaism and Jewish culture frequently influenced—albeit usually not in a significant way—by its contact with the Greeks, Romans, and, less often, Christians.[1] Sometimes condensed into the dichotomy "Judaism/Hellenism," this is a narrative of distinct cultures in conversation and conflict. Even a standard textbook of Jewish history from 1980 talks of the "confrontation" between Jewish and Greek "civilizations."[2]

Over the past twenty years, this narrative has begun to fray. In his introductory book, Shaye Cohen discusses his discomfort with a model that opposes Palestinian (i.e., "pure") Judaism to Hellenistic Judaism, and elsewhere he has argued that the very term of identity—"Jewish"—was not stable through antiquity.[3] Erich Gruen self-consciously rejects this

---

    1. The standard collection of essays along these lines is Henry A. Fischel, ed., *Essays in Greco-Roman and Related Talmudic Literature* (New York: Ktav, 1977).

    2. Robert M. Seltzer, *Jewish People, Jewish Thought: The Jewish Experience in History* (New York: Macmillan, 1980), 155. This narrative continues to be replicated. See, for example, Lee I. Levine, *Judaism and Hellenism in Antiquity: Conflict or Confluence?* (Seattle: University of Washington Press, 1988), whose very title assumes a model of distinct cultures in interaction.

    3. See Shaye J. D. Cohen, *From the Maccabees to the Mishnah* (Library of Early Christian-

model. Like Cohen, he believes that "[w]e can no longer contrast 'Palestinian Judaism' as the unadulterated form of the ancestral faith with 'Hellenistic Judaism' as the Diaspora variety that diluted antique practices with alien imports."[4] He calls for a new conception that recognizes that Jews were part and parcel of the Hellenistic societies in which they lived: "The Jewish intellectuals who sought to rewrite their past and redefine their traditions grew up in Diaspora or even Palestinian communities suffused with Hellenism. For them it *was* their culture. Their ideas and concepts expressed themselves quite naturally in Greek forms."[5] Seth Schwartz has developed a nuanced narrative of Jewish interaction in antiquity that highlights imperial power rather than alien culture.[6] Peter Schäfer, focusing on one particular moment of similarity between Jewish and Christian understandings of God, tries to avoid using "influence" and the underlying notion of opposing cultures as an explanatory model.[7] Yaron Eliav suggests a model that he calls "filtered absorption" or "controlled incorporation," a "quiet process of the absorption of outside cultural elements into ancient Jewish society through revision and adaptation."[8] Daniel Boyarin has demonstrated the fuzziness of boundaries even at the formative moment of rabbinic Judaism and "Orthodox" Christianity.[9]

These authors are part of a wider trend in Jewish and non-Jewish historiography. This historiography has recognized the inherent weakness of explanatory models that turn culture into static binary encounters, characterized by "conflict," "resistance," "influence," "assimilation," "acculturation," or "appropriation." It sees even the peoples whose history is told

---

ity 7; Philadelphia: Westminster, 1987), 34–45 (but see 43: "For most Jews the ideal solution was to create a synthesis between Judaism and Hellenism"); idem, *The Beginnings of Jewishness: Boundaries, Varieties, Uncertainties* (Hellenistic Culture and Society 31; Berkeley: University of California Press, 1999), esp. 69–106 and 140–74.

4. Eric Gruen, "Hellenistic Judaism," in *Cultures of the Jews: A New History* (ed. David Biale; New York: Schocken, 2002), 80. But see, for a partial defense of these categories, Daniel Schwartz, "From Maccabees to Masada: On Diasporan Historiography of the Second Temple Period," in *Jüdische Geschichte in hellenistisch-römischer Zeit: Wege der Forschung: Vom alten zum neuen Schürer* (ed. Aharon Oppenheimer; Munich: R. Oldenbourg, 1999), 29–40.

5. Gruen, "Hellenistic Judaism," 94 (original emphasis).

6. Seth Schwartz, *Imperialism and Jewish Society, 200 B.C.E. to 640 C.E.* (Jews, Christians, and Muslims from the Ancient to the Modern World; Princeton, NJ: Princeton University Press, 2001).

7. Peter Schäfer, *Mirror of His Beauty: Feminine Images of God from the Bible to the Early Kabbalah* (Princeton, NJ: Princeton University Press, 2002), 222, 229–35.

8. Yaron Z. Eliav, "The Roman Bath as a Jewish Institution: Another Look at the Encounter Between Judaism and the Greco-Roman Culture," *JSJ* 31 (2000): 416–54, quotation from 426 and 454; see also idem, "Viewing the Sculptural Environment: Shaping the Second Commandment," in *The Talmud Yerushalmi and Graeco-Roman Culture* (ed. Peter Schäfer; 3 vols.; Texts and Studies in Ancient Judaism 93; Tübingen: Mohr Siebeck, 2002), 3:411–33.

9. Daniel Boyarin, "Justin Martyr Invents Judaism," *Church History* 70 (2001): 427–61.

as themselves de-essentialized "imagined communities" continuously forming and reforming their collective identity.[10]

In his preface to *Cultures of the Jews: A New History*, David Biale attempts to apply these modern historiographical trends to Jewish history. Discussing an ornate fifteenth-century Jewish Italian casket, Biale writes:

> How should we label such adoption of non-Jewish culture? Does it suggest "assimilation" or, to use a less loaded term, "acculturation"? The Italian Jewish culture that produced our casket has frequently been described as one of the most assimilated or acculturated in all of pre-modern Jewish history. But perhaps the contemporary model of assimilation is misleading when applied to the Jews of Renaissance Italy. Here was a traditional community intent on drawing boundaries between itself and its Christian neighbors but also able to adopt and adapt motifs from the surrounding culture for its own purposes. Indeed, the Jews should not be seen as outsiders who borrowed from Italian culture but rather as full participants in the shaping of that culture, albeit with their own concerns and mores. The Jews were not so much "influenced" by the Italians as they were one organ in a large cultural organism, a subculture that established its identity in a complex process of adaptation and resistance. . . . [W]e may find it more productive to use this organic model of culture than to chase after who influenced whom.[11]

Historians of the Jews have certainly not been unaware of these "organic" models; in his essay in *Cultures of the Jews* on Jewish culture in Poland, and in a more programmatic essay, Moshe Rosman explicitly discards "influence" and "borrowing" as analytically useful terms.[12] Indeed, I suspect that Biale is here articulating the consensus of historians of early modern and modern Jews.[13]

The goal of this essay is to articulate and programmatically draw out the implications of this approach for the study of ancient Jews and Judaism. Building on the work of the scholars mentioned above, I will argue for a historiographical model that avoids the traditional dichotomy between "Jewish" and "alien" cultures and the language that this traditional model

---

10. See Benedict R. Anderson, *Imagined Communities: Reflections on the Origin and Spread of Nationalism* (rev. ed.; London: Verso, 1991).
11. David Biale, "Preface: Toward a Cultural History of the Jews," in Biale, *Cultures of the Jews*, xix.
12. Moshe Rosman, "Innovative Tradition: Jewish Culture in the Polish-Lithuanian Commonwealth," in Biale, *Cultures of the Jews*, 523–30. Cf. Moshe Rosman, "A Prolegomenon to the Study of Jewish Cultural History," *Jewish Studies: An Internet Journal* 1 (2002), http://www.biu.ac.il/JS/JSIJ/1-2002/Rosman.doc.
13. See David N. Myers, *Resisting History: Historicism and Its Discontents in German-Jewish Thought* (Jews, Christians, and Muslims from the Ancient to the Modern World; Princeton, NJ: Princeton University Press, 2003), 162–68. For a survey of some of this literature, see Moshe Rosman's essay in this volume.

most often uses to describe the relationship between them. Instead, I argue for an approach that recognizes Jews as subjective agents fully embedded within their cultural environments. There are four primary characteristics to this approach: (1) it focuses on people and their agency rather than on abstractions; (2) it recognizes the fluid nature of identity and identity formation; (3) it assumes similarities and seeks to explain difference; (4) and it explicitly justifies the linking of different types of data, such as using archaeology to interpret texts and vice versa.

Focus on People, Not Abstractions

One of the reasons that scholars of Jews in antiquity have been slow to abandon a historiographical model of static encounters between easily defined cultures has been that this model has such a long and venerable history that any departure from it—no matter how intellectually justified— seems radical. For this reason, it is important to trace, however briefly and insufficiently, the theological roots and assumptions of the model itself.

As told by the Bible, the history of Israel is a history of cultural struggle; the biblical etymology of "Israel," in fact, links its meaning to "struggle" (Gen 32:29). Legal, narrative, and historiographical sections of the Hebrew Bible all reinforce the notion that Israel is a "people apart," a group that has a particular essence marked by its relationship with and mode of devotion to its God. Legal sections of the Pentateuch, for example, construct a sexually promiscuous Canaanite Other, against which Israel's proper behavior is defined.[14] The Israelite origin narratives, from Abraham through Moses, are preoccupied with the theme of self-definition and identity formation.[15] In these stories, cultures emerge as sealed and unchanging, with an "essence" opposed to that of Israel.[16] The reality, as we now know, was far more complex, but no careful reader of the Bible can fail to be impressed by Israel's continuous struggle to retain its cultural distinctiveness amidst external and internal threats.

This biblical model was certainly influential on the Jewish author or epitomizer of 2 Maccabees, writing in the late second century B.C.E.[17] Yet

---

14. See most vividly Lev 18:1–4, 24–30. On the charge of cultic prostitution as a rhetoric of "othering," see Robert A. Oden, Jr., *The Bible without Theology: The Theological Tradition and Alternatives to It* (San Francisco: Harper & Row, 1987), 131–53.

15. This preoccupation can be embedded quite subtly. See Robert L. Cohn, "Before Israel: The Canaanites as Other in Biblical Tradition," in *The Other in Jewish Thought and History: Constructions of Jewish Culture and Identity* (ed. Laurence J. Silberstein and Robert L. Cohn; New Perspectives on Jewish Studies; New York: New York University Press, 1994), 74–80.

16. See Ronald S. Hendel, "Israel among the Nations: Biblical Culture in the Ancient Near East," in Biale, *Cultures of the Jews*, 43–75, esp. 43–46.

17. See Daniel R. Schwartz, "On Something Biblical about 2 Maccabees," in *Biblical Per-*

this author shifts the focus from a people, Israel, to their culture, "Judaism." 2 Maccabees uses the new term "Judaism" to denote a distinctive culture locked in eternal and mortal combat with "Hellenism."[18] This text thus sharpens the biblical conflict model: "Judaism" and "Hellenism" become opposites in a way that "Israelite" and "Moabite" never are.

To the extent that the rabbis had any historiographical model, they too understood their culture to be one locked in essential combat with that of the Greeks.[19] For the rabbis, the opposite of "Jew" is "Greek."[20] The opposite of the religion of Israel is *avodah zarah*, the strange worship exemplified by, although not limited to, the Greeks. For many rabbis, "Greek wisdom" is opposed to Jewish wisdom, and according to some rabbis is to be avoided completely.[21]

This traditional understanding of the relationship between "Jewish" and "non-Jewish culture," now preserved in biblical and rabbinic texts and reinforced by their study, parallels a strong Christian historiographical

---

spectives: Early Use and Interpretation of the Bible in Light of the Dead Sea Scrolls (ed. Michael E. Stone and Esther G. Chazon; Studies on the Texts of the Desert of Judah 28; Leiden: Brill, 1998), 223–32.

18. For the term "Judaism," see 2 Macc 2:21; 8:1; 14:38. For "Hellenism," see 2 Macc 4:13–15, which describes the "acme of Hellenism" in Jerusalem. On these terms, see Yehoshua Amir, "The Term Ioudaismos (*Ioudaismos*): A Study in Jewish-Hellenistic Self-Identification," *Immanuel* 14 (1982): 34–41; Jan Willem van Henten, *The Maccabean Martyrs as Saviours of the Jewish People: A Study of 2 and 4 Maccabees* (Leiden: Brill, 1997), 201–4; Shaye J. D. Cohen, "Religion, Ethnicity, and 'Hellenism' in the Emergence of Jewish Identity in Maccabean Palestine," in *Religion and Religious Practice in the Seleucid Kingdom* (ed. Per Bilde et al.; Aarhus: Aarhus University Press, 1990), 204–23; idem, "Ioudaios; 'Judaean' and 'Jew' in Susanna, First Maccabees, and Second Macabees," in *Geschichte–Tradition–Reflexion: Festschrift für Martin Hengel zum 70 Geburtstag* (ed. Peter Schäfer et al.; 3 vols.; Tübingen: Mohr Siebeck, 1996), 1:211–20, esp. 215–20. Cohen, against Amir, prefers "Jewishness" to Judaism as a translation of *ioudaismos*. See also Gabriele Boccaccini's article in this volume.

19. On the lack of rabbinic historiography, see Yosef Hayim Yerushalmi, *Zakhor: Jewish History and Jewish Memory* (Seattle: University of Washington Press, 1982), 16–26. For a more nuanced position on the ways that the rabbis were sensitive to history, see Isaiah M. Gafni, "Concepts of Periodization and Causality in Talmudic Literature," *Jewish History* 10 (1996): 21–38.

20. This position has never, to my knowledge, been systematically argued, but see, for example, *t. Ber.* 6:18, in which the rabbinic man is commanded to thank God each day for not making him a boor, a woman, or a non-Jew, each of which denotes a distinct and meaningful Other. For a more subtle conclusion, see Steven D. Fraade, "Navigating the Anomalous: Non-Jews at the Intersection of Early Rabbinic Law and Narrative," in Silberstein and Cohn, *Other in Jewish Thought and History*, 145–65.

21. See the essay by Saul Lieberman, "The Alleged Ban on Greek Wisdom," in Saul Lieberman, *Hellenism in Jewish Palestine: Studies in the Literary Transmission, Beliefs and Manners of Palestine in the I Century B.C.E.–IV Century C.E.* (New York: Jewish Theological Seminary, 1950), 100–114. Cf. Philip S. Alexander, "Hellenism and Hellenization as Problematic Historiographical Categories," in *Paul Beyond the Judaism/Hellenism Divide* (ed. Troels Engberg-Pedersen; Louisville: Westminster John Knox, 2001), 72–79.

tradition that opposed Judaism to Christianity. Early Christians sought to define themselves against the Jewish Other, constructing a category, "Judaism," that at times only marginally if at all described the beliefs and practices of real Jews.[22] Even the eighteenth-century *philosophes*, with their uneasy relationship to Christianity, continued to maintain an essentialized view of "Judaism" as Other.[23]

Jewish and Christian theological and historiographical trends converged in the nineteenth century. New Testament scholars divided the objects of their study into "Hellenism," "Judaism," and that odd hybrid, "Hellenistic Judaism."[24] Contemporary Jewish scholars found this division congenial.[25] By the middle of the twentieth century, the categories of "Judaism" and "Hellenism" were so entrenched that nearly all scholars of antiquity took them for granted, debating primarily about the relationships between them.[26] The category "Hellenistic Judaism" grew in the middle space to represent a phenomenon thought to be half-way from Judaism to Christianity.[27]

---

22. See Judith Lieu, *Image and Reality: The Jews in the World of the Christians in the Second Century* (Edinburgh: T&T Clark, 1996). For a particularly stunning example of the aporia between the heuristic construction of Judaism and its reality, see Jeremy Cohen, *The Friars and the Jews: The Evolution of Medieval Anti-Judaism* (Ithaca, NY: Cornell University Press, 1982).

23. See Arthur Hertzberg, *The French Enlightenment and the Jews: The Origins of Modern Anti-Semitism* (New York: Columbia University Press, 1968), 280–86; Allen Arkush, "Voltaire on Judaism and Christianity," *AJS Review* 18 (1993): 223–43; Adam Sutcliffe, "Can a Jew Be a Philosophe? Isaac de Pinto, Voltaire, and Jewish Participation in the European Enlightenment," *Jewish Social Studies* 6 (2000): 31–51.

24. See Dale Martin, "Paul and the Judaism/Hellenism Dichotomy: Toward a Social History of the Question," in Engberg-Pedersen, *Paul Beyond the Judaism/Hellenism Divide*, 29–61. See also the essay by Boccaccini in this volume.

25. See Maren R. Niehoff, "Alexandrian Judaism in 19th Century *Wissenschaft des Judentums*: Between Christianity and Modernization," in Oppenheimer, *Jüdische Geschichte in hellenistisch-römischer Zeit*, 9–28; Ismar Schorsch, *From Text to Context: The Turn to History in Modern Judaism* (Tauber Institute for the Study of European Jewry 19; Hanover, NH: Brandeis University Press, 1994), esp. 266–302.

26. The essays in Fischel, *Essays in Greco-Roman and Related Talmudic Literature* amply attest to the attractiveness of "influence" as an explanatory concept. The trend continues among many excellent modern scholars. Cf. Martin Goodman, "Jews and Judaism in the Second Temple Period," in *The Oxford Handbook of Jewish Studies* (ed. Martin Goodman, Jeremy Cohen, and David Sorkin; Oxford: Oxford University Press, 2002), 36–52, esp. 42. Exemplary is John J. Collins, "Cult and Culture: The Limits of Hellenization in Judea," in *Hellenism in the Land of Israel* (ed. John J. Collins and Gregory E. Sterling; Christianity and Judaism in Antiquity 13; Notre Dame, IN: University of Notre Dame Press, 2001), 38–61. Collins is clearly aware of the problems that these terms present, yet uses them uncritically in his analysis. In the same volume, Gregory E. Sterling, "Judaism Between Jerusalem and Alexandria," argues that "While all Jews were hellenized, the specifics of their Hellenization varied markedly" (264). My point is that there are better ways to frame the question that avoid the concept of "hellenization."

27. See Martin, "Paul and the Judaism/Hellenism Dichotomy."

Now, as Biale suggests and Schäfer has recently argued, there are two critical flaws with this historiographical model. The first is the reification of culture implied by categories such as "Judaism" and "Hellenism."[28] "Judaism"—as some kind of independent, unfolding tradition with its own inexorable logic—is not tangible; it is an abstract, second-order category.[29] For "insiders," Jews who identify themselves as religious practitioners, it is a functionally useful category that allows them to see a vast array of diverse religious practices as part of the same tradition. In Benedict Anderson's felicitous phrase, it reinforces an "imagined community."[30] Yet I am becoming increasingly convinced that particularly for historians of the Jews of antiquity, "Judaism" as an analytical category is more pernicious than useful. Terms such as "Judaism" or "Jewish culture" immediately imply a model of culture that separates "Jewish" from "non-Jewish" culture. Unless used with extensive qualifications, the terms obscure the ongoing messy negotiations that constitute culture. At the same time, they obscure agency. Jews exist, not Judaism.[31] Each Jewish community enters its own distinctive cultural negotiations with tradition, non-Jews, and other Jews.[32] It is perhaps more awkward but certainly more accurate to speak of how Jews wrestle with these issues, than how "Judaism" or "Jewish culture" responds to "Hellenism," "Christianity" or "non-Jewish" culture.

The second critical flaw with this model is the analytical terminology used to describe the relationships between the categories. "Syncretism" used to be commonly used to label the borrowing and incorporation of elements from one "culture" into another; Hellenistic Judaism was thus seen as a syncretistic phenomenon, combining "Jewish" and "Hellenistic"

---

28. See Alexander, "Hellenism and Hellenization."
29. See Schäfer, *Mirror of His Beauty*, 222, 229–35. I do not think that Schäfer himself goes far enough. He seems to want to preserve "influence" as an explanatory mechanism (thus talking of "varying grades and shades—or, better yet, different configurations—of what might be called, for strictly heuristic purposes, 'Hebraic' and 'Hellenic'" [p. 222]), but ultimately does not develop a new model of "influence" that overcomes its inherent limitations. Similarly, despite his dissatisfaction with current historiographical approaches, Israel Jacob Yuval uses "influence" as an explanatory model; see *"Two Nations in Your Womb": Perceptions of Jews and Christians* (Tel Aviv: Am Oved, 2000), esp. 41–43 (Heb.).
30. Anderson, *Imagined Communities*.
31. For some insightful theoretical comments on the relationship between such categories as religious traditions and agency, see Robert Ford Campany, "On the Very Idea of Religions (in the Modern West and in Early Medieval China)," *History of Religions* 42 (2003): 287–319.
32. It is, perhaps, only a marginal improvement to speak of "Jews" as a single, united corporate entity in antiquity that acts with a single "national" will. Some Zionist historiography uses this national model. See Seth Schwartz, "Historiography on the Jews in the 'Talmudic Period' (70–640 CE)," in Goodman, Cohen, and Sorkin, *Oxford Handbook of Jewish Studies*, 79–114, esp. 83–87.

culture. Syncretism, however, with its implied negative value judgment of inauthenticity, is hardly a neutral term; for this reason, contemporary scholars of Jews in antiquity have by and large abandoned it as a useful analytical category.[33] From around the mid-twentieth century until today, it has become more common to speak of the Greek, Hellenistic, Roman, Babylonian, or Christian "influence" on the Jews. In his monumental *Judaism and Hellenism*, Martin Hengel paradoxically demonstrated the deep "Hellenization" of "Jewish" culture in Palestine, and thus the difficulty of using "Hellenistic Judaism" and "Palestinian Judaism" as apposite categories, while at the same time implicitly justifying the analytical usefulness of the terms "Judaism" and "Hellenism."[34] "Influence," as a descriptor of similarities, is hardly better; its flaccidness and imprecision as an explanatory term have long been recognized.[35]

Thus, I think that it is critical to disentangle the concepts "Judaism" and "Jewish culture" from "the Jews." Scholars can and should use the category "Judaism" to denote the worldview and rituals of a particular group of Jews, but it is always important to remember that "Judaism" as we use the term is a heuristic construct, a category created and used by modern scholars for specific reasons.[36] Getting beyond the confusion that it has created in historiography of the Jews of antiquity requires shifting attention to the agents themselves, the Jews.

De-essentialize the Jews

"How do you know a Jew in antiquity when you see one?" Shaye Cohen asks in the subtitle of an essay.[37] The answer, of course, is that you don't—

---

33. On the history of "syncretism" as an analytical category in the study of religion and anthropology, see Rosalind Shaw and Charles Stewart, "Introduction: Problematizing Syncretism," in *Syncretism/Anti-Syncretism: The Politics of Religious Synthesis* (ed. Charles Stewart and Rosalind Shaw; London: Routledge, 1994), 1–26. Cf. David Chidchester, "Colonialism," in *Guide to the Study of Religion* (ed. Willi Braun and Russell T. McCutcheon; London: Cassell, 2000), 423–37, esp. 435–36.

34. Martin Hengel, *Judaism and Hellenism* (trans. John Bowden; Minneapolis: Fortress, 1974); idem, "Judaism and Hellenism Revisited," in Collins and Sterling, *Hellenism in the Land of Israel*, 6–37.

35. Edouard Will, "'Influence': note sur un pseudo-concept," in *Hellenica et Judaica; hommage à Valentin Nikiprowetzky* (ed. André Caquot, Mireille Hadas-Lebel, and Jean Riaud; Leuven: Peeters, 1986), 499–505.

36. I think that this basic conceptual confusion undermines Schwartz, *Imperialism and Jewish Society*; see his discussion on pp. 8–12.

37. Shaye J. D. Cohen, "'Those Who Say They are Jews and Are Not': How Do You Know a Jew in Antiquity When You See One?" in *Diasporas in Antiquity* (ed. Shaye J. D. Cohen and Ernest S. Frerichs; BJS 288; Atlanta: Scholars Press, 1993), 1–45.

at least not according to any obvious visual cues. Despite the strong self-assertions of many Jews that they were a distinctive people, and the legal recognitions of Jew by Greeks and Romans, Jewish identity throughout this time was more fluid than historical accounts of "the Jews" frequently reflect.[38]

The fluidity of Jewish identity in antiquity has only recently begun to receive sustained scholarly attention. Many inscriptions that used to be considered unproblematically "Jewish"—or unproblematically not Jewish—turn out to be far more complex than originally thought.[39] Seth Schwartz has argued that in second-century Palestine, there was little that was distinctively "Jewish" about "Jewish" urban culture.[40] Schwartz's position is admittedly controversial, but it does frankly acknowledge the lack of extant evidence for such a distinctive culture.[41] Even into the fourth century, the boundaries between "Judaism" and "Christianity" at times may have remained porous.[42]

"Jews," like "Judaism," should not be taken for granted. To be a Jew in antiquity could mean many different things to different people; to make a priori assumptions about who the "Jews" were is to obscure the ways in which Jewish identity could be fluid. Put differently, the ambiguity of the very criteria by which historians of the Jews gather their data (i.e., "Jew") needs to be recognized.

Theology accounts for the essentializing of Judaism, but Zionism is the more direct cause of modern historiographic essentializing of the Jews. Modern historical study of the Jews developed in nineteenth-century Germany, at a time of increasing state nationalism that, in its more romantic forms, attributed a unique essence to each *Volk*, or people. As the Jewish

---

38. Much of the extant Jewish literature in Greek is preoccupied with assertions of ethnic distinctiveness, and even superiority. See John J. Collins, *Between Athens and Jerusalem: Jewish Identity in the Hellenistic Diaspora* (2nd ed.; Bible Resource Series; Grand Rapids: Eerdmans, 2000). It is important not to forget that Jews were also defined from the outside. See Daniel R. Schwartz, "Antisemitism and other -ism's in the Greco-Roman World," in *Demonizing the Other: Antisemitism, Racism, and Xenophobia* (ed. Robert S. Wistrich; Amsterdam: Harwood, 1999), 73–87; Martin Goodman, "Nerva, the *Fiscus Judaicus*, and Jewish Identity," *JRS* 79 (1989): 40–44; Amnon Linder, ed., *The Jews in Roman Imperial Legislation* (Detroit: Wayne State University Press, 1987).

39. See Ross Kraemer, "On the Meaning of the Term 'Jew' in Greco-Roman Inscriptions," *HTR* 82 (1989): 35–53; Jan W. van Henten and Alice J. Bij de Vaate, "Jewish or Non-Jewish? Some Remarks on the Identification of Jewish Inscriptions from Asia Minor," *BO* 53 (1996): 16–28.

40. Schwartz, *Imperialism and Jewish Society*, 129–61.

41. See Yaron Z. Eliav, "The Matrix of Ancient Judaism: A Review Essay of Seth Schwartz's *Imperialism and Jewish Society 200 BCE to 640 CE*," *Prooftexts* 24 (2004): 116–28.

42. Daniel Boyarin, *Border Lines: The Partition of Judaeo-Christianity* (Divinations; Philadelphia: University of Pennsylvania Press, 2004).

manifestation of this nationalism, Zionism too returned to the biblical notion of "Israel" as a unique nation, set apart with its own essence.[43]

The assumption that there is a unique and identifiable people, Israel, with its own culture and history—*toledot am yisrael*—underlies nearly all Israeli historiography on Jews in antiquity (and beyond). Gedalyah Alon's lectures and study have had a decisive influence on later Israeli historiography, and its assumptions are thoroughly Zionist: the "Jews in their Land" strove for political and institutional autonomy.[44] The Jews, in this view, are a given; it is the historian's job to discover how they have expressed their national spirit through the ages.[45]

Any historiography that either explicitly or implicitly ascribes an "essence" or "spirit" to a people is not tenable in today's academy.[46] There were Jews in antiquity. Ancient Jews asserted their distinctiveness, in literary and epigraphic forms. The challenge for modern historians is to avoid imposing a static and essentialist definition of what it meant to be a Jew back onto identity formations that frequently were perspectival and in flux. Minimally, the scholar needs to state clearly what she or he means by using such concepts as "Jews" or "Jewish"; ideally, it is precisely the explication of these ancient strategies of Jewish identity formation that can be incorporated into nearly all historical studies.

Assume Similarity, Explain Difference

Over the last century scholarship on Jews in antiquity has tended to emphasize how alike Jews were to their neighbors. Many Jews in antiquity maintained their ethnic distinctiveness, but they were physically indistinguishable from, and socially integrated with, their non-Jewish neighbors.[47]

---

43. See David N. Myers, *Re-inventing the Jewish Past: European Jewish Intellectuals and the Zionist Return to History* (Studies in Jewish History; New York: Oxford University Press, 1995). In their essentialization of national identity Zionist historians were simply participating in wider historiographical trends. See Arielle Rein, "Patterns of National Historiography in B. Dinur's Work," *Zion* 68 (2003): 425–66 (Heb.).

44. See Schwartz, "Historiography on the Jews," 83–87; Yeshayahu Gafni, "On Gedaliahu Alon and His Role in the Study of Rabbinic Historiography," *Jewish Studies* 41 (2002): 75–83 (Heb.).

45. This assumption is not limited to Zionist historians. It underlies, for example, Judah Goldin, ed., *The Jewish Expression* (New Haven: Yale University Press, 1976).

46. Even Jacob Neusner sometimes comes close to essentializing the people of Israel. See Jacob Neusner, "Stable Symbols in a Shifting Society: The Delusion of the Monolithic Gentile in Documents of Late Fourth-Century Judaism," in *"To See Ourselves as Others See Us": Christians, Jews, "Others" in Late Antiquity* (ed. Jacob Neusner and Ernest S. Frerichs; Scholars Press Studies in the Humanities; Chico, CA: Scholars Press, 1985), 373–96.

47. See Cohen, "'Those Who Say They are Jews and Are Not.'" See the important qual-

They shared their "deep structures" of meaning.[48] Given the significant and growing indications that Jews shared much with the larger cultures in which they lived, these similarities cease to require explanation. The thing that needs explaining is difference: How and why are a given group of Jews different from those around them? How and why did they create their own distinctive ethnic identity?

The Greeks and Romans both recognized "ethnicity" as an organizing category of identity. Greek ethnography dates back to Herodotus and flourishes in the Hellenistic period.[49] Romans and Christians also developed ethnographies.[50] In addition, both Greek and Roman legal systems allowed ethnic groups to create corporate, legal identities.[51] At least some Jews in Egypt and Cyrene (modern-day Libya), like other contemporary ethnic communities, had their own semi-autonomous civic institutions, *politeumata*.[52]

I am suggesting that when these Greek-speaking Jews created their distinctive "imagined communities" from their cultural and traditional

---

ifications of Daniel R. Schwartz, "How at Home Were the Jews of the Hellenistic Diaspora?" *CP* 95 (2000): 349–57.

48. See Michael L. Satlow, *Tasting the Dish: Rabbinic Rhetorics of Sexuality* (BJS 303; Atlanta: Scholars Press, 1995), 315–20, 330–31; Eliav, "Viewing the Sculptural Environment."

49. See the classic essays of Arnaldo Momigliano, especially "Persian Historiography, Greek Historiography, and Jewish Historiography," in *The Classical Foundations of Modern Historiography* (Sather Classical Lectures 54; Berkeley: University of California Press, 1990), 5–28; and "The Herodotean and the Thucydidean Tradition," 29–53 in the same volume; idem, *Essays in Ancient and Modern Historiography* (Middletown, CT: Wesleyan University Press, 1977); idem, *Alien Wisdom: The Limits of Hellenization* (Cambridge: Cambridge University Press, 1975). On the method and influence of Herodotus, see François Hartog, *The Mirror of Herodotus: The Representation of the Other in the Writing of History* (New Historicism: Studies in Cultural Poetics 5; Berkeley: University of California Press, 1988). For more recent research, see Irad Malkin, ed., *Ancient Perceptions of Greek Ethnicity* (Washington: Center for Hellenic Studies, 2001).

50. On Christian ethnography, see Guy G. Stroumsa, "Philosophy of the Barbarians: On Early Christian Ethnological Representations," in Schäfer, *Geschichte–Tradition–Reflexion*, 3:339–68.

51. See Emil Schürer, *The History of the Jewish People in the Age of Jesus Christ* (rev. and ed. Geza Vermes, Fergus Millar, and Martin Goodman; 3 vols.; Edinburgh: T&T Clark, 1973–86), 3.1:107–25. Roman law was also flexible. See Greg Woolf, *Becoming Roman: The Origins of Provincial Civilization in Gaul* (Cambridge: Cambridge University Press, 1998), 71–72; Tessa Rajak, "Was There a Roman Charter for the Jews?" *JRS* 74 (1984): 107–23.

52. On the existence of Jewish *politeumata*, see Jean Juster, *Les Juifs dans l'empire romain: Leur condition juridique, économique et sociale* (2 vols.; Paris: Paul Geuthner, 1914), 2:1–27; Alfredo Mordechai Rabello, *Ha-Yehudim ba-Imperyah ha-Romit bi-re'i ha-hakikah: be-'ikvot mekharo shel G'an Yuster* (Jerusalem: Merkaz Dinur, 1987), 65–68; Schürer, *History of the Jewish People*, 3.1:86–107. For Egypt, see esp. James M. S. Cowey and Klaus Maresch, *Urkunden des Politeuma der Juden von Herakleopolis (144/3 – 133/2 v. Chr.) (P. Polit. Iud.)* (Papyrologica Coloniensia 29; Wiesbaden: Westdeutscher, 2001).

resources, they were, ironically, engaged in a more widespread process of identity formation. Groups, ethnic and otherwise, in the Greek and Roman worlds could maintain distinctive identities, and there were accepted strategies for marking these identities.[53] To Greeks and Romans, the Jews were little different from any other ethnic group. They had distinctive customs and ideas, but, as Martin Goodman has proposed, "the oddities of the Jews in the Graeco-Roman world were no greater than that of the many other distinctive ethnic groups, such as Idumaeans, Celts, or Numidians...."[54]

In this plan, then, the role of the historian is to recover within local Jewish communities the arenas in which they asserted their distinct identities as Jews, *how* they did so, and *why*. It is significant, for example, both that through most of antiquity most Jews did *not* use marriage as a locus in which to assert a distinctively Jewish identity, and that this began to change in late antiquity.[55] Outside of prescriptive rabbinic texts there is little evidence that Jews, from the Persian period through late antiquity, regularly used or were required to use a distinctive civil law.[56] Where precisely did Jews think it was important to mark their own identities as Jews?

Identity formation was a complex, variable, and messy enterprise that worked in the present but that drew upon the past, as understood in the present. There was no obvious or natural way to be a Jew, but that does not mean that all options were open.

Each Jewish community may have fashioned its own "culture" or expression of identity, but it did not make it up out of whole cloth. When Jewish communities, or individual Jews, chose to mark their identity as Jews, they drew upon the stuff of their tradition, as they understood it within their local cultural frame.[57]

In Rome, for example, six Jewish catacombs that together contain about six hundred burial inscriptions from late antiquity have been discovered.[58]

---

53. See Ramsay MacMullen, "The Unromanized in Rome," in Cohen and Frerichs, *Diasporas in Antiquity*, 47–64.

54. Martin Goodman, "Jews, Greeks, and Romans," in *Jews in a Graeco-Roman World* (ed. Martin Goodman; Oxford: Clarendon, 1998), 4.

55. See Michael L. Satlow, *Jewish Marriage in Antiquity* (Princeton, NJ: Princeton University Press, 2001); idem, "Slipping Towards Sacrament: Jews, Christians, and Marriage," in *Jewish Culture and Society under the Christian Roman Empire* (ed. Richard Kalmin and Seth Schwartz; Leuven: JTS Press and Peeters, 2003), 65–89.

56. See Hayim Lapin, *Early Rabbinic Civil Law and the Social History of Roman Galilee* (BJS 307; Atlanta: Scholars Press, 1995).

57. See Cohen, "'Those Who Say They Are Jews and Are Not.'" Cohen essentially argues that Jewish identity was voluntary and based on association and observance.

58. The classic, and still useful, discussion is by Harry J. Leon, *The Jews of Ancient Rome* (Philadelphia: Jewish Publication Society of America, 1960). Cf. Leonard V. Rutgers, *The Jews in Late Ancient Rome: Evidence of Cultural Interaction in the Roman Diaspora* (Religions in the Graeco-Roman World; Leiden: Brill, 1995), who corrects Leon's dating (although note the

Beyond Influence   49

All of the inscriptions are in Greek and Latin, and in form and language they are virtually indistinguishable from contemporary non-Jewish epitaphs. Yet several of the inscriptions from the Jewish catacombs also have etched on them some distinctive Jewish symbol, such as a menorah.⁵⁹ A few even have a Hebrew phrase at the end, typically "*shalom*."⁶⁰ One inscription reads in Greek: "Here lies Sabbatius, twice archon. He lived 35 years. In peace his sleep." Following this is a Hebrew phrase (שאלום על ישראל), with etchings of a shofar, menorah, and lulav.⁶¹ The phrase—misspelled in the Hebrew by someone who clearly had in mind a Greek phonetic system—together with its symbols clearly serve as a marker of ethnicity. Even in the most "Jewishly" marked of all graveyards, at Beit She'arim, some of the conventional Greek inscriptions contain short Hebrew phrases as ethnic markers.⁶²

Iconic artifacts demonstrate another strategy of identity formation. The content of the third-century C.E. synagogue mosaics in the Syrian border town of Dura Europos are distinctively Jewish; the scenes are drawn from the Bible.⁶³ The style is clearly drawn from the surrounding culture. Generally in antiquity the similarities between Jewish and non-Jewish material artifacts can be so strong that it is sometimes impossible to recover whether they were produced by Jews or Christians, as when, for example, the object draws either linguistically or iconographically from the Hebrew Bible.⁶⁴

Even Jewish understandings of the Torah offer yet another kind of example of the ways in which Jews filtered their traditions through their

---

problematic title!). The inscriptions have recently been republished by David Noy, *Jewish Inscriptions of Western Europe*, vol. 2, *The City of Rome* (Cambridge: Cambridge University Press, 1995).

59. See, e.g., *CII*, nos. 62, 86, 89, 105, 118, 234. On the menorah as a symbol of Jewish identity, see Rachel Hachlili, *The Menorah, the Ancient Seven-Armed Candelabrum: Origin, Form, and Significance* (Leiden: Brill, 2001), 204–9, where she also provocatively compares its use as an identity marker to that of the cross for contemporary Christians.

60. E.g., *CII*, nos. 319, 349.

61. *CII*, no. 397.

62. See, e.g., Moshe Schwabe and Baruch Lifshitz, *The Greek Inscriptions*, vol. 2 of *Beth She'arim: Report on the Excavations During 1936–1940* (New Brunswick, NJ: Rutgers University Press, 1973–76), nos. 178, 203. Cf. Seth Schwartz, "Language, Power, and Identity in Ancient Palestine," *Past and Present* 148 (1995): 3–47; Hayim Lapin, "Palestinian Inscriptions and Jewish Ethnicity in Late Antiquity," in *Galilee through the Centuries: Confluence of Cultures* (ed. Eric M. Meyers; Winona Lake, IN: Eisenbrauns, 1999), 239–67.

63. For an overview, see Erwin R. Goodenough, *Jewish Symbols in the Greco-Roman Period* (ed. Jacob Neusner; Princeton, NJ: Princeton University Press, 1988), 178–83.

64. See Johan H. M. Strubbe, "Curses against Violation of the Grave in Jewish Epitaphs from Asia Minor," in *Studies in Early Jewish Epigraphy* (ed. Jan Willem van Henten and Pieter W. van der Horst; Arbeiten zur Geschichte des Antiken Judentums und des Urchristentums 21; Leiden: Brill, 1994), 70–128.

local cultural contexts to construct identity. Both Philo and Josephus seem to understand "Torah" as a Jewish constitution analogous in all ways to other contemporary constitutions, only better.[65] Martin Goodman has suggested that many Jews in antiquity saw the physical object of the Torah as a sort of pagan idol.[66] At least some rabbis, I have argued, had a very different understanding of Torah, seeing it not as a national or ethnic constitution but as a source of wisdom analogous to non-Jewish philosophical classics, whose study mirrored the philosophical spiritual exercises so common throughout late antiquity.[67]

These brief linguistic, iconic, and conceptual examples illustrate the same process: Jews living fully within their local cultures while marking themselves as distinct according to the rules, or *"habitus,"* of those local cultures.[68] Many Jews in antiquity appear to have had the choice of whether to publicly identify themselves as Jews. What, for example, of the many thousands of dead Roman Jews who were not buried in the local Jewish catacombs? Do hundreds of other Jewish catacombs lurk underground, waiting to be discovered, or did Jews choose to be buried among non-Jews? Such questions take on meaning only within a framework that abandons a focus on systems and the influence between them.

Despite my emphasis thus far on focusing on Jews rather than Judaism, I do think that shifting our approach can open up productive ways of discussing the practices, beliefs, and worldviews of the Jews in antiquity. In his monumental *Jewish Symbols in the Greco-Roman World*, Erwin Goodenough highlighted the variety of Jewish religious expression in antiquity. Goodenough posited two primary types of "Judaism," one rabbinic and the other mystical and syncretistic. Jacob Neusner extended this insight to

---

65. See Reinhard Weber, *Das "Gesetz" bei Philon von Alexandrien und Flavius Josephus: Studien zum Verständnis und zur Funktion der Thora bei den beiden Hauptzegen des hellenistischen Judentums* (Arbeiten zur Religion und Geschichte des Urchristentums 11; Frankfurt am Main: Peter Lang, 2001), 68–114, 236–71.

66. Martin Goodman, "Sacred Scripture and the 'Defiling of the Hands,'" *JTS* 41 (1990): 99–107.

67. Michael L. Satlow, "'And on the Earth You Shall Sleep': Talmud Torah and Rabbinic Asceticism," *JR* 83 (2003): 204–25.

68. The concept, of course, is Pierre Bourdieu's. He defines *habitus* as "systems of durable, transposable *dispositions*, structured structures predisposed to function as structuring structures, that is, as principles of the generation and structuring of practices and representations which can be objectively 'regulated' and 'regular' without in any way being the product of obedience to rules . . ."; see Pierre Bourdieu, *Outline of a Theory of Practice* (trans. Richard Nice; Cambridge Studies in Social Anthropology; Cambridge: Cambridge University Press, 1977), 72 (original emphasis). Cf. Martha Himmelfarb, "Judaism and Hellenism in 2 Maccabees," *Poetics Today* 19 (1998): 19–40; Eliav, "Viewing the Sculptural Environment," esp. 433: "The rabbis' ruling on Roman statuary . . . reflects the discerning attitude of a minority group . . . that forged its own way of life out of a profound awareness of the environment in which it was living, defining its own uniqueness within this environment."

speak of the "Judaisms" of antiquity.[69] Although I think that Neusner errs by considering each *text* as representative of a distinctive form of Judaism, this model does suggest that the religious practices of each Jewish community need to be evaluated on their own terms.[70] Jonathan Z. Smith has taken this a step further, arguing for a polythetic definition of Judaism.[71] For Smith, the creation of any overarching definition of Judaism starts with, and must be inclusive of, the local "Judaisms." That is, the religious practices of local Jewish communities are the primary focus of first-order historical scholarship, and "Judaism" is a second-order scholarly term to accommodate them. First-order scholarship must thus focus not on an abstract notion of tradition but on the Jews and their religious practices in their distinct historical contexts.

Justify Data Selection

One of the reasons that scholars of the Jews of antiquity have been slow to adopt historiographical models like this with their focus on the "thick description" of local Jewish communities is evidentiary.[72] Cultural history, in the sense that it is practiced by modern historians, is out of the reach of all historians of antiquity. Only two Jewish societies in antiquity—the rabbis and the authors of the Dead Sea Scrolls—left anything approaching a significant body of evidence, and the extant evidence is frequently problematic. Otherwise, we know of Jewish communities for which we have very little direct evidence, and we have evidence that we cannot place within a particular community. For example, the synagogue and frescoes from Dura Europos are fascinating in their own right, but cannot be put into the larger context of Jewish life in Dura—there is no other evidence from this community.[73] The complex third- and fourth-century Jewish

---

69. "[T]here were many Judaisms," Neusner succinctly states in his foreword to Goodenough, *Jewish Symbols*, xxvii.

70. For discussions of this issue, see Shaye J. D. Cohen, "The Modern Study of Ancient Judaism," in *The State of Jewish Studies* (ed. Shaye J. D. Cohen and Edward L. Greenstein; Detroit: Wayne State University Press, 1990), 63–65, and Richard S. Sarason, "Response," in ibid., 74–79; Seth Schwartz, *Imperialism and Jewish Society*, 8–9.

71. Jonathan Z. Smith, "Fences and Neighbors: Some Contours of Early Judaism," in *Approaches to Ancient Judaism* (ed. Jacob Neusner; vol. 2; Chico, CA: Scholars Press, 1980), 1–25.

72. For a good survey of recent developments in the field, with explicit regard to issues of evidence, see Isaiah Gafni, "A Generation of Scholarship on Eretz Israel in the Talmud Era: Achievement and Recognition," *Cathedra* 100 (2001): 199–226 (Heb.).

73. For a brief review of the Jewish remains from Dura Europos, see Lee I. Levine, "The Hellenistic-Roman Diaspora CE 70–CE 235: The Archaeological Evidence," in *The Cambridge History of Judaism*, vol. 3, *The Early Roman Period* (ed. William Horbury, William D. Davies, and John Sturdy; Cambridge: Cambridge University Press, 1999), 1014–24.

graveyard in Beit She'arim presents a similar challenge: against what other evidence should we interpret it?[74] A stash of papyri in the Judean desert throws a fascinating light on the legal affairs of a few Jewish families in the second century C.E., but we know neither how representative these families were nor anything about other aspects of their lives.[75] On the other hand, much other evidence floats without a context. A significant corpus of Jewish literature written in Greek survives, but it is largely of unknown date and provenance.[76]

Clearly, any attempt at cultural history of the Jews in antiquity requires an unholy combining of evidence. Combinations of different types of data from antiquity are in no way obvious or natural. Although aware of the different perspectives and provenances of Jewish literature written in Greek, for example, Erich Gruen nevertheless combines these texts into a single argument about the state of "Diaspora" Jewry.[77] Ze'ev Weiss and Ehud Netzer have interpreted the iconography of a synagogue mosaic from Sepphoris against other literature that clearly was not produced in Sepphoris.[78] Whether or not these specific scholarly interpretations are compelling, they point to the need to articulate more fully the model that allows for such combinations of evidence. It is not at all obvious how the evidence from one Jewish community can or should be used with evidence from another Jewish community in antiquity.[79]

In fact, the historiographical shift that I have noted above implies that scholars should focus less on comparing evidence from different Jewish communities and more on using local non-Jewish evidence to create the primary context. Of course scholars have always used pagan and Chris-

---

74. See Zeev Weiss, "Social Aspects of Burial in Beth She'arim: Archeological Finds and Talmudic Stories," in *The Galilee in Late Antiquity* (ed. Lee I. Levine; New York: Jewish Theological Seminary of America, 1992), 357–71, who unselfconsciously juxtaposes rabbinic and archaeological data.

75. See Hannah M. Cotton, "The Rabbis and the Documents," in Goodman, *Jews in a Graeco-Roman World*, 167–79: "I maintain, therefore, that they are representative of Jewish society as a whole in the period under discussion. They present a faithful picture of the realities of life at the time that they were written" (p. 172). It is unclear which "Jewish society" Cotton has in mind.

76. See Ross Shepard Kramer, *When Aseneth Met Joseph: A Late Antique Tale of the Biblical Patriarch and His Egyptian Wife, Reconsidered* (New York: Oxford University Press, 1998), 303–5.

77. Erich S. Gruen, *Diaspora: Jews amidst Greeks and Romans* (Cambridge, MA: Harvard University Press, 2002).

78. Ze'ev Weiss and Ehud Netzer, *Promise and Redemption: A Synagogue Mosaic from Sepphoris* (Jerusalem: Israel Museum, 1996). Cf. Schwartz, *Imperialism and Jewish Society*, 248–61, for a critique of the interpretation of Weiss and Netzer.

79. See the discussion of conflation of evidence in Goodman, "Jews and Judaism in the Second Temple Period," 44–48.

tian evidence in their histories of the Jews of antiquity, often with great effectiveness. Frequently, however, this evidence provides a secondary rather than primary context. If the Jews were more a part of their larger local cultures than they were part of a trans-Mediterranean Jewish culture, then the *comparanda* should be sought locally. To interpret the mosaics of Dura, for example, we need to look primarily at the city and its immediate environs rather than at Philo or the rabbis. When scholars do move further afield—which they frequently should do—they are nevertheless obligated to justify this move explicitly. What, in particular, justifies the elucidation of a particular material artifact with a particular text?

*   *   *

For many scholars of ancient Jews and Judaism, "culture" is a noun rather than a verb. "Jewish culture," "rabbinic culture," and "Greco-Roman culture," for example, are frequently understood as transparent categories needing little explicit justification. No matter how precise the cultural category (e.g., Palestinian amoraic culture) or nuanced the description of the interaction between the cultures, the assumption that culture exists as a static category is severely limiting. When Erich Gruen, for example, asserts that Jewish ideas "expressed themselves quite naturally in Greek forms," he seems to assume that one can speak meaningfully of distinct Jewish culture, however subtle and fluid the interactions between this and "other" cultures.

I have argued here that as an analytic category "culture" works better as a verb.[80] It is an ongoing, shifting, highly complex set of negotiations. Throughout antiquity Jewish identity was largely voluntary, with Jews deeply embedded within their wider environments. Many Jews self-consciously identified as Jews and marked themselves in various, shifting, and unpredictable ways as Jews. To describe "rabbinic culture," for example, is to unpack the ways in which the rabbis filtered their traditions through their deep structures of meaning, which were themselves largely the products of the broader material, intellectual, religious, and social worlds in which they lived. The goals of this essay have been both to articulate the assumptions that might underlie such an approach to "culture" and to argue for its potential utility reframing the study of the Jews of antiquity.

---

80. In Homi Bhabha's oft-quoted formulation, culture is "the 'inter'—the cutting edge of translation and negotiation, the *in-between* space . . ."; see Homi K. Bhabha, *The Location of Culture* (London: Routledge, 1994), 38 (original emphasis).

2

Hellenistic Judaism

Myth or Reality?

GABRIELE BOCCACCINI

יהוה קנני ראשית דרכו
κύριος ἔκτισέν με ἀρχὴν ὁδῶν αὐτοῦ (LXX)
ὁ θεὸς ἐκτήσατό με πρωτίστην τῶν ἑαυτοῦ ἔργων (Philo)
The Lord (God) acquired (made) me as the beginning of His work(s)
(Prov 8:22a)

The Myth of Hellenistic Judaism

The term "Hellenism," indeed, the very concept of it, is a construct of modern scholarship. It was coined by Johann Gustav Droysen (1808–1884) in his *Geschichte des Hellenismus* (published in Hamburg between 1836 and 1843) to describe the period after the conquest of Alexander the Great. He saw it not as a time of decadence following the golden age of Hellenic civilization, but as the creative age of *mixing* of Hellenic and Eastern thought into new cultures and ways of life. Since Droysen, the term and concept of Hellenism have become an established hermeneutical category in the study of ancient philosophy and civilization.[1]

The idea that Alexander's conquest produced a mixing of cultures was not foreign to ancient sources. The treatise "On the Fortune or the Virtue

---

1. Amélie Kuhrt and Susan Sherwin-White, eds., *Hellenism in the East: The Interaction of Greek and non-Greek Civilization from Syria to Central Asia after Alexander* (London: Duckworth, 1987); Frank W. Walbank, *The Hellenistic World* (Fontana History of the Ancient World; London: Fontana, 1981); William W. Tarn and Guy T. Griffith, *Hellenistic Civilization* (3rd ed.; London: Arnold, 1959); Michael Rostovtzeff, *The Social and Economic History of the Hellenistic World* (3 vols.; Oxford: Clarendon, 1941).

of Alexander" in Plutarch's *Moralia* offers already an enthusiastic description of "Hellenistic" society as a melting pot in which "people from everywhere . . . united and mixed as in one great loving cup" (ἐν κρατῆρι φιλοτησίῳ). Plutarch gives all the credit for this revolution to Alexander's genius, and praises Alexander's independence of character and strong determination:

> Alexander did not follow Aristotle's advice to treat the Greeks as if he were their leader, and other peoples as if he were their master; to have regard for the Greeks as for friends and kindred, but to conduct himself toward other peoples as though they were plants or animals, for to do so would have been to cumber his leadership with numerous battles and banishments and festering seditions. But, as he believed that he came as a heaven-sent governor to all, and as a mediator for the whole world, those he could not persuade to unite with him, he conquered by force of arms, and he brought together into one body all men everywhere, *uniting and mixing in one great loving cup, as it were, men's lives, their characters, their marriages, their very habits of life.* (Plutarch, *Alex. fort.* 2.329 bc [Babbitt, LCL; my emphasis])

The trouble with the modern term and concept of "Hellenism" is that the verb *hellēnizō* and the noun *hellēnismos* were never used in ancient sources to denote the mixing of cultures, but rather the contribution given by Hellenic culture to the new civilization.[2] Plutarch was no less enthusiastic in celebrating the "Hellenization" of the East, that is, the assimilation of the "uncivilized" peoples to Hellenic literature, law, and religion:

> O wondrous power of Philosophy, that brought the Indians to worship Greek gods, that brought the Scythians to bury their dead, not to devour them! . . . When Alexander was civilizing Asia, Homer was commonly read, and the children of the Persians, of the Susianians, and of the Gedrosians learned to chant the tragedies of Sophocles and Euripides . . . [t]hrough Alexander Bactria and the Caucasus learned to revere the gods of the Greeks. . . . Alexander established more than seventy cities among savage tribes, and sowed all Asia with Grecian magistracies, and thus overcame its uncivilized and brutish manner of living. . . . Hundreds of thousands have made use of Alexander's law, and continue to use them. Those who were vanquished by Alexander are happier than those who escaped his hand; for these had no one to put an end to the wretchedness of their existence, while the victor compelled those others to lead a happy life. (Plutarch, *Alex. fort.* 2.328c-e [Babbitt, LCL])

The peoples of the East (including the Jews) were much less enthusiastic about being so graciously civilized from their "brutish manner of liv-

---

2. Hans Windisch, "'Ἕλλην," *TWNT* 2:501–13.

ing" and the "wretchedness of their existence." Many felt the spread of Hellenic customs as an imposed colonization—a menace to their own ways of life and religion.³ 1 Maccabees describes the coming of Alexander and his successors as the source of all evil:

> Alexander . . . advanced to the ends of the earth, and plundered many nations. When the earth became quiet before him, he was exalted, and his heart was lifted up. . . . Then his officers began to rule, each in his own place. They all put on crowns after his death, and so did their descendants after them for many years; and they caused many evils on the earth. From them came forth a sinful root, Antiochus Epiphanes. . . . In those days certain renegades came out from Israel and misled many, saying: Let us go and make a covenant with the Gentiles around us. . . . So they built a gymnasium in Jerusalem, according to Gentile custom. . . . They joined with the Gentiles and sold themselves to do evil. (1 Macc 1:1–15)⁴

Commenting on the establishment of the gymnasium in Jerusalem, the author of 2 Maccabees called it "a peak of Hellenization and assimilation to foreign customs" (ἀκμή τις Ἑλληνισμοῦ καὶ πρόσβασις ἀλλοφυλισμοῦ) (2 Macc 4:13). It is clear that by the noun *hellēnismos* he meant something different from the modern term and concept of "Hellenism," namely, the shifting "over to the Greek way of life" (πρὸς τὸν Ἑλληνικὸν χαρακτῆρα) (2 Macc 4:10), or the adoption of "the Greek constitution" (τὴν Ἑλληνικὴν πολιτείαν) (Josephus, *Ant.* 12.240–41). In short, *hellēnismos* was the opposite of *ioudaismos* ("the Jewish constitution and way of life"), not the mixing and synthesis of Jewish and Hellenic thought we now indicate with the term "Hellenism."

In their approach to "Hellenism," Judaic studies have been somehow misled not only by the way the noun *hellēnismos* was used in ancient Jewish sources but also by the theological assumption that at that time "the Jewish way of life" (ἰουδαϊσμός) consisted of a normative, monolithic set of customs, untouched by any foreign influence. Scholars began to measure the influence of Hellenistic (not Hellenic) thought and customs on Jewish thought and customs (which they derived essentially from rabbinic sources), as if Judaism were not part of, and were not shaped by, the Hellenistic world. A sharp scholarly distinction separated those Jews who were affected by the new culture and those who remained faithful to traditional

---

3. Doron Mendels, *The Rise and Fall of Jewish Nationalism* (Anchor Bible Reference Library; New York: Doubleday, 1992); Shaye D. J. Cohen, *The Beginnings of Jewishness: Boundaries, Varieties, Uncertainties* (Hellenistic Culture and Society 31; Berkeley: University of California Press, 1999).

4. Here and throughout this essay, translations from the Bible (both the Jewish and Christian) and the so-called Apocrypha are taken from the New Revised Standard Version, at times with slight alterations.

Judaism. "Hellenistic Judaism" became the label to describe the religion and way of life of those Jews who had given up their Jewishness and adopted Hellenic ideals and ways of life. The Maccabean revolt was thus interpreted as the heroic fight through which Palestinian Jews rejected not assimilation to "the Hellenic way of life" (ἑλληνισμός) but "Hellenism" *toutcourt* and regained their cultural, religious, and political "purity." In contrast, scholars believed that the western Diaspora under the Ptolomies and later, the Romans remained exposed to the (corrupting) Hellenistic influence. But at the roots of the term and concept of "Hellenistic Judaism" is a myth—the myth of a "Hellenized" diasporic Judaism as distinct from a pure, uncontaminated Palestinian Judaism.

The scholarly debate was complicated and often made bitter by religious concerns about the value or danger of cultural assimilation to the Christian world during post-Enlightenment emancipation.[5] The curse of 1 Maccabees against "those renegades from Israel" was read either as a perennial warning against any improper concession or as evidence, now and then, of *démodé* obscurantism. No middle ground seemed possible. The theology of Hellenistic Judaism and the way of life of Hellenistic Jews were either despised (by Orthodox Jews) as a degeneration of, or deviation from, normative Judaism due to Gentile influence; or praised (by Reform Jews) as a highly philosophical development that challenged the legalistic religion of the rabbis; or even exalted (by Christians) as an act of divine providence that prepared the minds and hearts of Gentiles and Jews of the Diaspora for the spread of Christianity.[6]

Contemporary research has finally shown how fragile and groundless the myth of Hellenistic Judaism is. The exposure to Hellenic civilization was not limited to a particular Jewish group or to a particular geographical area.[7] In this sense all Judaisms of late antiquity (including Rabbinic Judaism and Christianity) were "Hellenistic," since they were all influenced by Hellenic culture, and, in various ways, all contributed to defining that synthesis of Western and Eastern thought that we now call Hellenis-

---

5. Menahem Mor, ed., *Jewish Assimilation, Acculturation and Accommodation: Past Traditions, Current Issues and Future Prospects* (Lanham, MD: University Press of America, 1983).

6. On the history on research of Second Temple Judaism, see Gabriele Boccaccini, *Portraits of Middle Judaism in Scholarship and Arts: A Multimedia Catalog from Flavius Josephus to 1991* (Turin: Zamorani, 1992).

7. The change became apparent with the work of Martin Hengel, *Judaism and Hellenism: Studies in Their Encounter in Palestine during the Early Hellenistic Period* (trans. John Bowden; 2 vols.; Philadelphia: Fortress, 1974) and is firmly established in all recent contributions, notably, John J. Collins, *Between Athens and Jerusalem: Jewish Identity in the Hellenistic Diaspora* (2nd ed.; Grand Rapids: Eerdmans 2000); Eric S. Gruen, *Heritage and Hellenism: Reinvention of Jewish Tradition* (Hellenistic Culture and Society 30; Berkeley: University of California Press, 1998); Martin Hengel, *The Hellenization of Judaea in the First Century after Christ* (London: SCM, 1989).

tic civilization. It became then apparent that the term "Hellenistic Judaism" could no longer be used to signal the presence of Hellenic influence (all Jews were in fact "Hellenized"), nor as a geographical term denoting the religion of the Diaspora (Palestinian Judaism was in fact no less "Hellenistic" than diasporic Judaism, and diasporic Judaism was no less diverse than Palestinian Judaism).[8] Even the attempt to recycle the term as an abbreviation for "Judaism in the Hellenistic times" looked desperate as it had to compete with much more successful terms such as "Second Temple Judaism" or "Judaism in Late Antiquity." Should we then resign ourselves to seeing "Hellenistic Judaism"—such a glorious term—erased from our vocabulary, deemed obsolete and useless?

I believe that the term may continue to be used, with some caveats. Contemporary scholars recognize the diversity of Second Temple Judaism, divided as it is in competing movements of thought.[9] Many even find it useful to use the plural (Judaisms) to denote the existence of varied intellectual trends and the absence of a normative tradition.[10] If we talk of Judaisms (such as Zadokite, Enochic or Sapiential Judaism, and later early Christianity or Rabbinic Judaism) we do not have to intend a single organized institution, or a single social group, or a homogeneous theological system; we can be referring to intellectual trajectories that are to Jewish thought as Aristotelianism, Platonism, or Epicureanism are to Greek thought. Each "Judaism" is a proliferation of groups, individuals, and ideas, which shared some basic principles, competed with, influenced and were influenced by other movements of thought.[11]

Among the varieties of ancient Judaism, scholars have long identified a particular "intellectual tradition" present both in the Diaspora and in the land of Israel and characterized by a particular concept of Wisdom (and of her relation with the Torah). Such an "intellectual tradition" (commonly known as "wisdom tradition") is rooted in the ancient wisdom of the Near East, but particularly developed in Hellenistic times, when it was "combined with Hellenistic thought in the interest of a theological conceptual-

---

8. An outstanding example of a book on "diasporic Judaism" is John M. G. Barclay, *Jews in the Mediterranean Diaspora: From Alexander to Trajan (323 BCE–117 CE)* (Edinburgh: T&T Clark, 1996).

9. Paolo Sacchi, *The History of the Second Temple Period* (JSOTSup 285; Sheffield; Sheffield Academic Press, 2000); Lester L. Grabbe, *Judaic Religion in the Second Temple Judaism* (London: Routledge, 2000); George W. E. Nickelsburg, *Ancient Judaism and Christian Origins: Diversity, Continuity, and Transformation* (Minneapolis: Fortress, 2003).

10. The publication of Jacob Neusner, William S. Green, and Ernest S. Frerichs, eds., *Judaisms and Their Messiahs at the Turn of the Christian Era* (Cambridge: Cambridge University Press, 1987) marks the introduction of the concept of Judaisms in the study of Second Temple Judaism.

11. Gabriele Boccaccini, *Roots of Rabbinic Judaism: An Intellectual History, from Ezekiel to Daniel* (Grand Rapids: Eerdmans, 2002), 1–41.

ity."[12] The evidence for such development is provided by literary works from the fragments of Aristobulos to the *Letter of Aristeas,* and from the Wisdom of Solomon to the works of Philo of Alexandria; it also seems to be consistent with what we know from the art and inscriptions of the many ancient synagogues,[13] and from the historical information provided by ancient testimonies such as Josephus, Paul, or the Acts of Apostles. We do not, however, know what this movement of thought was called, or what it called itself (if it even had the awareness to name itself), in antiquity. However, since this movement was the one most directly engaged in a conscious dialogue with Hellenic culture and in finding a recognized role for Judaism within it, the term "Hellenistic Judaism" seems quite appropriate as a modern label for the development of the wisdom tradition after the conquest of Alexander the Great.[14] This suggestion was first made by Erwin R. Goodenough in 1935 in his work *By Light, Light: The Mystic Gospel of Hellenistic Judaism.*[15] Goodenough was followed by a long series of scholars engaged in reconstructing the history and theology of "Hellenistic Judaism" not as a Hellenized (or corrupted) form of normative Judaism but as an autonomous variety of Judaism. Within this group we should mention Harry A. Wolfson, Peter Dalbert, Burton Lee Mack, and more recently, Louis H. Feldman and Peder Borgen.[16] Thanks to the works of these scholars, the term "Hellenistic Judaism" has survived, beyond its myth, as the name for one of the Judaisms of the Second Temple period.

---

12. For a survey of contemporary research on the Jewish wisdom tradition, see Burton L. Mack and Roland E. Murphy, "Wisdom Literature," in *Early Judaism and Its Modern Interpreters* (ed. Robert A. Kraft and George W. E. Nickelsburg; Bible and Its Modern Interpreters 2; Atlanta: Scholars Press, 1986), 371–410 (quotation from p. 372), and Dianne Bergant, *What are They Saying about Wisdom Literature* (New York: Paulist, 1984). For the developments of the Jewish wisdom tradition in late antiquity, see John J. Collins, *Jewish Wisdom in the Hellenistic Age* (Old Testament Library; Louisville: Westminster John Knox, 1997); James H. Charlesworth and Michael A. Daise, eds., *Light in a Spotless Mirror: Reflections on Wisdom Traditions in Judaism and Early Christianity* (Faith and Scholarship Colloquies 4; Harrisburg, PA: Trinity Press International, 2003).

13. Erwin R. Goodenough, *Jewish Symbols in the Graeco-Roman Period* (13 vols.; New York: Pantheon, 1953–68).

14. We can leave the term "Sapiential Judaism" to denote the earlier stage.

15. Erwin R. Goodenough, *By Light, Light: The Mystic Gospel of Hellenistic Judaism* (New Haven: Yale University Press, 1935).

16. Harry A. Wolfson, *Philo: Foundations of Religious Philosophy in Judaism, Christianity and Islam* (2 vols.; Cambridge, Mass.: Harvard University Press, 1945); Peter Dalbert, *Die Theologie der hellenistisch-jüdischen Missionsliteratur unter Ausschluss von Philo und Josephus* (Theologische Forschung; Hamburg-Volksdorf: Reich, 1954); Burton L. Mack, *Logos and Sophia: Untersuchungen zur Weisheitstheologie in hellenistischen Judentum* (SUNT 10; Göttingen: Vandenhoeck & Ruprecht, 1973); Carl R. Holladay, *THEIOS ANER in Hellenistic Judaism: A Critique of the Use of This Category in New Testament Christology* (SBLDS 40; Missoula, MT: Scholars Press, 1977); Louis H. Feldman, *Studies in Hellenistic Judaism* (Arbeiten zur Geschichte des Antiken Judentums und des Urchristentums 30; Leiden: Brill, 1996); Peder Borgen, *Early Christianity and Hellenistic Judaism* (Edinburgh: T&T Clark, 1996).

The identification of any variety of Judaism (including Hellenistic Judaism) requires an interdisciplinary approach, in which the disciplines of the social sciences, history, archaeology, philosophy, religion, literature, and the arts work together to identify trajectories of thought from the scraps of material culture and the literary remains of intellectual activities. As Marc Bloch writes, "The good historian resembles the ogre of the fairy-tale; where he scents the human flesh, he knows that his prey is there."[17] This witty remark reminds us that ours is a dirty job that does not have to do with anonymous and aseptic "systems of thought" but with the actual life and temperamental behavior of flesh-and-blood people who expressed their identity and beliefs through the production of artifacts, documents, and ideas. In the words of Eugenio Garin, the intellectual historian's task is

> to be aware of the plurality of philosophies, understand the many voices, put them in context, identify the relations with the social groups in which they emerged, assess what they meant for these groups, how they acted if they acted, how they changed, and how they declined—human thoughts, how they were created by people, how they changed people.[18]

This article does not aim for a comprehensive reconstruction of Hellenistic Judaism. Rather, it highlights the contribution that one aspect—the study of the literary remains of intellectual activity—can provide to our efforts of historical reconstruction. It focuses in particular on two questions: how the concept of Wisdom became central in Hellenistic Judaism, while remaining marginal in other competing varieties of Judaism; and how in later times such a concept was transformed and exploited within Christianity and Rabbinic Judaism to become the foundation for the preexistence of the Messiah and the Torah, respectively.

The Concept of Wisdom in the Ancient Sapiential Tradition

The lineage of Hellenistic Judaism goes back to the polytheistic roots of Israelite religion in the monarchic period before the Babylonian exile. The heavenly and preexistent nature of Wisdom is a concept that the Jews inherited from the religious world of the ancient Near East, as witnessed by the sayings of Ahiqar: "From Shamayn the peoples are favored; Wisdom is of the gods. Indeed she is precious to the gods, her kingdom is

---

17. Marc Bloch, *Apologie pour l'histoire; or, Métier d'historien* (Paris: Colin, 1949), 35; for the English translation, see idem, *The Historian's Craft* (trans. Peter Putman; New York: Knopf, 1953).
18. Eugenio Garin, "Osservazioni preliminari a una storia della filosofia," *Giornale critico della filosofia italiana* 38 (1959): 1–55 (quotation from p. 41).

et[er]nal. She has been established by Shamayn; yea, the Holy Lord has exalted her" (6:13).[19] Wisdom is a goddess ("of the gods"); she is also "precious to the gods" and inaccessible to human beings. Her special relationship with Baal Shamayn, the Canaanite Lord of Heaven, seems to allude to divine marriage; her enthronement is a sign of Shamayn's benevolence toward humankind. Divine Wisdom rules forever as the queen (and mother) of the created universe.

The language of postexilic Jewish texts, such as Job 28 and Proverbs 1–9, is still largely polytheistic, although now in the context of a henotheistic exaltation of the God of Israel, who is not yet seen as the only God but is viewed as the most powerful of all gods.[20] In Job 28, four former gods of the Canaanite pantheon (Tehom, Yam, Abaddon, and Muet) are summoned to testify to the inaccessibility of Wisdom. What people and other gods cannot do, the God of Israel can: Elohim/Yhwh found her and "established" her and made her beneficial to humankind. Proverbs 1–9 emphasizes the role that Wisdom played in creation. She "was set up, at the first, before the beginning of the earth" (8:23), and through her God gave order to the primordial chaos (8:30). Through creation, God made the inaccessible Wisdom close to humans, desirable to their eyes, necessary to their well-being (8:31). The key verse is Proverbs 8:22a: "Yhwh acquired (קנה) [Wisdom] as the beginning (ראשית) of his work." Not only does Proverbs confirm that Wisdom is divine and uncreated, but by calling Wisdom "the beginning" (ראשית; ἀρχή), it also reinterprets the *incipit* of Genesis 1:1 (בראשית; ἐν ἀρχῇ) in light of the principles of Sapiential Judaism: God created the heavens and the earth not "in" the beginning but "by means of" the beginning, that is, Wisdom.[21]

To put it simply, in pre-Hellenistic Jewish literature, Wisdom (חכמה) is essentially a (female) divine being. Nobody possesses Wisdom; no human being, no rival god but the God of Israel alone "acquired" her and used her to create the universe. The language itself betrays the ancient polytheistic concept of marriage among gods, the very same language that we find also in Genesis, where the creation narrative is introduced as "the genera-

---

19. On the Book of Ahiqar, see James M. Lindenberger, "Ahiqar," *OTP* 2:479–507, here 499.

20. On the emergence of Jewish monotheism from polytheism through henotheism, see Diana V. Edelman, ed., *The Triumph of Elohim: From Yahwisms to Judaisms* (Grand Rapids: Eerdmans, 1996).

21. On the concept of Wisdom in Second Temple Judaism and its cultural environment, see Ulrich Wilckens and Georg Fohrer, "σοφία," *TWNT* 7:466–528. On Job 28, Proverbs 1–9 and the early wisdom tradition, see John G. Gammie and Leo G. Purdue, eds., *The Sage in Israel and the Ancient Near East* (Winona Lake, IN: Eisenbrauns, 1990); Roland E. Murphy, *The Tree of Life: An Exploration of Biblical Wisdom Literature* (2nd ed.; Grand Rapids: Eerdmans, 1996); Boccaccini, *Roots of Rabbinic Judaism*, 103–11.

tions (תולדות) of Heaven and Earth" (Gen 2:4), to which "the book of the generations (ספר תולדת) of Adam" would follow (5:1). In pre-Hellenistic Jewish literature, nothing is said about the origin of Wisdom; her existence is simply taken for granted. Seeking Wisdom and conforming to Wisdom are the essence and the goal of religious life for all those who "fear God." Further, as the universe is an orderly cosmos shaped by God through Wisdom, experience is the main tool to understand God's will, and the wise are the elders, or those who hand down their teachings. The result is a rich legacy of parental and traditional teaching passed on from one generation to the next, from parents to children and from teachers to disciples, in families and in schools, outside the religious boundaries of the Mosaic covenant (and the ethnic boundaries of the Jewish people) and outside the control of the priesthood. As witnessed by both Jeremiah 18:18 and Ezekiel 7:26, "the *torah*" (תורה) and "the proverb" (עצה) originated in ancient Israel (outside the prophetic environment) as two separate forms of religious knowledge connected to "the priest" (כהן), and "the wise" (חכם; Ezekiel: "the elders," זקנים), respectively.[22] It is no surprise, therefore, that nothing is said about the relation between Wisdom and the Mosaic Torah, a problem that is completely ignored in the ancient wisdom literature. Born autonomously, and existing within different social groups, Torah and Wisdom would meet only later in the Jewish experience.

Competing Developments in the Hellenistic-Roman Period

In the Jewish literature of Hellenistic times, after the conquest of Alexander the Great, we encounter three parallel developments, three different understandings of the nature (either heavenly or divine) of Wisdom and of her relationship with the Torah. Some of the documents here examined are now confined in the obscure collections of Old Testament Apocrypha and Pseudepigrapha and are excluded by the modern religious canons of Christianity and Judaism, as happened to most of the Jewish literature from the Second Temple period. This destiny of religious oblivion must not make us forget that these documents were not the product of marginal sects but the expression of mainstream communities and, at the time in which they were written, enjoyed large popularity and well-established reputation.[23]

---

22. Joseph Blenkinsopp, *Sage, Priest, Prophet: Religious and Intellectual Leadership in Ancient Israel* (Library of Ancient Israel; Louisville: Westminster John Knox, 1995); Lester L. Grabbe, *Priests, Prophets, Diviners, Sages: A Socio-Historical Study of Religious Specialists in Ancient Israel* (Valley Forge, PA: Trinity, 1995).

23. For a survey of Jewish literature in the Second Temple period, see George W. E. Nick-

In our first development we see how the wisdom tradition gradually penetrated the priestly circles, where the idea of the Mosaic Torah had first originated.[24] At the end of the third century B.C.E., the book of Tobit states that the faithful Jew should live according to both the teaching of the Mosaic Torah and the sayings of the wisdom tradition.[25] The sapiential document repeatedly appeals to the authority of the Jerusalem priesthood and to the authority of the Zadokite Torah (Tob 1:8; 6:13; 7:11–13). Even more striking, the wise Tobit claims that his righteousness is based on both "the ordinance decreed concerning it in the Law of Moses and according to the instructions of Deborah, the mother of my father Tobiel" (Tob 1:8). This is the first time that the two sets of traditions, the priestly and the familial, are put on the same level, thus opening the path to a more sophisticated understanding of the relation between Wisdom and Torah.

A few decades later, the book of Sirach proposed what would prove to be an ingenious and fortunate solution.[26] According to Sirach, Wisdom is not a goddess or a divine attribute, but a heavenly being created by God and used by God as a tool in creation (Sir 1:4, 7–8). Wisdom lived in heaven with the angels, but asked God for a dwelling place on earth (24:1–7). This dwelling place is Israel, more specifically the Temple (24:8–12). There, Wisdom manifested herself in an embodied form, namely, "the book of the covenant of the Most High God, the Law that Moses commanded us as an inheritance for the congregations of Jacob" (24:23). The concept would later be reiterated in similar terms by the book of Baruch (3:9–4:4).[27] This does not mean that Wisdom and Torah are identical, as some commentators have claimed.[28] Identity is a transitive relation, in which the two elements bear the same properties. In Sirach and Baruch, Wisdom and Law are not interchangeable, and their relationship is still conceived in strongly asymmetrical terms.[29] The connection between Wisdom and Torah is the result

---

elsburg, *Jewish Literature between the Bible and the Mishnah: A Historical and Literary Introduction* (2nd ed.; Minneapolis: Fortress, 2005).

24. Boccaccini, *Roots of Rabbinic Judaism*, 113–50 ; Collins, *Jewish Wisdom*.

25. On the book of Tobit, see Carey A. Moore, *Tobit: A New Translation with Introduction and Commentary* (AB 40A; Garden City: Doubleday, 1996).

26. See Patrick W. Skehan and Alexander A. Di Lella, *The Wisdom of Ben Sira: A New Translation with Notes* (AB 39; Garden City, NY: Doubleday, 1987).

27. See Carey A. Moore, *Daniel, Esther and Jeremiah: The Additions: A New Translation with Introduction and Commentary* (AB 44; Garden City, NY: Doubleday, 1977), 255–316.

28. *Pace* Eckhard J. Schnabel, *Law and Wisdom from Ben Sira to Paul: A Tradition Historical Enquiry into the Relation of Law, Wisdom, and Ethics* (WUNT 2; Tübingen: Mohr Siebeck, 1985).

29. Gabriele Boccaccini, *Middle Judaism: Jewish Thought, 300 BCE to 200 CE* (Minneapolis: Fortress, 1991), 81–99; idem, "The Preexistence of the Torah: A Commonplace in Second Temple Judaism or a Later Rabbinic Development?" *Henoch* 17 (1995): 329–50; see also Collins, *Jewish Wisdom*, 61; Roland E. Murphy, "The Personification of Wisdom," in *Wisdom in Ancient Israel: Essays in Honour of J. A. Emerton* (ed. John Day et al.; Cambridge: Cambridge University Press, 1995), 227.

of a one-way process. Wisdom manifested herself in Torah. It is not the other way around. Torah does not gain either the autonomy or the cosmic functions of the heavenly and preexistent Wisdom. It is not preexistent; it is not heavenly; on the contrary, it simply does not exist before it was given on Sinai.

The implications of this view of the relationship between Wisdom and Torah are remarkable. Not only is there no wisdom without the practice of Torah (as in Tobit), but observance of Torah is also the propaedeutically indispensable condition by which people become worthy of receiving the gift of wisdom. Torah gains a solid link with the order of creation, but Wisdom loses her divine status and much of her cosmopolitan dimension of being immediately accessible to human experience, even apart from the mediation of Torah and outside the boundaries of the covenantal community of Israel. Simultaneously, human experience loses much of its nonconformist and autonomous power of revelation, and its ability to criticize Torah, which we see so powerfully in the books of Job, Jonah, and Qohelet.

Sirach's and Baruch's understanding of the relation between Wisdom and Torah, and their reduction of Wisdom from the divine to the heavenly realm, or from a goddess to a created, angelic being, did not become commonplace in Second Temple Judaism. The nature of Wisdom remained a highly controversial issue. In our second line of thought, we see that the covenantal understanding of the relationship between Wisdom and Torah was explicitly rejected by yet another movement of Second Temple Judaism, the so-called Enochic Judaism.[30] In the Book of Dream Visions (second century B.C.E.) the anxiety about Wisdom leaving her divine status is already apparent, symbolized by this declaration of her enthronement: "Wisdom does not escape you, and she does not turn away from your throne, nor from your presence" (1 En. 84:3).[31] One century later, at the end of the first century B.C.E., in the Book of the Parables, Enochic Judaism gave the most direct attack on the priestly conception of Wisdom:

> Wisdom could not find a place in which she could dwell; but a place was found (for her) in the heavens. Then Wisdom went out to dwell with the children of the people, but she found no dwelling place. (So) Wisdom returned to her place and she settled permanently among the angels. Then Iniquity went out of her rooms . . . and dwelt with them. (1 En. 42)[32]

---

30. On Enochic Judaism as one of Second Temple Judaisms, see Paolo Sacchi, *Jewish Apocalyptic and Its History* (Sheffield: Sheffield Academic Press, 1997); George W. E. Nickelsburg, *1 Enoch: A Commentary on the Book of 1 Enoch* (Minneapolis: Fortress, 2001); Gabriele Boccaccini, ed., *The Origins of Enochic Judaism* (Turin: Zamorani, 2002 = *Henoch* 24 [2002]); idem, ed., *Enoch and Qumran Origins* (Grand Rapids: Eerdmans, 2005).

31. Unless stated otherwise, translations from the book of *Enoch* are from George W. E. Nickelsburg and James C. Vanderkam, eds., *1 Enoch: A New Translation* (Minneapolis: Fortress, 2004).

32. E. Isaac, *OTP* 1:33.

The text is an explicit rebuttal of Sirach and Baruch. It takes up the myth that Wisdom searched for a dwelling place, but denies its happy ending. The disappointing outcome of Wisdom's search fits the Enochic idea that the world has become the place of evil as a consequence of a cosmic rebellion of angels. There is no room in this world for the salvific role of Wisdom or Torah.

Dwelling in heaven, Wisdom is connected with the eschatological Messiah of the Book of the Parables of Enoch, the "Son of Man," a heavenly creature who shares the same preexistent nature as Wisdom.[33] The Son of Man has a special relation with Wisdom, for "in him dwells the spirit of Wisdom" (*1 En.* 49:3). In particular, he would be her revealer at the end of times, sitting with her on God's throne: "In those days, (the Elect One) shall sit on my throne, from the conscience of his mouth shall come out all the secrets of wisdom, for the Lord of the Spirits has given them to him and glorified him" (*1 En.* 51:3).[34]

The implications of this view are equally remarkable. Wisdom does not dwell in this world, which is the place of iniquity, and there is nothing resembling an embodiment of her in this world. God rules unchallenged in heaven, but not as much on earth—at least not since the angelic sin—and won't again until the end of times. The heavenly Wisdom is an eschatological gift, and the Mosaic Torah no more than a feeble image of God's will on earth.

The Enochians were not the only ones to remain unconvinced by the transformation of the divine Wisdom into a heavenly being created by God, and by the view of the Mosaic Torah as Wisdom on earth. While sharing the priestly idea of the universe as an orderly cosmos, a series of Second Temple Jewish texts exemplify our third line of thought, which also preferred to keep Wisdom unambiguously connected with the divine. Here, Wisdom is a hypostasis of God and not one of his creatures, is generated rather than created by God, and shares the same divine nature. This is the position consistently expressed in the documents of Hellenistic Judaism.

For the first-century book of the Wisdom of Solomon,[35] Wisdom "is a kindly spirit . . . the spirit of the Lord" (Wis 1:6–7); she is "an aura of the might of God and a pure effusion of the glory of the Almighty . . . she is the refulgence of eternal light, the spotless mirror of the power of God, the image of His goodness" (7:25–26). Unlike Sirach, for whom Wisdom is heavenly, the Wisdom of Solomon speaks of the divine *sophia*, who, as in the tradition of Enoch, "sits" on the throne by God (Wis 9:2). Unlike the

---

33. See Sabino Chialà, *Il libro delle Parabole di Enoc* (Brescia: Paideia, 1997); George W. E. Nickelsburg, "Son of Man," *ABD* 6:137–50.

34. Isaac, *OTP* 1:37.

35. See David Winston, *The Wisdom of Solomon: A New Translation with Introduction and Commentary* (AB 43; Garden City, NY: Doubleday, 1979).

tradition of Enoch, however, Wisdom in not relegated to heaven, but "comes from God" (Wis 9:6). She is not at all an eschatological gift, but rather a constant salvific presence in the history of Israel. So Solomon prays to God, "Send her forth from the holy heavens, and from the throne of your glory send her, that she may labor at my side, and that I may learn what is pleasing to you" (Wis 9:10).

The direct link between the ancient wisdom tradition and Hellenistic Judaism is proved by the reference to Wisdom as the "mother" of the universe. Behind Philo's mystical interpretation, the ancient idea of the godly marriage is still very vivid in his reading of Proverbs 8:22a as a powerful metaphor. Philo even presents a Greek translation (ἐκτήσατο) that is much closer to the meaning of the original Hebrew (קנני) than the Septuagint version (ἔκτισεν).

> The Architect of the universe is also the father of his creation, and the mother was the knowledge of the Creator with whom God uniting, not as a man unites, became the father of creation. And this knowledge having received the seed of God, when the day of her travail arrived, brought forth her only and well-beloved son, perceptible by the external senses, namely this world. Accordingly Wisdom is represented by some one of the beings of the divine company as speaking of herself in this manner: God acquired me first of His works and before the beginning of time He established me [Prov 8:22]. (Philo, *Ebr.* 30–31)[36]

Philo explicitly identifies Wisdom (σοφία) with the Word (λόγος) of God: "By using many words for it Moses has already made it manifest that the sublime and heavenly Wisdom is of many names; for he calls her beginning (ἀρχή), and image (εἰκών) and vision of God.... The *sophia* of God is the *logos* of God" (*Leg.* 1.43, 65). The *logos* was an equally uncreated and powerful divine hypostasis, whose creative power was recognized by the ancient Jewish tradition.[37] Particularly in the early targumic tradition of Aramaic translation of the Hebrew Scriptures, the concept of the Word (מימרא) of God had developed from being a way to obviate anthropomorphism into a quite sophisticated theology. While in the proto-rabbinic traditions no relation could be established between the divine Word and the heavenly Wisdom, in Hellenistic Judaism the two divine hypostases soon became interchangeable: "You have made all things by your Word, and by your Wisdom have formed humankind" (Wis 9:1–2).

---

36. Cf. Philo, *Fug.* 109. Translations from Philo are based, with some alterations, on Colson and Whitaker, LCL.

37. Ps 33:6: "By the Word of the Lord the heavens were made"; cf. Genesis 1. On the concept of Word (*logos*) in Second Temple Judaism and its cultural environment, see Albert Debrunner, et al., "λέγω," *TWNT* 4:69–198.

Compared to *sophia*, the *logos* had the advantage, in Philo's eyes, to already be part of the Hellenistic philosophical discourse. Even under the new name, however, the concept of Wisdom remained largely unchanged. The *logos-sophia* is the "image (εἰκών) of God through whom the whole universe was framed" (Philo, *Spec.* 1.81). The Creator, like an architect building a city, generated in his mind an archetypal model, so that he might use it to build the megalopolis, the universe.

> When a city is being founded to satisfy the soaring ambition of some king . . . there comes forward now and again some trained architect who, observing the favourable climate and convenient position of the site, first sketches in his own mind wellnigh all the parts of the city that is to be wrought out. . . . Thus after having received in his own soul, as it were in wax, the figures of these objects severally, he carries about the image of a city which is the creation of his mind. Then . . . like a good craftsman he begins to build the city of stones and timber, keeping his eye upon his pattern and making the visible and tangible objects correspond in each case to the incorporeal ideas. Just such must be our thoughts about God. (Philo, *Opif.* 17–19)

In Philo's reading of Genesis 1:27, Adam was made not "in the image of God" but as a copy of the image of God: "Nothing is more godlike than man, the all-beautiful copy of an all-beautiful model, a representation admirably made after an archetypal rational idea" (Philo, *Spec.* 3.83; cf. *Opif.* 25). As Adam, so the entire universe: "If the part is an image of an image, it is manifest that the whole is so too, and the whole creation . . . is a copy of the divine image . . . the *logos* of God" (*Opif.* 25). In Philo's philosophical view, the transcendent God needs a demiurge, a "second god" (*Leg.* 2.86), generated not created, a "son" (*Agr.* 51), who would function as a mediator between the Creator and the corporeal world, as a "tool" in creation (*Abr.* 6; *Cher.* 127) but also as a representative of creation before God:[38]

> To His *logos*, His chief messenger, highest in age and honour, the Father of all has given the special prerogative, to stand on the border and separate the creature from the Creator. This same *logos* both pleads with the immortal as suppliant for afflicted mortality and acts as ambassador of the ruler to the subject. He glories in this prerogative and proudly describes it in these words "and I stood between the Lord and you" [Deut 5:5], that is neither uncreated as God, nor created as you, but midway between the two extremes, a surety to both sides. (Philo, *Her.* 205–6)

The transcendence of God's *logos-sophia* clearly makes it impossible to identify Wisdom with Torah. Contrary to the ancient wisdom tradition, however, Hellenistic Judaism recognized an important role for Torah,

---

38. This figure is presented both as a "high priest" (Philo, *Gig.* 52) and a "lawyer" (Philo, *Mos.* 2.133).

although not in the terms articulated by Sirach and Baruch. While the natural order of Wisdom is preexistent and eternal, the eternity of the Mosaic Law does not overcome the boundaries of history: "its enactments . . . remain firm and lasting from the day on which they were first promulgated [on Sinai] to the present one" (Philo, *Mos.* 2.14). The Law neither equals nor embodies Wisdom. Rather, the Law was created "in harmony with the cosmos. . . . The man who observes the Law is constituted thereby a loyal citizen of the cosmos, regulating his doings by the purpose and will of nature, in accordance with which the entire cosmos itself is administered" (Philo, *Opif.* 3).

The implications of this concept of Wisdom (and of her relation with Torah) are, once again, remarkable. In this view, Judaism is not a Temple-centered or Torah-centered religion but a Wisdom-centered religion. As such, Judaism is not simply the religion of the Jewish people but more properly the religion of the universe, and the Jews, who are taught by Torah to live according to the order of the universe, are by education a nation of sages who follow the highest form of natural philosophy. Moreover, the Jews are by birth the priests of humankind: "A priest has the same relation to a city that the nation of the Jews has to the entire inhabited world" (Philo, *Spec.* 2.163). While obedience to Torah is not abolished, and the distinction between Jews and Gentiles is maintained, "God-fearing" Gentiles are accepted in the Hellenistic-Jewish communities as the equivalent of "laypeople" in relation to the "priests." Besides, as the longing for wisdom is universal, the door is open even to those who want to go further and join the priestly order. Philo confirms the enormous possibilities of this strand of Judaism when he writes, "[Moses] receives all persons of a similar character and disposition, whether they were originally born so, or whether they have become so through any change of conduct, having become better people, and as such entitled to be ranked in a superior class. . . . These last he calls proselytes" (*Spec.* 1.51)

Wisdom in Christianity and Rabbinic Judaism

With three different views of Wisdom competing in Second Temple Judaism, the newly formed movements of Christianity and Rabbinic Judaism could not ignore her presence; they were compelled to find a place for her in their theological worldviews, even at the cost of denying her existence. Although neither of these Jewish movements was born from Hellenistic Judaism, both of them would be profoundly influenced by it.

We should begin by acknowledging that the Jesus movement was at its inception little more than a variant of Enochic Judaism.[39] As Enochic Jews,

---

39. Gabriele Boccaccini, *Beyond the Essene Hypothesis: The Parting of the Ways between*

the first Christians rejected any connection between Wisdom and Law and regarded Wisdom as a divine, eschatological gift. In their faith in the coming of the heavenly Son of Man, however, they presented Jesus as filled with a wisdom that is not of this world (Mark 6:2; Matt 13:54). Through the Son of Man, Wisdom had somehow found her way to earth, but this would also mark the beginning of her end. In their claim for the preexistence of Christ, Christians began using the imagery of Wisdom for christological purposes (see, e.g., 1 Cor 1:24). When eventually, at the end of the first century, Christians began to claim that their Messiah was not only heavenly but divine, they began looking at the relationship between God and God's uncreated Wisdom (or *logos*), established by Hellenistic Judaism, as a useful model.

The prologue of the Gospel of John is a masterpiece of synthesis. It identifies Jesus with the uncreated, divine *logos*;[40] *logos* in turn is identified with Wisdom, as we have seen in Hellenistic Judaism, as the tool used by God in the act of creation.[41] Compared to *sophia*, the *logos* had the advantage, in Christian eyes, of being masculine and thus making the gender identification with Jesus of Nazareth much easier. *Logos* had also the advantage, besides being an established concept in Hellenistic thought, of referring to Judaism's long tradition of the creative power of the Word of God—a divine hypostasis that, unlike Wisdom, had never been turned into a heavenly creature. In the term *logos* (instead of *sophia*) the divinity of Jesus and the masculinity of the incarnated Messiah were unambiguously stated and thus clearly understood by both the Jewish and the Gentile readers of the Gospel of John.

While stressing the divinity of the *logos-sophia*, Christians nevertheless retained an element of the previously discussed Sirach-Baruch model in order to explain the incarnation of the preexistent *logos*.[42] In the new Christian formulation, Jesus took the place of Torah. This stance dismisses the Sirach-Baruch notion that Torah is the perfect manifestation of Wisdom on earth: Jesus, not Torah, is the earthly embodiment of the heavenly Wisdom.[43]

The prologue of John finally alludes to the Enochic myth in its insis-

---

Qumran and Enochic Judaism (Grand Rapids: Eerdmans, 1998); idem, "Uomo, angelo o Dio? Alle radici del messianismo ebraico e cristiano," in *Il messia tra memoria e attesa* (ed. Gabriele Boccaccini; Brescia: Morcelliana, 2005), 15–48.

40. John 1:1: "In the beginning was the *logos*, and the *logos* was with God, and the *logos* was divine."

41. John 1:2–3: "He was in the beginning with God. All things came into being through him, and without him not one thing came into being."

42. John 1:14: "And the *logos* became flesh and lived among us."

43. John 1:17: "The Law was given through Moses; grace and truth came through Jesus Christ."

tence on the rejection of the *logos*.⁴⁴ Jesus-*logos-sophia*, however, did not go back to heaven empty-handed. The first coming of Jesus marks the beginning of redemption, as forgiveness of sin is assured to those who believe in his heavenly power.⁴⁵

In the second century, many Christian writers, such as Theophilus of Antioch, were still wavering between *sophia* and *logos*, not knowing exactly what to make of these two distinct hypostases. Theophilus, for example, gives voice to these difficult deliberations when he writes: "God, then, having his own *logos* internal with his own bowels, begat him, emitting him along with his own *sophia* before all things. [God] had this *logos* as a helper . . . and by him [God] made all things. . . . God's *sophia* was in [God] and his holy *logos* was always present with [God]" (*Autol.* 2:10; *ANF* 2:98). With the *logos* clearly taking all the attributes of *sophia*, there was no more room or autonomy for Wisdom as a distinct concept. Eventually the solution provided by the prologue of John (i.e., the identification of *logos* and *sophia*) would prove to be the most effective; Wisdom would become nothing more than poetic imagery, a metaphor for the divine *logos*-Christ. Generated not created, preexistent, the Christ is, as Justin says, "the beginning" (ראשית; ἀρχή). Quoting Proverbs 8:22a, he says:

> God has begotten as a Beginning (ἀρχή) before all His creatures a kind of Reasonable Power from Himself, which is also called by the Holy Spirit the Glory of the Lord, and sometimes Son, and sometimes Wisdom (σοφία), and sometimes Angel, and sometimes God, and sometimes Lord and Word (λόγος). . . . [Jesus is] the *logos* and *sophia* and Power and Glory of God who begat and spoke as follows by Solomon: The Lord made me the beginning (ἀρχή) of His ways for His works. (*Dial.* 61:1–3)⁴⁶

Wisdom's role in Rabbinic Judaism changed radically as well. The rabbinic concept of Wisdom developed directly from the tradition of Sirach; this book was rejected in the rabbinic canon for its priestly roots but was held in great esteem by the rabbis. Echoes of the position of Sirach can still be found in rabbinic literature, most explicitly in a saying attributed to R. Abin: "The incomplete form of the heavenly light is the orb of the sun; the incomplete form of the heavenly wisdom is the Torah" (*Gen. Rab.* 17:5).⁴⁷ Here Wisdom and Torah still maintain, as in Sirach, their separate

---

44. John 1.11. "He [the *logos*] came to what was his own and his own people did not accept him."

45. John 1:12: "But to all who received him, who believed in his name, he gave power to become children of God."

46. See Giuseppe Visonà, ed., *Giustino: Dialogo con Trifone* (Rome: Paoline, 1988); translations are mine.

47. *Midrash Rabbah: Genesis* (trans. H. Freedman and M. Simon; 2 vols.; London: Soncino, 1939), 1:136; cf. ibid. 44:7.

identities, Torah being an inferior, earthly, and quite late manifestation of the heavenly Wisdom on earth.

But this is no more than the last, inert relic of what used to be the predominant position in proto-rabbinic traditions. The absence of any discussion or controversy within a tradition that was quite open to debate and dissent makes it clear that this was not only the position of *some* rabbis but came to be regarded as normative within Rabbinic Judaism. The uniqueness of R. Amin's saying within the rabbinic body of literature confirms the general rule of Rabbinic Judaism, which constantly and consistently replaced Wisdom with Torah and took all references to the heavenly Wisdom as a reference to Torah.

The second century C.E. was the turning point. The problem of the preexistence of Torah apparently did not arise until it became an argument used by Christians against the Jews. In the middle of the second century, Justin could still observe that since righteousness was reckoned by God even before the gift of Torah, the salvation of the ancient patriarchs must have relied on something else—namely, the grace of the preexistent Christ (*Dial.* 19:5; 23:1). But soon after, we can see how rabbinic texts changed to face this Christian challenge and began to refer explicitly to the preexistence of Torah. From the second half of the second century, a passage in *Targum Neofiti* may well be the earliest surviving evidence of the idea that "two thousand years before the world was created, [God] created the Torah . . . the Garden of Eden for the righteous and Gehenna for the wicked" (*Tg. Neof.* Gen 3:25).[48] In this new formulation, then, since the beginning the Law has been the only and exclusive criterion of salvation for humankind.

The importance of the wisdom tradition for the development of the concept of the preexistence of Torah is apparent in the reference to the "two thousands years" preceding the creation of the world. This figure is the result of a subtle reading of Proverbs 8:30, in light of Psalm 90:4. In Proverbs 8:30, Wisdom claims that before creation she "was beside [God] . . . and was daily [His] delight." "Daily" implies the succession of at least two days, and since from Psalm 90:4 we learn that "one thousand years in [God's] sight are like yesterday," it means that Torah-Wisdom had to be created at least "two thousand years" before the creation of the world in order to have stood "daily" before God.

In this way the rabbis were finally able to emancipate Torah from its dependence on Wisdom, and themselves from competition with Hellenis-

---

48. See Alejandro Díez Macho, *Neophyti 1* (6 vols.; Madrid: Consejo Superior de Investigaciones Científicas, 1968–78); Roger Le Déaut, *Targum de Pentateuque* (4 vols.; Paris: Cerf, 1978–80); cf. Gabriele Boccaccini, "Targum Neofiti as a Proto-Rabbinic Document: A Systemic Analysis," in *The Aramaic Bible: Targums in Their Historical Context* (ed. Martin McNamara and Derek R. G. Beattie; Sheffield: Sheffield Academic Press, 1994), 260–69.

tic Jews. At the same time, the rabbis repelled Christianity's insidious challenge. This effort was so successful that by the beginning of the third century C.E., the argument of the lateness of the Torah could no longer be used in Christian anti-rabbinic treatises. Tertullian's *Adversus Judaeos*, for example, acknowledged that "the Law of God already existed before Moses . . . for the first time in Paradise" (2:9; my translation). Even more, the rabbis strengthened the centrality of the Torah, endowing it with a new and unique status: it was now a heavenly, preexisting, self-sufficient being created by God in order to make the world. While *Neofiti* still grants both Wisdom and the *logos-memra* a central role in creation and the function of hypostases,[49] for the post-mishnaic treatise *Avot*, Torah—not Wisdom—is "the precious instrument by which the world was created" (*m. Avot* 3:15; Danby, 452).

Gradually, rabbinic literature would adopt a very similar stance to Christian writings, and Wisdom would become nothing more than poetic imagery. Instead of Christ, the rabbis saw Wisdom as a metaphor for the preexistent Torah. "Seven things were created before the world was created: [the first being] the Torah . . . for it is written: The Lord made me as the *reshit* of His way [Prov 8:22a]" (*b. Pesah.* 54a [Epstein]). Still, there is a major difference between the concept of Wisdom in Hellenistic literature and the concept of Torah in Rabbinic Judaism. According to *Genesis Rabbah*:

> The Torah says, I was the instrument of the Holy One, blessed be He. As a rule when an earthly king builds a palace, he does not build it by himself, but calls an architect; and the architect does not plan the building in his head, but he makes it of rolls and tablets. Even so the Holy One, blessed be He, looked in the Torah and created the world. And the Torah declares: By means of the *re'shit* (בראשית) God created and *re'shit* means no other than the Torah as it is written: The Lord made me the *re'shit* of his work [Prov 8:22a]. (*Gen. Rab.* 1:1)[50]

The passage follows the sapiential interpretation of Genesis 1:1, but here Torah has replaced Wisdom. The passage also echoes almost verbatim the words of Philo, but only to reverse the relation between Wisdom and Torah. While in Hellenistic Judaism Torah was made in harmony with the order of the universe, the rabbis claim that the opposite occurred: the world was created according to Torah and endures for the sake of Torah.

The same destiny of oblivion occurred to the *logos-memra*, a phenomenon that is apparent in the textual history of the targumic tradition itself.[51]

---

49. *Tg. Neof.* Gen 1:1: "From the beginning with Wisdom [the Word of] God created and perfected the heavens and the earth."

50. Translation from Freedman and Simon, with changes.

51. Domingo Muñoz León, *Dios-Palabra: Memra en los Targumim del Pentateuco* (Granada: Santa Rita, 1974).

It is certainly striking to notice how carefully the rabbis separated the concept of the Word of God from any speculation about the preexistence of Torah. Rabbinic literature knew the creative and autonomous power of the Word of God and to a certain extent elaborated on it,[52] but became increasingly aware of the danger of mixing a function of God with God's creature. Like Wisdom, the Word of God was preexistent and played a role in creation, yet the Word was uncreated and divine. The heavenly Wisdom of Proverbs, "created" according to the interpretation of Sirach and Baruch, offered a less insidious ground than the Word of Psalm 33:6, on which the preexistence of Torah could be founded. Eventually, Rabbinic Judaism censored the *logos-memra* theology, as any "heresy" that would posit "two powers in heaven" by granting a quasi-divine status to any mediator or messiah.[53]

In the end, Christ and Torah would play a similar role, each within its own system of thought. This result was not the consequence of a direct replacement, but rather came through the mediation of a complex series of influences. Christianity was not born from Rabbinic Judaism, nor Rabbinic Judaism from Christianity.[54] The concept of a clash between the new Christian faith and traditional Judaism is one of the foundational myths of both Christianity and Rabbinic Judaism, but is not borne out by the history of their origins. Jesus and his followers were not as innovative as they claimed, nor the rabbis as conservative as they claimed. Neither movement parted from its roots in Second Temple Judaism; both parted from each other.[55]

As we have seen, the Christians developed the Enochic idea that Wisdom had her dwelling place in the heavens, first making the Son of Man stand side by side with the divine, preexistent Wisdom and then replacing the divine Wisdom with the preexistent and divine Christ. The rabbis, on

---

52. Daniel Boyarin, "The Gospel of the Memra: Jewish Binitarianism and the Prologue to John," *HTR* 94 (2001): 243–84.

53. Daniel Boyarin, "Two Powers in Heaven; or, The Making of a Heresy," in *The Idea of Biblical Interpretation: Essays in Honor of James L. Kugel* (ed. Hindi Najman and Judith H. Newman; Brill: Leiden, 2004), 331–70; Alan F. Segal, *Two Powers in Heaven: Early Rabbinic Reports about Christianity and Gnosticism* (Studies in Judaism in Late Antiquity 25; Leiden: Brill, 1977).

54. On Christianity and Rabbinic Judaism as "fraternal twins," see Alan F. Segal, *Rebecca's Children: Judaism and Cristianity in the Roman World* (Cambridge: Harvard University Press, 1986); Hershel Shanks, ed., *Christianity and Rabbinic Judaism: A Parallel History of Their Origins amd Early Developments* (Washington, DC: Biblical Archaeology Society, 1992).

55. The "Parting of the Ways" was between Christianity and Rabbinic Judaism; see James D. G. Dunn, *The Partings of the Ways between Christianity and Judaism and Their Significance for the Character of Christianity* (London: SCM Press, 1991); idem, ed., *Jews and Christians: The Partings of the Ways, AD 70 to 135* (Grand Rapids: Eerdmans, 1992). For the possibility that the ways between Christianity and Judaism never parted, see Adam H. Becker and Annette Y. Reed, eds., *The Ways That Never Parted: Jews and Christians in Late Antiquity and the Early Middle Ages* (Texte und Studien zum Antiken Judentum 95; Tübingen: Mohr Siebeck, 2003).

the other hand, developed the idea that Torah was the earthly embodiment of the heavenly, preexistent Wisdom, first making Torah stand side by side with the heavenly Wisdom and then replacing Wisdom with the preexistent and heavenly Torah.

In the process, both Christianity and Rabbinic Judaism met Hellenistic Judaism. The rabbis gave to the Torah all the attributes—preexistence, heavenly status, creative role, and so on—given by Hellenistic Judaism to Wisdom *except* her divine nature; the Christians gave to Christ all the attributes given by Hellenistic Judaism to Wisdom *including* her divine nature. In both cases the centrality of Torah and Christ left no room for Wisdom. The disappearance of Wisdom was certainly no accident; it was a deliberate act of censorship, which the Christians and the rabbis perpetrated consciously in order to stress the centrality of their own mediator to God.

Conclusion: The Legacy of Hellenistic Judaism

The movements of Hellenistic Judaism, Christianity, and Rabbinic Judaism were all, in one way or another, influenced by the legacy of the ancient wisdom tradition; each movement developed it in an original and competing way. In all three trajectories of thought, as we have seen, the concept of Wisdom is provided by a different interpretation of the same key verse: Proverbs 8:22a. In Hellenistic Judaism the concept of divine Wisdom blossomed in a sophisticated theology that put the law of nature at the center of Judaism. By contrast, in Rabbinic Judaism and Christianity, the centrality of the Torah and the Messiah, respectively, overshadowed Wisdom. In Rabbinic Judaism, the heavenly Wisdom lost any autonomy and became merely a metaphor for the Torah. In Christianity the divine Wisdom was identified with the divine *logos* and became only a metaphor for the Messiah.

As proved by the production of a sophisticated literature and by the magnificent art of the so-called Jewish-Hellenistic synagogues, the idea of Judaism as the religion of the cosmos and of the Jews as the priests of humankind was a powerful and attractive concept during the Second Temple period, and even after the destruction of the Temple, when it was still able to attract large crowds of God-fearing Gentiles. Hellenistic Judaism was limited in its expansion in the Roman world by the spread of anti-Semitism and by the success of Christianity (as the state religion of Rome), and it was challenged by the strength of rabbinic propaganda; nevertheless, it remained a well-established presence in the western Diaspora alongside Christianity and Rabbinic Judaism up to the Muslim conquest.[56] It was then

---

56. Nicholas De Lange, ed., *The Illustrated History of the Jewish People* (New York: Harcourt, 1997).

that Rabbinic Judaism finally expanded from its eastern strongholds to the west, from the Middle East to North Africa to Spain to northern Europe, and gradually confined Hellenistic Judaism to some small pockets of resistance (especially strong in Italy). Although silenced in its autonomy by the success of its siblings, the heritage of Hellenistic Judaism has survived both in Christianity and Judaism as a respectable legacy. Every time Jewish thinkers have to face the encounter with the outside world, they find in the cosmopolitan experience of Hellenistic Judaism an inexhaustible source of inspiration. It would be enough here to mention the examples of Yehudah Abrabanel (Leone Ebreo, 1460–1521) during the Italian Renaissance; Moses Mendelssohn (1721–1786), the father of the Jewish Haskalah; and Isaac Mayer Wise (1819–1900) at the foundation of the American Reform movement. Yet, in spite of its historical importance and its influential legacy, Hellenistic Judaism is still a rather neglected and ill-defined subject in contemporary scholarship and even more in the historical self-understanding of contemporary Jews and Christians.

The time is ripe for the myth of Hellenistic Judaism to be replaced by its reality—as one of the most influential ancient Judaisms, one that played an essential role in late antiquity as an autonomous movement, and that has remained an influential tradition of thought both in Christianity and in Rabbinic Judaism. What a challenge indeed for Christians and Jews today! They are just recently, and not without reservations, growing accustomed to seeing one other as siblings,[57] and now are asked to acknowledge the presence in the family of yet another forgotten sibling.

---

57. Segal, *Rebecca's Children*.

3

"He Was Renowned to the Ends of the Earth" (1 Maccabees 3:9)

Judaism and Hellenism in 1 Maccabees

MARTHA HIMMELFARB

The depiction of Judaism and Hellenism as opposing entities goes back to 2 Maccabees, an account of the Maccabean revolt (167–163 B.C.E.) written not long after. According to 2 Maccabees, the revolt, which marked the end of foreign rule and the beginning of Jewish sovereignty, was not only a military conflict but also a battle between Jewish values and Greek values. Yet despite the influence of this idea on Western thought, the actual relationship between Judaism and Hellenism during and after the revolt proves to be far more complicated. To begin with, the triumphant Maccabee brothers and their descendants can hardly be said to have rejected Hellenism. Even after they won independence from their Seleucid overlords, no area of the life of their kingdom, from coinage to literature to religion, was untouched by Greek culture. Indeed, Elias Bickerman argues that Judaism as we know it today was shaped to a considerable extent by Greek ideas, and that it was precisely the success of the revolt that made it possible for ancient Jews to transform Greek culture for their own purposes.[1]

---

1. See especially the second portion of Elias Bickerman, *From Ezra to the Last of the Maccabees: Foundations of Post-Biblical Judaism* (New York: Schocken, 1962). In *From Ezra*, Bickerman draws on his groundbreaking work *Der Gott der Makkabäer: Untersuchungen über Sinn und Ursprung der makkabäischen Erhebung* (Berlin: Schocken, 1937); ET: Elias Bickerman, *The God of the Maccabees: Studies on the Meaning and Origin of the Maccabean Revolt* (trans. Hoerst R. Moehring; Leiden: Brill, 1979). On Bickerman's contribution to the discussion of Judaism and Hellenism, see Martha Himmelfarb, "Elias Bickerman on Judaism and Hellenism," in *The Jewish Past Revisited: Reflections on Modern Jewish Historians* (ed. David N. Myers and David B. Ruderman; Studies in Jewish Culture and Society; New Haven/London: Yale University Press, 1998), 199–211.

Further, though the understanding of the revolt as a confrontation between Judaism and Hellenism comes to us from 2 Maccabees,[2] this text itself is deeply indebted to Hellenism. While it represents the situation that leads to young priests abandoning the temple precincts for the gymnasium as "the height of Hellenism" (2 Macc 4:13 [my translation])[3] and describes its heroes as "those who strove zealously on behalf of Judaism" (2 Macc 2:21), it is written in an elevated Greek style reflecting familiarity with Greek literature and the conventions of contemporary Greek historiography. Bickerman referred to 2 Maccabees' "synthesis of narrowly orthodox theology with the most powerful Hellenistic rhetoric."[4] More recently Christian Habicht judged 2 Maccabees "purely Jewish" in its theology, though "primarily Greek" in its literary form.[5] But the relationship of Jewish elements and Greek in 2 Maccabees is more complex than the division into Greek form and Jewish content suggests. In my view, 2 Maccabees depicts its heroes in terms drawn from Greek ideals of heroism and gentlemanliness, transformed in light of Jewish values.[6] I shall return to 2 Maccabees' conception of heroism below.

The subject of my discussion here is the relationship between Judaism and Hellenism in 1 Maccabees, another ancient history of the revolt that, despite its title, is unrelated to 2 Maccabees. At some point in antiquity, Jews stopped copying the two histories, and both have reached us as part of the Christian Bible. But in contrast to the language of 2 Maccabees, the Greek of 1 Maccabees is similar to that of other books of the Greek Bible translated from Hebrew, and it is thus widely accepted that Hebrew was the original language of the work.[7] The two works also differ in scope.

---

2. While previously "Hellenism" was used to mean Greek language, 2 Maccabees provides the first attestation of the term with the meaning, Greek culture; it may have coined the term "Judaism" to serve as Hellenism's opposite. See Christian Habicht, "Hellenismus und Judentum in der Zeit des Judas Makkabäus," *Jahrbuch der Heidelberger Akademie der Wissenschaften für das Jahr 1974* (1975): 98; Martin Hengel, *Judaism and Hellenism: Studies in Their Encounter in Palestine during the Early Hellenistic Period* (trans. John Bowden; 2 vols.; Philadelphia: Fortress, 1974), 1:1–2.

3. Unless otherwise indicated, all translations of 1 Maccabees and other texts from the Bible and Apocrypha are taken from Revised Standard Version. In my quotations from 1 Maccabees, however, I consistently change the RSV's "Judas," which reflects the spelling of the Greek, to "Judah," in keeping with the Hebrew original.

4. Elias Bickerman, "Makkabäerbucher (I. und II.)," PW 14:792, quoted approvingly by Hengel, *Judaism and Hellenism*, 1:98.

5. Christian Habicht, *2. Makkabäerbuch* (Gütersloh: Gerd Mohn, 1976), 185.

6. See Martha Himmelfarb, "Judaism and Hellenism in 2 Maccabees," *Poetics Today* 19 (1998): 19–40.

7. See Jonathan A. Goldstein, *I Maccabees: A New Translation with Introduction and Commentary* (AB 41; Garden City, NY: Doubleday, 1976), 14–21, for Hebrew as the original language, including a discussion of the evidence from Origen and Jerome.

While 2 Maccabees treats the events leading up to the revolt and the revolt itself, focusing on Judah alone of all his family and concluding with his triumph against Nicanor, 1 Maccabees follows the fortunes of Judah's entire family, from his father Mattathias through Jonathan and Simon, the brothers who succeeded him as leaders, into the reign of John Hyrcanus, who succeeded his father in 134 B.C.E. Since it alludes to a chronicle of the reign of John Hyrcanus (1 Macc 16:23–24), it was probably written sometime after John's death in 104 B.C.E.; its picture of the Romans as friends (1 Macc 8) requires a date before the Roman takeover in 63 B.C.E.

Unlike 2 Maccabees and despite the behavior of the Hasmoneans themselves, 1 Maccabees continues to be read as more or less untouched by Greek culture.[8] In part this is because it was composed in Hebrew and draws extensively on biblical models.[9] Further, unlike 2 Maccabees, which depicts the dire effects of the attraction of Hellenism on the Jewish elite before the revolt, 1 Maccabees says nothing specific about Greek culture. Rather, for 1 Maccabees it is the embrace of the ways of the "Gentiles" by renegade Jews that leads to the persecution and revolt. While the primary Gentile institution of which 1 Maccabees takes note is the gymnasium (1:14), it does not draw the conclusion of 2 Maccabees, that there is something uniquely problematic with Greek culture.[10] Indeed, much of its hostility is directed not at the Greeks, that is, the ruling Seleucids, but rather at neighboring peoples, often named in terms that recall more ancient times: "sons of Esau" for the Idumeans (5:1–3), "nobles of Canaan" for local Arab tribes (9:37).[11] Still, I shall argue here that the usual reading of 1 Maccabees is mistaken, that it too is deeply indebted to Greek culture, though in a rather different way from 2 Maccabees.

Let me begin by noting that 1 Maccabees is hardly a straightforward

---

8. See, e.g., Félix-Marie Abel, *Les livres des Maccabées* (Études bibliques; Paris: Lecoffre, 1949); Diego Arenhoevel, *Die Theokratie nach dem 1. und 2. Makkabäerbuch* (Mainz: Matthias-Grünewald, 1967); Goldstein, *1 Maccabees*.

9. I use the terms "Bible" and "biblical" for convenience. In the last centuries before the turn of the era, most of the texts of what would become the Hebrew Bible were already viewed as having some kind of authoritative status, but a single well-defined corpus is still some distance in the future at the time 1 Maccabees was written. See Goldstein, *1 Maccabees*, 6–11, for biblical models for many episodes in 1 Maccabees; some are more persuasive than others.

10. On 1 Maccabees, see Seth Schwartz, "Israel and the Nations Roundabout: 1 Maccabees and the Hasmonean Expansion," *JJS* 42 (1991): 22–23. On 2 Maccabees, see Himmelfarb, "Judaism and Hellenism," 24–29.

11. Schwartz argues that 1 Maccabees' strikingly hostile attitude toward non-Jewish neighbors must be earlier than the assimilation of some of those neighbors into the Jewish people as a result of John Hyrcanus's conquests. He suggests a date around 130 B.C.E.; see Schwartz "Israel and the Nations," 16–38. But perhaps 1 Maccabees' expressions of hostility are actually a defense of the expansion, insisting on the Hasmoneans' record of opposition to Gentile neighbors, thus providing cover for the absorption of these Gentiles.

account of the revolt. Rather, it is propaganda for the Hasmonean dynasty. For 1 Maccabees, Mattathias and his sons were chosen by God for the task of liberating Israel from its oppressors. Thus, when two of Judah's officers attempt to lead their troops into battle without Judah's authorization, it suggests that the outcome should have been foreseen:

> The people suffered a great rout because, thinking to do a brave deed, [the officers] did not listen to Judah and his brothers. But they did not belong to the family of those men through whom deliverance was given to Israel. (1 Macc 5:61–62)

1 Maccabees concludes with the death of Simon, the last of Judah's brothers, and a notice of the ascent to power of his son, John Hyrcanus (16:16–24). With the transfer of power to the third generation, a dynasty has been established.

As I have already noted, 1 Maccabees takes biblical works as its literary models, particularly the books of Judges, Samuel, and Kings with their warrior heroes. The first hero in its narrative of resistance to Seleucid persecution is Mattathias, Judah's father, who is depicted as a second Phinehas, zealously fighting idolatry in Israel (Num 25:6–11; 1 Macc 2:26). On his deathbed, Mattathias entrusts leadership to the two sons who ultimately had the most glorious careers, Judah and Simon (1 Macc 2:65–66).

Much of 1 Maccabees is an account of Judah's military successes. Judah is 1 Maccabees' David, and the account of his days as a guerilla leader clearly recalls David's days as an outlaw on the run from Saul (1 Macc 3–5; 1 Sam 21–31). The people of Israel mourn Judah's death with words drawn from David's lament over the deaths of Saul and Jonathan: "How is the mighty fallen!" (1 Macc 9:21).[12] But 1 Maccabees continues with words the books of Samuel would hardly have applied to Saul and Jonathan: "How is the mighty fallen, the savior of Israel."

1 Maccabees also invokes the Book of Kings to take the measure of Judah's significance at his death. The standard notice on the death of a king in the Book of Kings runs, "Now the rest of the acts of X and all that he did, are they not written in the Book of the Chronicles of the Kings of Judah [or Israel]?"[13] Sometimes, as with King Jehoshaphat, the notice is more enthusiastic: "Now the rest of the acts of Jehoshaphat, and his might that he showed, and how he warred, are they not written in the Book of the Chronicles of the Kings of Judah?" (1 Kgs 22:45). But the notice after Judah's death in 1 Maccabees trumps even that one: "Now the rest of the acts of Judah, and his wars and the brave deeds that he did, and his greatness, have not been recorded, for they were very many" (1 Macc 9:22).

---

12. In 2 Sam 1:19, the lament is plural: "How are the mighty fallen."
13. E.g., Rehoboam in 1 Kgs 14:29.

With the death of Judah, another brother, Jonathan, became the leader of the rebels. After his first successful military campaign, 1 Maccabees describes his assumption of leadership in terms drawn from the book of Judges: "Thus the sword ceased from Israel. And Jonathan dwelt in Michmash. And Jonathan began to judge the people, and he destroyed the ungodly out of Israel" (1 Macc 9:73).[14] Michmash is a particularly appropriate seat for Jonathan; it recalls the defeat of the Philistines there at the hands of the earlier Jonathan, Saul's son, as reported in 1 Samuel 14.

After Jonathan is treacherously murdered by a pretender to the Seleucid throne (1 Macc 12:42–48), Mattathias's deathbed admonition is fulfilled, and the people acclaim Simon their leader (13:1–9). Like Judah and Jonathan, Simon won military victories and thus expanded the land under Jewish control (13:10–11, 43–53), but his most important achievement was the realization of independence: "In the one hundred and seventieth year the yoke of the Gentiles was removed from Israel, and the people began to write in their documents and contracts, 'In the first year of Simon the great high priest and commander and leader of the Jews'" (13:41–42). The new state of affairs is marked also by the decree of the Jewish people appointing Simon high priest (14:27–48).

1 Maccabees praises Simon's achievements with a poem (14:4–15), one of several at important points in its narrative. So too in the Book of Samuel, poems attributed to David mark the death of Saul (2 Sam 1) and the end of David's own life (2 Sam 22, 23). The twelve verses of the poem in praise of Simon make it by far the longest poem in 1 Maccabees, an indication of the importance of Simon's achievement. The poem begins with an allusion to the formula by which the book of Judges describes the peaceful periods after the Israelites have been liberated from their oppressors (e.g., Judg 3:30; 5:31): "The land had rest all the days of Simon" (1 Macc 14:4). After recounting Simon's military and political achievements, it goes on to depict the era of peace and prosperity over which he presided:

> They tilled their land in peace;
>   the ground gave its increase,
>   and the trees of the plains their fruit.
> Old men sat in the streets;
>   they all talked together of good things;
>   and the youths donned the glories and garments of war.
> . . . .
> He established peace in the land,
>   and Israel rejoiced with great joy.
> Each man sat under his vine and fig tree,
>   and there was none to make them afraid. (1 Macc 14:8–12)

---

14. On 1 Maccabees' view of the Hasmoneans as judges, see Arenhoevel, *Theokratie*, 47–50.

The picture of these verses resembles the picture of the end of days of Micah 4 and Zechariah 8, though at most points without close verbal similarities.[15] The language of the last verse quoted here, however, suggests that the original Hebrew was a quotation of Micah 4:4. But for Micah, "each man under his vine and fig tree" is a prediction of the future, while 1 Maccabees implies that Simon has achieved the conditions the prophet promised.[16] The glorious garments of war (1 Macc 14:9) appear to be an inappropriate intrusion into this idyllic scene of peace and prosperity.[17] I shall suggest below that they reflect the heroic ideal of the Greeks. The poem concludes by noting Simon's zeal for the Torah and his contributions to the temple, which are perhaps intended to recall the reign of Solomon, builder of the first temple and king over the land at its greatest extent (1 Macc 14:14–15).

1 Maccabees concludes with the transfer of power to the third generation of the family, Simon's son John Hyrcanus. Like his brother Jonathan, Simon was the victim of murder, in this case, a conspiracy led by his own son-in-law, who did not, however, succeed in his plan to kill John as well (16:11–22). After noting John's escape, 1 Maccabees does not go on to recount his career. Rather, it concludes with a summary modeled on the notices of the deaths of kings in the book of Kings:

> The rest of the acts of John and his wars and the brave deeds which he did, and the building of the walls he built, and his achievements, behold, they are written in the chronicles of his high priesthood, from the time that he became high priest after his father. (1 Macc 16:23–24)

There can be no doubt, then, that 1 Maccabees consciously takes as its models the books of Judges, Samuel, and Kings, and that it is deeply informed by prophetic literature. Yet there can also be no doubt that 1 Maccabees is a distinctively Hellenistic creation. To begin with, many of the acts of the Jewish protagonists of 1 Maccabees cannot be understood apart from international Hellenistic culture: the crowns and shields with which the victorious rebels decorate the rededicated temple (4:57), the establishment of annual celebrations of the rededication of the temple (4:59)[18] and the victory over Nicanor (7:49),[19] the monument Simon builds for the fam-

---

15. Goldstein suggests several specific parallels to the poem from these chapters and other places in prophetic literature and the Hebrew Bible more generally. I find many of them too vague to be convincing; see *1 Maccabees*, 491.

16. Goldstein suggests that such echoes are intended to claim fulfillment of earlier prophecies in the Hasmoneans without the risk of saying so outright; see *1 Maccabees*, 12–13.

17. Goldstein's translation "glorious garments" is surely to be preferred to the RSV's hyperliteral "glories and garments."

18. Bickerman, *From Ezra*, 121–22.

19. Ibid., 131.

ily tomb at Modein (13:27–30),[20] the proclamation of the people naming Simon "leader and high priest" (14:41),[21] or the exchange of letters with the Spartans and the Romans (1 Macc 8; 12:1–23; 14:16–24; 15:15–24). One might argue that even the recourse to biblical models is characteristically Hellenistic, similar to the interest in ancient stories evident in the Greek literature of the period. Any of these aspects of 1 Maccabees would merit further discussion.[22]

But I want to focus on a different aspect. I have stressed 1 Maccabees' debt to Judges, Samuel, and Kings, but 1 Maccabees departs from these books in its treatment of its heroes. Judges, Samuel, and Kings all form part of the Deuteronomic history; they were composed by editors who drew on earlier texts and traditions but shaped them in conformity with the characteristic concerns of the Deuteronomic school, a theory of history that reads any instance of defeat or subordination to other peoples as the result of disobedience to the covenant, and insistence on Jerusalem as the only legitimate cult site. Even kings were not exempt from the requirements of the covenant, as we learn from the speeches of prophets condemning royal misdeeds such as David's adultery with Bathsheba (2 Sam 12:1–15) or Ahab's seizure of Naboth's vineyard (1 Kgs 21:17–24), and the notices in the book of Kings at the beginning of reigns evaluating the piety of the monarch in question.[23]

The Deuteronomic history, then, does not shy away from condemning the behavior even of David, except for Josiah, the greatest of its heroes. 1 Maccabees, on the other hand, never judges its heroes negatively. Perhaps it could not afford to, given the close chronological proximity of the author of 1 Maccabees to the controversial rule of the Maccabean heroes, in contrast to the Deuteronomist's more distant (and safe) account of the Davidic dynasty. But whatever the reasons, it is important to note that the author of 1 Maccabees drew on aspects of the Deuteronomic history that enabled him to glorify his heroes and present them as a suitable replacement for the Davidic dynasty while ignoring the Deuteronomist's willingness to criticize members of the chosen line.

---

20. Steven Fine, "Art and Identity in Latter Second Temple Period Judaea: The Hasmonean Royal Tombs at Modi'in" (The Twenty-Fourth Annual Rabbi Louis Feinberg Memorial Lecture in Judaic Studies, May 10, 2001), 3–8; idem, *Art and Judaism in the Greco-Roman World* (Cambridge: Cambridge University Press, 2005), 61–65.

21. Bickerman, *From Ezra*, 157–58. Goldstein, suggests that the decree is also influenced by "Hebrew and Aramaic patterns"; see *1 Maccabees*, 501. Tessa Rajak also sees "biblical patterns" in the decree ("Hasmonean Kingship and the Invention of Tradition," in *The Jewish Dialogue with Greece and Rome: Studies in Cultural and Social Interaction* [Arbeiten zur Geschichte des Antiken Judentums und des Urchristentums 48; Leiden: Brill, 2001], 54).

22. For a recent discussion of Hasmonean Hellenism, see Rajak, "Hamonean Kingship," 39–60; eadem, "The Hasmoneans and the Uses of Hellenism," in *Jewish Dialogue*, 61–80.

23. E.g., 1 Kgs 15:3 (Abijam); 15:11–15 (Asa); 15:26 (Nadab).

1 Maccabees does not neglect to evaluate its heroes, but they are never found wanting. The most important criteria for its judgments, heroism in battle and the glory it brings, are quite different from those of the Deuteronomic history just noted. The Greek *doxa* ("glory") and the verb *doxazō* ("glorify") play a central role in 1 Maccabees. It seems likely that they most often translate the Hebrew *kavod* and verbs from the root *kbd*, as is typically the case in the Greek Bible.[24] But *doxa* and *doxazō* translate other Hebrew expressions as well, as will be seen below in the Wisdom of Ben Sira.[25] Since the Hebrew of 1 Maccabees has not survived, we have no way of knowing how consistent the Greek translators were in their choices of equivalents and we can never be certain of the Hebrew behind the Greek. Nor are modern English translations consistent. In the RSV of 1 Maccabees, "glory" is the most common equivalent for *doxa*, although "honor" is an important alternative, especially in contexts where *doxa* is conferred on someone. Thus, in what follows, I take *doxa* and *doxazō* in 1 Maccabees as one element pointing to the themes of heroism, honor, and glory, but I do not restrict my discussion to passages in which they appear.

Warfare plays no small role in the biblical histories so important to 1 Maccabees, and success on the battlefield does sometimes bring fame. The women of Israel fill Saul with fury by singing, "Saul has slain his thousands, and David his ten thousands" (1 Sam 18:7–8), and Deborah warns Barak that he will forfeit his chance to win glory (תפארת) by the defeat of the Canaanites if she leads the way (Judg 4:9). The term *kavod* is sometimes used to refer to military power—"The Lord is bringing up against them the waters of the River, mighty and many, the king of Assyria and all his glory" (Isa 8:7)—or to political power—thus, Joseph sends his brothers to get their father with the words, "You must tell my father of all my splendor (כבוד) in Egypt" (Gen 45:13). But these examples are exceptions. As a glance at a concordance demonstrates, when *kavod* appears in the construct in the Bible, its possessor is almost always the Lord. Indeed, "the glory of the Lord" is often used of the Lord's presence among the people (e.g., Exod 16:7, 10; 24:16, 17; Lev 9:6, 23). Only the wisdom tradition does not hesitate to grant glory to human beings: "The wise will inherit glory (כבוד; RSV: honor)" (Prov 3:35).

For the priestly narrative, a central purpose of the exodus is to provide the Lord with the opportunity to acquire glory and to display his majesty to the Egyptians. Thus the prolongation of the process of punishing the

---

24. As is clear from a glance at Edwin Hatch and Henry A. Redpath, *A Concordance to the Septuagint and the Other Greek Versions of the Old Testament (Including the Apocryphal Books)* (3 vols.; Oxford: Clarendon Press, 1897; repr. Grand Rapids: Baker, 1983), 1:341–44.

25. And as indicated ibid., 1:341.

Egyptians, which gives God the opportunity to demonstrate his power to them:

> I will harden Pharaoh's heart, and though I multiply my signs and wonders in the land of Egypt, Pharaoh will not listen to you; then I will lay my hand upon Egypt and bring forth my hosts, my people the children[26] of Israel, out of the land of Egypt by great acts of judgment. And the Egyptians shall know that I am the Lord. (Exod 7:3–5)

Further, in the priestly strand of the account of the climactic defeat of the Egyptians at the Red Sea, the Lord "gets glory" (כבד) over Pharaoh and the Egyptians (Exod 14:4, 17, 18).

So too when we look beyond the term *kavod* to the depiction of victory on the battlefield and the renown it brings, we find that the Bible regularly attributes them to the Lord. Thus, as David confronts Goliath, he announces to the assembled Israelite and Philistine armies, "War belongs to the Lord, and he has given you into our hands" (2 Sam 17:47). To be sure, a share of the glory often comes to rest on the Lord's human agents, as is evident in the refrain, "Saul has slain his thousands, and David his tens of thousands." Yet the Bible's emphasis is undoubtedly on the Lord.

In the book of Joshua, for example, the Israelites' victories are never merely human: the walls of Jericho fall down (chapter 7); the sun stands still at Gibeon (10:1–14). Even at Ai, where a clever ambush secures victory, Joshua guarantees its success by stretching out his arm toward Ai while holding a javelin at God's command (8:18). The laws governing warfare in the Torah also make it quite clear that victory belongs to the Lord, whether by demanding that a set share of the booty be offered to him (Num 31:25–31) or by insisting that only the wholehearted are permitted to serve in the Lord's army (Deut 20:1–9).

Despite its debt to the Deuteronomic history, 1 Maccabees offers a very different understanding of its heroes' success in battle. Let me begin with its account of the career of Judah. Mattathias's last words single out Judah for leadership because of his military prowess (1 Macc 2:66), and 1 Maccabees wastes no time in declaring the glory and lasting fame of its new hero in one of its poems:

> He extended the glory (δόξα) of his people. . . .
> He embittered many kings,
> but he made Jacob glad by his deeds,
> and his memory is blessed for ever. . . .
> He was renowned to the ends of the earth. . . . (1 Macc 3:3, 7, 9)

Indeed, Judah is so successful that "his fame reached the king, and the Gentiles talked of the battles of Judah" (1 Macc 3:26). After further victories,

---

26. RSV translates "sons" rather than "children."

"The man Judah and his brothers were greatly honored (δοξάζω) in all Israel and among all the Gentiles, wherever their name was heard" (1 Macc 5:63).

It is worth contrasting this account with the story of the harlot Rahab in the book of Joshua. In explaining her protection of the Israelite spies who lodge with her in Jericho, Rahab refers to the report she has heard of the Lord's mighty deeds on behalf of the Israelites (Josh 2:8–13). 1 Maccabees certainly does not discount God's role in Judah's victories; indeed, it is important for its claims that God is on Judah's side, that he is the ultimate source of Judah's success. Yet while it takes pains to show Judah exhorting his troops that the few can triumph over the many because all battles are in God's hands (1 Macc 3:17–22; 4:8–11) and depicts him engaged in prayer and other pious practices before and during battle together with his men,[27] it is of Judah's deeds, not of God's, that the Gentiles hear.

Judah's death in battle was a problem for the view that God always supported the Maccabee brothers, but 1 Maccabees could not avoid it (9:18). It makes the best of the problem by using Judah's death to demonstrate yet again his greatness. Despite the desertion of much of his army in the face of a force far superior in size, Judah is unwilling to flee: "Far be it from us to do such a thing as to flee from them. If our time has come, let us die bravely for our brethren and leave no cause to question our honor (δόξα)" (9:10). It is striking that 1 Maccabees does not represent Judah as concerned about obedience to God's will or the salvation of his people. Rather, it suggests, honor (or glory) is the ultimate concern, and its account secures Judah's honor. So too when Eleazar, the first Maccabee brother to die, falls in battle after attacking the elephant on which he believed Antiochus rode: "he gave his life to save his people and to win for himself an everlasting name" (1 Macc 6:44).

Jonathan succeeds Judah as leader of the revolt (1 Macc 9:28–31). His glory is the glory of the statesman, not the military hero. With the death of Antiochus, he is soon negotiating terms of peace and playing off the two claimants to Antiochus's throne against each other (chapter 10). 1 Maccabees emphasizes the honor shown Jonathan by the would-be king Alexander. When a group brings accusations against Jonathan to Alexander in Ptolemais where Jonathan was attending him, Alexander has Jonathan clothed in purple and brought into the middle of the city while

---

27. 1 Macc 3:46–56; 4:30–33, 38–41; 5:28, 33. Most of the practices reported in 1 Maccabees, such as prayer and fasting, are not enjoined by the Torah's laws of warfare. There are two instances in which Judah's preparation for war reflects the military legislation in the Torah: Judah sent home the categories of men excluded from participation in battle (Deut 20:5–8), an act that 1 Maccabees explicitly calls "according to the law" (1 Macc 3:56); Judah and his army killed all males in the city of Bozrah, located east of the Jordan (1 Macc 5:28, following the legislation for warfare against a distant city in Deut 20:10–15).

Alexander's officers proclaim that no one is to make accusations against him or otherwise trouble him (10:59–63). The description of Jonathan's treatment by Alexander recalls the book of Esther's description of the way Ahasuerus honored Mordecai to reward him for saving his life (Esth 6).

1 Maccabees passes over Jonathan's death at the hands of Trypho, a newly emerged claimant to the Seleucid throne, as quickly as possible (13:23). There is little opportunity for honor or glory for the victim of treachery. But, as noted above, the monument Simon builds at the family tomb serves to memorialize the family's military exploits (13:25–30), and the occasion for building the monument is the deposit of Jonathan's bones in the tomb.

Though Judah is the greatest of the military heroes, it is Simon, as we have seen, who presides over the restoration of the fortunes of his people. I noted above that the poem in praise of his reign, which offers a picture of peace and prosperity in language drawn from the prophets, also contains a rather jarring mention of youths putting on the glorious garments of war (1 Macc 14:9). Indeed, honor and glory are central concerns of the poem:

> The land had rest all the days of Simon.
> He sought the good of his nation;
> his rule was pleasing to them,
> as was the honor (δόξα) shown him, all his days.
> To crown all his honors (δόξα, sg.) he took Joppa for a harbor. . . .
> He extended the borders of his nation. . . .
> and there was none to oppose him. . . .
> He supplied the cities with food,
> and furnished them with means of defense,
> till his renown (lit., the name of his δόξα) spread to the ends of the earth.
> He established peace in the land,
> and Israel rejoiced with great joy.
> Each man sat under his vine and fig tree,
> and there was none to make them afraid.
> No one was left in the land to fight them,
> and the kings were crushed in those days.
> He strengthened all the humble of his people;
> He sought out the law,
> and did away with every lawless and wicked man.
> He made the sanctuary glorious (δοξάζω),
> and added to the vessels of the sanctuary. (1 Macc 14:4–15)

The glory of Simon's political achievements cannot be separated from the glory of his military might, for it is the military might that makes the political achievements possible. Thus, the glorious garments of war, so out of place in the ideal state envisioned by the biblical prophets, are crucial to the polity over which Simon rules and to the ideal of 1 Maccabees. But the poem insists that Simon's achievements extend to his loyalty to the Torah and the temple, and the term "glory," as just noted, is also applied to Simon's contribution to the temple. Simon's own glory and the glory he bestows on the land and his people are affirmed by a letter from Sparta that follows the poem. It refers to its ambassadors' report of "your (pl.) glory (δόξα) and honor (τιμή)" (14:21). The plural "your" must refer to Simon and his people.

Glory and honor are also themes of the proclamation of the people declaring Simon "leader and high priest forever" until a prophet arises. The proclamation is modeled on Greek honorific decrees.[28] The proclamation notes the people's awareness of "Simon's faithfulness and the glory (δόξα) which he had resolved to win for his nation" (1 Macc 14:35). It notes also the honor (δόξα) conferred on Simon by Demetrius and by the Romans (14:39–40), and it reserves for Simon alone of all the Jews the right to "be clothed in purple and wear gold" (14:43–44).

The passages from 1 Maccabees I have just examined offer a very different understanding of glory from the biblical view that glory belongs to the Lord. In Greek culture from archaic times forward, however, the glory earned by great men is a central theme. The standard is set by the heroes of the Homeric poems, who gain glory and fame from their prowess in battle.[29] This heroic ideal with its aristocratic individualism was problematic for the social and political values of the polis. By the Hellenistic era it was virtually obsolete, and many have commented on the inversion of heroic values in the works of writers such as Apollonius of Rhodes.[30] Nonetheless, the ideal continued to be invoked throughout later Greek literature, including poetry and orations in praise of heroes in battle, political leaders, athletic victors, and other notable figures.[31]

Isocrates (436–338 B.C.E.), the great Athenian orator who was a contemporary of Plato and Xenophon, was a particularly influential practitioner of the rhetoric of praise.[32] I quote below two passages from his orations that show clearly the importance of glory for this Greek tradition:

> Men of ambition and greatness of soul . . . prefer a glorious (εὐκλεῶς) death to life, zealously seeking glory (δόξα) rather than existence, and doing all

---

28. For different opinions on the cultural background of the decree, see Fine, "Art and Identity," 3–8; idem, *Art and Judaism*, 61–65. On honorific decrees and inscriptions in Hellenistic cities, see Bradley H. McLean, *An Introduction to Greek Epigraphy of the Hellenistic and Roman Periods from Alexander the Great down to the Reign of Constantine (323 B.C.–A.D. 337)* (Ann Arbor: University of Michigan Press, 2002), 228–45.

29. See, e.g., Walter Donlan, *The Aristocratic Ideal in Ancient Greece: Attitudes of Superiority from Homer to the End of the Fifth Century* (Lawrence, KS: Coronado, 1980).

30. See, e.g., Peter Green, *Alexander to Actium: The Historical Evolution of the Hellenistic Age* (Berkeley/Los Angeles: University of California Press, 1990), 201–15.

31. For a convenient discussion of this literature, see Thomas R. Lee, *Studies in the Form of Sirach 44–50* (SBLDS 75; Atlanta: Scholars Press, 1986), 103–206.

32. Ibid., 143–48.

that lies in their power to leave behind a memory of themselves that shall never die. (*Evag.* 3 [van Hook, LCL])³³

Bear in mind that, although the body that we all possess is mortal, by means of commendation, praise, fame, and the memory that attends us with the course of time we partake of immortality, which we ought to strive after as far as we are able, and to endure anything to attain it. You may see even the most respectable private individuals, who would risk their lives for nothing else, ready to die in battle in order to win honourable renown (δόξα), and, generally, those who show themselves desirous of still greater honour (τιμή) than they enjoy, are commended by all, while those who exhibit an insatiable longing for anything else whatever are considered to be proportionately inferior and lacking in self-control. (*Phil.* 134–35 [Norlin, LCL])

The reference to the desire for glory of even "private individuals" is worth dwelling on for a moment. The need to include them explicitly highlights the fact that Isocrates and his audience take for granted the link between political leadership and the glory conferred by heroic deeds. This link is very much in evidence in 1 Maccabees.

I do not wish to suggest that the author of 1 Maccabees was familiar with the writings of Isocrates. There is nothing in the structure or style of the work, which, as we have seen, imitates the biblical histories, to suggest such knowledge. Furthermore, similar sentiments can be found in a variety of other texts spanning many centuries, from Homer to Xenophon to historians and orators closer to his own time. And it is also quite possible that Greek heroic ideals reached the author of 1 Maccabees and his audience through channels other than literary works. Greek cities, including those of the Hellenistic empires, regularly inscribed decrees honoring kings, benefactors, and eminent citizens on stone so that they would be visible to any resident of the city or visitor to it.³⁴ Judeans would not have had to travel very far to encounter such inscriptions, and by the time of Simon they were engaging in the practice themselves, inscribing the decree that named Simon "leader and high priest for ever" on bronze tablets for all to see.³⁵ The language of diplomacy is another channel through which the language of glory and honor reached Judeans. In a letter preserved in 1 Maccabees, Antiochus VII Sidetes writes to Simon, offering many concessions in a bid for his support against Trypho (15:2–9). The letter concludes, "When we gain control of our kingdom, we will bestow great honor (δοξάζω, δόξα) upon you and your nation and the temple, so that your glory (δόξα) will become manifest in all the earth" (15:9).

---

33. This passage is quoted by Lee, *Studies*, 197.
34. McLean, *Introduction*, 236–44.
35. 1 Macc 14:41–48; quotation, v. 41. On this decree, see Gregg Gardner, "Jewish Leadership and Hellenistic Civic Benefaction in the Second Century B.C.E.," *JBL* 126 (2007): 332–37.

Since the achievements of heroes and rulers were thus marked and acknowledged throughout the world in which 1 Maccabees was written, it is perhaps not surprising that the passages from 1 Maccabees considered above show no awareness that the conceptions of glory and honor they embrace are characteristically Greek. Indeed, there is nothing in these passages to suggest that 1 Maccabees recognizes these conceptions as in any way foreign to Jewish tradition, despite their profound difference from biblical ideas.

1 Maccabees was not the first Jewish text to go beyond biblical precedent in attributing glory to individual human beings. The Wisdom of Ben Sira, a collection of proverbs and reflections modeled on the biblical book of Proverbs, concludes with a history of Israel centered on the glory achieved by great men of the past:[36]

> These were men of mercy,
> whose righteous deeds have not been forgotten. . . .
> Their posterity will continue forever,
> and their glory will not be blotted out.
> Their bodies were buried in peace,
> and their name lives to all generations. (Sir 44:11–14)

Joshua ben Sira lived in Palestine and wrote his book in the first decades of the second century B.C.E., shortly before the Hellenistic reform and the Maccabean revolt. Proverbs and the other works that form part of the biblical wisdom tradition bear little resemblance to the dominant themes of the rest of the Bible, such as the covenant between God and Israel and the story of God's deeds on behalf of Israel's ancestors. Ben Sira's Praise of the Fathers, as the section of his book came to be known, is part of his effort to integrate these covenantal themes into the wisdom tradition. The original Hebrew of the book survives in part,[37] but the complete work survives in the Greek translation made by Ben Sira's grandson in Egypt (after 132 B.C.E.). Sometimes the surviving Hebrew appears to reflect later revision; thus even when the Hebrew is preserved, the Greek must be taken into account.

Glory plays a central role in the hymn in praise of creation (Sir 42:15–43:33) that immediately precedes the Praise of the Fathers, which announces as its central theme: "The work of the Lord is full of his glory" (42:16).

---

36. On glory in the Praise of the Fathers, see Burton L. Mack, *Wisdom and the Hebrew Epic: Ben Sira's Hymn in Praise of the Fathers* (Chicago: University of Chicago Press, 1986), 128–37, 168–9. I indicate Greek only when it is something other than *doxa* or *doxazō* and Hebrew only when it is something other than *kavod* or *kbd*.

37. For the Hebrew, see *Sefer Ben Sira: Ha-maqor, qonqordantsiah, ve-nituah 'otsar ha-millim* (Jerusalem: Academy of the Hebrew Language and Shrine of the Book, 1973).

"He Was Renowned to the Ends of the Earth" (1 Maccabees 3:9)   91

Throughout the Greek version of the hymn *doxa* figures prominently; it translates not only *kavod* (42:16, 17; 43:12), but also *hod* (42:25; 43:1) and *hadar* (43:9).[38] The placement of the Praise of the Fathers immediately after this hymn shows the daring of Ben Sira's claim that the fathers had a share of glory—glory belongs to the Lord—but also softens it: the Lord can confer it on his creations.[39]

The catalyst for the Praise of the Fathers' attribution of glory to human beings was probably Ben Sira's knowledge of the tradition of praise for heroes in Greek culture.[40] But Ben Sira follows biblical precedent in associating glory with wisdom and the temple. In the first part of the book, glory serves as the reward of the wise, as in traditional wisdom literature: "Whoever holds [Wisdom] fast will obtain glory" (4:13). In the Praise of the Fathers, Ben Sira pays special attention to the glory of priests, an association that reflects the priestly and prophetic descriptions of God's presence in the temple as *kavod*. But, as in the hymn to creation, where the Greek repeatedly uses *doxa* and *doxazō*, the Hebrew has not only *kavod* and the root *kbd*, but other Hebrew terms as well. Nonetheless it is clear that Ben Sira is deeply influenced by the biblical associations of glory and temple.

Not all of the figures to whom the Praise of the Fathers attributes glory are priests.[41] It is perhaps not surprising that Ben Sira grants glory to both Abraham and Moses;[42] indeed Moses is said to equal the angels in glory. Joshua, like the Maccabees, is glorious (נהדר) in war (46:2). The prophet Elijah is glorious (נורא) for his wonders (48:4). With no specifics at all, Ben Sira recalls toward the end of the poem that Shem and Seth were glorious among men (49:16).[43]

But the two figures who receive the most attention in the Praise of the

---

38. The Hebrew of 43:11 appears to contain the word *kavod*, though it is fragmentary; the Greek does not contain *doxa*.

39. On the relationship between the hymn to creation and the Praise of the Fathers, see Mack, *Wisdom*, 189–93.

40. Ibid., 128–37, 168–69, following Lee's dissertation, now published as *Studies*.

41. I omit from consideration the judges, whose names are called glorious in the Greek (Sir 46:12) but not in the Hebrew because it appears that the Greek has imported the opening of the following passage about Samuel (Sir 46:13–20) into the passage about the judges. While the Hebrew of Sir 46:13 praises Samuel, it lacks the language of glory; see Patrick W. Skehan and Alexander A. Di Lella, *The Wisdom of Ben Sira: A New Translation with Notes* (AB 39; Garden City, NY: Doubleday, 1987), 517. I also omit Ezekiel's vision (Sir 49:8), a vision of glory in Greek, of "the kinds of the chariot" in Hebrew; even in the Greek, it is the vision, not the prophet, that is glorious.

42. Abraham: 44:19; Moses: 45:2–3 according to the Greek; the Hebrew is fragmentary and corrupt.

43. Thus the Greek; the Hebrew reproduces the verb of the previous verse, "are cared for." Skehan and Di Lella suggest that the text be emended in conformity with the Greek (*Ben Sira*, 542), and this certainly yields better sense.

Fathers are Aaron, the first Israelite priest, and Simon, the high priest of Ben Sira's youth.[44] It is clearly Aaron's role as founder of the priestly line that interests Ben Sira. Thus, he devotes a great deal of attention to the priestly garments that can be seen as defining the office: "Before his time there never were such beautiful things./No outsider ever put them on,/but only his sons/and his descendants perpetually" (45:13).[45] Despite some differences between Hebrew and Greek, the picture of Aaron's almost royal glory is clear.[46] Ben Sira also emphasizes God's covenant with Aaron (45:7, 13, 15, 20–22); God "add[s] glory" to Aaron by giving him and his descendants the right to firstfruits and sacrifices (45:20–21). Ben Sira also insists that priesthood is reserved for Aaron's descendants alone (45:13, 18–19).

Ben Sira's account of Simon's career marks him as even greater than his ancestor, for, unlike Aaron, he is ruler as well as priest. The passage introduces Simon as "the greatest of his brethren and the glory (תפארת) of his people" (50:1).[47] It goes on to describe his achievements as ruler: repairing the temple, fortifying temple and city, constructing a reservoir (50:1–4). But most of the passage is devoted to a description of Simon performing his duties in the temple that begins, "How glorious (נהדר) he was when the people gathered round him/ as he came out of the inner sanctuary" (50:5). There follows a series of similes comparing Simon's to instances of nature's beauty. Then Ben Sira turns to Simon's garments, even more glorious than Aaron's, and the glory he brings to the sanctuary:

Wearing his splendid [Greek: δόξα; Hebrew: כבוד] robes,
and vested in sublime magnificence [Greek: καύχημα; Hebrew: תפארת].
As he ascended the glorious [Greek: ἅγιος; Hebrew: הוד] altar
and lent majesty [Greek: δοξάζω; Hebrew: הדר] to the court of the
    sanctuary. (50:11)[48]

The praise of Simon as he officiates in the temple is clearly meant to recall not only his ancestor Aaron but also the figure of Wisdom herself, whom Ben Sira earlier represented as serving in the temple (24:8–12). Just as Simon's splendor is compared to a series of natural phenomena, Wis-

---

44. On priests in the Praise of the Fathers, see Martha Himmelfarb, "The Wisdom of the Scribe, the Wisdom of the Priest, and the Wisdom of the King according to ben Sira," in *For a Later Generation: The Transformation of Tradition in Israel, Early Judaism and Early Christianity* (ed. Randal A. Argall, Beverly A. Bow, and Rodney A. Werline; Harrisburg, PA: Trinity Press International, 2000), 94–97.

45. Thus the Greek; the Hebrew is fragmentary here, but appears to support the Greek.

46. See esp. 45:12; Himmelfarb, "Wisdom," 95; Pancratius C. Beentjes, "'The Countries Marvelled at You': King Solomon in Ben Sira 47:12–22," *Bijdragen, Tijdschrift voor filosofie en theologie* 45 (1984): 12.

47. My translation. Although these phrases are missing from the Greek, the RSV includes them: "The leader of his brethren and the pride of his people."

48. Translation of Skehan and Di Lella, *Ben Sira*, 546, which reflects a critical text that follows the Hebrew but at one point corrects it in accordance with the Greek (p. 549).

dom compares herself to a series of trees and plants (24:13–17). Thus, Simon emerges as a sort of human counterpart of Wisdom,[49] and Simon's glory turns out to derive not only from his priestly association with the glory of God's presence but also from the glory wisdom offers to the wise.

Ben Sira also places considerable emphasis on the glory of the priestly line as a whole. Following Aaron in the priesthood is his grandson Phinehas, whose zeal earns the eternal covenant of priesthood for his descendants (Num 25:10–13; Sir 45:24). Phinehas is "the third in glory" (Sir 45:23),[50] presumably following Moses and Aaron, and Ben Sira underlines the glory of his descendants (45:25 [Heb.], 26 [Greek]).[51] At the other end of priestly history come the sons of Aaron, who stand about Simon as he stands before the altar; they too are glorious (50:13).

But if priesthood is intimately connected to glory, kingship is not. Toward the end of the Praise of the Fathers, Ben Sira chastises all the kings of Judah for giving their glory to foreigners, with three exceptions: David, Hezekiah, and Josiah (49:4–5). Yet it is far from clear that Ben Sira views David as glorious. David is said to have proclaimed the Lord's glory (47:8), but this pious activity does not necessarily make David himself glorious. The Greek calls both David's crown and his throne glorious (47:6, 11); the Hebrew, which reads rather differently at both points, lacks any mention of glory, and even in the Greek the glory belongs not to David but to the royal office. The only point at which Ben Sira's poem attributes glory to David himself is in an allusion in the Greek version to the biblical account of the praise of David's prowess as a warrior by the women who ranked his exploits above Saul's (47:6; cf. 1 Sam 18:7); the Hebrew alludes to the women's song in somewhat different language without the verb "glorify." If Ben Sira betrays a certain lack of enthusiasm for David, he views Solomon in clearly negative terms, as his absence from the list of kings who did not give their glory to foreigners indicates. Solomon was once called by "that glorious name which was conferred upon Israel," that is, the name of God (Sir 47:18).[52] But despite his wisdom, which Ben Sira does not neglect to praise (47:14–17), Solomon sullied his glory through the idolatry inspired by his wives (47:20).[53] Finally, while Ben Sira praises Hezekiah and Josiah, they are awarded their glory only negatively in the passage noted above, in which they appear with David as exceptions.[54] The description of their reigns does not mention glory.

---

49. Himmelfarb, "Wisdom," 97.

50. Thus the Greek; the Hebrew is fragmentary here.

51. The Greek and Hebrew differ substantially.

52. Translation of Skehan and Di Lella, *Ben Sira*, 523. The mention of glory is missing from the Greek, but the Hebrew is probably original; see ibid., 527.

53. For a somewhat different reading of Ben Sira's criticism of Solomon, see Beentjes, "Countries," 9–10.

54. Hezekiah: Sir 48:17–22; Josiah: Sir 49:1–3.

It is hard to escape the conclusion that for Ben Sira the truly glorious institution, the institution whose occupants were worthy of it, was priesthood, not kingship.[55] If Solomon, the wisest of kings, could not resist temptation, perhaps the institution itself was fatally flawed. Simon, on the other hand, performed all his duties, as ruler and as priest, piously and well. The selective conferral of glory on great figures of Israel's past, then, serves Ben Sira's effort to make the case that rule by high priest is to be preferred to rule by king. Yet while Ben Sira's attribution of glory to human beings goes beyond biblical precedent, his association of glory with wisdom and the priesthood is in tune with the biblical tradition. There is much greater tension with biblical precedent in 1 Maccabees' attribution of glory to warrior heroes; for the biblical texts, as we have seen, victory belongs to the Lord.

1 Maccabees' embrace of Greek ideas of glory and honor also stands in striking contrast to 2 Maccabees' transformation of Greek ideas in its depiction of the martyrs as exemplars of heroism, a topic I have discussed elsewhere at some length.[56] For 2 Maccabees, the martyrs are almost as important to the victory of Judaism as Judah is. Judah's military successes begin only after the terrible sufferings and martyrs' deaths of the aged scribe Eleazar (2 Macc 6) and the mother and her seven sons (2 Macc 7), stories that 2 Maccabees recounts in great detail. The last of Judah's victories reported in 2 Maccabees, the defeat of Nicanor, follows the gruesome suicide of the pious elder Razis, who throws himself on his own sword to avoid capture by Nicanor's men (14:37–46); 2 Maccabees clearly understands Razis's death as martyrdom despite the fact that it is self-inflicted.

2 Maccabees' descriptions of the deaths of the martyrs draw liberally on the language of heroism on the battlefield. Because 2 Maccabees, unlike 1 Maccabees, was composed in Greek, it is easier to identify the sources of its language of heroism. 2 Maccabees' favorite adverb for describing the actions of the martyrs is *gennaiōs*, literally, "nobly," and it uses the adjectival form as well.[57] While the adjectival form of this root is in wide use in Greek literature, the adverbial form is less common. It is, however, a favorite adverb of the historian Polybius, a contemporary of the events 2 Maccabees describes. He uses it for military and death scenes, where it clearly means "bravely," and 2 Maccabees also uses it in this sense (8:16; 13:14; 15:17). But elsewhere 2 Maccabees effects a transformation of the meaning of bravery by using *gennaiōs* also of those whose courage consists of enduring suffering without fighting back (6:28, 31; 7:5, 11).[58] The extent

---

55. For more detail, see Himmelfarb, "Wisdom"; and Beentjes, "Countries."
56. Himmelfarb, "Judaism and Hellenism," 31–38.
57. Ibid., 33–35.
58. The adjectival form appears in 1 Macc 7:21 with the same meaning.

of the transformation can be seen by considering who the martyrs are: two old men, a woman, and seven boys who have not reached adulthood. 2 Maccabees claims that people unqualified for heroism on the battlefield are capable of a different type of heroism. Indeed 2 Maccabees explicitly attributes masculine courage to both the mother and the aged Razis (7:21; 14:43). With Polybius in mind, we can see that the usage of 2 Maccabees represents a transformation of the bravery the Greeks admire. The new kind of bravery is displayed not only by Judah but also by those who are very distant from the heroism of the battlefield. This concept, then, so central for 2 Maccabees, is a reinterpretation of a Greek ideal in light of loyalty to "Judaism."

Only in one passage in 1 Maccabees do we find some indications of a similar transformation. In Mattathias's address to his sons before his death, he exhorts them, "Remember the deeds of the fathers, which they did in their generations; and receive great honor (δόξα) and an everlasting name" (1 Macc 2:51). The language in which 1 Maccabees introduces Mattathias' examples recalls the introduction to Ben Sira's Praise of the Fathers; and, as in the Praise of the Fathers, 1 Maccabees' choice of fathers to single out for praise reflects political concerns. It is quite possible that the author of 1 Maccabees knew the Wisdom of Ben Sira, though outside of this passage, 1 Maccabees' treatment of glory shows no trace of a reading of Ben Sira.[59]

Mattathias goes on to invoke the examples of Abraham, Joseph, Phinehas, Joshua, Caleb, David, Elijah, Hananiah, Azariah, Mishael, and, finally, Daniel (1 Macc 2:52–60). The invocation of Phinehas and David serves the propaganda goals of the Hasmonean dynasty: Phinehas's zeal against idolatry won him and his descendants an eternal covenant to serve as priests, while David, the great military hero, was party to a covenant of eternal kingship (2:54, 57). Elijah's zeal for the law echoes Phinehas's (2:58). Joshua was a great military hero, the leader of the conquest of the land of Canaan (2:55); his deeds are prototypes of those of Mattathias' sons. But the heroism of Hananiah, Azariah, and Mishael in the fiery furnace and Daniel in the lions' den is the same type of heroism the martyrs of 2 Maccabees display (1 Macc 2:59–60). The achievements attributed to Abraham and Joseph are particularly telling. Abraham could have been depicted as a great warrior on the basis of his role in the war of the five kings against the four kings, and Joseph could certainly have been credited with many achievements of statecraft. But the speech praises them in quite different terms: Abraham was "found faithful when tested, and it was reckoned to him as

---

59. Rajak suggests that before they claimed kingship for themselves, the Hasmoneans' understanding of their role as high priests was influenced by the kind of picture of the high priest that we find in Ben Sira ("Hasmonean Kingship," 44).

righteousness," while Joseph "in the time of distress kept the commandment, and became lord of Egypt" (2:52–53). The speech concludes with Mattathias urging his sons, "Be courageous and grow strong in the law, for by it you will gain honor (δοξάζω)" (2:64). The courage of allegiance to the Torah could perhaps be exhibited on the battlefield, but it is also the courage of the martyrs. 1 Maccabees makes only brief mention of the martyrs of Antiochus's persecution, but Mattathias's speech suggests that a transformation of notions of heroism was under way in 1 Maccabees as well.

Thus 1 Maccabees' attitude toward glory and heroism is not entirely uniform. Most of the book, I have argued, adopts Greek ideals of heroism and glory more or less unaltered, although it sets them in a narrative written according to biblical models. In Mattathias's speech, on the other hand, these ideals undergo a process of adaptation to reflect specifically Jewish concerns very much as they were transformed in 2 Maccabees. It is remarkable that these ideals could be admitted, even briefly, into a work of propaganda for a family that won its right to rule precisely through its military exploits. Their presence suggests that martyrdom and suffering out of allegiance to the Torah were widely recognized as conferring prestige.

For Jews in Europe in the Middle Ages, the boundaries between Jewish culture and the larger culture were relatively clear. Jews were, if not the only minority, then the most obvious one, and the intimate and complex relationship between Judaism and Christianity meant that a certain tension between Jews and Christians was almost inevitable. For Jews in antiquity, on the other hand, the boundaries were far less clear. Jews were only one minority among many, and while they stood out for their eccentric religious beliefs, their relationship to the dominant culture was not nearly as fraught. Still, even in pre-Constantinian antiquity, relations were hardly symmetrical. Jews could not escape the fact that theirs was a minority culture and that the culture of the majority, or rather of the dominant group, exerted a pull on them—and other minorities—that their traditions did not exercise on others.

The author of 2 Maccabees worries a great deal about Hellenism and its effect on Jews. To be sure, his transformation of Greek ideas of heroism can be seen as blurring the boundaries between Judaism and Hellenism, but at the same time his use of old men, a woman, and boys to exemplify the new heroism reflects both an awareness of what was characteristically Greek and an effort to avoid it. 1 Maccabees was composed in Hebrew, and thus it must have been intended for a Jewish audience. While conceptions drawn from Greek culture play a crucial role in its narrative, it appears to make use of these conceptions quite unself-consciously. It gives no hint of anxiety that its embrace of the categories of glory and honor represents a departure from the traditions of Israel's past or even that it recognizes these categories as a foreign import. Only in Mattathias's speech does it appear to have made a conscious effort to transform it in light of Jewish values. In its simultaneous pride in Jewish power and embrace of the values of the world around it, 1 Maccabees reflects well the cultural synthesis of the Hamoneans, whose rule it was written to praise.[60]

---

60. I have tried in this formulation to avoid the pitfalls in describing the influence of one culture on another, to which Peter Schäfer has recently pointed; see Peter Schäfer, *Mirror of His Beauty: Feminine Images of God from the Bible to the Early Kabbalah* (Princeton, NJ/Oxford: Princeton University Press, 2002), 229–35. See also the article by Michael Satlow in this volume.

4

Roman Statues, Rabbis, and Greco-Roman Culture

YARON Z. ELIAV

Public sculptures were the "mass media" of the Roman world. They populated urban centers throughout the empire, serving as what art historians call a "plastic language" that communicated political, religious, and social messages.[1] Sculptural displays evoked a complex spectrum of emotions, from fear and loathing to aesthetic admiration, and of ideas, from reflections on the nature of the divine to the implications of social hierarchy, patronage, and power. Most prominent were the three-dimensional sculptures—some life-sized, others colossal representations of mythological figures and real people. They were carved from marble or other stone, cast in bronze, and shaped out of wood, and throughout the Roman world could be found on tall pedestals, atop arches, and in special niches and *aediculae*. Alongside was a profusion of relief sculptures that enlivened both the exteriors and interiors of public buildings and temples, animated column capitals, and decorated entablatures of all sorts of architectural structures along the street, from the *nymphaea* (water fountains) to the *tetrapyla* (colonnaded, arched structures that marked the intersection of streets in the Roman city). Sculpted images were omnipresent in the urban landscape of the Roman realm.[2]

This article is a revised, second version of an earlier study of mine; see Yaron Z. Eliav, "Viewing the Sculptural Environment: Shaping the Second Commandment," in *The Talmud Yerushalmi and Graeco-Roman Culture III* (ed. Peter Schäfer; Texte und Studien zum Antiken Judentum 93; Tübingen: Mohr Siebeck, 2002), 411–33. In preparing it I benefited from the comments of Elise Friedland and Anita Norich; many thanks to both.

1. See most recently Yaron Z. Eliav, Elise Friedland, and Sharon Herbert, eds., *The Sculptural Environment of the Roman Near East: Reflections on Culture, Ideology, and Power* (Interdisciplinary Studies in Ancient Culture and Religion; Peeters; forthcoming).

2. Most recently, although focused mostly on the western part of the Roman Empire, see Peter Stewart, *Statues in Roman Society: Representation and Response* (Oxford: Oxford University Press, 2003).

The closest (although of course not identical) parallel in the modern world is the huge billboards ubiquitous along the main streets of many cities, carrying our own political and cultural messages. It seems to me that the fascination of a small-town visitor walking into Times Square, stunned by its enormous images and neon signs, is probably somewhat analogous to the experience of the author of the Acts of the Apostles when he described Athens as *kateidōlos* (17:16). (The literal meaning is "full of idols," but I think Nigel Spivey, and Richard Wycherley before him, were on target when they creatively translated this phrase as "a forest of idols.")[3]

In the Roman Near East — the provinces of Syria, Palestine, Arabia, and Egypt — statues surrounded people wherever they went and were an integral part of the physical environment in which they lived. Anyone walking in a typical city in Palestine during this period, from Caesarea Maritima, Scythopolis, and Samaria, to Paneas and Eleutheropolis, would encounter Roman sculpture every step of the way. There is no reason to believe that major cities in regions heavily settled by Jews, such as Sepphoris or Tiberias, were any different. The archaeological evidence, the varied discussions of statues in rabbinical literature (some of which will be discussed below) and even their incidental mention in non-Jewish sources all support this claim.[4]

How did the Jews function within this visual environment? Modern scholars have tended to examine the relationship between Judaism and the Greco-Roman world in terms of the conflicts and tensions that purportedly divided them.[5] Roman sculpture, in particular, seems to embody this envisioned clash between the two cultures. After all, what could be more representative of the pagan trajectory than their "idols"? What could be more contradictory to the second commandment's prohibition against the

---

3. See Nigel Spivey, *Understanding Greek Sculpture: Ancient Meanings, Modern Readings* (London: Thames & Hudson, 1996), 13; Richard E. Wycherley, "St. Paul in Athens," *JTS* 19 (1968): 619. I owe this last reference to my student Jason von Ehrenkrook.

4. Moshe L. Fischer, *Marble Studies: Roman Palestine and Marble Trade* (Xenia: Konstanzer Althistorische Vorträge und Forschungen 40; Konstanz: UVK, 1998), provides the most comprehensive summary of statuary in Roman Palestine, though this monograph focuses solely on marble. See also Zeev Weiss, "Sculptures and Sculptural Images in the Urban Galilean Context," in Eliav, Friedland and Herbert, *Sculptural Environment*; Yaron Z. Eliav, "The Desolating Sacrilege: A Jewish-Christian Discourse on Statuary, Space, and Power," in Eliav, Friedland and Herbert, *Sculptural Environment*.

5. In another paper in this volume Michael Satlow surveys these paradigms in nineteenth- and twentieth-century research and elucidates their difficulties; I have devoted a few studies to this question as well. See Michael L. Satlow, "Beyond Influence: Toward a New Historiographic Paradigm," in this volume; Yaron Z. Eliav, "The Roman Bath as a Jewish Institution: Another Look at the Encounter between Judaism and the Graeco-Roman Culture," *JSJ* 31 (2000): 416–54.

creation of images than the three-dimensional figures that inhabited the ancient world? In the centuries that followed antiquity, and arguably still in our own day, the apprehension toward and the rejection of statues came to epitomize the Jewish (disapproving) stance toward the outside world in general and art in particular.

The term "conflict," however, can be deceptive. In describing two cultures as "conflicting," we need to clarify which aspects of society manifest this hostility. Who in fact are the opposing parties? Are their ideologies inimical to each other? Is the hostility evident on the social level, among the common people, or is it only the leaders and cultural elite inflaming these differences? Enmity is an age-old tool to define identity, retain elite power, and strengthen unity. Thus, we must proceed with scholarly skepticism. When characterizing the "multicultural atmosphere" in a particular time and place, awareness of the divergent, even seemingly contradictory, attitudes of each group becomes mandatory. In the sphere of culture and religion, conflict and amity both coexist and intertwine. Shifting attention, therefore, from the fixed category of inexorable and everlasting discord between "Athens" and "Jerusalem," and concentrating instead on everyday Jewish life in Roman Palestine and on the material culture of its landscape, may provide an alternative, less ideologically fraught, perspective on the encounter between Jews and their surroundings in antiquity.

Like other Jews in Palestine, especially those living in urban centers, the sages who produced the tannaitic and amoraic literature (usually referred to as "rabbis") were well aware of the "sculptural environment," and alluded to it quite freely in their writings. Not only did the rabbis repeatedly mention statues by name, such as Aphrodite, Mercury, the figures (icons) of kings and emperors, or even the "faces which spout out water in the towns" (*t. Avod. Zar.* 6:6),[6] they were also conscious of the social and political dynamics associated with the positioning of statues as well as the cultural milieu in which they functioned. They were acutely aware of the customs, myths, and emotions that revolved around these graven images.

For example, the use of statues for imperial propaganda, and the procedures of *damnatio memoriae* that stemmed from it, provided the context for the following rabbinic parable: "A king of flesh-and-blood entered a province and [the people] set up icons [of him], made statues [of him] and struck coins in his honor. Later on they upset his portraits, broke his statues and defaced his coins, thus diminishing the likenesses of the king." It likewise supplied the background for the story about the artisan "who [started to] fashion the icon of the king" but the king was "replaced" by another before he had a chance to complete his work (*Mek. R. Ishmael*, trac-

---

6. Ed. Zuckermandel, 469.

tate *Bahod.* 8).⁷ Frequent changes of rule during the political turmoil of the third century C.E. undoubtedly provided many opportunities to watch such events unfold in real time, whether at a formal declaration of the former emperor as *hostes* or simply when such actions transpired spontaneously in the heat of the moment.

Elsewhere, the rabbis mention the customs of family statuary. One tradition reads, for example, "[A person] goes to a sculptor and says to him, 'Make me a likeness of my father'"; another says, "When the eldest [son] of one of them died they made an icon of him and placed it in their house." As is well known, although less emphasized by scholars, private statues and masks of family leaders (*imagines maiorum*) or children who died prematurely were extremely popular with affluent families (*Mek. R. Ishmael,* tractate *Pisha* 13).⁸ Rabbinic literature mentions many other details distinctive of Greco-Roman sculpture—and not only in a negative tone. The engraved inscription that accompanies a statue, for example—a crucial factor in the way onlookers engage it—surfaces in second-century rabbinic terminology as nothing more than "[a]n inscription that runs under figures and icons." Tannaitic halakah forbids Jews to inspect the inscription on the Sabbath, apparently as part of the general prohibition against reading texts other than scripture on that day (*t. Shabb.* 17:1).⁹ Another example relates to the importance of personal statues in the estate of the deceased— a subject that comes up occasionally in Roman law as well. The rabbis raise it in regard to the case of a convert who inherited them from his father (*m. Demai* 6:10; *t. Demai* 6:13).¹⁰ Rather unexpectedly, the sages also allude to even more spiritual aspects of sculptures, such as the animistic beliefs associated with them, not to mention the aesthetic appreciation of their beauty.

In general, the rabbis' close acquaintance with these aspects of Roman culture should not be startling. After all, like their fellow Jews, they did not disengage themselves from the Greco-Roman domain, and so it is natural that the world they lived in should be reflected in their literary work. The important question is therefore not whether rabbis were familiar with the Roman world but how they assessed it. Cyril Mango, in his influential

---

7. Ed. Horovitz and Rabin, 233; translation with slight changes based on Jacob Z. Lauterbach, *Mekilta de-Rabbi Ishmael* (3 vols.; Philadelphia: Jewish Publication Society of America, 1933), 2:262. For the association of this text with the *damnatio memoriae*, see already Saul Lieberman, *Tosefta Kifshutah: A Comprehensive Commentary on the Tosefta* (10 vols.; Jerusalem: Jewish Theological Seminary, 1955–88), 3:281 n. 3; *Lev. Rab.* 23:12 (ed. Margulies, 547). Here and throughout the paper, if not otherwise noted, the translations are mine.

8. Ed. Horovitz and Rabin, 44; ibid., tractate *Besallah* 8 (ed. Horovitz and Rabin, 144). See Harriet Flower, *Ancestor Masks and Aristocratic Power in Roman Culture* (New York: Clarendon; Oxford: Oxford University Press, 1996).

9. Ed. Lieberman, 80.

10. Ed. Lieberman, 96; *Dig.* 34.2.1, 14 (ed. Mommsen and Krueger, 522–23).

essay about Byzantine perspectives on statuary, maintains that the Byzantines' position regarding statuary can be indicative of that society's overall approach to antiquity and Greco-Roman culture in general.[11] The same model may apply to the Jews as well. In the current essay, I study rabbis as a particular Jewish group from the ancient world whose literature survived and thus allows us a glimpse into their worldview.

Chapter 3 of the Mishnah tractate *Avodah Zarah* (Idolatry) presents the rabbis' "working assumptions," which forms the basis of all discussions about statuary in rabbinic literature. It reads as follows:

> "All statues are forbidden because they are worshipped once a year," such is the statement of R. Meir. [But] the [other] sages say, "[a statue] is not forbidden except one that has a stick or a bird or a ball." R. Simeon b. Gamaliel says, "[a statue] which bears anything in its hand [is forbidden]." (*m. Avod. Zar.* 3:1)[12]

Evidently, R. Meir and the sages disagree about the extent of the prohibition of idolatry in regard to statues—whether "all" are included or only some.[13] The problem arises with the causative clause adjacent to R. Meir's statement that provides his rationale. The link it creates between the noun "statues" and the verb "are worshiped" makes it apparent that the issue at the root of R. Meir's view involves the actual Greco-Roman practice of idol worship, through sacrifice, libation, and other conventional practices, to which the rabbis allude on various occasions (e.g., *m. Sanh.* 7:6). So R. Meir's inclusive rejection of statues is explained by the "fact" that they are all worshiped.

Such a concept—that *all* statues were worshiped as idols—already perplexed the amoraic, third-century sage R. Hiyya b. Abba, who questioned its accuracy in the Palestinian Talmud (the so-called Yerushalmi). He reinterpreted the reason for the prohibition by stating that statues "were wor-

---

11. Cyril Mango, "Antique Statuary and the Byzantine Beholder," *Dumbarton Oaks Papers* 17 (1963): 55.

12. Based on MS Kaufmann (Budapest: Hungarian Academy of Sciences MS A 50; facsimile edition, Jerusalem, 1968).

13. The question in dispute here—that is, the extent of the prohibition against idolatry (which statues are included)—should not be confused with another issue that the rabbis discuss and disagree about, namely, the manner of implementing the ban (i.e., how to behave with a statue that is considered an idol), although the same criterion—whether the statue is worshiped—plays an essential role in that discussion as well. Consider, for example, the rabbinic dispute in *Sifra Kedosh.* 1 (ed. Weiss, 87a): "'Do not turn to idols'—do not turn aside to worship them; R. Judah says: certainly do not turn aside even to look at them"; trans. Jacob Neusner, *Sifra: An Analytical Translation* (BJS 138–40; 3 vols.; Atlanta: Scholars Press, 1988), 3:88. The issue of "looking at statues" has to do with the broader topic of aesthetics, to which, as mentioned above, I plan to devote a separate study.

shiped in the big city of Rome twice in seven years" (*y. Avod. Zar.* 3:42b). But this explication did not satisfy another talmudic sage, who asked logically, "and where they are not worshiped they are permitted?" To solve this problem he employed a principle of another rabbi, R. Jose: "since they were forbidden in one place they are forbidden everywhere" (ibid.). Apparently, R. Meir's sweeping ruling confused these amoraim, because they knew that some statues were *not* worshiped. Their desire to preserve R. Meir's stance in its exact formulation, a common manoeuver in rabbinic hermeneutics, forced the amoraim to validate it using a faraway, almost mythological, place—Rome—in which, at least in their minds, people worshiped all statues.[14]

A modern, and at times sneering, reader of such rabbinic deliberations might be inclined to see them as mere argumentative casuistry, perhaps associated with some speculative exegesis of biblical commandments, but with minimum connection to notions and concepts prevailing outside their isolated legalistic world. Repeatedly, commentators have applied the rather superficial categories "lenient" and "stringent" to sum up rabbinic positions and in general have viewed them as alienated from and rejecting of their hostile, idolatrous surroundings. In fact the opposite is true: in their rulings here and elsewhere, the rabbis engage in the prevailing cultural discourse of their time by utilizing commonly held cultural notions to design their sophisticated positions. A closer view of how these specific rabbinic statements worked will illustrate the intimate connections between the rabbis and the cultural environment in which they lived and wrote.

A student of early periods must, of course, always remain cognizant of the fundamental differences that separate the modern era from previous ages. This is particularly true with regard to the study of religion. The dramatic advances in the natural sciences, the technological-industrial revolution, and the replacement of devout belief by secularism have radically transformed the religious experience. In ancient times, people perceived the whole scope of reality through categories that we would today call religious.

The cosmology of the Greco-Roman Mediterranean basin was replete with divine beings—deities, goddesses, spirits, souls, angels, demons, and mythological monsters.[15] Today these entities are the province of special

---

14. The fantastic nature that underlines these amoraic positions was already observed by Martin Goodman, "Palestinian Rabbis and the Conversion of Constantine to Christianity," in *The Talmud Yerushalmi and Graeco-Roman Culture II* (ed. Peter Schäfer; Texte und Studien zum Antiken Judentum 79; Tübingen: Mohr Siebeck, 2000), 6.

15. An illuminating articulation of this all-embracing religious spirit that prevailed in the ancient world, with an emphasis on the period under discussion here, can be found in Peter

effects and Hollywood cinema, but in the classical era they surrounded people wherever they were, from the heights of the temples on Mount Olympus, to the abstractions of philosophical writings, to the lowest of the latrines in which people relieved themselves. One of these latter facilities, for example, discovered almost intact in Pompey, contains a fresco of the goddess Fortuna in all her glory. The graffiti to her right reads, *cacator cave malum* ("shitter, beware of evil"), and under it a man crouches over nothing less than a small altar, suggesting that he is defecating. To the people of that time, this resembled neither a sacrilege nor a derisive caricature. On the contrary, the elementary human function of excretion, with the odors and physical exertion involved, demanded expression—as bathroom graffiti, for all its humorous and scatological intent, demonstrate even in our day. In the ancient mind, the act registered in the language of religion, incarnated in the Roman case in the guise of Fortuna. Keith Hopkins succinctly captures this phenomenon in the title of his last book—*A World Full of Gods*.[16]

Pervasive and invasive, a religious mentality shaped the lens through which people of the Roman world viewed their surroundings and everyday routines. Religious vocabulary and imagery seeped into every strata of language, assisting people in mediating, explaining, and interpreting their interactions with their environment. Myths, legends, and folk beliefs, even the names and characteristics of gods, all fashioned the cognitive templates that explained and consequently validated both natural phenomena and human situations, just as scientific truth shapes the contours of our world today. Religion—or to be more precise, what we today call religion—encompassed all.

In contrast to this sweeping and unbounded religious landscape, a fundamental human tendency, going back to the earliest origins of civilizations, strives to define and delineate boundaries, especially with regard to physical space and artefacts. Just as human beings have always distinguished, for example, between private and public domains, so the Roman world established, at least in the public sphere, a fairly clear—although somewhat permeable—divide between *locus consecratus* (consecrated space, also known as the *locus sacer*, sacred space) and *locus profanus* (non-

---

Brown's extensive writing. See, e.g., the chapter on religion in Peter Brown, *The World of Late Antiquity AD 150–750* (London: Norton, 1971), 49–112; and his recent article "Christianization and Religious Conflict," in *Cambridge Ancient History*, vol. 12, *The Crisis of Empire, A.D. 193–337* (ed. Averil Cameron and Peter Garnsey; Cambridge: Cambridge University Press, 1998), 632–64. There he characterizes the "religious common sense" of the period as "a spiritual landscape rustling with invisible presences—with countless divine beings and their ethereal ministers" (p. 632).

16. Keith Hopkins, *A World Full of Gods: The Strange Triumph of Christianity* (New York: Plume, 1999). The wall painting from Pompey is reproduced there in plate 1.

consecrated space). The Romans devised clear-cut and precise procedures, known as *consecratio*, for turning a pre-(*pro*)holy place (*fanum*) into a consecrated space, which then received the status of *templum*. This category included the architectonic structure that we now identify as a temple — what they called *aedes sacra* — but also comprised a much wider range of venues. For example, the judicial seat of the magistrate known as the *praetor* and the space in which it was placed, as well as the Senate's chamber, were also *templa*. By the same token, a reverse process, *exauguratio*, restored a site to its profane status.[17] It is difficult to know to what extent people on the margins of the empire followed this formal modus operandi, but it seems that its basic elements were standard and familiar, even if not always performed according to the institutionalized Roman formula.[18] In any case, it is fairly clear that people identified the sacred places in their world with relative ease, and were able, without too much difficulty, to distinguish between them and the profane realm.[19]

The two sides of this complex, at times contradictory equation apply also to sculpture. Only a formal process of *consecratio* imbued a statue with the "holy spirit" — the *pneuma* (or the *numen*, that is, the divine power and will) of one of the gods or, alternatively, the *numen* or the *genius* of one of the emperors — making it sacred (*res sacra*). These statues of gods and deified emperors enjoyed an orderly, well-developed ceremonial system including sacrifices, libations, gifts, and processions, and sometimes even special priests or priestesses. Non-worshiped statues did not merit these privileges. Thus, built into the rituals and liturgy that developed around sacred statues was a means to distinguish between sacred and nonsacred statues.[20]

---

17. For a concise but complete summary of these processes, along with a bibliography, see John E. Stambaugh, "The Functions of Roman Temples," *ANRW* 2.16.1 (1978): 554–608. On the various meanings of *templum* and its basic etymology as a demarcation of space, both in the heavens and on earth, as a place set aside for sacred purposes, see Pierangelo Catalano, "Aspetti spaziali del sistema giuridico-religioso romano: Mundus, templum, urbs, ager, Latinum, Italia," *ANRW* 2.16.1 (1978): 467–79.

18. See, e.g., Mary Beard, John North and Simon Price, *Religions of Rome* (2 vols.; Cambridge: Cambridge University Press, 1998), 1:320–22.

19. On the comparative aspect of the definition of holy sites, and a survey of them across disparate times, regions, and cultures, see, e.g., David L. Carmichael et al., eds., *Sacred Sites, Sacred Places* (One World Archaeology 23; London/New York: Routledge, 1994). See also Ton Derks's precise definition: "Cult places are spaces *intended* for the worship of one or more cosmological powers, *separate* from the profane world, in which the members of the cult community *regularly* gather in order to perform their personal or collective rituals before a ritual focus" (Ton Derks, *Gods, Temples and Ritual Practices: The Transformation of Religious Ideas and Values in Roman Gaul* [Amsterdam Archaeological Studies 2; Amsterdam: Amsterdam University Press, 1998], 133; my emphases).

20. For a more comprehensive description and analysis of this system, see Stewart, *Statues*, 184–222.

On the other hand, this does not mean that individuals could not themselves set apart statues to gods—a process known as *dedicatio*—or that they could not interact ritually (e.g., by making a sacrifice) with a statue lacking a holy spirit. Such informal practice, even if fundamentally distinct from official consecration, was an inseparable part of religious experience in those times. Varying in intensity and commitment, this private and unofficial worship took place in daily routines, through, for example, an endless series of gestures directed toward a statue—any statue. Waving one's hand, touching, kissing, to some more elaborate gestures that required preparation, all could be perceived as a "religious" act.[21] This could culminate in the erection of a small, informal altar, dedicated to a specific statue, which, after receiving the sanction of the authorities (under the guidelines of the *lex area*, the set of laws regulating the usage of public space), placing the altar in a city street, in the forum, or in a bathhouse. All in all, to the (admittedly limited) extent that we can refer to a shared perception of the ancients, they did not view these artefacts as *res sacra*, and a long list of regulations distinguished them from consecrated statues. As one example among many, a person who damaged such a figure was not guilty, under Roman law, of sacrilege, *sacrilegium*. Still, the intricacies of these everyday practices meant that the demarcating lines could be blurred.

Along with the contextual distinctions between the sacred and the profane came the "plastic language" that identified the different statues, what we today call iconography. The repertoire of sculpture in Greco-Roman civilization was astoundingly varied and constantly changing. Greek gods of the pantheon, legendary heroes, and other mythological figures—who either acquired Roman identity or were syncretized with Near Eastern deities—accounted for a large share of the sculpture industry, along with statues of the emperors and their families, who were deified in the process of emperor worship. These figures were placed both in temples and in the public domain. At the same time, a ramified system of other statues existed that represented almost every possible aspect of life in antiquity. The streets were filled with visual expressions of the various elements that shaped people's lives: images of local public figures, athletes, and cultural icons, from orators and philosophers to historians and poets; recreation of battle scenes, both real and mythological, and artistic depictions of all the stages of life, expressing almost every familiar human emotion, joy and pain, elation and innocence. Spectators were not indifferent to these scenes, and this resulted in an interactive system integrating emotional and spiritual symbolism and fostering a plastic language rich in themes and nuances.[22]

---

21. E.g., Jan T. Bakker, *Living and Working with the Gods: Studies of Evidence for Private Religion and Its Material Environment in the City of Ostia (100–500 AD)* (Dutch Monographs on Ancient History and Archaeology 12; Amsterdam: J. C. Gieben, 1994), 15.

22. See Spivey, *Understanding Greek Sculpture* (although focusing on a wider and slightly

In order to understand this plastic language somewhat better we must not confine ourselves to modern encounters with these figures, which usually take place in museums, and define them as "art" (in the modern sense). We need to consider their broader function in the context of the Roman world. In that milieu, statues could be many things at the same time: they were declarations and promoters of power and social status, they marked individual and familial rank just as they symbolized the ineffable, they were commemorators as well as "memories," and they functioned as beckoners as well as trumpeters. In a world that did not distinguish clearly between "religious" and "secular," every sort of artistic expression, even those that seem neutral to the modern viewer, acquired meaning within a conceptual system that we now call "religious." For the people of antiquity this was the only language they knew. Thus, for example, even the vegetal reliefs on the exterior of the *Ara pacis* (the celebrated altar of the Roman goddess peace commissioned by the emperor Augustus) were seen as representing "images of abundance and fruitfulness intended to evoke the blessings of the pax Augusta" and also a "visual embodiment of the returning Golden Age, a new era of blessedness in which the limitless flowering of the earth is contingent upon the efficacious presence of a divinely appointed sovereign, Augustus himself."[23]

However, all this does not imply that Greco-Roman sculptures were all of the same type. Quite the contrary. Within the plethora of existing statues, several varieties could be distinguished. Two of the major categories were statues of gods and those that were not. In the first century B.C.E., for example, Cicero furnished an explicit expression of this division. In an essay discussing the various methods prevalent in his day for understanding the divine nature (*De natura deorum*), he maintains that "from our childhood Jupiter, Jove, Minerva, Neptune, Vulcan and Apollo have been known to us by the appearance [*facies*] with which painters and sculptors have chosen to represent them; and not with that appearance only, but having that equipment, age and dress" (1.29.81 [Rackham, LCL]).[24] The literary context of this passage is illuminating, since Cicero's argument is that precisely because the gods are presented in human form (anthropomorphic) those artistic attributes that allow the viewer to differentiate between

---

earlier chronological range than discussed here); Jaś Elsner, *Art and the Roman Viewer: The Transformation of Art from the Pagan World to Christianity* (Cambridge: Cambridge University Press, 1995); Stewart, *Statues*.

23. David Castriota, *The Ara Pacis Augustae and the Imagery of Abundance in Later Greek and Early Roman Imperial Art* (Princeton, NJ: Princeton University Press, 1995), 12. See also Paul Zanker, *The Power of Images in the Age of Augustus* (trans. Alan Shapiro; Ann Arbor: University of Michigan Press, 1988).

24. I preferred to translate *facies* in this context as "appearance" rather than Rackham's "aspect." See Charlton T. Lewis and Charles Short, *A Latin Dictionary* (1879; repr., Oxford: Clarendon, 1962), 714, s.v. *facies*.

deities and humans are essential. Later on, statues of gods and of human beings as clearly defined categories are repeatedly referred to, for example, in the segments Pliny the Elder devoted to statues in his first-century C.E. encyclopedic work *Naturalis Historia* (e.g., 34.38). Similarly, references to this differentiation reappear some 150 years later throughout Philostratus's essay on images. In echoing the commonly held conventions of his time that were used to evaluate works of art, he mentions the artists' techniques for endowing their works with the identity of a god (*Imag.* 1.15.2). As noticed by many art historians, these details are not mere *schemata*, but rather are meant to convey meaning, thus forming the "plastic language" and consequently shaping the public's perception of statues.[25]

Placed within this convoluted context of the Greco-Roman sculptural environment, the various rabbinic views in the Mishnah gain new meaning. I would like to suggest that, similar to Cicero and Pliny, the rabbis present a position about their surroundings—that is, they set out to shape the way in which people perceive the reality that surrounded them. The majority view in the Mishnah disagrees with R. Meir's assertion that all statues are worshiped, and claims that "[a statue] is not forbidden except one that has a stick or a bird or a ball." This position should be read in light of remarks such as Cicero's about the ability to identify the gods and differentiate them from the many statues that surrounded them by using widely known attributes, iconography, that the artists assigned to the figures. In other words, the rabbis are utilizing the common "plastic language" in order to create their own differentiation between statues that are worshiped (*res sacra*) and those that are not worshiped.

Ultimately, the rabbis are defining their own process of *consecratio*. The items listed by the sages in the Mishnah—the stick, the bird, and the ball—were, at least in their eyes, identifying signs of a deity. In the Tosefta other elements are added to the list, such as a sword, a crown, a ring, and a snake (*t. Avod. Zar.* 5:1).[26] This tannaitic stance results in a more lenient prohibition than does the position of R. Meir, because it qualifies which statues are forbidden. According to the explanation presented here, however, it is not primarily the number of forbidden statues about which the sages differed with R. Meir, but rather the criteria he suggested to define the interdiction, namely, that all the statues are to be seen as worshiped.

Understanding the dispute in this way suggests that both sides agreed that in order for a statue to be prohibited it had to be a "worshiped idol."

---

25. Michael Koortbojian, *Myth, Meaning and Memory on Roman Sarcophagi* (Berkeley: University of California Press, 1995), 9–22, and the literature he lists in n. 27.

26. Ed. Zuckermandel, 468. The position of the third tanna in the Mishnah, R. Simon b. Gamaliel, could be explained as expanding the boundaries of the prohibition to include any kind of attribute.

However, R. Meir, voicing his position about the all-inclusive nature of Roman religiosity, maintained that all statues were considered "worshiped idols," whether they were actually consecrated or not. The majority of the sages, on the other hand, did not agree with him and argued for a more restricted view of the religious experience; they concluded that only statues originally created to be deities, and thus given an identifying "tag" (attribute), were forbidden. The disputed designations help create an iconographic language that the two rabbinic parties use to classify the statues they saw around them and differentiate between divine figures and nondivine figures. R. Meir and the other rabbis did not debate the actual situation (as it might seem from the language of the Mishnah, "because they are worshiped"). Rather, they presented two views regarding how to perceive and evaluate the sculptural environment.

The various perspectives on statues prevalent in the Roman world shed light on the general rabbinic approach that divides statues into "worshiped" and "non-worshiped." It might also assist in further clarifying the difference between R. Meir, who deemed all statues to be idols, and the sages who classified them more specifically. Close reading of Greco-Roman descriptions of their sculptural environment reveals two rather incompatible ways of looking at statues, which parallel the two positions in rabbinic literature.[27] A comparison between the accounts of the first-century author and encyclopedist Pliny the Elder with those of the second-century traveler and geographer Pausanias may illustrate these divisions further.[28]

A modern reader following Pliny's writing on statues could mistake him for a contemporary art dealer. Pliny enlightens his readers with the historical backgrounds of these pieces, shares gossipy minutiae about the artists, and acknowledges with respect (even veneration) the statues' monetary values. His primary criterion in evaluating statues is their aesthetics—their beauty. This allows him to embrace all types, whether gods or not. Even though Pliny, in accordance with the all-encompassing sensibilities of Roman religiosity, applied different terminology for statues of deities and nondeities, he did not privilege either of the groups, and he definitely did not show a preference for one over the other. When it comes to the financial worth of statuary, what counts is the fame and talent of the

---

27. In the following discussion I rely heavily on the theoretical model for understanding the diverse modes of viewing as presented in David Freedberg, *The Power of Images: Studies in the History and Theory of Response* (Chicago: University of Chicago Press, 1989). And also on the formulations developed in Elsner, *Art*.

28. Note that despite their different cultural backgrounds, literary agendas, and the gap in time that separates them, these two authors shared thorough and first-hand acquaintance with the Roman Mediterranean basin and its realities. Lionel Casson labels these common grounds as the "one world" notion (*Travel in the Ancient World* [Toronto: Hakkert, 1974; repr., Baltimore/London: John Hopkins University Press, 1994], 115–27).

sculpture, or the beauty and artistic value of the piece, but the question of whether a statue was worshiped or not becomes irrelevant.[29]

In contrast, Pausanias's *Periegesis* suggests that the great majority, if not all, of the statues pervading the Greco-Roman world either were those of gods or were other sculpture that was placed in their sanctuaries. Consistently, although not definitively, Pausanias neglects most of the nondivine statuary and directs his attention toward either sculpture located in consecrated enclosures and temples or divine figures placed along the streets. This is the case, for example, when he takes the reader along the streets of Corinth and depicts, in the typical jargon of the *ciceroni* (the tour guides), spiced with legends and myths, a visual panorama of the route. The literary tour winds from the eastern port through the city gates to the agora, and then twists back and forth along its main streets. However, despite the realistic impression created by Pausanias's writing, it is hard to accept his description at face value—to believe that the center of second-century Corinth contained only statues of divine figures such as those of Artemis, Dionysus, Athena, and the like (*Descr.* 2.2.6ff.). Intensive archaeological excavations in the area show that at the time of Pausanias, dozens of diverse statues crowded that section of town.[30]

This is not to discredit (as did many nineteenth-century scholars) the reliability of Pausanias, or to denounce him as distorting reality, but only to claim that he does not give the whole picture. As he himself explicitly states at the beginning of the above passage about Corinth, his text describes only "the things worth mentioning." Despite the multitude of statues he saw, his gaze, and consequently his narrative, was transfixed only on statues of the gods or those that populated sanctuaries. His description, then, reflects his own perspective on a more crowded and complicated scene. Nigel Spivey labels this "visual theology," and in Jaś Elsner's unembellished but accurate formulation, "Pausanias' interest is almost obsessively (though not exclusively) in things religious."[31]

The polychromatic scenario painted by Pliny, in which statues of gods and of humans are found side by side, is reduced to a one-sided, although lively and charming, depiction by Pausanias, with the statues of the gods and those located in sanctuaries dominating the entire stage. In this regard, Pausanias and Paul, who "saw" in Athens nothing but a forest of idols (see

---

29. See, e.g., Pliny the Elder, *Nat.* 34.63; 36.18, 27–28. See also Miranda Marvin, "Copying in Roman Sculpture: The Replica Series," in *Roman Art in Context: An Anthology* (ed. Eve D'Ambra; Englewood Cliffs, NJ: Prentice Hall, 1993), 161–88.

30. Franklin P. Johnson, *Corinth: Results of Excavations Conducted by the American School of Classical Studies at Athens IX: Sculpture 1896–1923* (Cambridge, MA: Harvard University Press, 1931).

31. Spivey, *Understanding Greek Sculpture*, 13–14; Elsner, *Art*, 130 (I would change Elsner's phrasing a bit into "things that we now consider religious").

above p. 100), shared a similar "perspective: in the sense that though evaluating the scene in opposite terms, they were looking at reality in the same way.

Without delving into the reasons that led Pliny to see the world in one way and Pausanias (and Paul) to see the same thing in such a different way,[32] we can draw parallels between these two viewpoints and our two rabbinic approaches. R. Meir's perception of the "sculptural environment," which led him to envision all statues as "worshiped," corresponds to Pausanias walking in Corinth and "seeing" only statues of gods and goddesses. In contrast, the sages' distinction between worshiped and non-worshiped statues resonates with Cicero's and Pliny's perspective, in which a "plastic language" distinguishes between the various types of statues.

Following the dispute between R. Meir and the sages, the Mishnah offers an anecdote about Rabban Gamaliel in the "Aphrodite bathhouse." This portion, which might seem at first unrelated to the previous discussion, actually further develops the same halakic/cultural issues. It reads as follows:

> Proklos the son of Plaslos asked Rabban Gamaliel in Acre while he was bathing in the bath of Aphrodite [and] he said to him "it is written in your law 'and nothing of the *herem* shall stick to your hand' (Deut 13:17) why [then] are you bathing in the bath of Aphrodite? He [R. Gamaliel] replied: "it is not allowed to answer in the bath." When he came out he said to him: I did not come within her limits; she came within my limits. [People] do not say "let us make a bath for Aphrodite," but [rather] she, Aphrodite, is made an ornament for the bath. Furthermore, [even] if you are given a large sum of money, [would] you enter in to your idolatry naked, [or] polluted from semen, [or would you] urinate in front of her?! And she [Aphrodite] is standing by the drainage and all the people are urinating in front of her. It is said only "their gods" (Deut 12:3), [i.e.] that which he treats as a god is prohibited, [but] that which he does not treat as a god is permitted. (*m. Avod. Zar.* 3:4–5)[33]

Rabban Gamaliel's position takes the above-mentioned distinction of the rabbis a step further, adding the practical function, what I called before the "identifying context," of a statue to the plastic-language criterion of the

---

32. Many scholars have noticed the difference between the two but interpreted it rather differently. See, e.g., Karim W. Arafat, "Pausanias' Attitude to Antiquities," *Annual of the British School at Athens* 87 (1992): 387–409; Elsner, *Art*, 129–32; Stewart, *Statues*, 184–85.

33. Based on ms Kaufmann.

34. E.g., Seth Schwartz, *Imperialism and Jewish Society, 200 BCE to 640 CE* (Princeton, NJ: Princeton University Press, 2001), 169–74; and my critique of his view in Yaron Z. Eliav, "The Matrix of Ancient Judaism: A Review Essay of Seth Schwartz's *Imperialism and Jewish Society 200 BCE to 640 CE*," *Prooftexts* 24 (2004): 116–28.

sages. Even though Aphrodite was surely a "worshiped deity" (in the sense defined by the sages above) with other statues of her kind receiving rituals, placed in temples, and so on, Rabban Gamaliel maintains that a statue in a given location is forbidden only if that particular one operates in ritual worship.

The two explanations that the Mishnah ascribes to Rabban Gamaliel to justify his visit to the Aphrodite bathhouse support this interpretation. The first claims that "[People] do not say 'let us make a bath for Aphrodite,' but [rather] she, Aphrodite, is made an ornament for the bath." Here Rabban Gamaliel appeals to the general opinion, to the view on the street, to prove that people did not apprehend the particular statue of Aphrodite that stood in the bathhouse as a worshiped idol. He did not reason that Aphrodite and the other statues were "mere decorations," as some scholars believe,[34] but he based his view on the ritual status of this particular statue. This view uses the adornment of the statue only as an indicator of its lack of ritual status. The Romans too applied the same designation—"decorative" (what they called *ornamentum*, and what the Mishnah in the story about Rabban Gamaliel labels *noy*)—to classify a statue as not formally consecrated (e.g., Suetonius, *Tib.* 26).

The second justification in the Rabban Gamaliel story lists the debased acts that people performed before the statue of Aphrodite in the bathhouse—urinating, walking around naked, and the like—linking this with a midrash on the verse in Deuteronomy (12:3), "cut down the images of their gods," which asserts "that which he treats as a god is prohibited, [but] that which he does not treat as god is permitted." Rabban Gamaliel's position may be formulated as follows: even a statue of a deity like Aphrodite is not forbidden if people do not treat it with the respect reserved for the gods. Here too, it was not the particular conduct of people—urinating or exposing themselves—that "secularized" the statues, but rather what such actions reflected about how the public perceived these sculptures. Significantly, the Tosefta uses the same verse to reach the opposite conclusion: "Whether one treats it as a deity or whether one does not treat it as a deity, it is forbidden" (*t. Avod. Zar.* 5:6).[34] These legal prescriptions represent opposing responses to the question of what determines the ritual nature of a statue—whether it is the objective identity or the subjective function of the particular statue.

Another well-known and much-debated tradition in the Yerushalmi can be explained along similar lines. In the passage describing this incident, the famous third-century amora, R. Simeon b. Lakish, encountered a group of people sprinkling liquids in honor of a statue of Aphrodite in the bathhouse of Bostra. According to the talmudic report, after relating this

---

34. Ed. Zuckermandel, 468.

incident to his colleague R. Yohanan, the latter permitted it retroactively (i.e., he ruled that the act did not turn the statue into an idol and consequently the bath into a prohibited location), and asserted "A thing of the public is not forbidden" (*y. Sheb.* 8.8b-c).[35] It seems to me that this anecdote further elaborates the halakic principle developed in the above story of Rabban Gamaliel, and both advance beyond the legal regulations of the tannaitic sages in their dispute with R. Meir. According to the position presented in the anecdote here, not only is a statue of a deity that is standing outside of a ritual context not considered a forbidden idol (R. Gamaliel's position), but even the actual performance of an informal ritual deed in its honor does not revoke its previous nonidolatrous status. The explanation provided for this ruling—"A thing of the public is not forbidden"—conveys the reasoning behind R. Yohanan's interdiction. According to his view, if a statue of a god stands in a public, noncultic context and is considered nonidolatrous (*profanus*), the unofficial *dedicatio* of individuals cannot change its unsanctioned status. This statement should be seen against the background of the ancient world as depicted above, where informal veneration of statues, including processions, semi-pagan games and celebrations, were very common.

To conclude: the rabbinic differentiation between the various statues, based on whether they were worshiped or not, is anchored in the conceptual framework of the Roman world. These are not some peculiar classifications of the rabbis that would have sounded ridiculous to the people of the time, whether Jewish or not; rather they are halakic formulations of accepted, widespread conceptions stemming from the various ways of "viewing" statuary. Furthermore, seeing this distinction in the broad cultural context presented here overturns the commonly held characterization of the attitudes of the sages, and of Jews in general, toward Greco-Roman culture as unrelentingly hostile and overwhelmingly confrontational. At least from the standpoint of their daily contact with the statues of Roman cities, it seems that the sages did not hold a single, fixed position but rather a diverse, wide range of ideas that were based on common ways of looking at statues in those days. While some, like R. Meir, perceived the entire sculptural environment as homogeneous, as made up solely of idols, others classified statues into different categories, distinguishing between those that transgress Jewish norms and those that did not constitute a problem. This halakic formula allowed those who accepted it to live a "normal" Jew-

---

35. For a detailed discussion of this passage in the context of rabbinic attitudes toward the bathhouse and for bibliographical references regarding the various readings that were suggested for this text, see Eliav, "Roman Bath," 433–34 and n. 37.

ish life in the presence of Roman sculpture. The rabbis' ruling on Roman statuary, far from expressing hostility toward all manifestations of the dominat culture, instead reflects the discerning attitudes of a minority group within the Roman world, a group that strove to shape its own way of life by utilizing its profound awareness of the cultural and physical landscapes in which it was living.

5

The Ghetto and Jewish Cultural Formation in Early Modern Europe:

Towards a New Interpretation

DAVID B. RUDERMAN

The myth of the ghetto as a site of Jewish cultural isolation, notwithstanding a wealth of contrary evidence to explode this myth, remains very much alive. We are still accustomed to reading how ghettoized Jews gained enlightenment and emancipation by overcoming a hermetically sealed and alienated existence wrought by their social and political disabilities, and ultimately gained a fuller state of integration and social equality with their non-Jewish majorities. This narrative of the triumphant journey from ghetto to emancipation, whose most important architect was Heinrich Graetz,[1] has not only dominated modern Jewish historiography since the nineteenth century but also entered the essential vocabulary of Jewish memory with such terms as " the age of the ghetto," "ghetto mentality," "ghetto Jew," or "out of the ghetto." In this common understanding, ghetto is synonymous with parochialism and insularity, while emancipation implies the desirable condition of maximal freedom, creativity, and self-determination. Myths die hard and we are conditioned to accept the dichotomy despite the efforts of several generations of historians to blunt its sharp edges and ultimately to challenge the very opposition of closure versus openness that ghettoization and emancipation imply.

Within the confines of this brief essay, I would like to consider the place of the ghetto in Jewish history, a subject I have previously addressed, by adding two significant components to my analysis.[2] In the first place, I need

---

1. See Heinrich Graetz, *Divrei yemei yisra'el* (ed. and trans. Saul P. Rabinowitz; vols. 6–8; Warsaw: Ahisefer, 1916).
2. See David Ruderman, "The Cultural Significance of the Ghetto in Jewish History," in

to situate my own thinking in the context of previous historical treatments of the subject. A historiographical review, albeit incomplete and cursory, will then allow me to suggest a somewhat new perspective by underscoring the cultural significance of the phenomenon of the ghetto—that is, that unique communal structure that emerged first in Venice in 1516 and spread throughout the Italian peninsula by the late sixteenth and early seventeenth centuries—for Jewish life throughout Europe in the era we usually call the early modern period.[3]

As early as 1928, the then young historian Salo W. Baron, in his classic essay "Ghetto and Emancipation," sought to challenge the regnant explanation of Graetz.[4] Baron emphatically rejected the idea that the emancipation represented "the dawn of a new day after a nightmare of the deepest horror."[5] He perceptively observed that nineteenth-century Jewish historians considered the "dark ages" for Jews not the European Middle Ages, which they viewed more positively but rather the period immediately preceding the emancipatory period, that is, the sixteenth through eighteenth centuries.[6] For Baron, this age of the ghetto was one of relatively full autonomy, one in which social services for the members of the Jewish community flourished. Technically, Baron admitted, the ghetto was the direct result of the Counter-Reform policies of the Catholic Church, but he chose to define the ghetto in this essay much more loosely, as "an institution that the Jews had found it in their interest to create themselves,"[7] as a means of Jewish self-defense. In this form of ghetto existence, Jews were able to live a full, rounded life in a kind of territory of their own. Ignoring the actual ghettos of Venice and Rome, Baron called the Frankfort Judengasse "the most typical ghetto in the world" with its highly successful banking

---

From *Ghetto to Emancipation: Historical and Contemporary Reconsiderations of the Jewish Community* (ed. David Myers and William Rowe; Scranton, Pa.: University of Scranton Press, 1997), 1–16, and translated into Dutch as David Ruderman, *De culturele betekenis van het getto in de joodse geschiedenis* (trans. Ruth Peeters and Emile Schrijver; Amsterdam: Vossiuspers, 2003). In this essay, I explore the dynamic and open cultural experience of the ghetto by offering four examples from Venice, Padua, and Modena, focusing especially on political apologetics, university education, music in the synagogue, and clerical control of local customs and traditions. See also my introduction to David Ruderman, ed., *Essential Papers on Jewish Culture in Renaissance and Baroque Italy* (New York: New York University Press, 1992).

3. For a useful and succinct summary of the subject, see Benjamin Ravid, "From Geographical Realia to Historical Symbol: The Odyssey of the Word Ghetto," in Ruderman, *Essential Papers*, 373–85.

4. Salo W. Baron, "Ghetto and Emancipation," *Menorah Journal* 14(1928): 515–26; republished in *The Menorah Treasury* (ed. Leo W. Schwarz; Philadelphia: JPS of America, 1964), 50–63. My citations are from the latter volume.

5. Baron, "Ghetto and Emancipation," 50.

6. Ibid., 51, note.

7. Ibid., 55.

houses.⁸ Emancipation, Baron concluded, had not brought the golden age, since at least some Jews had already created for themselves in those allegedly "dark ages" a viable and productive social and economic system of their own.

Baron's revisionist perspective on the ghetto was useful in seeing the positive dimensions of early modern Jewish life and in de-emphasizing the rupture between the premodern and the modern ages. Ghetto for him meant, however, not the specific walled enclosure created by Italian municipal authorities at the urging of the papacy but rather all forms of contemporaneous Jewish self-government, including those in Eastern and Central Europe. This loose usage of the term also characterized Jacob Katz's classic account of modernity, aptly titled *Out of the Ghetto*, where "ghetto" was synonymous with traditional society. Katz's purview was exclusively Ashkenazic culture, primarily in Germany. Eschewing the negativity of Graetz in describing this traditional society, Katz nevertheless reintroduced the sharp divide between premodern and modern, where formally a social cleavage between Jews and Christians actually existed along with a double moral standard defining the relations of the two communities. In the course of one or two generations, all of this radically changed, as the most traditional of European communities was transformed by the end of the eighteenth century, taking its first bold steps toward integration into the mainstream of European society and culture. For Katz, this critical alteration came about from the top down, that is, through the impact of the ideologies articulated by such German Enlightenment thinkers as Moses Mendelssohn, Gotthold Ephraim Lessing, Naftali Herz Wessely, Christian Wilhelm von Dohm, and others.⁹

Only among the Italian Jewish historians, specifically Moses Avigdor Shulvass, Attilio Milano, and Cecil Roth, did the term "ghetto" receive its extensive treatment in its original Italian context.¹⁰ For all three historians, the ghetto emerged as a result of the repressive policies of a Counter-Reform papacy, accompanying the burning of the Talmud and other forms of aggressive missionizing and social deprivation. In contrast to the

---

8. Ibid., 59.

9. Jacob Katz, *Out of the Ghetto: The Social Background of Jewish Emancipation 1770–1870* (Cambridge, Mass.: Harvard University Press, 1973); consider especially the critique of Todd Endelman, "The Englishness of Jewish Modernity in England," in *Toward Modernity: The European Jewish Model* (ed. Jacob Katz; New Brunswick, N.J.: Transaction Books, 1987), 225–46, who challenged the assumption that modern Jewish history began in Berlin and that it should be primarily focused on intellectuals as agents of change.

10. Moses A. Shulvass, *The Jews in the World of the Renaissance* (Leiden: Brill, 1973); Attilio Milano, *Storia degli ebrei in Italia* (Turin: Giulio Einaudi, 1963); Cecil Roth, *The History of the Jews in Italy* (Philadelphia: JPS of America, 1946); idem, *The Jews in the Renaissance* (New York: Harper and Row, 1959).

relatively tolerant Renaissance period that preceded it, with its open social relations between elite Christians and Jews, intellectual encounters, and economic opportunities for Jewish banking families and their dependents, the ghetto engendered a deterioration of economic and social life for Jews now cramped in crowded ghetto neighborhoods, in the lessening of social liaisons between Jews and Christians, and in the decline of Jewish intellectual life, reflected in the revival of kabbalistic spirituality within the closed walls of Jewish communal existence. While the ghetto era heralded the decline of the creative impulses of the Renaissance ambiance for these historians, their portrait was not thoroughly one-sided. Roth especially could find in the ghetto era signs of Jewish cultural vitality, communal solidarity, and even intellectual creativity.[11] Since some of the ghetto figures he portrayed appeared more like products of the Renaissance than belonging to this supposed era of cultural decline, he was at times rather ambiguous about when the Renaissance began and when it actually ended.[12] Nevertheless, for the most part, Jewish culture for him and for the others was most vital and engaging when stimulated by the outside during the Renaissance and displayed signs of decline and stagnation when forced to turn to its own internal resources during the ghetto era.

In 1986, Robert Bonfil first delivered a paper that was later published in journal form and then incorporated into his book on Jewish life in Renaissance Italy.[13] Reacting directly to the outer-directed historiography of Roth and Shulvass, which he sometimes exaggerated to suit his polemical purposes,[14] he nevertheless offered a highly original and perspicuous view of what the ghetto, specifically the ghettos of the Italian city-states, meant in transforming Jewish culture and society from the late sixteenth century on. For Bonfil, the imposed closure and enforced segregation of the ghetto hardly arrested social and cultural change at all. On the contrary, it triggered a cultural, literary, and liturgical revolution of the first magnitude. For Jews, the ghetto became the site of cultural revitalization. Perhaps betraying the impact of his Jerusalem teachers Yizhak Baer and Haim Hil-

---

11. See his long chapter called "The Age of the Ghetto" in Roth, *The History of the Jews of Italy*, 329–420.
12. See the preface in Roth, *The Jews in the Renaissance*, ix–xiii.
13. Robert Bonfil, "Changes in the Cultural Patterns of a Jewish Society in Crisis: Italian Jewry at the Close of the Sixteenth Century," *Jewish History* 3 (1988): 11–30; reprinted in Ruderman, *Essential Papers*, 401–25; Robert Bonfil, *Jewish Life in Renaissance Italy* (Berkeley: University of California Press, 1994). See also Robert Bonfil, "Lo spazio culturale degli ebrei d'Italia fra Rinascimento ed eta barocca," in *Storia d'Italia: Gli ebrei in Italia* (ed. Corrado Vivanti; vol. 11; Turin: Giulio Einaudi, 1996), 411–73.
14. See especially Robert Bonfil, "The Historian's Perception of the Jews in the Italian Renaissance," *Revue des etudes juives* 143 (1984): 59–82; compare David Ruderman, "Cecil Roth, Historian of Italian Jewry: A Reassessment," in *The Jewish Past Revisited* (ed. David N. Myers and David Ruderman; New Haven, Conn.: Yale University Press, 1998), 128–42.

lel Ben Sasson,[15] Bonfil insisted that when the Jews were empowered by the political and social conditions the ghetto offered them, they were more in control of their own destiny, and rather than simply react to the larger environment, they naturally created their own.

For Bonfil, the starting point for reevaluating the ghetto period was to acknowledge that it constituted a kind of paradox in Jewish–Christian relations and in defining "the self" in relation to "the other." No doubt Jews confined to a heavily congested area surrounded by a wall shutting them off from the rest of the city except for entrances bolted at night were subjected to considerably more misery, impoverishment, and humiliation than before. Nevertheless, as Benjamin Ravid noticed, "the establishment of ghettos did not lead to the breaking off of Jewish contacts with the outside world on any level, much to the consternation of church and state alike."[16] Moreover, the ghetto provided Jews with a clearly defined area within Christian society. In other words, despite the obvious negative implications of ghetto life, there was also a positive side: the Jews were granted a legal and natural residence within the legal boundaries of Christian space. The difference between being expelled and being ghettoized represented the difference between having no right to live in Christian society and becoming an organic albeit inferior and occasionally beleaguered part of the society. In this sense, the ghetto, despite its negative associations, could also connote a change for the better; a formal acknowledgment by Catholic society, revolutionary from the perspective of previous policies of expulsion, that Jews did formally belong to the Christian body politic.[17]

Bonfil extended this analysis by arguing that the creation of the ghetto precipitated a radical shift in the Jewish mentality. During the fifteenth and early sixteenth centuries, Jews lived throughout Italy in widely scattered, miniscule, and vulnerable Jewish settlements. In this earlier Renaissance period, Jewish life was essentially abnormal. Jews felt the constant need to justify their continued existence before despots and democratic communes alike. They were constantly subjected to the darker side of Renaissance culture: Franciscan attacks against Jewish moneylenders, crowd violence, even blood libels such as the infamous one in Trent during the height of the Renaissance. Jews were merely tolerated because they offered a palliative to the poor through their moneylending services, performing in Bonfil's

---

15. Compare my review of Bonfil's book in *Renaissance Quarterly* 49 (1996): 850–53, and that of Anthony Molho, "Robert Bonfil: A 'Modern' Historian's Moral Imperative," *Jewish History* 9 (1995): 113–8. Molho notes Bonfil's post-Shoah sensibility while I suggest his strong Zionist orientation in his creative attempt to re-define the collective self-identity of Italian Jews in the ghetto era.

16. Ravid, "From Geographical Realia," 384.

17. Some of the language in this paragraph and the next two is borrowed from Ruderman, "The Cultural Significance," 7–8.

dramatic simile, like prostitutes, a despised but necessary service. Given this stark reality, the high culture of the Renaissance, its new literary forms and new modes of thinking, had little impact on Jewish cultural consciousness.

The erection of the ghetto system, in contrast, had a noticeable impact on the patterns of Jewish culture and society. Jews became more urbanized, more concentrated in the heart of Italy's largest cities, more polarized both economically and socially, more attuned to the sights and sounds and tastes of the Christian majority, and more secure in their new neighborhoods, despite the squalor and congestion. In the ghetto, Bonfil pointed out, the Kabbalah, the esoteric and mystical traditions of Judaism, performed the paradoxical function of mediating between the past and the present, between medievalism and modernity, restructuring religious notions of space and time, separating the secular from the sacred, even serving as "an anchor in the stormy seas aroused by the collapse of medieval systems of thought," and simultaneously, "an agent of modernity." In exerting a wider impact on Jewish society through the public sermon and more popular moralistic writing, in encouraging revisions and additions to Jewish liturgy, in proposing alternative times and places for Jewish worship and study, and in stimulating the proliferation of religious confraternities and their extra-synagogal activities, the Kabbalah of the ghetto era deeply affected the religious sensibilities of Italian Jews. In fact, in demarcating the religious from the secular, a clear mark of a modern consciousness, the new spirituality left its most enduring mark.[18]

Bonfil's insightful reconstruction of the social and cultural dimensions of the ghetto has had an enormous impact on recent historiography and perhaps constitutes his most important reconceptualization of the period. Nevertheless, as I have indicated elsewhere, it is not immune to some criticism and refinement.[19] In the first place, Bonfil's depiction of the negative impact of Renaissance culture on its Jewish minority is exaggerated and one-sided. No doubt the dialogue between Christians and Jews prior to the ghetto period was limited primarily to intellectuals of each community. But as the case of the circle of Giovanni Pico della Mirandola testifies, the mutual impact was profound and long-lasting. In contrast to previous periods, contemporaneous Jewish culture, especially the Kabbalah, left a lasting impact on a significant number of Christian thinkers, writers, and artists. And new modes of Christian thinking about ancient Judaism, Christianity, paganism, magic, rhetoric, and science left their mark on Jewish self-conception as well.[20]

---

18. See especially Bonfil, "Change in the Cultural Patterns."
19. See my review and essay mentioned in notes 14 and 15 above.
20. This is not the place to fully document these generalizations. In recent years the

In the second place, the explosion of new forms of Jewish cultural production in the ghetto period itself should be seen more clearly for what it was: the result of a more profound and intimate encounter with Catholic society, on the one hand, and a more direct engagement with other Jewish communities throughout Europe and the Middle East, on the other. I refer primarily to the ghettos of Venice, although other Italian ghettos were similarly affected in one way or another. Instead of becoming more innerdirected, more independent or defiant of the values and norms of the Catholic majority, a larger number of Jews living in close proximity to their Christian neighbors absorbed more readily patterns of thought and behavior stemming from the Christian society that surrounded them. Their synagogues became more cathedral-like; their wedding feasts, their iconography, their entertainment, their liturgical music, their confraternal piety, and their intellectual tastes and political loyalties all reflected those of the world they shared with the Christian majority.

It has become unfashionable in our own day to speak about "the influence of the majority upon the minority" or to describe the social processes of the ghetto as assimilatory with respect to the Jewish minority, and Bonfil creatively invents a new vocabulary to understand the complex interactions between Jews and Christians in Italy.[21] I find it simpler and more comprehensible, nevertheless, to see the new neighborhoods for what they were: incubators of new social and cultural liaisons between a Catholic majority and its minority populations, including the Jews. The Christian planners of the ghetto had conceived these enclosed neighborhoods as a means of isolating Jews in a kind of "urban condom,"[22] diminishing their ability to pollute the Catholic majority while leading them eventually to see the truth of the Christian faith through baptism. Although they succeeded in converting a small number of vulnerable Jews, especially impoverished ones, the overwhelming majority remained firmly anchored in their ancestral faith. The ghetto in this sense did not attenuate Jewish

---

study of Christian kabbalah and Christian Hebraism during the Renaissance and in later centuries has attracted much new scholarship. See especially Moshe Idel, "The Magical and Neoplatonic Interpretations of Kabbalah in the Renaissance," in *Jewish Thought in the Sixteenth Century* (ed. Bernard Cooperman; Cambridge, Mass., Harvard University Press, 1983), 186–242; reprinted in Ruderman, *Essential Papers*, 107–69, and most recently in *Hebraica Veritas? Christian Hebraists and the Study of Judaism in Early Modern Europe* (ed. Allison P. Coudert and Jeffrey S. Shoulson; Philadelphia: University of Pennsylvania Press, 2004).

21. See especially Bonfil, *Jewish Life in Renaissance Italy*, xi, 101–24. See now the useful but, by now, hardly controversial remarks of David Myers on "influence" in Jewish cultural history in David Myers, *Resisting History: Historicism and its Discontents in German-Jewish Thought* (Princeton: Princeton University Press, 2003), 157–72.

22. The phrase is borrowed from the Richard Sennert's interesting account of the Venetian ghetto in Richard Sennett, *Flesh and Stone: The Body and the City in Western Civilization* (New York: W. W. Norton, 1994), 212–51.

loyalties; it often fortified them. But in ways unknown to either the Catholic authorities or their ghettoized subjects, they did succeed in remaking the Jews into a community more like them than they ever had imagined.

The ghetto, especially the Venetian one, also became a meeting place of Jews from all over Europe, beginning with its own designated subcommunities: Tedeschi, Ponentini, and Levantini, that is, Ashkenazic, Converso, and Ottoman Jews, but including other visitors from the far corners of the Jewish world. The ghetto, through its printing presses—often joint enterprises between Jews and Christians—its international trade, and through its great pull of Jewish students of medicine from across the continent, became an entrepot of goods and ideas, an open and cosmopolitan center where Jews and non-Jews lived side by side, observing and usually tolerating the other. All of this reinforces the dynamic portrait of ghetto society Bonfil paints but places a greater emphasis on the ways Jewish thinking and behavior patterns more closely approximated those of their Catholic neighbors while simultaneously molded in the context of a growing awareness of other Jewish communities, customs, practices, and ideas generated far from the demarcated space of ghetto existence.

This last observation might serve as a starting point in offering some additional reflections in this paper about the overall cultural significance of the ghetto of Venice, surely stimulated by Bonfil's analysis but attempting to move beyond it. We might recall the loose and imprecise usage of earlier scholars like Baron and Katz who equated the ghetto with all forms of communal organization outside of Italy such as those in Frankfort or Prague in the early modern period, or simply saw the ghetto as synonymous with traditional Jewish society. The historians of Italian Jewry situated the term in its precise political and cultural context, thus underscoring its unique creation as a result of Catholic reform policies at the end of the sixteenth century. While the term eventually evolved into more general usage, their analysis provided a much needed corrective about the origins and novelty of ghetto organization. In accepting this more precise definition and historical context, might one still compare the specific structure in which most Italian Jews lived with those found in the rest of Europe? If the Italian ghetto was not identical with other forms of Jewish communal organization, did it share with them some common features, and might we see in the emergence of the ghetto an Italian expression of a much broader phenomenon characteristic to some degree of all Jewish communities of early modern Europe? This seems to be the intention of Jonathan Israel in his broad survey of Jewish societies in early modern Europe, first published in 1985, in which he presents the program of ghettoization in Italy alongside other manifestations of Jewish communal consolidation throughout Europe.[23]

---

23. Jonathan I. Israel, *European Jewry in the Age of Mercantilism 1550–1750* (Oxford:

The Ghetto and Jewish Cultural Formation in Early Modern Europe 125

For some years now, in response to Israel's pioneering effort, I have attempted to search in my own way for those common features that might allow us to define roughly the period of the sixteenth, seventeenth, and eighteenth centuries as a specific cultural epoch in Jewish history. Despite the significant regional differences separating Jewish life in Italy from that in Eastern and Central Europe, the Ottoman Empire, and the Sephardic communities of Amsterdam, Hamburg, and London, I remain convinced that we can speak of a transnational Jewish culture in early modern Europe, a period distinct from the Middle Ages and also distinct from a modern age, however we choose to define the latter era. Any scheme of periodization is fraught with difficulties and can be challenged by specialists who might readily point out the exceptions to any generalized notion of what a period might represent. This is not the place to defend my effort at offering a tentative definition of what "early modern" might mean for Jewish culture or how this might contribute, however modestly, to a clearer definition of the muddled early modern period in European or world history.[24]

I offer as a working hypothesis the following five key ingredients for any attempt to define a Jewish culture in early modern Europe: constant mobility and social mixing; the powerful drive toward greater communal cohesiveness accompanied by a decline of rabbinic authority and the rising power of lay oligarchies; an explosion of knowledge precipitated by the technology of print, by Christian readers of Jewish books, by an expanded curriculum of Jewish learning, and by the conspicuous entrance of Jewish elites into the university; a subsequent crisis of traditional authority engendered by many factors but often expressed through messianism, radical enthusiasm, and heresy; and finally, intimately connected to the last factor, the blurring of religious identities, specifically the emergence of the conversos, of individual Jewish converts to Christianity, of philo-Semitism and syncretism in European culture. It is obvious that each of the aforementioned factors did not affect all Jewish communities with the same intensity and during the same time frame. Nevertheless, one might argue that the entire Jewish world—east and west, north and south—was affected in some way by each of these factors.

Clarendon Press, 1985), 72–73. Israel also calls Frankfort a ghetto on p. 74. Compare Ravid's careful formulation in "From Geographical Realia," 381–2, and also Alfred Haverkamp, "The Jewish Quarters in German Towns during the Late Middle Ages," in *In and Out of the Ghetto: Jewish-Gentile Relations in Late Medieval and Early Modern Germany* (ed. R. Po-Chia Hsia and Hartmut Lehmann; Cambridge: Cambridge University Press, 1995), 13–15, 25–28. The Jewish quarter was recently the subject of an entire conference in Frankfort on May 16–18, 2004, entitled "Die Franfurter Judengasse: Judisches Leben in der Fruhen Neuzeit," with papers by Ravid and others.

24. While I have addressed this subject in several oral presentations and received important feedback, my forthcoming book on the subject emerges quite slowly and deliberately.

Without denying the unique conditions that account for the erection of the Italian ghettos, the latter should not be studied in isolation from Jewish communities in the rest of Europe. Jonathan Israel then is correct in underscoring the common features of ghetto existence with those of the rest of European Jewry, especially in Eastern Europe, in Germany, in the Ottoman Empire, and in the port cities of Western Europe populated by former converso families. We might add that the ghetto not only reveals the powerful forces of communal solidarity evident among all early modern Jewish communities; it also reveals their patent weaknesses. The Jewish communities in Italy as well as elsewhere became stronger at the expense of the rabbis, who witnessed an erosion of their authority. The latter were forced to acknowledge the real power of lay elites, who generally controlled the affairs of their community, including in many cases the rabbis and their livelihood as well. The Italian case of circumscribed rabbinic power is fully documented in Robert Bonfil's first book, which lends itself to a favorable comparison with Jewish communal structures elsewhere.[25]

Beyond the one factor of communal cohesiveness and diminution of rabbinic power, I would like to propose that the ghetto of Venice (and to a lesser degree those in other Italian cities) exemplifies the other four factors as well. With its repeated waves of Jewish immigrants from Germany, other Italian Jewish communities, France, Spain, and the Ottoman Empire, Venice was surely an important magnet of Jewish migrants and immigrants and for intense social and cultural mixing. With the rise of powerful oligarchic families in the ghetto, the social, cultural, and economic divisions between haves and have-nots was an essential feature of Venetian Jewish life. Venice, through its significant printing industry pioneered by Daniel Bomberg and others, became a central link between disparate Jewish communities and their readerships and between Jews and Christians. With the publication of such significant books as the Babylonian Talmud, the Rabbinic Bible and the *Shulhan arukh*, Venice assumed a major role in shaping a transnational early modern Jewish culture. Venice also claimed the first and most important university to regularize the admission of Jewish students in its midst, the University of Padua. In its training and granting degrees to hundreds of Jewish students from as far away as Poland, Germany, and the Iberian Peninsula, along with many from other Italian communities, Venice simultaneously assumed the role of forming an intellectual elite of Jewish physicians, who collectively and individually became mediators between Jewish and non-Jewish cultures and between Jewish communities throughout Europe.

The ghetto of Venice was hardly immune to the intense debate over

---

25. Robert Bonfil, *Rabbis and Jewish Communities in Renaissance Italy* (London: Littman Library of Jewish Civilization, 1993).

the messiahship of Shabbetai Zevi and the heretical charges leveled against his enthusiastic followers. Debates over the validity of the Kabbalah, over the oral law, and over the viability of traditional forms of Jewish belief also marked the cultural ambience of Venetian Jewry by the late seventeenth century. And the testimony of the Venetian inquisition makes abundantly clear to what degree Venice became a site of mingled and contested identities with the influx of conversos and the allegations of heterodoxy and heresy which they faced from both orthodox Catholic and Jewish authorities.[26]

In sum, the five factors I would stress in defining the common features of a European Jewish identity in early modern Europe existed simultaneously and with particular intensity in the ghetto of Venice during the sixteenth through eighteenth centuries. Indeed, given its intimate connections with Jews to the east and to the west, to Prague and Krakow, as well as to Constantinople, Amsterdam, and Jerusalem, it would be fair to conclude that the ghetto experience in Venice represented a quintessential nub of early modern Jewish cultural formation, a dramatic microcosm of the larger cultural landscape in which European Jews, whatever their origins and regional loyalties, were participants. When viewing the ghetto of Venice in its proper transregional and global perspective, it assumes a central and critical place in the history of European Jewry as a whole.

---

26. This is not the place to document my broad generalizations with multiple references. For the time being, see the many essays in Gaetano Cozzi, ed., *Gli ebrei e Venezia secoli XIV-XVIII* (Milan: Edizioni Comunità, 1987); and in Robert C. Davis and Benjamin Ravid, eds., *The Jews of Early Modern Venice* (Baltimore: Johns Hopkins University Press, 2001). See also Talya Fishman, *Shaking the Pillars of Exile: 'Voice of a Fool,' and Early Modern Critique of Rabbinic Culture* (Stanford: Stanford University Press, 1997); David Ruderman, *Jewish Thought and Scientific Discovery in Early Modern Europe* (New Haven, Conn.: Yale University Press, 1995; repr., Detroit: Wayne State University Press, 2001).

6

Hybrid with What?

The Variable Contexts of Polish Jewish Culture: Their Implications for Jewish Cultural History and Jewish Studies

MOSHE ROSMAN

Often, in reading contemporary scholarship on Jewish cultural history, it seems to me that it has developed two "meta-solutions" that are applied to virtually any question: "influence" and "pluralism." That is, if the question is why Jewish family life is organized in a particular configuration, or why Jews eat specific foods, or how certain institutions of communal governance evolved, or what the basis for Jewish prayer rituals is, or any of a multitude of issues, the answer almost invariably relates to influence of the surrounding culture, the existence of competing and cooperating Judaisms, or both.[1]

With regard to the "influence" meta-solution, there is a firm article of faith shared by practically all of today's academic Judaica scholars that in all times and places premodern or "traditional" Jews lived in intimate interaction with surrounding cultures to the point that they may be termed embedded in them and, consequently, culturally speaking, indebted to them. This contrasts with an older approach to Jewish culture (now usually deemed outmoded), which represented Jews as living in at least semi-isolation from the Gentile world, animating their lives with an original,

---

My thanks to Gershon Bacon, Miriam Bodian, Richard Cohen, Edward Fram, Anita Norich, Elhanan Reiner, David Ruderman, Michael Satlow, Scott Spector, Adam Teller, and Shira Wolosky for their comments and criticisms on various drafts of this article.

1. See virtually all of the chapters in David Biale, ed., *Cultures of the Jews: A New History* (New York: Schocken, 2002), and the critical, and somewhat tendentious, review by David Roskies, "Border Crossings," *Commentary* 115 (2003): 62–66.

autonomous and authentically Jewish culture that functioned according to its own dynamic.²

In the following sections my first objective is to demonstrate, by utilizing the example of Polish-Jewish cultural history, that there are more than these two possible approaches to the history of Jewish culture and that these two themselves should be understood in a more sophisticated way. I then will assert that the first approach (universal cultural influence — in its incarnation as hybridity theory), when applied automatically, unimaginatively and uncritically, can be as ideological, dogmatic, and inappropriate as the second (Jewish cultural autonomy) often has been. Next I propose to contemplate the metahistories implied by the various approaches to Jewish cultural history and their relationship to intellectual presuppositions for engaging in Jewish studies in the academy.

Conceptions of Polish-Jewish Culture

There have been four distinct historiographical approaches to writing the Jewish cultural history of the Polish-Lithuanian Commonwealth of the early modern period. The first was characteristic of the classic Jewish historians of pre-Holocaust Poland, Majer Balaban, Ignacy Schiper, Mojzes Schorr, and to some extent the generation that followed them, Emanuel Ringelblum and Raphael Mahler. Perhaps surprisingly, while conversant in Jewish and especially Polish sources, these scholars gave but pro forma acknowledgment to both the traditional nature of Polish-Jewish culture (its derivation from, continuity and coherence with medieval Ashkenazic [i.e., German-Jewish] and other versions of traditional Jewish culture) as well as to the influences of Polish culture on and parallels with Polish-Jewish institutions, mores, customs, and so on. These historians chose instead to emphasize, indeed to celebrate, the ramified articulation of Jewish culture in Poland: new style *yeshivot*, Council of Four Lands, kahal, taxation expedients, charity arrangements, synagogue architecture, Jewish clothing and jewelry, Jewish language, music, and theater.

Despite the fact that, like us, these early Polish-Jewish historians easily rejected the postulate that Jewish culture existed in splendid isolation, the issues of origins, precursors, influences, and precedents were at most of secondary importance. These men were all accomplished scholars of Polish history and worked primarily with Polish material. They indubitably

---

2. For example, Haim H. Ben-Sasson, ed., *A History of the Jewish People* (London: Weidenfeld & Nicolson, 1976); Louis Finkelstein, ed., *The Jews: Their History*, vol. 2, *The Jews: Their Religion and Culture* (New York: Schocken, 1970–71).

recognized the background intimacy, embeddedness, and indebtedness of Jewish culture relative to Polish and other European cultures. Unlike today's scholars, however, they detected no overriding significance in this. It was a fully expected mundane detail, not a novel insight worthy of elaborate research and presentation. For them, the central point, the exciting discovery, was the vibrancy, comprehensiveness, and power of Polish Jewish culture, irrespective of its possible genetic links to non-Jewish culture.[3]

These scholars dwelled on what Polish Jewry had wrought through an ingenious resourcefulness, often in the face of legal and other obstacles. The conclusion implied by their depiction is that Polish-Jewish culture was a unique array of cultural institutions and behaviors that outstripped its Ashkenazic progenitors in quality and quantity; matched or outmatched other Jewish subcultures in authenticity and integrity; and compared favorably to Polish culture in terms of originality, creativity, vitality, and sophistication.

While this approach has much to teach us, in describing in loving detail the values, symbols, and institutions of Polish Jewry it raises the question of the extent of the cause-and-effect connections between Jewish culture and Polish culture. For the pre-Holocaust Polish-Jewish scholars, the essential question was one not of cultural genesis but of *juxtaposition* and *comparison* of the two cultures. Rather than utilizing the three metaphors of intimacy, indebtedness, or embeddedness (the latter two of which imply hierarchy and dependence) to conceptualize the relationship between the two cultures, they recognized two distinct entities, intertwined but independent and functionally equal. For them, it was important to understand that the Jewish as configured in Poland could hold its own vis-à-vis the Polish; outside or mutual influences, taken for granted, were largely beside the point.[4]

---

3. See comments made in passing by, e.g., Majer Balaban, *Historja i literatura zydowska ze szczegolnem uwzglednieniem historji Zydow w Polsce: dla klas wyzszych szkol srednich* (3 vols.; Lwów: Ossolinskich, 1925; repr., Warsaw: Wydawnictwa Artystyczne i Filmowe, 1982), 3:188, 205–6, 232. For the Hebrew version, see Israel Halperin, ed., *Bet yisrael be-polin* (2 vols.; Jerusalem: ha-Mahlakah, 1948–53), 1:45–46, 50, 55, 69. Also Raphael Mahler, *Toldot hayehudim bepolin* (Merhavia: Sifriat poalim, 1946), 74, 188–89, 191, 202, 360–61, 381. See also the references in n. 4.

4. For example, Balaban, *Historja*, 3:183–259; Halperin, *Bet yisrael*, 1:44–80. Ignacy Schiper, *Kultur-geshikhte fun Yidn in Poyln beysn mitlalter* (Warsaw: Brzoza, 1926); Ignacy Schiper, Aryeh Tartakower, and Aleksander Hafftki, eds., *Zydzi w Polsce odrodzonej* (2 vols.; Warsaw: Nakl. Wydawn, 1932–35), 1:81–110, 213–374, with various sections written mainly by Schiper, but also by Balaban and Jeremiah Frenkel. Schiper devoted much of his attention (not always to the best advantage) to Jewish language, arts, and literature; see, e.g., on Jewish theater in Poland from earliest times, Ignacy Schiper, *Geshikhte fun der yiddisher teater-kunst un drame* (3 vols.; Warsaw: Kultur-lige, 1927–28); and chapters on Jewish-language folk literature, plastic arts, music, theater decoration, graphic arts, and sculpture in Poland in Schiper,

The second approach to the description of Polish-Jewish culture was that of Jewish nationalist, Zionist, and what might be termed intellectual historians (where these groups are not mutually exclusive). This began with Simon Dubnow, who, based on his master narrative of shifting culturally hegemonic centers of the Diaspora, crowned Polish Jewry as the co-hegemon (along with the rest of Yiddish-speaking Jewry in Ashkenaz) of world Jewry in the early modern period.[5]

This notion of a worldwide, interconnected, nationally self-conscious, transnational Jewish people with a common history, culture, and fate was continually cultivated by such historians as Haim Hillel Ben-Sasson, who termed the Polish-Lithuanian Commmonwealth "a *province* of Jewish Society and Culture," the "outside" influences on which came from other *Jewish* communities.[6] Jacob Katz's famous *Tradition and Crisis* took it axiomatically

---

Tartakower, and Hafftki, *Zydzi w Polsce odrodzonej*, 1:225–35, 308–36; and 2:114–47; also Mahler, *Toldot*, 50, 188–215, 357–95. It should be noted that Mahler's presentation of Jewish life in the Polish-Lithuanian Commonwealth was much less sanguine than that of his predecessors.

5. Simon Dubnow, *Vsemirnaya istoriya yevreiskovo naroda*, vol. 1 (Berlin: Izd-vo "Gesher," 1924), xx-xxv: "Periodizatsia i raspredeleniye materiala" [lit., Periodization and Distribution of the Material]; see esp. p. xxii on the period of joint Ashkenazic-Polish hegemony; German edition: Simon Dubnow, *Weltgeschichte des jüdischen Volkes*, vol. 1 (trans. Aaron Steinberg; Berlin: Jüdischer Verlag, 1925), xxiii-xxx: "Periodisierung und Stoffverteilung," esp. p. xxv; English edition: Simon Dubnow, *History of the Jews*, vol. 1 (trans. Moshe Spiegel; New York: T. Yoseloff, 1967), 33–38: "Periodicity and System of Hegemonies," esp. p. 35. Hebrew edition: Simon Dubnow, *Divrei yemei am olam*, vol. 1 (trans. Baruch Karu; Tel Aviv: Devir, 1958), 6–11: "Keviat hatekufot vesiddur hahomer" [Setting the Periods and Organizing the Material], esp. p. 8; and note subtle differences in formulation among the various translations. For analysis of Dubnow's historiographical theory and its ramifications and applications, see Jonathan Frankel, "Assimilation and the Jews in Nineteenth Century Europe: Towards a New Historiography?" in *Assimilation and Community: the Jews in Nineteenth Century Europe* (ed. Jonathan Frankel and Steven J. Zipperstein; Cambridge: Cambridge University Press, 1992), 1–37. For an introduction to the development of the nationalist school in Eretz Israel, see Israel J. Yuval, "Yitzhak Baer and the Search for Authentic Judaism," in *The Jewish Past Revisited: Reflections on Modern Jewish Historians*, ed. David N. Myers and David B. Ruderman; New Haven: Yale University Press, 1998), 77–87; David N. Myers, "Between Diaspora and Zion: History, Memory and the Jerusalem Scholars," in Myers and Ruderman, *Jewish Past Revisited*, 88–103.

6. Haim H. Ben-Sasson, *Trial and Achievement: Currents in Jewish History* (Jerusalem: Keter, 1974), 144. As to the influence of other Jewish communities, see, e.g., Haim H. Ben-Sasson, *Hagut vehanhagah* (Jerusalem: Mosad Byalik, 1959), 14–16. At times Ben-Sasson, like the generation of Polish-Jewish historians before him did emphasize the uniqueness of Polish-Jewish culture and how it broke in some ways with Ashkenazic precedents (e.g., *Hagut vehanhagah*, 152–53, 155–56). Nevertheless, he announced, "In the end the western Ashkenazi culture became dominant" (*Trial and Achievement*, 144); and, "In the 16th and 17th centuries Poland-Lithuania became the main center of Ashkenazi culture" (ibid., 162). In *Hagut vehanhagah* he was even more emphatic that Polish Jewry was the direct cultural descendant of Ashkenazic Jewry, and especially *Hasidei ashkenaz* (e.g., Ben-Sasson, *Hagut vehanhagah*, 11–13); but cf. Haym Soloveitchik, "Piety, Pietism and German Pietism: *Sefer Hasidim I* and the Influence of *Hasidei Ashkenaz*," *JQR* 92 [2002]: 484–88). Note that Ben-Sasson was well aware

that "[a]ll Jews, whether in Poland or Yemen, Holland or Palestine, saw themselves as members of a single nation."[7] However, this nation was geographically divided into various centers, and one of them, stretching from the Loire to the Dniepr, was in Jewish terms an expanded Ashkenaz (in the early modern period no longer just the Germanic areas, but also including Poland-Lithuania), a single cultural domain.[8] Jacob Elbaum highlighted the profound effects of non-Ashkenazic Jewish subcultures on Polish-Jewish culture in the wake of the spread of printing, and implied that Polish culture itself impinged on the Jews barely at all.[9] Chone Shmeruk vividly demonstrated the cultural alienation between Polish and Jewish cultures with his analysis of their versions of the Esterke myth, which stemmed from independent sources (according to the Polish version, the Jewish Esterke was King Kazimierz the Great's mistress; in the Jewish version, Esterke was the king's queen).[10]

---

of Polish sources and knew that some individual Jews were subject to Christian intellectual influences. He lent this little significance (e.g., Ben-Sasson, *Hagut vehanhagah*, 30, 38–39, 78), while Gentile parallels with Jewish culture he took not as evidence of a cause-and-effect relationship of Polish influence on Jewish culture, but merely as proof of correlations reflecting third factors that acted on both cultures and subjected them to some of the same conditions, pressures, and demands (e.g., ibid., 52–54, 60, 65, 89, 101, 117, 150, 240, 249, 250). Ben-Sasson believed that for Polish Jewry Gentiles represented a halakic problem but not a cultural one (e.g., ibid., 56, 60, 104). There might be a question as to how to deal with Gentiles on their holidays, but they did not pose any challenges to Jews' life assumptions. By the way, Ben-Sasson's manner of evaluating cultural parallels may prove to be a fruitful alternative to the paradigm of embeddedness, aiding, for example, in explaining the simultaneous recrudescence of religious fundamentalism in the late twentieth century among mutually alien cultures—e.g., Iran and the United States Baptist Belt—that hardly can be said to be embedded one within the other.

7. Jacob Katz, *Tradition and Crisis: Jewish Society at the End of the Middle Ages* (trans. Bernard D. Cooperman; New York: New York University Press, 1993), 5; see also pp. 6–8. Cf. David Biale's remarks cited below n. 44.

8. Ibid., 6.

9. Jacob Elbaum, *Openness and Insularity* (in Hebrew; Jerusalem: Magnes, 1990), esp. 30–32, 63–64, 179–80. Western readers might instinctively assume that the "openness and insularity" to which Elbaum referred were relative to non-Jewish culture. However, as deeply imbued as he was with the Zionist approach to Jewish culture, Elbaum reflexively used these terms to denote cultural relations between the Polish-Jewish and other Jewish communities. In his book the relationship between Jewish and non-Jewish culture is deep in the background.

10. Chone Shmeruk, *The Esterke Story in Yiddish and Polish Literature* (Jerusalem: Zalman Shazar Center, 1985). Many others contributed to the conception of a transnational and transtemporal autonomous Jewish culture, including some of the classic Jewish historians of the past as well as some of the most recent ones; e.g., Simha Assaf, Ben-Zion Dinur, Israel Halperin. The latest example of this approach is Mordechai Breuer, *The Tents of Torah: The Yeshiva, Its Structure and History* (in Hebrew; Jerusalem: Merkaz Zalman Shazar, 2003). Tellingly, this book is organized not geographically or chronologically but thematically, by aspects of the yeshiva as an institution (curricula, methodology of study, administration, etc.),

All of these scholars, and many others, presumed that Polish-Jewish culture was, at base, an elaboration of a traditional, authentic, autonomous Jewish culture that had developed organically at least from talmudic times and probably even beginning with the Bible. It was a culture that was continuous and coherent over time and geography; its essential core recognizable through all of its myriad permutations. This culture was, of course, subject to alien influences, but these were either insignificant, ultimately eschewed, or so Judaized as to make the question of origins moot.

The concept of an isolated culture with a dynamic of its own, as noted above, was abandoned a generation or more ago. Interestingly, however, just as this view was losing favor with many Jewish historians of the premodern periods, it was reinforced from unexpected directions. In his 1988 essay "Jewish Continuity in an Age of Discontinuity: Reflections from the Perspective of Intellectual History," the modernist intellectual historian Paul Mendes-Flohr attempted to define the universal, if variably inflected, ingredients of Jewish culture that made for an unambiguous, self-evident, and unproblematic Jewish continuity up until the age of secularization, and that everywhere resisted co-optation. These he archly dubbed the Seven C's: Creed, Code, Cult, Community, Culture, Cognitive, and Covenant.[11]

A more historical, detailed, and closely argued claim appeared in *European Jewry in the Age of Mercantilism*, where Jonathan Israel, theretofore primarily a historian of early modern Holland and Spain, boldly asserted that there was

> a distinctive Jewish culture within Europe. . . . Hispanization of Levantine, and Germanization of east European Jewry . . . imparted a remarkable degree of cohesion to a people scattered in small groups over vast distances in a score of lands. What is more, the two spheres, the Hispanic and the Germanic, were now brought into a high degree of interaction . . . [A]t a deeper level the two spheres developed intellectually and spiritually largely as one.[12]

---

as if to say that the yeshiva embodies and symbolizes a universal Jewish culture, the individual expressions of which in various times and places are but specific examples of an abiding, timeless, even essential, Jewish culture. Several younger scholars, such as Elhanan Reiner, Edward Fram, and Zev Gries have kept to the basic idea of Polish-Jewish culture as developing, cultivating, and further articulating general Ashkenazi and earlier Jewish culture, but they have tried to explain the mechanisms of this process and explicate the resultant differences between the progenitors and the filiation in a nuanced, sophisticated, and complex way.

11. Paul Mendes-Flohr, "Jewish Continuity in an Age of Discontinuity: Reflections from the Perspective of Intellectual History," *JJS* 39 (1988): 261–68; reprinted in Paul Mendes-Flohr, *Divided Passions: Jewish Intellectuals and the Experience of Modernity* (Detroit: Wayne State University Press, 1991), 56–59.

12. Jonathan I. Israel, *European Jewry in the Age of Mercantilism* (Oxford: Clarendon, 1985), 31.

Moreover, with respect to influences from the surrounding cultures, the "unified and integrated Jewish culture . . . was increasingly remote from that of the peoples among whom Jews lived."[13]

Israel said nothing about the eras preceding the sixteenth century and regarded this "maximum cohesion in the history of Jewish culture" as a product of the early modern period.[14] Still, it is striking how his—and Mendes-Flohr's—evaluations lend credence to the idea of an early modern traditional, coherent Jewish culture standing as an equal among and apart from other cultures; not embedded within one or another of them; certainly ever *less* indebted to them; and, while itself modulated into various subcultures, still laying claim to be an integral, continuous whole.

Whether propounded by nationalists or others, this approach has the virtue of proffering a reasonable explanation for two seemingly fundamental aspects of Polish-Jewish culture: first, much of early modern Polish- (and other-)Jewish culture is an iteration of earlier Ashkenazic and even talmudic forms that often defies attempts at historicist analysis aiming to identify features that make it a specific product of its Polish milieu. Most of the halakic rulings of the sixteenth-century Polish rabbi Moses Isserles,

---

13. Ibid., 33.
14. Ibid., 184; see also p. 71 and the introduction to the book. One might also infer the existence of a coherent, worldwide Jewish culture in the early modern period in dialogue with local Jewish cultures or subcultures from Miriam Bodian's description of the "rejudaization" of the "Portuguese Nation," i.e., the descendants of the Portuguese conversos, who emigrated from the Iberian peninsula in the seventeenth century, settling in Amsterdam and elsewhere. These people worked toward the objective "of a collective 'return' to mainstream Jewish life and historical experience . . . integration into the wider Jewish world" while still cultivating an Iberian informed way of life; see Miriam Bodian, *Hebrews of the Portuguese Nation: Conversos and Community in Early Modern Amsterdam* (Bloomington: Indiana University Press, 1997), 19 (where the previous citation appears), 30, 45, 47, 89–92, 96–131, 132–33, 138, 146, 148, 152, 155–56. Perhaps the strongest case for the existence of an autonomous Jewish culture in the early modern period juxtaposed to the non-Jewish "outside" culture was made by Robert Bonfil, *Jewish Life in Renaissance Italy* (Berkeley: University of California Press, 1994), although his argument was limited to Italy. Bonfil variously asserted, e.g.: "I have tried instead to point out the component elements of the subject's [i.e., the Jews] *different* culture and the implications of that *difference* for the complex process of the insertion of the Jew into the sociocultural fabric of the Italian cities of the period"(p. xi); "the structural opposition between the two societies was absolute and fundamental"(p. 123); "the *importation* of elements of the outside culture must be understood as the adoption and manipulation of contents considered as 'neutral' as far as their potential impact on their consciousness of a Jewish identity—perceived as different from, or better yet, *opposed* to Christian identity—was concerned"(p. 151); see also pp. 3, 103, 104, 108–9, 110, 115, 124, 151, 152, 284. In a similar spirit, Gershon D. Hundert (*Jews in Poland-Lithuania in the Eighteenth Century: A Genealogy of Modernity* [Berkeley: University of California Press, 2004]), while seeing Polish Jews as both insular and integrated into the society in which they lived, maintained that "Polish society held no attraction for Jews"(p. 238), and that Jews' insistence on determining their own identity and their refusal to be defined by others is the "defining . . . element in the modern Jewish experience"(p. 240).

for example, were restatements or recastings of the decisions of earlier, non-Polish authorities. The extent to which they reflect and react to Polish conditions is not self-evident.[15]

The second aspect is that on numerous counts the mutual cultural alienation of Gentiles from Jews in Poland is patent. As illustrated by such expressions as legislation and economic behavior, Poles and Jews each regarded the members of the other group as most definitely "Other," to be suspected, feared, and often demonized or worse. Linguistically, there was no real common language. Boundary markers, differential calendars, food restrictions, and various distinguishing religious rituals carefully delineated the respective cultural space of each group. Contact between cultural elites was limited and, where it existed, was usually negative. Although living physically intermixed to a significant degree, each group had its own institutional infrastructure that functionally, and—one might argue—redundantly, duplicated that of the other group. Even ostensibly shared cultural possessions, such as the Esterke myth alluded to earlier, proved to have different origins. In general, it is fair to say that the cultural creations

---

15. Moshe Rosman, "A Prolegomenon to the Study of Jewish Cultural History," *Jewish Studies: An Internet Journal* 1 (2002): 113–15, www.biu.ac.il/JS/JSIJ/. This is not to say that Isserles' rulings were not characteristic of Polish-Jewish culture. As an anthology, the *Mappah*, Isserles' glosses on the Sephardic Joseph Karo's halakic code, the *Shulhan Arukh*, presents a particular cultural canon that guided the society Isserles lived in. However, the elements anthologized in this canon came largely from Ashkenaz. Moreover, some of Isserles' statements and rulings are historicizable; but the process of separating halakic precedent and standard practices from contingencies and extralegal concerns that sixteenth-century Polish circumstances gave rise to is a complex and arduous one that is not guaranteed to produce results. For examples of successful analysis of this type and, by implication, how exceptional it appears to be, see Edward Fram, *Ideals Face Reality: Jewish Law and Life in Poland, 1550–1655* (Monographs of the Hebrew Union College 21; Cincinnati: Hebrew Union College Press, 1997), index, under "Isserles, Moses"; idem, "Two Cases of Adultery and the Halakhic Decision-Making Process," *AJS Review* 26 (2002): 277–300; cf. Elbaum, *Openness and Insularity*, 15, 27–28, 222, 376. Joseph Davis ("The Reception of the *Shulhan 'Arukh* and the Formation of Ashkenazic Identity," *AJS Review* 26 [2002]: 251–76), has averred, based on his interpretation of criticism of Isserles' work by R. Hayyim ben Bezalel of Prague and his own understanding of Isserles' use of the term "these lands" [*medinot ellu*], that Isserles intended his code specifically for the Polish-Jewish community (see esp. pp. 262–65) and that "[t]he 'customs of these lands' that Isserles codified in his notes to the *Shulhan 'Arukh* were the customs of the Polish Jews" (p. 265). Even if this is the case, it still is incontrovertible that most of what Isserles wrote in the *Mappah*, and most of the halakic practice of Polish Jewry, had earlier Ashkenazic precedents, making it difficult to prove a Polish *origin*—as opposed to *audience* and *practitioners*—for the contents of the *Mappah*. Moreover, Ashkenaz is not a monolith. As Eric Zimmer has pointed out, there are various streams—French, Rhenish, "Ostreikh" and Byzantine—within Ashkenazic tradition (*Society and Its Customs* [in Hebrew; Jerusalem: Merkaz Zalman Shazar, 1996], 296–98). Both Zimmer and Fram have suggested to me in personal communications that the "Polish" customs Isserles was advocating (and that R. Hayyim ben Bezalel was objecting to) probably derived from "Ostreikh" and did not originate in Poland.

of Poles and Jews to a great extent stemmed from different sources and usually developed along different lines.[16]

Both the difficulty of historicist analysis and the mutual cultural alienation of Jews and their neighbors are much easier to understand and contend with historiographically if Polish-Jewish culture is viewed as primarily Jewish, deriving from Jewish antecedents outside of Poland and in constant reference to contemporary Jewish cultural communities all over the world. Such a conception clashes, however, with the now conventional belief that Jewish culture was always embedded in and indebted to the local culture where it was found.

An additional approach to Polish-Jewish culture is what we might call the "early American school." This was espoused by ex-Europeans, in particular, Salo W. Baron and Bernard Dov Weinryb, who made their home in the United States and adopted its ways. They took Baron's general paradigm for Jewish history[17]—which can be characterized as an ellipse whose contours are determined by two foci, one internal, one external—and applied it to the Polish case. As Weinryb put it:

> As a minority[18] [the Jews] absorb elements of their environment, but they are also conditioned by the heritage of their own history, religion, and culture, as well as by the possibility of contacts with their places of origins and kindred Jewish groups. This leads to a distinctive Jewish existence, which in the case of Polish Jewry embodied elements of both Jewishness and Polishness. Jewish history in Poland thus deals with these two processes: Polish history and Jewish life, often with emphasis on the latter.[19]

---

16. Moshe Rosman, "Innovative Tradition: Jewish Culture in the Polish-Lithuanian Commonwealth," in Biale, *Cultures of the Jews*, 523–25, 527; idem, "Jewish Perceptions of Insecurity and Powerlessness in 16th–18th Century Poland," *Polin* 1 (1986): 21–25; idem, "A Minority Views the Majority: Jewish Attitudes Towards the Polish-Lithuanian Commonwealth and Interaction with Poles," *Polin* 4 (1989): 36–39; Hundert, *Jews in Poland-Lithuania*, introduction, afterword, and passim. Cf. Roskies, "Border Crossings," 65. Overt Polish cultural influence on Jews can be detected in the areas of dress, diet, music, and book illustrations; see Nisson E. Shulman, *Authority and Community: Polish Jewry in the Sixteenth Century* (New York: Yeshiva University Press, 1986), 80; Chone Shmeruk, *The Illustrations in Yiddish Books in the 16th–17th Centuries* (in Hebrew; Jerusalem: Akademon Press, 1986); David Assaf, "The World of Torah in Poland" (in Hebrew), *Polin* 5–6 (1990): 93–99.

17. Baron explicated his view of the relationship between Jewish and general history in two articles republished in Salo W. Baron, *History and Jewish Historians* (compiled by Arthur Hertzberg and Leon A. Feldman; Philadelphia: Jewish Publication Society of America, 1964): "World Dimensions of Jewish History" (pp. 34–42); and "Newer Emphases in Jewish History" (pp. 100–105).

18. Hundert contends that applying the term "minority" to Jews in early modern Poland is inappropriate (*Jews in Poland-Lithuania*, 21–31).

19. Bernard D. Weinryb, *The Jews of Poland: A Social and Economic History of the Jewish Community in Poland from 1100 to 1800* (Philadelphia: Jewish Publication Society of America, 1973), ix.

Although Weinryb claimed to privilege what he called "Jewish life," in his book he gave Jewish heritage short shrift while focusing on the importance of the Polish setting in determining the circumstances of Jewish existence in many ways. He devoted most of his efforts to describing how, thanks to the structures of Polish society and culture, the Jews were largely well situated, comfortable, and successfully adapted in Poland.[20]

"Embedded" would certainly be a fair epitome of Weinryb's characterization; however, his discussion largely omitted any systematic consideration of Jewish culture. Glaringly missing are Polish-Jewish halakic development, rabbinic culture, and the educational system. He managed to treat the hoary and, to most scholars, cardinal subject of Jewish communal organization in the shortest chapter in the book (numbering but eight pages) and denied that Sabbatianism exercised a significant impact in Poland, thus undercutting what for Zionist historians was the classic proof for the existence of a world Jewish culture.[21]

Baron, for his part, gave so much weight to the Polish focus of the Polish-Jewish ellipse that in many places the reader of his book will be forgiven for thinking that he is reading a textbook on Polish history that happens to highlight the Jewish angle.[22] Moreover, under the rubric "Extraordinary Creative Elan," where one might rightfully expect a full-blown exposition of the achievements of Polish-Jewish culture and how each of the two foci determined the profile of this culture, Baron wrote a bare two and a half pages devoted mainly to the subject of religious toleration in Poland, while noting merely in passing how Polish Jews "achieved a cultural level which exceeded anything known in Ashkenazic Jewry since the days of the Tosafists."[23]

As was true of the nationalist approach, the two-foci perspective on Polish-Jewish history in the early modern period has been continued by a

---

20. Weinryb, *Jews of Poland*, 156–76.

21. Ibid., 71–78, 228–31; cf. Gershom Scholem, *Sabbatai Sevi: The Mystical Messiah* (Princeton, NJ: Princeton University Press, 1973), who portrayed the Jewish reaction to Sabbatai Sevi as simultaneous, similar, and synergetic worldwide; see esp. pp. 591–602 on Poland. Cf. Moshe Rosman, "Reflections on the State of Polish-Jewish Historical Study," *Jewish History* 3 (1988): 118–19.

22. Salo W. Baron, *Late Middle Ages and Era of European Expansion, 1200–1650: Poland-Lithuania 1500–1650*, vol. 16 of *A Social and Religious History of the Jews* (New York: Columbia University Press, 1976). Note rubrics such as: "Poland's Golden Age," "The Last Jagiellonians," "Two Interregna and Bathory," "Protestant Sectarianism," "Poland-Lithuania on a High Plateau," "Poland's Eastern Drive," where there is much to learn about Polish history, irrespective of the Jews. Like Dubnow before him, Baron was convinced that Polish Jewry attained cultural hegemony in the Jewish world: "In sum: the Jewish community of the dual Commonwealth could now assume the communal and cultural leadership of Ashkenazic, and in some respects of all world, Jewry" (p. 163).

23. Baron, *Late Middle Ages*, 75–77.

somewhat unexpected group—Polish-born and trained historians who have chosen to devote their efforts to the elucidation of the history of the Jews in Poland. They have naturally highlighted the Polish focus of the ellipse and are supplying a steady stream of sources and information that shed an ever brighter light on the conditions of life for Jews in the Commonwealth as shaped by the Polish context.[24]

Intuitively—for our consciousness is still similar to theirs—Baron's and Weinryb's (and their successors') assertion of the importance of the Polish context seems all too obviously correct. While they are, however, convincing that Polish policy and actions toward the Jews and the Jews' parameters of existence cannot be understood except within a Polish context and largely on the basis of Polish sources, they did not, and have not, successfully tackled the question of the relationship between Polish and Jewish cultures. The conclusion of Baron's discussion of the effects of Polish culture on the Jews is that there was a lack of significant impact, certainly no relationship of either embeddedness or indebtedness. He even intimated that the Jews made more of an impression on Polish culture than the other way around.[25] Baron and his intellectual heirs failed to solve the problems of elusive historicist analysis and obvious mutual cultural alienation in a way that makes Polish culture seem to be a significant element in the

---

24. The pioneer in this regard was Jacob Goldberg, who was trained in Poland but settled in Israel; see, e.g., his collection of articles, *The Jewish Society in the Polish Commonwealth* (in Hebrew; Jerusalem: Merkaz Zalman Shazar, 1999). For a bibliographic discussion of renewed Polish interest in writing Jewish historiography, see Moshe Rosman, "Historiography of Polish Jewry: 1945–1995" (in Hebrew), in *The Broken Chain: Polish Jewry through the Ages*, vol. 2 (ed. Israel Bartal and Israel Gutman; Jerusalem: Merkaz Zalman Shazar, 2001), 718–21, and esp. nn. 28–30. In the 1990s a new generation of Polish historians dealing with the history of the Jews in this period emerged, including such scholars as Adam Kazmierczyk, Hanna Wegrzynek, Michal Galas, Magda Teter (although her doctorate is from Columbia University in the United States). Also in this group is Anna Michalowska, *Miedzy demokracja a oligarchia: wladze gmin zydowskich w Poznaniu and Swarzedzu*, (Warsaw: Wydawn, 2000), which is, however, atypical of the trend in that it utilizes mainly Jewish sources and explains the working of the autonomous Jewish community in a way that is reminiscent of the Balaban et al. approach discussed at the beginning of this essay, although the audience today is obviously Polish and not Jewish. For later periods one might add Natalia Aleksiun, Alina Cala, and Marcin Wodzinski. Also noteworthy is Andrzej Kaminski, *Historia Rzeczypospolitej wielu narodow* (Lublin: Instytut Europy Srodkowo Wschodniej, 2000), which stresses the multiethnic character of the Polish-Lithuanian polity and regards the Jews as one of its bona fide constituent groups. See Norman Davies, *God's Playground: A History of Poland* (2 vols.; Oxford: Clarendon, 1981), 1:32.

25. Baron, *Late Middle Ages*, 52–77, esp. 79. Note his comment on p. 89: "In fact next to the Greek Orthodox and Uniate groups concentrated in the eastern parts of Poland, the Jews remained the principal dissenting minority; and because of their dispersion throughout the country and their economic vitality, they continued to play a role in Polish and Lithuanian affairs far in excess of their ratio in the population."

shaping of Jewish culture, let alone serve as the soil that gave it life. Because our intellectual convictions predict such a solution, this failure rankles.

In response came the fourth approach to the Polish-Jewish cultural nexus, which we may designate "late (North) American." This demonstrated an abiding belief in Baron's basic assumption, and determined to get around the problem with it by evaluating cultural contact more subtly. If culture be defined not as the fruit of creative production—as all of our previous examples had done—but in Geertzian terms (notwithstanding recent criticism of Geertz's approach, which has demoted it from its former canonical status[26]) as meaning and the ways in which it is expressed, then on the level of meanings taken for granted, the unspoken assumptions that served as the substratum for daily behavior, Jews really could be seen as sharing in Polish culture.

This perspective was dramatically enunciated by Gershon Hundert when he entitled a chapter of his book *The Jews in a Polish Private Town*, "Jews and Other Poles." By this he meant that Polish-Jewish identity was "incontestably Polish," differentiated from other Jewish communities— even the rest of Katz's Ashkenaz to the west—and perceived by non-Jews, as well, as a permanent and integral part of the Polish social landscape.[27] Jews were embedded literally and figuratively in Poland.

In my own work I sought to explore the possibilities of this idea further, claiming not only that was there a distinctive, identifiable Polish-Jewish cultural style with regard to such things as Jewish ritual observance and communal organization, but also that phenomena such as the Jews' mental universe, aesthetic sensibilities, material culture, and political behavior all indicate a profound identification with Polish categories and values. To cite a telling example: the various myths that place Jews as kings, kingmakers, or powers behind the throne in Poland all signify that for Jews in Poland meaningful empowerment had to be legitimate in Polish terms. In general Jews placed a premium on Polish modes of cultural validation.[28] In addition, Jews and Poles shared a common Western heritage (with roots in late antiquity) in connection with political, civic, economic, gender, sci-

---

26. Sherry B. Ortner (ed.), *The Fate of Culture: Geertz and Beyond* (Berkeley: University of California Press, 1999), esp. 1–13; cf. Miri Rubin, "What Is Cultural History Now?" in *What Is History Now?* (ed. David Cannadine; New York: Palgrave Macmillan, 2002), 80–94. My thanks to Eyal Mizrahi for this reference.

27. Gershon D. Hundert, *The Jews in a Polish Private Town: The Case of Opatów in the Eighteenth Century* (Johns Hopkins Jewish Studies; Baltimore: Johns Hopkins University Press, 1992), 37–39.

28. Rosman, "Innovative Tradition," 525–28; cf. Hayah Bar-Itzhak, *Jewish Poland: Legends of Origins* (Detroit: Wayne State University Press, 2001); Hundert, *Jews in Poland-Lithuania*, 8–11.

entific, and legal theory and practice; popular ideas about causation and medicine; and principles of theurgy.²⁹

This response to the question of the nature of the Polish-Jewish cultural connection acknowledged that many components of Jewish culture were indeed unconnected to Polish culture, that on a conscious level there was unquestionably a significant degree of mutual antagonism and alienation, but that these coexisted with various shared cultural axioms and behaviors. As we have been taught, upon close inspection virtually all dichotomies dissolve. So the issue is not whether Jewish culture is separate from or part of Polish culture, because both Polish and Jewish cultures were polysystems, that is, open, dynamic, *heterogeneous* cultural systems. Their elements' origins are various and in constant interaction with one another in multiple ways at multiple intersections within the systems.³⁰

Metaphorically speaking, Polish and Jewish cultures were at times separate, at times intertwined, at times embedded, and at times coincident with each other along broad bands. They each generated multiple vectors that did not need to be consistent with each other.³¹ Contradictions (e.g., the grant of autonomy to Jewish *kehalim* that were physically part of self-governing towns and cities) put stresses on each polysystem, stresses that could result in creative solutions (e.g., multiple arrangements for adjudicating legal cases involving Jews) or, at the other end of the spectrum, frustrations (e.g., over the lack of effective political control of Jews), resulting in violence. Gentile consultations on health problems with Jewish *ba'alei shem* (shamans) or Jewish consultations with their Polish or Ukrainian equivalents posed no challenge to the rarefied discussions of the fine points of talmudic law carried out in the *yeshivot* far from the eye and understanding of Catholic canon lawyers.³²

Was Jewish culture embedded? Yes. Was it autonomous? Also, yes. This fourth approach to the relationship between the two cultures appreciates the influences of one culture on another, but recognizes that not all is influence. One facet of the polysystemic quality of each culture is its own autonomous dynamic. Most importantly, the cultural interrelationship is

---

29. Rosman, "Innovative Tradition," 528–30; cf. Shmuel Shilo, "Influences of the European Legal Tradition on Jewish law," in *European Legal Traditions and Israel: Essays on Legal History, Civil Law and Codification, European Law, Israeli Law* (ed. Alfredo M. Rabello; Jerusalem: Nevo Pub., 1994), 27–38.

30. For definition and discussion of polysytems, see Itamar Even-Zohar, *Polysystem Studies* (Poetics Today 11; Durham, NC: Duke University Press, 1990), esp. 9–26.

31. See ibid., 12: ". . . in order for a system to function uniformity need not be postulated."

32. Moshe Rosman, *Founder of Hasidism: A Quest for the Historical Ba'al Shem Tov* (Contraversions 5; Berkeley: University of California Press, 1996), 57–60.

fluid and requires description at various points of contact rather than one all-embracing characterization.[33]

Hybridity and the Jewish Problem

At this point, I shift to slippery ground by predicting the evolution of a fifth approach. I must emphasize that while this seems to be an outgrowth of the "influence-is-the-answer" view discussed at the beginning of this paper, it has not yet been explicitly articulated in the scholarly literature. However, judging from what is being written about Jewish cultural history in general and from certain adumbrations specifically connected to Polish Jewry (although it is still too soon to say how these will turn out), the wave seems to be cresting.[34]

I am referring to the school of Jewish historical cultural analysis that, drawing either intuitively or consciously on postcolonial discourse, and in particular on the theories of Homi K. Bhabha, sees traditional premodern Jewish communities as subaltern peoples, and Jewish culture everywhere, like the cultures of modern colonized peoples, as primarily hybrid with the culture of the majority. In other words, Jewish culture develops within frameworks laid down by the hegemonic culture and is limited by it, as well as trying sometimes to resist it.

According to my reading, Bhabha's work[35] is inseparable from the gestalt of modern colonialism and the issues it engenders, such as discrimination, racism, and slavery; intentional, planned, yet disavowed cultural domination; culture as political struggle; the threat that hybridity poses to the colonial power; postcolonial liberation and the contra-modernity or non-modernity that accompanies it; and the proposition that it is the postcolonial process that is the mainspring of *modern* culture.[36] While he does make an occasional bow in the direction of history, Bhabha's analysis relies predominantly on modern literary, linguistic, and philosophical associations rather than historical ones.[37]

---

33. See Rosman, "Prolegomenon," 116–19.
34. For example, see the cautious treatments of this topic by Gershon D. Hundert, "On the Problem of Agency in 18th Century Jewish Society," *Scripta Hierosolymitana* 38 (1998): 82–89; idem, *Jews in Poland-Lithuania*, xv, 37–38.
35. References here are to Homi K. Bhabha, *The Location of Culture* (London: Routledge, 1994); cf. Bill Ashcroft, Gareth Griffiths, and Helen Tiffin, eds., *The Post-Colonial Studies Reader* (London: Routledge, 1995); Gyan Prakash, "Subaltern Studies as Postcolonial Criticism," *AHR* 99 (1994): 1475–90; Florencia E. Mallon, "The Promise and Dilemma of Subaltern Studies: Perspectives from Latin America," *AHR* 99 (1994): 1491–1515; Frederick Cooper, "Conflict and Connection: Rethinking Colonial African History," *AHR* 99 (1994): 1516–45.
36. Bhabha, *Location of Culture*, 6, 34–35, 38, 55, 110–11, 114, 115, 152, 251.
37. Bhabha repeatedly cited many fiction writers such as Toni Morrison, Salman

It is not simple to apply his theories to early modern Jewish societies (as Bhabha's Jewish epigones are beginning to do), including Poland's. These were dominated by forms of political-economic organization other than colonialism and characterized by different types of social structures. The exercise of interpreting them from the perspective of colonial hybridity risks anachronism and reductionism.[38]

However, those who do attempt this task are willing to brave these problems, seemingly because of its powerful attraction on one key plane. Bhabha offered an antidote to the "invented tradition" and "imagined communities"–type critiques of nationalism and its cultures.[39] Not that he tried to resurrect the idea of homogeneous, authentic, essentialist, national culture, but he made it possible to pick up the shards the criticism left behind and conceptualize a new way to construe national culture: hybridity. As the critics asserted, there never is a preexistent, homogeneous, authentic, essentialist national culture; but Bhabha pointed out that there is a continually evolving hybrid one. More important, Bhabha emphasized that cultural hybridity is not "a third term that resolves the tension between two cultures. . . . [C]olonial hybridity is not a *problem* of genealogy or identity between two *different* cultures which can then be resolved as an issue of cultural relativism." The hybrid is not a compromise between cultures, but a product of domination and discrimination. It is something new, related to the group's precolonial history only by, what I would call, a palimpsest.[40]

For our purposes, the first implication of this conception is that—as opposed to the Balaban-Schiper school, for example—Jewish culture is

---

Rushdie, Derek Walcott, and Joseph Conrad, as well as thinkers and critics such as Jacques Derrida, Walter Benjamin, and especially Frantz Fanon.

38. See Dan V. Segre, "Colonization and Decolonization: The Case of Zionist and African Elites," in *Comparing Jewish Societies* (ed. Todd M. Endelman; Ann Arbor: University of Michigan Press, 1997), 219, on the dangers of "thesis mongering, that is, mixing ideology, political fashion, and academic evidence; differences in historical experiences must continuously be borne in mind. The impact of Europe on the Jews, even on those of Eastern Europe, who kept a separate social identity much longer than did the Jews of the West, was totally different from the impact of European culture on African colonial societies." Segre points out that comparisons of Jews and blacks are already to be found in the classic works on colonialism of Frantz Fanon and Albert Memmi (219, 231 n.6).

39. I am referring here to the by now standard treatments of Eric J. Hobsbawm and Terence O. Ranger, eds., *The Invention of Tradition* (Cambridge: Cambridge University Press, 1983); in this volume, see esp. Eric J. Hobsbawm, "Introduction: Inventing Traditions" (pp. 1–14), and idem, "Mass-Producing Traditions: Europe 1870–1914" (pp. 263–307); Benedict Anderson, *Imagined Communities: Reflections on the Origin and Spread of Nationalism* (London: Verso, 1983; rev. and extended ed., 1991); Ernest Gellner, *Nations and Nationalism* (Ithaca, NY: Cornell University Press, 1983), and the others who have further cultivated these critiques; see Bhabha, *Location of Culture*, 5–6, 37, 149, 152, 172–73.

40. Bhabha, *Location of Culture*, 113–14 and 5, 35–36, 38, 54–55, 58, 113–14, 126, 162–63, 172–73, 177, 224, 251; quotation from pp. 113–14.

always in a hierarchical relationship with the culture of the Other. It is always, even when resisting and subverting the hegemonic culture, both embedded and indebted, owing its evolution primarily to energy supplied by the encounter with the hegemon.

A second implication is that Jewish culture is always a *local* phenomenon. In terms of content, there is no universal, essential, core, authentic, autonomous Jewish culture that informed Jewish life everywhere and that always stood in independent relationship to the hegemonic culture of any given place.[41] The presumption is that there is, rather, a plurality of Jewish cultures, each of which is an aspect of its place of origin—Spain, Poland, Yemen—not of some putative Jewish culture; and certainly more linked to its locale than to other Jewish communities, either contemporaneously or through history. The common Jewishness of these communities tends to be reduced to artifacts of religion.

In short, what animates Jewish culture is the dynamic interplay of minority and majority in each particular place; not vestiges, like food restrictions or sexual practices, which for unexplained reasons have survived in one variation or another over the ages. Probe virtually any aspect of a given Jewish culture and you will find some practice, belief, or value of the majority at its root. Jewish culture is so embedded in the majority culture that it is of a piece with it, distinguished, perhaps, as a subculture colored by its religious difference. It certainly cannot be understood except in terms of the foundation non-Jewish culture that both helps to unleash its vital forces and subordinates it.

Compare this stance with Robert Bonfil's summary of the relationship between Italian Jewish culture—often considered to be the most "embedded and indebted" of Jewish subcultures—and Italian culture: "it is also possible to read the history of the Jews of the Renaissance in a modern perspective—that of the complex question of the definition of an identity in the context of a nascent awareness of the Self as organically interrelated with the Other, *without for all that being confused with the Other, still less annihilated by it*" (emphasis added). Like others, Bonfil also recognized that the encounter with the culture of the Other was an important source of Jewish cultural creativity. As opposed to the hybridity construct, however, he stressed that the Other's culture was filtered and transformed by a strong, vital, self-conscious, and lasting Jewish culture.[42]

---

41. See Mendes-Flohr and Israel above, nn.11–12; Robert Bonfil, *Jewish Life in Renaissance Italy*, esp. xi, 3, 103, 104, 108–9, 110, 123, 151–52, 284.

42. Bonfil, *Jewish Life in Renaissance Italy*, 115, 116, 151, 152; quotation from p. 286. For other scholars who have grappled with this problem, see Ivan G. Marcus, *Rituals of Childhood: Jewish Acculturation in Medieval Europe* (New Haven: Yale University Press, 1996), 4, 8–13; Biale's preface to *Cultures of the Jews*, xix; Hundert, *Jews in Poland-Lithuania*, introduction, after-

The hybridity construct holds that the key factor is not the people, the Jews—whom, according to Mendes-Flohr, Franz Rosenzweig characterized as mastering and melding "an ensemble of cultures"[43]—but a deterministic cause-and-effect mode. Human choices are, if not preordained, then pushed along certain vectors by the overriding processes of initial embedding followed by hybridization.

This proposition is latent in many of the chapters of the recent award-winning cultural history of the Jews edited by David Biale, *Cultures of the Jews,* and, emblematically, in the plural of its title—and of the title of the conference, "Jewish Literatures and Cultures—Context and Intertext," that spawned this book. As one of the authors of *Cultures of the Jews,* I can testify that the "*s*" in "Cultures" was the subject of a lively e-mail debate when it was proposed, with the authors deeply divided on the issue.[44] The pros contended that it was essential to emphasize that Jewishness was always pluralistic and multivocal. The cons insisted that by denying the existence of a common Jewish culture at some basic level, the book was denying the existence of a Jewish people and negating the legitimacy of the entire project—for what might define such a people except its shared culture? Moreover, even if the plurality of Jewish cultures be granted, one is still left with the question of how each of them is to be recognized as indeed "Jewish." What common characteristic(s) define them as part of that cultural category?

As one of the "cons" in this controversy, I dare to suggest, after jettisoning the teleology and rigid essentialism of the nationalist approach, how we can still attempt to define a continuing, interlinked Jewish culture.

---

word, and passim; Stephen Sharot, "Religious Syncretism and Religious Distinctiveness: A Comparative Analysis of Pre-Modern Jewish Communities," in Endelman, *Comparing Jewish Societies,* 23–60, esp. 23–25; and Michael Satlow's article in this volume.

43. Paul Mendes-Flohr, "The Jew as Cosmopolitan," in *Divided Passions,* 420.

44. It is instructive to take note of the attempt by Biale to coordinate the two positions on this issue: "Both high literary culture and material culture, from the way Jews dressed to the way they looked and behaved, from their natural landscapes to the architecture of their homes and communal institutions, differed radically from period to period and from place to place. Culture would appear to be the domain of the plural: we might speak of Jewish cultures instead of culture in the singular. And, yet, such a definition would be missing a crucial aspect of Jewish culture: the continuity of both textual and folk traditions throughout Jewish history and throughout the many lands inhabited by Jews.... [T]he Jews throughout the ages *believed* themselves to have a common national biography and a common culture. These beliefs are also an integral part of the history of Jewish culture.... [W]e can speak of a dialectic between, on the one hand, the *idea* of one Jewish people and of a unified Jewish culture, and, on the other, the history of multiple communities and cultures.... On both the elite and popular levels, then, the Jewish people were, at once, one *and* diverse"; see Biale, *Cultures of the Jews,* xxiv-xxv; see also Salo W. Baron, "Problems of Jewish Identity from an Historical Perspective: A Survey," *Proceedings of the American Academy for Jewish Research* 46–47 (1979–80): 64–65.

Such a definition would contain not only ideas and beliefs of the culture about itself but also a constellation of behavioral elements that show up in different numbers, in different permutations, and in combination with elements of other constellations in each era and location. A constellation of this type might be termed a "disjunctive description" of Jewish culture, where all of the elements of the constellation are never present simultaneously in any given historical example of Jewish culture, but where varying combinations of them always are. Taking a similar tack, borrowing from biology, Jonathan Z. Smith has called this a "polythetic" taxonomy, where "a class is defined as consisting of a set of properties, each individual member of the class to possess 'a large (but unspecified) number' of these properties, with each property to be possessed by 'a large number' of individuals in the class, but no single property to be possessed by every member of the class."[45]

What might be the elements in this Jewish cultural constellation? This is a subject for a full-scale research project; but we can tentatively suggest, beginning with Baron's common descent, common history, common faith, common fate; Biale's traditions, ideas, and beliefs; Shaye Cohen's intra-Jewish association and ritual sancta; Jacob Neusner's group solidarity and Jewish religion; Diaspora experience and minority status; and variations on Mendes-Flohr's Seven C's.[46]

To return to the issue of applying hybridity to the Jewish case, a historical example that at first glance appears appropriate as an illustration of hybridity is the phenomenon of "The Men of the Nation," that is, the Portuguese crypto-Jews and their descendants who underwent rejudaization

---

45. Jonathan Z. Smith, *Imagining Religion: From Babylon to Jonestown* (Chicago: University of Chicago Press, 1982), 4–8, 18 (my thanks to Michael Satlow for introducing me to Smith's work); cf. Morton Beckner, *The Biological Way of Thought* (New York: Columbia University Press, 1959). Although I believe that such an approach, allowing for a limited variety, can lend a measure of stability to the concept of Jewish culture, Smith seems to maintain the opposite; see Smith, *Imagining Religion*, 14.

46. Baron, *History and Jewish Historians*, 12–13, 21–22; Biale, *Cultures of the Jews*, xxlv-xxv (see n. 42 above); Shaye Cohen, "'Those Who Say They are Jews and Are Not': How Do You Know a Jew in Antiquity When You See One?" in *Diaspora in Antiquity* (ed. Shaye J. D. Cohen and Ernest S. Frerichs; BJS 288; Atlanta: Scholars Press, 1993), 1–45, esp. 26–35; cf. Jay Berkovitz, *Rites and Passages: The Beginnings of Modern Jewish Culture in France 1650–1860* (Philadelphia: University of Pennsylvania Press, 2004), beginning sections of chapters 3 and 9. See also the discussions in Bryan Cheyette and Laura Marcus, eds., *Modernity, Culture, and 'the Jew'* (Cambridge: Polity Press, 1998); and Jacob Neusner, review of Ben-Sasson, *A History of the Jewish People*, AHR 82 (1977): 1030–31. It might be interesting to compare the definitions of Jewish culture proffered by historians who are themselves personally committed to halakah and those who are not. The question of the problematics of cultural definition is not unique to the Jewish case; see Brian Porter, "Is the Pope Catholic: Defining Roman Catholicism" (unpublished lecture delivered at the University of West Virginia, November 2002).

to one degree or another. These people developed an ethnic identity that both doubled and subverted the hegemonic culture and accompanying persecution—both physical and cultural—that they experienced in the Iberian Peninsula. The difficulty is that they did this largely *after* their emigration; once their contact with the hegemonic Iberian culture was reduced to a minimum or severed completely. Moreover, since their "native culture" was fundamentally non-Jewish, they might be seen as constructing a hybrid with Jewish culture at the same time they were doing so with respect to Iberian culture.[47]

In writing on Poland, the subject that keeps coming up as a candidate for illustrating the idea of Jewish hybridity with the hegemonic culture is Hasidism. Since Torsten Ysander in the1930s, there have been (thus far signally unsuccessful) attempts to link Hasidism to contemporary Russian Orthodox schismatic sects.[48]

Anticipating the future, however, and assuming that there will be numerous attempts to apply at least parts of hybridity theory to Polish-Jewish history, I would suggest that hybridity theory can be understood somewhat differently from the way I think it is being brought to bear on the Jewish case in lectures and essays (see below). There can be hybridity that is combination without hierarchy. There can be hybridity of one culture with multiple other cultures. Hybridity is not always at work in every context. Therefore I propose a few caveats to be considered by those preparing to hike the hybridity trail.

First, I don't think we should assume that to the extent to which there is some kind of partial cultural hybridity in the context of the precolonial period it must always be a function of political subordination and power relationships. For example, hybridity can be "Western," resulting from the adoption of established cultural models from other places that had no political claim on the Jews. Here I would again call attention to the general European heritage common to Jews and Poles referred to previously.[49]

Second, hybridity may be with other Jewish communities. For example, if Israel, Elbaum, and others were correct that the sixteenth and seventeenth centuries marked a high point of Jewish intercommunal cultural cohesion, then why was it not hybridity with Sephardic Jewry that led the Polish Jews to attempt to coordinate, compete, or—if the Sephardim be the Jewish cultural hegemons and the Ashkenazim, the Jewish subalterns of the era—mimic and double them in hybrid fashion?[50] In a different vein, as

---

47. Bodian, *Portuguese Nation*, esp. 20, 77–79, 85–95; and above n.12.
48. Torsten Ysander, *Studien zum B'estschen Hasidismus in seiner religionsgeschichtlichen Sonderart* (Uppsala: A.-B. Lundequistska Bokhandeln, 1933). For discussion of this issue, see Rosman, *Founder of Hasidism*, 56–60; Hundert, *Jews in Poland-Lithuania*, 176–79.
49. See nn. 29–30 above; Hundert, *Jews in Poland-Lithuania*, 176–77.
50. For an example, as late as the eighteenth century, of Sephardic claims to superiority

intimated above, might the Jewish culture amalgamated with Portuguese ethnicity, developed by the "Hebrews of the Portuguese Nation" in Amsterdam, be considered hybrid with "Old Sephardic" or hegemonic rabbinic Jewish culture of the time?[51]

Third, as Hundert has already observed, hybridity, or what he called the "dialectical relationship between Jews and surrounding cultures," might be selectively operative. He argued that with regard to Polish Jewry it applied to economic and political processes, but much less to culture.[52]

If hybridity is to be added to the armamentarium of Jewish cultural interpretation, it must be done with due diligence. Scholars may not assume that hybridity is a given that can serve as a standard explanatory framework for virtually any cultural phenomenon. Rather, they should be required to prove its presence in each separate historical circumstance, and to delineate carefully how it functions as a factor and what its limits are.

A possible example is the phenomenon of roughly simultaneous projects of codification of law in the sixteenth century in Europe in general, in Poland, in the Polish-Jewish community and among Sephardic Jewry. Research here might offer an instructive example of how each of these cultural spheres impinged on or was independent of the others. In other words, this might serve as a test case for the applicability of hybridity theory to the Jewish sphere, testing as well the three caveats I have proposed.[53]

---

over Ashkenazim, see Isaac de Pinto, *Apologie pour la nation juive . . .* (Amsterdam, 1762); translated and excerpted in Paul Mendes-Flohr and Jehuda Reinharz, *The Jew in the Modern World: A Documentary History* (New York: Oxford University Press, 1980), 253–55. Cf. Bodian, *Portuguese Nation*, 125–31, 133, 158, 195–96, n. 154; Ismar Schorsch, "The Myth of Sephardic Supremacy," *Leo Baeck Institute Year Book* 34 (1989): 47–66.

51. Bodian, *Portuguese Nation*, 85–95, 96–131, 152–56; and above n. 12. There are other examples of early modern intra-Jewish cultural hybridity, such as Italy, Safed, and Istanbul.

52. Hundert, "On the Problem of Agency," 89.

53. To my knowledge it was Adam Teller who first noted the simultaneity of interest in legal codification on the part of Jewish rabbis and Polish legal experts; see Adam Teller, "A View from the East: The Legal Status and the Legal System of Polish Jewry in the 16th-18th Centuries," in *Von den Rechtsnormen zur Rechtspraxis: Ein neuer Zugang zur Rechtsgeschichte der Juden im Alten Reich* (ed. Andreas Gotzmann and Stephan Wendehorst; Frankfurt am Main, forthcoming). See also Davis, "Shulhan 'Arukh," 252–53, and literature cited there. In addition, on Polish codification (and its possible links to more general European activity), see Henryk Lowmianski, ed., *Historia Polski*, vol. 1.2 (Warsaw: Panstwowe Wydaw, 1958), 370–77; Juliusz Bardach, Boguslaw Lesnodorski, and Michal Petrzak, *Historia Panstwa i Prawa Polskiego* (Warsaw: Panstwowe Wydaw, 1979), 193–95; Waclaw Uruszczak, *Próba kodyfikacji prawa polskiego w pierwszej polowie XVI wieku: korektura praw z 1532 r.* (Warsaw: Panstwowe Wydaw, 1979), 11–70; Waldemar Voise, *Andrzej Frycz Modrzewski, 1503–1572* (Wroclaw: Zaklad Narodowy im. Ossolinskich, 1975), 8, 33, 36, 51, 91, 231, 258. On general European codification, see Manlio Bellomo, *The Common Legal Past of Europe, 1000–1800* (trans. Lydia G. Cochrane; Washington, DC: Catholic University of America Press, 1995), 206, 215–16, 223, 224; O. F. Robinson, T. D. Fergus, and William M. Gordon, *European Legal History* (London: Butterworths, 1994), 106; John M. Kelly, *A Short History of Western Legal Theory* (Oxford: Clarendon,

Which Metahistory to Choose?

It does not require much effort to connect each of these five approaches to Jewish cultural history in Poland to more general metahistories which they appear to represent and reinforce. In describing the Polish case, historians were and are also making larger claims about the nature of Jewish history and Jewish existence.

For the Polish Jewish historians who reached their prime between the world wars the objective was, in a sense, Warsaw—to demonstrate how deeply rooted the Jews were in Poland. They aimed both to give Jews pride and confidence in their rightful claim to Polish citizenship combined with Jewish national consciousness, and to counter anti-Semitic critics who called for a Polish Poland and for Jews to go to Palestine. As Schiper put it, the historian's task was to "forge a sword for battle out of knowledge."[54] Their metahistory was that Jews, while possessing their own national culture and not being ethnically Polish, were still Polish natives whose made-in-Poland culture gave them legitimacy and the right to see themselves as not just in Poland but of it, and the prerogative to make demands on government and society.[55]

For the nationalist portrayal of Polish-Jewish culture it was the nation and its culture fashioned in the once and future capital of Jerusalem that Polish Jewry was cultivating and preparing for return to Zion. This explains the tremendous emphasis by nationalists on the institutions of Polish-Jewish autonomy and on the legal and literary legacy of Polish Jewry. Autonomy proved that Jews were politically adept long after their formal state was dissolved, and this political tradition could easily be applied in establishing a new Jewish political entity. Law codes and elite literature provided ready-made, genuinely Jewish civic culture and elite

---

1992), 180; Arrigo D. Manfredini, "Codes and Jurists: Historical Reflections," in Rabello, *European Legal Traditions and Israel*, 17–18. On Sephardic and Polish Jewish codification, see Chaim Tchernowitz, *History of the Jewish Codes*, vol. 3 (in Hebrew; New York: Va'ad ha-yovel, 1947), 1–191; Isadore Twersky, " The Shulhan 'Aruk: Enduring Code of Jewish law," in *The Jewish Expression* (ed. Judah Goldin; New York: Bantam Books, 1970), 322–43; Stephen M. Passamaneck, "Toward Sunrise in the East, 1300–1565," in *An Introduction to the History and Sources of Jewish Law* (ed. Neil S. Hecht et al.; Oxford: Clarendon, 1996), 323–53; Edward Fram, "Jewish Law from the Shulhan Arukh to the Enlightenment," in Hecht, *History and Sources*, 359–77; Louis Ginzberg, *On Jewish Law and Lore* (Philadelphia: Jewish Publication Society of America, 1955), 180–84; Moses A. Shulvass, *Jewish Culture in Eastern Europe: The Classical Period* (New York: Ktav, 1975), 52–70, 120–22; Elchanan Reiner, "The Ashkenazi Elite at the Beginning of the Modern Era: Manuscript versus Printed Book," *Polin* 10 (1997): 93–98.

54. Cited in Jacob Litman, *The Economic Role of Jews in Medieval Poland: The Contribution of Yitzhak Schipper* (Lanham, MD: University Press of America, 1984), 233.

55. Ibid., 232–35, 251, and passim.

culture that could serve as the foundation for a renewal of national collective life. Polish Jews were a key component of an always existing Jewish nation that—as Polish Jewry itself demonstrated—possessed virtually all of the accoutrements of nationhood except territoriality. When the time came to move to the territory, Polish Jewry would be ready to do its part in reconstituting the Jewish nation.

The two-foci approach to Jewish cultural history set its sights, I think, on New York. It assured Jews and Gentiles alike that Jews could be both Jewish and American without jeopardizing either identity. Jewish life in the Diaspora continues because the internal focus of the metaphorical historical ellipse is ever-present; but the external focus will always lead Jews to accommodate to the larger environment. The two foci working together promise not contradiction but mutual enrichment. Attending synagogue and rooting for the Yankees can be two sides of the same coin. As already observed, Jews have much experience at mastering an ensemble of cultures. Jewish culture has an unlimited capacity to expand and embrace what is new, yet always remaining true to itself.

The fourth approach, positing that, despite obvious differences, on the level of deep structures there is shared meaning among contiguous groups, seems best suited to a belief in moderate, liberal, individualist, Western-style multiculturalism. That is, it recognizes that any group, Jews included, has the right to define an identity for itself that results from a process of recombining the strands of cultural DNA that it has acquired in various ways. The origins of the strands, or metaphorical genotype, are not important; their recombination and its resultant phenotype are. Moreover, within each group's DNA are elements that it shares in common with all the other groups with which it also shares a territory, a government, a society. So everyone has a right to a seat at the table, everyone has something to bring to the table that the others can respect, but everyone can also be trusted not to overturn the table. This might be a viable strategy for holding together the culturally ever more variegated countries of the Western world, including Israel, where the disaffections and dissonances among constituent groups are all too obvious, while unifying factors seem to be fading away.

The fifth approach, Jewish culture as locally evolved hybrid, has its roots, I believe, in Jacob Neusner's rejection of what he termed the "peoplehood-and-history theory of Jewish historiography" and along with it the proposition that "a single, clearly defined entity, 'the Jewish people'" has produced what he caricatured as "a unitary and linear history, 'Jewish history,' which extends back to the time of Abraham."[56] For him there is in

---

56. Neusner, review of Ben-Sasson, *History of the Jewish People*, 1030–31.

fact no "Jewish history," only "the history of Judaism."[57] The latest twist on this I hear in the corridors is, "not Jewish history, but history of the Jews," or alternatively, "history of Jews." What we should be writing about is individual Jewish communities in the only context that had meaningful historical reality, and that context is as an integral component of whatever larger society they belonged to.

Neusner asserted that there is no canonical definition of the traits that define Jews and Jewishness. There is no fixed content to Jewish culture, and Jewish religion is always historicizable. With regard to metahistory, this premise, touting a haphazard and absolute Jewish pluralism, facilitates dissociation from a now, to its proponents, much more than embarrassing, or merely politically incorrect, Jewish nationalism and, especially, Zionism, while confirming the primacy of the Diaspora experience in the history of the Jews. It also undermines Orthodox triumphalist religious claims to be *the* loyal and true bearers of Jewish heritage and reaffirms the *essential* multivariety and multivocality of the Jewish experience.

Neusner's successors have taken his approach to its logical conclusion, as represented by a recent conference and book devoted to the subject of "Modernity, Culture, and 'the Jew,'"[58] which put the last term in quotation marks. The editors have, however, filled the vacuum caused by the lack of any fixed content to Jewishness with the processes that create the vacuum, what they term the creative disruptiveness and unfixity of Jewishness.[59]

The significance of Jewish history is that while in all of their diasporas they have undoubtedly been part of the larger civilizations that incorporated them, the Jews always challenged and discomfited those civilizations.[60] In addition, the Jews confound the conventional ways of studying and constructing those civilizations. The value of studying Jewish history and culture is that they "are able to disrupt and to cross received gendered, sexual and racial boundaries. . . . [T]he specificity and incongruity of Jewish

---

57. Jacob Neusner, "The Problematic of 'Jewish History' as an Academic Field," in *The Academic Study of Judaism: Essays and Reflections* (2nd series; New York: Ktav, 1977), 106–28, esp. 107–8, 112–14, 124, 125–28. This essay originally appeared as Jacob Neusner, review of Michael A. Meyer, *Ideas of Jewish History*, in *History and Theory* 14 (1975): 212–26. For a different view of the problems of the unity and continuity of Jewish history, see Michael Meyer, *Ideas of Jewish History* (New York: Behrman House, 1974), 5–6, 23–42.

58. Cheyette and Marcus, *Modernity, Culture, and 'the Jew.'* Strictly speaking, this book treats the modern period and not the early modern period, which is my subject here. However, just as colonial and postcolonial approaches in general have been imposed on the historiography of the early modern period in various contexts, so will the positions of the authors of *Modernity, Culture, and 'the Jew'* probably be transposed to the earlier period.

59. Ibid., x. Note the depiction and criticism of the position I am advocating by Paul Gilroy in his afterword to the book, ibid (p. 296).

60. Ibid., e.g., 3, 9–10, 287–88.

history and culture will both encourage the critique of an empty western universality and help to break down, on all sides, an increasingly untenable and divisive identity politics."⁶¹ Evidently, Jews are valuable to the extent that they problematize and complicate political and cultural discourse.

The foreword to *Modernity, Culture, and 'the Jew'*, written by none other than Homi K. Bhabha himself, catches the spirit of the enterprise when it states:

> The "Jew" *stands for* that experience of a lethal modernity, shared by the histories of slavery and colonialism, where the racist desire for supremacy and domination turns the ideas of progress into a *danse macabre*. In the half-century since the Shoah, we have had to stand too often with, or in the place of, "the Jew," taking a stance against the spread of xenophobic nationalism. . . . The editors urge their collaborators to represent the "present history of the Shoah" in the voices of the excluded, written from the margins.⁶²

The Jew, representative par excellence of diaspora, of alterity, of dissident culture, of discrimination and exclusion, can serve as the basis "to build bridges across supposedly different histories of diaspora."⁶³ The Jew is the perfect metaphor or allegory for telling the story of what is wrong with modern civilization.⁶⁴ The Torah the Jews have to offer the world comes not from Zion but from the location of the ultimate Diaspora experience, Auschwitz.⁶⁵

---

61. Ibid., 2; see also x, 3, 12, 17, 18, 294–96, and passim.
62. Ibid., xv-xvi, xx (emphasis added).
63. Ibid., 2; cf. 285–88, 290–91, 294, 295.
64. E.g., ibid., x: "It is precisely the fraught interrelationship between 'the Jew' as metaphor and Jews as historical agents that this collection addresses." While many of the writers in the book subscribe to the approach of Jew as trope, allegory, or metaphor, it is partially protested against in Max Silverman's article, "Re-Figuring 'the Jew' in France" (pp. 197–207), although even he could not refrain from retaining the quotation marks: "conceiving of 'the Jew' neither simply as an open-ended signifier nor as an unproblematic signified but as a real hybrid between the two, a 'Jew' in inverted commas but with an upper case 'J'" (p. 205). There are rhetorically self-conscious, postmodern scholars, interested in clarifying the Jewish contribution to postcolonial discourse, Diaspora studies, and multiculturalism, who have strongly resisted the tendency to reduce the Jewish experience to an allegory. See Daniel Boyarin and Jonathan Boyarin, "Diaspora: Generation and the Ground of Jewish Identity," *Critical Inquiry* 19 (1993): 693–725, and many of the essays in the collection *Insider/Outsider: American Jews and Multiculturalism* (ed. David Biale, Michael Galchinsky, and Susannah Heschel; Berkeley: University of California Press, 1998).
65. Note the candid remarks of Colin Richmond in his "Introduction: The Jews in Medieval England," *Jewish Culture and History* 3 (2000): 3: "Jewish Studies . . . has ghoulish roots because it seems to the writer that it is the Holocaust that detonated the explosion . . . it is difficult to think of non-Jews, like the writer, becoming interested without the Holocaust to concentrate his mind."

Why Jewish Studies?

Each of these approaches to Jewish cultural history not only has implications for the study of that subject and for its practitioners' larger metahistories; each also can determine the direction, content, and style of Jewish studies today.

My critical evaluation of hybridity should not obfuscate my belief that a syncretistic, pluralistic, nondogmatic view of culture has something to offer; anyone who is familiar with my work knows that I have drawn from this well. However, in my view, Jewish studies is at a crossroads. It can, like the hybrid approach of *Modernity, Culture, and 'the Jew'*, see the object of its study, Jewish culture, as a subset, appendage, or example of something else that has the potential to shed much light on that entity, or even go a step further, as did the editors of *Modernity, Culture and 'the Jew,'* and regard the most valuable aspect of the Jewish experience to be its utility as an allegory for the circumstances of other peoples and their cultures.[66] To me, this is a postmodern version of the venerable but discredited "contribution approach" to Jewish history.[67]

If, however, this be the justification for its study, the usefulness of Jewish studies will soon be exhausted and interest in it will quickly run its course. Soon, more apt examples will be found and more cogent allegories developed.

Moreover, this instrumentalist view of Jewish studies implies that it does not require a profound, rigorous, integrated, knowledge of the components of Jewish culture, since they are essentially illustrations of something more important and therefore that larger something is more important to master.

In my opinion, the academic study of Jewish culture should not be instrumentalist, whether for the sake of better understanding other cultures (although such understanding will certainly be a by-product of this study, just as it can be of the study of any particular culture) or for the sake of constructing or reinforcing a contemporary Jewish identity (the exploration of which is beyond the scope of this essay). There lies the path to a modern kind of apologetics, seeking to please the dons of the hegemonic

---

66. For a more moderate view, which sees Jewish studies both as having intrinsic value and as shedding light on other cultures, see David Biale, Michael Galchinsky, and Susannah Heschel, "Introduction: The Dialectic of Jewish Enlightenment," in Biale, Galchinsky, and Heschel, *Insider/Outsider*, 1–13; Susannah Heschel, "Jewish Studies as Counterhistory," in ibid., 17–33; Sara R. Horowitz, "The Paradox of Jewish Studies in the New Academy," in ibid., 101–30.

67. There are Library of Congress subject headings: "Jews: Contribution to Civilization"; "Civilization: Jewish Influences."

culture or of the organized Jewish community, and ultimately to irrelevancy as standards and intellectual tastes shift.

Jewish studies in the university, while certainly having the potential to contribute to other fields of knowledge, should be engaged in primarily on the basis of the belief that Jewish culture in all of its manifestations has an intrinsic value that requires no justification other than its existence as a constituent part of human culture, equal to all the other constituents and therefore deserving of consideration on its own terms, with the knowledge and by the methods most appropriate to unlocking its secrets.

7

Idols of the Cave and Theater

A Verbal or Visual Judaism?

KALMAN P. BLAND

Economists study the marketplace of commodities, goods, and services. Historians of culture study the marketplace of ideas and art forms. These marketplaces are not dissimilar. When the number of producers or vendors is small, conditions are ripe for the emergence of "oligopoly," "cartel," and "monopoly."[1] These structures manipulate the market and eliminate potential rivals in order to control prices and quality of product. Economists acknowledge that this control may be unfavorable to the customer. Historians of culture discern analogous phenomena in the marketplace of ideas and art forms. Examples taken from the modern study of Judaism are instructive. They indicate that partisans of literature have come to behave monopolistically.

Prior to the publication of Gershom Scholem's *Major Trends in Jewish Mysticism* in 1941,[2] how might professors have prepared aspiring scholars for the study of Kabbalah? In the 1930s, faced with this very problem, Scholem himself informed students that "nowadays one had to read Franz Kafka's writings first, particularly *The Trial*."[3] Reading Kafka undoubtedly offered efficacious introductions to the Kabbalah, but several weeks of supervised experimentation with alternate states of consciousness might have offered something equally effective, if not more germane. Scholem nevertheless recommended reading Kafka's tales.[4]

---

1. For technical definitions, see the relevant entries in David. W. Price, ed., *The MIT Dictionary of Modern Economics* (Cambridge, MA: MIT Press, 1992).
2. Gershom G. Scholem, *Major Trends in Jewish Mysticsm* (Jerusalem: Schocken, 1941; repr., New York: Schocken, 1961).
3. Gershom Scholem, *Walter Benjamin: The Story of a Friendship* (trans. Harry Zohn; Philadelphia: Jewish Publication Society of America, 1981), 125.
4. Scholem subsequently added Walt Whitman and William Blake to the list of secular,

Yosef Hayyim Yerushalmi is another witness to the prestige and power of storytelling. Yerushalmi, a critical historian, ruefully reminds us that

> it is not modern Jewish historiography that has shaped modern Jewish conceptions of the past. Literature and ideology have been far more decisive.... Many Jews today are in search of a past, but they patently do not want the past that is offered by the historian.... The Holocaust has already engendered more historical research than any single event in Jewish history, but I have no doubt whatever that its image is being shaped, not at the historian's anvil, but in the novelist's crucible.[5]

Fixing his eye on novelists, Yerushalmi is undoubtedly on target, but it is odd that he excludes other artists who create equally powerful images of the Holocaust: musicians, photographers, film makers, painters, sculptors, architects who design memorials and museums, and curators who stage exhibits.[6]

To mention the storytellers while ignoring all the rest is indeed odd. It is also typical. If the authorities are to be believed, when all is said and done, it all boils down to literature, texts, and storytelling. Let Harold Bloom, the distinguished literary critic, testify: "Yet we can hardly resign the term [culture] to the conceptual contexts of anthropologists and sociologists. We [Jews] *were* a text-centered people, perhaps as much as any people ever has been. If we still *are* a people, it can only be because we have some texts in common."[7]

Let Gershom Scholem testify again. Consider his comments in the final chapter of *Major Trends in Jewish Mysticism*. The chapter is devoted to

---

propaedeutic readings. For bibliographic references and discussion, see Steven M. Wasserstrom's introductory remarks in Gershom Scholem, *The Fullness of Time: Poems* (trans. Richard Sieburth; Jerusalem: Jewish National and University Library and Ibis Editions, 2003), 38, 139.

5. Yosef Hayyim Yerushalmi, *Zakhor: Jewish History and Jewish Memory* (Seattle: University of Washington Press, 1982; repr., New York: Schocken, 1989), 96–98.

6. Merely to mention the popularity and heated controversy surrounding Claude Lanzmann's documentary *Shoah* and Steven Spielberg's film *Schindler's List* ought to suffice. For a particularly striking survey of artists and sculptors at work, see Norman L. Kleeblatt, ed., *Mirroring Evil: Nazi Imagery/Recent Art* (New York: Jewish Museum, 2001). For a foundational discussion of museums and memorials, see James E. Young, *The Texture of Memory: Holocaust Memorials and Meaning* (New Haven: Yale University Press, 1993). Scholarly research regarding musical representations of the Holocaust lags behind research related to the visual media. Judah Cohen (New York University), a musicologist, is presently at work closing this gap. In forthcoming publications, he will study a wide array of formats, including musical scores for such films and theatrical plays as *The Producers, The Sound of Music, Cabaret,* and *The Diary of Anne Frank* as well as any number of concert and chamber music works.

7. Harold Bloom, "Jewish Culture and Jewish Identity," in *Poetics of Influence: Harold Bloom* (ed. John Hollander; New York: Henry R. Schwab, 1988), 347–68; quotation from p. 348.

Hasidism, the "living organism,"[8] the social reality that Scholem described as the last of the "main tendencies of Jewish mysticism as we know them."[9] Scholem declares:

> When all is said and done, it is this myth which represents the greatest expression of Hasidism. In the place of theoretical disquisition, or at least side by side with it, you get the Hasidic tale. . . . To tell a story of the deeds of the saints has become a new religious value, and there is something of the celebration of a religious rite about it. Not a few great Zaddikim . . . have laid down the whole treasure of their ideas in such stories. Their Torah took the form of an inexhaustible fountain of story-telling. Nothing at all has remained theory, everything has become story.[10]

Consistent with the epistemological principle that "everything has become story," Scholem clinched the argument for the significance of storytelling in Hasidism by telling one. He repeated a story "as he heard it told by that great Hebrew novelist and storyteller, S. J. Agnon," a "story of which the subject, if you like, is the very history of Hasidism itself."[11] Here is the story's conclusion:

> When Rabbi Israel of Rishin was called upon to perform the task, he sat down on his golden chair in his castle and said: We cannot light the fire [lit by the Baal Shem Tov], we cannot speak the prayers [uttered by the Maggid of Mezeritch], we do not know the place [known by Rabbi Moshe Leib of Sassov], but we can tell the story of how it was done. And, the story teller adds, the story which he told had the same [successful] effect as the actions of the other three.[12]

To this tale within a tale Scholem appended a talmudic gloss informed by the subtle logic of "say if you will or say if you will": "You can say if you

---

8. Gershom G. Scholem, "The Science of Judaism—Then and Now," in *The Messianic Idea in Judaism and Other Essays on Jewish Spirituality* (New York: Schocken, 1971), 306.
9. Scholem, *Major Trends in Jewish Mysticism*, 350.
10. Ibid., 349. For historiographical dangers entailed by overreliance on Hasidic tales, see Gershom Scholem, "Martin Buber's Interpretation of Hasidism," in *Messianic Idea in Judaism*, 228–50. For a critical review of the Buber–Scholem debate and a thoughtful attempt to situate the emergence of the written Hasidic tale in its historical context, see Ira Robinson, "Hasidic Hagiography and Jewish Modernity," in *Jewish History and Jewish Memory: Essays in Honor of Yosef Hayyim Yerushalmi* (ed. Elisheva Carlebach, John M. Efron, and David N. Meyers; Tauber Institute for the Study of European Jewry 29; Hanover, NH: Brandeis University Press, 1998), 405–12. For a more general and intriguing account of the controversial narrative impulse in modern historiography, see Hayden White, *Metahistory: The Historical Imagination in Nineteenth-Century Europe* (Baltimore: Johns Hopkins University Press, 1973) and idem, *Tropics of Discourse: Essays in Cultural Criticism* (Baltimore: Johns Hopkins University Press, 1978).
11. Scholem, *Major Trends in Jewish Mysticism*, 349.
12. Ibid., 350.

will that this profound little anecdote symbolizes the decay of a great movement. You can also say that it reflects the transformation of all its values, a transformation so profound that in the end all that remained of the mystery was the tale."[13] The first "say if you will" is unambiguous; it uses the reduction of Hasidism to mere storytelling for proof that Hasidism underwent sociological entropy or historical degeneration. The second "say if you will" is enigmatic. Does it merely paraphrase the first "say if you will," doubling the notion of "decay"? Or does it balance the critique of social degeneration with praise for the prodigious Hasidic genius in storytelling? Mindful of Scholem's high regard for Kafka's writings, I tend to favor the second reading. Scholem seems to have preferred Hasidic tales over its living mysteries. He seems to suggest that an indefinite number of sociological realities attain perfection when they disappear from the stage of history and transmute into verbal narrative. He certainly conceded that the omnipotent tales and living mysteries of Hasidism were functionally equivalent.

Going far beyond the self-effacing chore of disinterested scholarly description, Scholem pinned his hopes for the future on the story. In 1938, why else would he have ended his lecture series on Jewish mysticism by saying, "This is the position in which we find ourselves today, or in which Jewish mysticism finds itself. The story is not ended . . . and the secret life it holds can break out tomorrow in you or me."[14] This prophecy suggests that scholarly exposition and hagiographic recitation are surrogate repositories, both holding as much secret life as the social reality of Jewish mysticism itself. If so, Scholem was indeed smitten by storytelling. In 1938, on the brink of the "great cataclysm now stirring the Jewish people more deeply than in the entire history of Exile,"[15] why else would he have overlooked Hasidism's seemingly inexhaustible social vitality, its revolutionary sociological implications,[16] its zestful performance of ritual, or its repertoire of soulful melodies, choosing instead to designate the Hasidic tale as "the greatest expression of Hasidism"?[17]

That Scholem was infatuated with storytelling, especially spellbinders, is no surprise. That he equated storytelling with social reality, ascribing to them equal power, is troubling. After all, who more cogently than Scholem warned us against the "genteel," bourgeois, romantic tendency of the scientific study of Judaism to "reduce Judaism to a purely spiritual, ideal phe-

---

13. Ibid.
14. Ibid.
15. Ibid.
16. See Jacob Katz, *Tradition and Crisis: Jewish Society at the End of the Middle Ages* (New York: Free Press of Glencoe, 1961), 233–44.
17. Despite his affinity for the Hasidic tale, Scholem was later to take pains to distinguish his own views from those of Martin Buber; see Scholem, "Martin Buber's Interpretation of Hasidism," 228–50.

nomenon"?[18] Who more dramatically than Scholem lamented the tendency of nineteenth-century Jewish scholarship to disembody, "deactualize," and sentimentalize the hustle and bustle of historical realities, to "cast a kind of spell over Jewish history itself, a spell which expressed itself in a certain kind of idyll, a peculiar etherialization"?[19] The apotheosis of the omnipotent Hasidic tale in Scholem's account seems precisely the kind of apologetic and idealistic etherialization of Jewish life that he himself so passionately decried.

Recognition of this inconsistency in Scholem's scholarship reinforces the discovery of irreconcilable tensions between the philological-historical and metahistorical trends in his idealistic thinking.[20] Recognition of Scholem's fixation on textuality and storytelling also displays a relatively undetected aspect of his magisterial scholarship: adoption of conventional wisdom. For the past two centuries, the glorification of literature and Jewish literary art, both religious and secular, has been a prominent feature on the landscape of Jewish life in Central Europe, Western Europe, and America. Among literature's chief advocates in recent scholarship are Harold Bloom, already cited above, and Moshe Halbertal. Bloom champions Jewish survival in America by invoking premodern Jewish "text-centeredness or even text-obsessiveness."[21] In the monograph *People of the Book*, Halbertal "seek[s] to understand the Jewish tradition as a text-centered tradition." He insists that "the essence of Judaism" is to be found in "the shared commitment to certain texts and their role in shaping many aspects of Jewish life and endowing the tradition with coherence."[22]

That Bloom and Halbertal have articulated alluring and influential ideas is beyond doubt. They are widely quoted. Moshe Idel, the distinguished and staunchly contrarian scholar of Jewish mysticism, for example, cites them without demurral. Bloom and Halbertal support his contentions that Judaism, "a text-centered community," made the transition "from a Geographical to a Textual Center" and that "the renomadization of postbiblical Judaism is characterized by its novel gravitation toward books and their study."[23]

Let two more examples of the monopolistic apotheosis of textuality,

---

18. Scholem, "Science of Judaism-Then and Now," 305.
19. Ibid., 307.
20. For compelling accounts of these tensions, see David N. Meyers, *Re-Inventing the Jewish Past: European Jewish Intellectuals and the Zionist Return to History* (New York: Oxford University Press, 1995), 167-76 and Steven M. Wasserstrom, *Religion after Religion: Gershom Scholem, Mircea Eliade, and Henry Corbin at Eranos* (Princeton: Princeton University Press, 1999).
21. Harold Bloom, *Agon: Towards a Theory of Revisionism* (New York: Oxford University Press, 1982), 319.
22. Moshe Halbertal, *People of the Book: Canon, Meaning, and Authority* (Cambridge, MA: Harvard University Press, 1997), 1.
23. Moshe Idel, *Absorbing Perfections: Kabbalah and Interpretation* (New Haven: Yale University Press, 2002), 3, 493.

literature, and storytelling suffice: Franz Rosenzweig and Franz Kafka. They represent two very different sorts of Germanophone Jews. In his theological masterpiece, *Star of Redemption*, Rosenzweig proclaimed that

> poetry ... comes to be the truly vital art, and a certain human maturity is even more indispensable for the great poet than for the painter or musician.... As a result, oral revelation, beginning with Moses, has never confronted visual art ... without some misgivings. No such misgivings apply to poetry.... It is not necessary for every person to have a taste for music or painting, to be an amateur producer or reproducer in the one or the other. But every complete human being must have a taste for poetry; indeed he must be an amateur poet himself. At the very least he must have once written poetry. Even if, at a pinch, one can be human without composing poetry, one cannot become human without having done so for a time.[24]

The second example is Gustav Janouch's recollection of *Conversations with Kafka*. If Janouch is a reliable witness, Franz Kafka, the master of fiction, was not inattentive to the visual arts. According to Janouch, Kafka's young friend, Kafka replied to the question "Don't you like the cinema?" with this typically Kafkaesque answer:

> As a matter of fact I've never thought about it. Of course it's a marvelous toy. But I cannot bear it, because perhaps I am too "optical" by nature. I am an Eye-man. But the cinema disturbs one's vision. The speed of the movements and the rapid change of images force men to look continually from one to another. Sight does not master the pictures, it is the pictures which master one's sight. They flood one's consciousness. The cinema involves putting the eye into uniform, when before it was naked.[25]

Kafka's attention to the visual arts was not restricted to the cinema. On another occasion, Janouch showed Kafka a portrait painted by Vladimir Sychra. Janouch reports that Kafka, "delighted with the portrait," said several times, "The drawing is wonderful. It is filled with truth." Janouch asked, "Do you mean that it is true to life as a photograph is?" Kafka replied: "What are you thinking of? Nothing can be so deceiving as a photograph. Truth, after all, is an affair of the heart. One can get at it only

---

24. Franz Rosenzweig, *The Star of Redemption* (trans. William Hallo; Boston: Beacon Press, 1972), 245–46. For discussion of the Germanophone, Jewish context of this passage, see Kalman P. Bland, *The Artless Jew: Medieval and Modern Affirmations and Denials of the Visual* (Princeton, NJ: Princeton University Press, 2000), 19. For a comprehensive analysis of the central place of aesthetics in Rosenzweig's thought, see Leora Batnitzky, *Idolatry and Representation: The Philosophy of Franz Rosenzweig Reconsidered* (Princeton, NJ: Princeton University Press, 2000).

25. Gustav Janouch, *Conversations with Kafka* (trans. Goronwy Rees; New York: Frederick A. Praeger, 1953), 88–89.

Idols of the Cave and Theater   161

through art."[26] Janouch also quotes Kafka making this declaration: "Actual reality is always unrealistic. . . . Look at the clarity, purity, and veracity of a Chinese coloured woodcut. To speak like that—that would be something."[27] On another occasion, Kafka and Janouch visited an exhibition of French paintings. They stood before "some pictures by Picasso: cubist still-lifes and rose-coloured women with gigantic feet." Janouch remarked that Picasso "is a willful distortionist." To which Kafka the "Eye-man," replied, "I do not think so. . . . [Picasso] only registers the deformities which have not yet penetrated our consciousness. Art is a mirror, which goes 'fast,' like a watch—sometimes."[28]

On yet another occasion, Janouch and Kafka were discussing illustrations drawn by George Grosz. Gazing upon one of them, Kafka is reported to have said, "This is the familiar view of Capital[ism]—the fat man in a top hat squatting on the money of the poor." Noticing that the image did not depict the fat man as a victim, Kafka was critical of the artwork. Kafka observed that "the picture is not complete. For that reason it is not good. Capitalism is a system of relationships, which go from inside to out, from outside to in, from above to below, from below to above. Everything is relative, everything is in chains. Capitalism is a condition both of the world and of the soul." Janouch challenged Kafka, exclaiming, "Then how would you picture it?" Janouch reports Kafka's response: "Doctor Kafka shrugged his shoulders and smiled sadly. 'I don't know. In any case we Jews are not painters. We cannot depict things statically. We see them always in transition, in movement, as change. We are story tellers."[29] When Kafka, who described himself as "optical by nature," claimed that "we Jews are not painters . . . we are story-tellers," what did he mean and for whom was he speaking? The assimilated German-speaking Jews of Prague, all the Jews of Central and Eastern Europe, all the Jews of Europe, or all the Jews of every place and every time?

Perhaps Kafka was speaking only for himself. One day, Janouch and Kafka were looking at reproductions of pictures by Van Gogh. Janouch reports:

> Kafka was delighted with them. "This restaurant garden with the violet night in the background is very beautiful," Kafka said. "The others are lovely too. But the restaurant garden is wonderful. Do you know his drawings?" Janouch replied, "No, I do not." [Kafka:] "What a pity! They are in the book *Letters from the Asylum*. Perhaps you will find the book somewhere. I should so like to be able to draw, [Kafka continued], as a

---

26. Ibid., 87.
27. Ibid.
28. Ibid., 85.
29. Ibid., 86–87.

matter of fact, I am always trying to. But nothing comes of it. My drawings are purely personal picture writing, whose meaning even I cannot discover after a time."[30]

Generalizing from the personal I to the collective We is a familiar habit. All of us indulge in similar projections, rhetorically aggrandizing our personal histories, rationalizing our peculiar strengths and weaknesses, perhaps none of us so artfully as Kafka. Kafka, the assimilated German-speaking Jew of Prague, the frustrated visual artist, and the accomplished author of fictions, might therefore only have been speaking for himself when he said, "We Jews are not painters . . . we are story tellers."

On the other hand, the line may be the figment of Janouch's imagination, an apocryphal invention of Janouch's understanding of what Jews are capable of doing. Janouch may merely have been speaking on behalf of the consensus, merely repeating what so many others scholars, museum curators, and critics, both Gentile and Jewish, have been saying since the nineteenth century: "There is no such thing as Jewish art." "Jews are not painters."

The conventional wisdom articulated by Scholem, Yerushalmi, Bloom, Halbertal, Rosenzweig, and Janouch displays three notable features. First, it originated 160 years ago among Germanophone Jewish intellectuals, and it continues to flourish today. Second, it presupposes that the literary arts express the quintessence of Judaic culture or religion. The conventional wisdom thereby elevates literature and Jewish literary art to a preeminence equal to Jewish theological axioms, ethics, or ritual observance of the commandments. Third, concomitant with the elevation of Jewish literature, the conventional wisdom either denigrates the visual arts, viewing them as inferior or antagonistic to the spirit of Judaism, or simply ignores them. The logic of the conventional wisdom is peculiar. It resembles a funicular installed on the slope of Mount Sinai. Traveling in that alpine cable car, the literary arts perpetually ascend while the visual arts forever descend.[31]

In its most extreme and widely disseminated form, the conventional wisdom proclaims that Judaism prohibits the visual arts. Recently, one critic confidently asserted that "[Steven Spielberg was the first mainstream Hollywood Jewish filmmaker to break] the taboo of explicitly imagining the Holocaust and the gas chamber as its ultimate sacred center and horrifying metaphor. In essence, Spielberg violated the ancient Jewish biblical prohibition against creating images as it had been unconsciously resurrected in the moral taboo on representing the Holocaust."[32] Even more

---

30. Ibid., 77.
31. For detailed historical and conceptual analyses of these three features and their alpine logic, see the introduction and first three chapters in Bland, *Artless Jew*.
32. The source is Yosefa Loshitzky as quoted by Janet Wolff, "The Iconic and the Allu-

recently, on December 8, 2002, the University of Pennsylvania sponsored a symposium dedicated to the memory of Chaim Potok. The audience was informed that "Picasso's *Guernica* was a central element of [Potok's] life.... The fact is that an artist deals in images, and the Jewish tradition, embodied in the Second Commandment, was against image-making because image-making was part of ancient worship."[33]

To state bluntly the epistemological status of this conventional wisdom, it smacks of dogma and idolatry as defined by Francis Bacon at the dawn of the scientific revolution. According to Bacon, "there are four classes of idols [or false notions] which beset men's minds." Among them are the "Idols of the Cave" and the "Idols of the Theater." "Idols of the cave are the idols of the individual man. For everyone . . . has a cave or den of his own, which refracts and discolors the light of nature; owing either to his own proper and peculiar nature or to his education and conversation with others; or to the reading of books, and the authority of those whom he esteems and admires." By "Idols of the Theater, " Bacon meant errors and fallacies "which have immigrated into men's minds from the various dogmas of philosophies." According to Bacon, "all the received systems are but so many stage-plays, representing worlds of their own creation after an unreal and scenic fashion. . . . Neither again do I mean this only of entire systems," Bacon continued, "but also of many principles and axioms in science, which by tradition, credulity, and negligence have come to be received."[34]

Historians strive to minimize the roguish harm inflicted by these idols. Historians of Judaism understand that both the apotheosis of literature and the related claim of a biblical taboo against visual art are based on an egregious misperception of Jewish aesthetic practices and theories.[35] As the

---

sive," in *Image and Remembrance: Representation and the Holocaust* (ed. Shelley Hornstein and Florence Jacobwitz; Bloomington: Indiana University Press, 2003), 157.

33. Daniel Walden, "Chaim Potok: A Zwissenmensch ("Between Person") in the Cultures," in *Chaim Potok and Jewish-American Culture: Three Essays* (Philadelphia: Jewish Studies Program, University of Pennsylvania), 10.

34. Francis Bacon, *Novum Organum* [Aphorisms 38–44] as reprinted in *The English Philosophers from Bacon to Mill* (ed. Edwin A. Burtt; New York: Modern Library, 1939), 34–35.

35. For a mere sampling of documentary and artifactual correctives to the mistaken conventional view, see Bland, *Artless Jew*; and idem, "Defending, Enjoying, and Regulating the Visual," in *Judaism in Practice: From the Middle Ages through the Early Modern Period* (ed. Lawrence Fine; Princeton, NJ: Princeton University Press, 2001), 281–97; Vivian Mann, *Jewish Texts on the Visual Arts* (New York: Cambridge University Press, 2000); Bezalel Narkiss, "On the Zoocephalic Phenomenon in Medieval Ashkenazi Manuscripts," in *Norms and Variations in Art: Essays in Honour of Moshe Barasch* (ed. Moshe Barasch; Jerusalem: Magnes, 1983), 49–62; Joseph Gutmann, *Hebrew Manuscript Painting* (New York: George Braziller, 1978); Bezalel Narkiss, *Hebrew Illuminated Manuscripts* (Jerusalem: Keter, 1992); and Grace Cohen Grossman, *Jewish Art* (New York: Hugh Lauter Levin Associates, 1995).

following example is meant to show in minute detail, the conventional wisdom also ruins the pleasure of accurately beholding the artifacts of fully embodied Jewish creativity.

The story of this example and its misconstrual of Jewish culture begins with an episode from Sholem Aleichem's charming novel, *Motl Peysi dem Chazans*. Its hero is an adventurous and slightly mischievous young fellow, an orphan, a cantor's son who loves to draw and sculpt three-dimensional figures. In Vienna, Motl notices that his older brother

> Elye's beard has grown by leaps and bounds on the way to America. It looks more like a broom now. I'd love to sketch it. I once drew Pinye's portrait on some paper. And I drew Brokheh [Elye's wife] with a piece of chalk on a table. Did I get a licking! Brokheh said it was the spit and image of her. She hollered for Elye and he whacked me. He would have murdered me long ago if it weren't for my mother. I get shellacked (*geshlogen*) each time he catches me drawing (*mahlen*). I've liked to draw since I was little. At first I drew on walls with coal. I got shellacked for that, too. Then I drew on the doors with chalk and got shellacked again. Now I draw with pencil and paper. Elye says: "What's this, more of your figurative doodles (*menschelakh*)?" I get shellacked even harder for modeling (*keneten*). I like to make little pigs (*hazirmelakh*) out of bread. Elye lets me have it when he sees them. Pinye comes to the rescue and says, "What do you want from him? Let him model! Let him draw! Maybe he was destined (*bashert*) to be a painter (*mahler*)." Elye lets Pinye have it too. "An artist? You mean a paint smearer? You want him to decorate churches? To doodle on walls? To go around with stained hands like a greasy drayman (*baal agolah*)? He's better off singing for a cantor. God willing, I'll apprentice him as soon as we get to America. He's a soprano." "Why not teach him a trade (*baal melokhah*)?" Pinye says. "In America everybody works at a trade." That's all my mother needs to hear. "What? A common workingman? My enemies won't live to see the day when Cantor Peysi's boy becomes a workingman?" [36]

This is a delicious passage in many respects. How might unbiased readers with a sophisticated smattering of our planet's lore respond to it?

---

36. Sholom Aleichem, *Adventures of Mottel the Cantor's Son* (trans. Tamara Kahana; New York: Henry Schuman, 1953), 155–56. For the original Yiddish, see Sholem Aleichem, *Motl Peysi dem Hazns* (2 vols.; New York: Morgen-Freiheit, 1937), 1:223–24. For the translation offered here, equally faithful to the original, see Sholem Aleichem, *The Letters of Menakhem-Mendl and Sheyne-Sheyndl and Motl, the Cantor's Son* (trans. Hillel Halkin; New Haven: Yale University Press, 2002), 205. On the basis of the original Yiddish, I have slightly revised Halkin's translation of this passage and the ones that follow. For perceptive discussions of the novel and the trope of travel in modern Jewish literature, see Hillel Halkin's introduction to the above translation, and Sidra Dekoven Ezrahi, *Booking Passage: Exile and Homecoming in the Modern Jewish Imagination* (Berkeley: University of California Press), 8–9, 16, 30–31, 103–30, passim.

Following the lead of Peter Burke, the sociologically minded historian of culture, they might

> begin by assuming that artistic and other creative abilities are randomly distributed among the population. In conditions of perfect opportunity, a cultural elite, that is, the people whose creative abilities are recognized in that society, would be in all other respects a random sample of the population. In practice this never happens. Every society erects obstacles to the expression of some group, and Renaissance Italy was no exception.... It is unlikely that social forces can produce great artists, but it is plausible to suggest that social obstacles can thwart them.[37]

Among those social obstacles are gender and geographic location. Social bias is another obstacle. Throughout human history, impartial readers might add, many pragmatic elders have looked unkindly upon youngsters who decline to follow the family business, who refuse to indulge the ambitions of a "stage-door" parent, or who display too much autonomy.

Listening to Sholem Aleichem's descriptions of Motl, impartial readers might be prompted to remember Benvenuto Cellini, the justly celebrated sixteenth-century Florentine goldsmith and sculptor. In his autobiography, Cellini reports that his grandfather Andrea and father Giovanni were master architects and engineers, but that his father's true love and avocation were music, especially for playing the flute. Anxious to encourage Benvenuto's musical talents, his father began "teaching [him] to play the flute and to sing ... at the tender age when children love blowing whistles and playing with toys of that kind." Benvenuto explained that "he hated every moment of it and would only sing or play the flute to obey him." Benvenuto also explained that

> in those days musicians were all members of the most respected trades, and some of them belonged to the greater guilds of silk and wool. That was why my father was not ashamed to follow such a profession. And his greatest ambition as far as I was concerned was to turn me into an accomplished musician; and I was never more miserable than when he used to talk to me about it, saying that I showed so much promise that if I wanted I would outshine anyone in the world.

Eventually and reluctantly, Benvenuto's father relented and allowed his son to satisfy his overwhelming passion for designing and goldsmithing, as long as Benvenuto continued his musical training. This is precisely what the lad did. He reports that in Bologna he apprenticed himself to a

---

37. Peter Burke, *The Italian Renaissance: Culture and Society in Italy* (Princeton, NJ: Princeton University Press, 1986), 43, 48.

goldsmith and continued taking daily lessons on the flute, "making very good progress in that cursed art." Still in Bologna, he lived and worked for another "miniaturist called Sciopone Cavaletti . . . and there I started doing designs and working very profitably for a Jew called Graziado."[38]

Even closer to hand, borrowing a reference directly from Peter Burke, impartial readers might recall another lad, another budding artist like Sholem Aleichem's Motl, who aroused his family's slap-happy opposition to painting and three-dimensional modeling. The biographer reports that when this lad

> was old enough to be sent to grammar school . . . , he was so obsessed with drawing that he used to spend on it all the time he possibly could. As a result he used to be scolded and sometimes beaten by his father and the older members of the family, who most likely considered it unworthy of their ancient house for [the lad] to give his time to an art that meant nothing to them.[39]

The biographer was Giorgio Vasari, and the lad was none other than Michelangelo Buonarotti. With Michelangelo, Benvenuto Cellini, and Sholem Aleichem's Motl in mind, impartial readers who are unburdened by the conventional wisdom might deduce that Eastern European Jewish and Italian Renaissance cultures were remarkably similar: both cultures fostered diverse arts, producing gifted musicians, painters, and sculptors, despite occasional parental opposition. Impartial readers would therefore not be startled by the conclusion that there must have been an Eastern European Jewish affinity for visual art. To corroborate their conclusion, impartial readers might turn to Irving Howe's informative description of energetic Eastern European Jewish behavior in the early twentieth-century art world of New York City.[40]

Not all readers are impartial, however. Some take Sholem Aleichem's novel and reach twisted conclusions that are predetermined by the conventional wisdom that negates visual art in Jewish culture. After the interlude in Vienna, in Antwerp, still on the way to America, Motl

> drew a huge foot with chalk, a real monster. Leave it to Brokheh to decide it's hers. How come? Because no one else, she says, has such big feet. She wears size thirteen galoshes, that's a fact. She ratted to Elye and he yelled: "More doodling? Are you back to your *menschelakh*, your precious little

---

38. Benvenuto Cellini, *The Autobiography of Benvenuto Cellini* (trans. George Bull; New York: Penguin, 1998), 4–12.

39. Giorgio Vasari, *Lives of the Artists* (trans. George Bull; New York: Penguin, 1965), 326–27.

40. Irving Howe, *World of Our Fathers: The Journey of the East European Jews to America and the Life They Found and Made* (New York: Simon & Schuster, 1976), 573–85.

human figures again?" I swear, even a foot by him is an entire human figure. He can drive you crazy, Elye can. But it's true that the drawing bug is getting stronger and stronger. I go around with a crayon I got from an emigrant's son. . . . In exchange for the colored crayon which he gave me on the train, I gave him a picture I made of his face with the big, fat cheeks. I made him promise not to show it to anyone, because I didn't want Elye laying into me. So naturally he goes straight to my brother Elye and waves it in his face. "This looks like my brother's work! Just wait till I get my hands on the little doodler!" That's what Elye said, running off to look for me.[41]

Seth Wolitz, a professor of Jewish studies and of French and Slavic studies at the University of Texas in Austin, observes that this passage provides hefty evidence for Judaism's native antipathy to the visual arts. Wolitz declares, "We must never forget that the act of figurative drawing for Jews automatically and dramatically violated a taboo inscribed in their traditional culture. Sholem Aleichem's little hero, Mottel, for example, is severely reprimanded for drawing."[42]

Bear with me as I dissect this prejudicial and parochial reading, this product of misguided and distorting conventional wisdom. The reading might have been strengthened by referring to the episode in Vienna which highlights Motl's more transgressive preference for modeling three-dimensional piglets. The episode also records Elye's physical rather than verbal reprimand. In fact, the novel recounts numerous episodes of Motl's drawing and Elye's slap-happy reprimands.[43] The prejudicial reading fails to cite any of them. It only knows chapter 17, "The Wonders of Antwerp."

The prejudicial reading suffers from other, more serious defects as well. It fails to notice that Elye slaps Motl for almost everything. At the very beginning of the novel, for example, Motl is playing with Menye, the neighbor's calf.

> Menye . . . stuck his black moist muzzle into the refuse heap, shuffled the earth three times with his foreleg, lifted his tail, hopped, and gave voice to a hollow *Me-e-eh!* This *Me-e-eh* seemed so comical to me that I simply had to laugh and mimic it. Evidently this pleased Menye, because he at

---

41. Aleichem, *Letters*, 211; idem, *Adventures of Mottel*, 165–66.
42. Seth Wolitz, "Experiencing Visibility and Phantom Experience," in *Russian Jewish Artists* (ed. Susan Tumarkin Goodman; New York: Jewish Museum, 1995), 14–15.
43. See, e.g., Aleichem, *Adventures of Mottel*, 194: "draws ship with a gang of emigrants"; 196: Elye reprimands Motl for idleness and drawing figures; 238: Motl wants to draw the adorable three-year child, "Pussy"; 243: Motl regrets not having the equipment needed to draw the mass of huddled immigrants on Ellis Island; 286: Motl yearns to draw the various personalities at a meeting of the tailors' union; 309: Motl wants to draw Brocha reading, mother sleeping, and Taibel weeping, but forgoes the drawing because the day is the Sabbath; 319: Motl wants to draw a domestic scene of the family sitting at the table.

> once repeated it in the same fashion, accompanied by the same hop. Naturally, I also repeated the procedure—the same sound and the same hop. Thus several times: a hop for me, a hop for the calf; a *Me-e-eh* for me, a *Me-e-eh* for the calf.... Who knows how long the game would have lasted if not for a chop on the nape of my neck. It originated from all the five fingers of my brother Elye's hand. "You ought to sink in the ground! A boy almost nine years old, dancing with a calf! Back to the house, you rascal! You'll catch it from father!!"[44]

To be consistent, critics adhering to the logic entailed by the conventional wisdom would have to conclude that Elye's severe reprimand reminds us never to forget that there were traditional Jewish taboos against laughing, hanging around barnyards, mimicking animal sounds and movements, dancing, and all sorts of children's play. But, of course, no such taboos were ever inscribed in Eastern European Jewish culture.

Equally fatal, the prejudicial and parochial reading fails to notice that there must also have been a traditional taboo inscribed in Eastern European Jewish culture against workingmen, music, and especially musicians. One day, attending his brother's wedding, Motl is too busy to notice the newlyweds. "[He has] to attend to the musicians (*kle zemer*). Not so much the musicians, but their instruments (*kelim*)." Motl muses: "Oh, if mother were really a good mother she'd let me be a musician. But I know she'll never allow it. Not because she's a bad mother but because she won't allow the son of Cantor Peysi to become a musician. Neither a musician (*kle zmer*) nor a workingman (*baal melokhah*)."[45] The logic seems impeccable: if Elye's reprimands for drawing pictures prove the existence of austere Eastern European Jewish taboos against the visual arts, then the refusal to allow Motl to become a musician must be proof of similar taboos against music. Such traditional and stringently observed taboos against music, in weddings and other social settings, of course, hardly existed. It is nevertheless as instructive as it is odd that a prejudicial and parochial critic of Sholem Aleichem's novel fails to remind us that Eastern European Jews disparaged the musical arts.

Equally fatal, the prejudicial and parochial argument fails to notice that Elye finally comes around and finds pleasure in Motl's artistic ventures. Late in the novel, after Motl and his entourage had settled in America, Motl is inspired by the Yiddish idiom *hakt a chaynik*, literally "to hack, rattle, or pound the teapot." Figuratively, the idiom means "to exaggerate," or as Tamara Kahana, Sholom Aleichem's granddaughter, the English

---

44. Aleichem, *Adventures of Mottel*, 4–5; idem, *Letters*, 107–8; idem, *Motl Peysi*, 10–11 [Yiddish].

45. Aleichem, *Adventures of Mottel*, 52; idem, *Letters*, 132; idem, *Motl Peysi*, 68–69 [Yiddish].

translator put it, "to tell a cock and bull story." Motl draws a picture of Bereh the shoemaker, the teller of "tall stories (*guzmos*) . . . a 'bluffer.'" Motl prefers the Yiddish idiom to the English loanword "bluffer," so that when he translates the idiom into a picture,

> he drew (*oisgemahlt*) the shoemaker with a hammer in his hand. On the table stands a huge teapot, and [Bereh] is pounding away at it. Everyone who saw the picture (*bild*) rolled with laughter. Even my brother Elye produced something resembling a smile. He has stopped punishing me for making pictures. Now he merely utters, "When there's nothing to do, drawing is also a job."[46]

In America, Elye finally catches up to Pesye, Motl's friendly neighbor, "a very nice woman, only a little too fat. She has three chins." Once, while they were still in the Old Country, Motl "got her down on paper several times." Pesye's son, nicknamed Vashti, "tore the drawing (*gemahlekhtes*) from [Motl's] hand and showed it to his mother. She laughed. But then [Elye] got wind of this and would have, as usual, paid me off for my *menschelakh*, my little figures. Luckily, Pesye took [Motl's] part. She said, 'Children like to fool around (*narisch*), but that's no reason to tear one's heart out.'"[47] By the novel's end, therefore, the traditional taboo is forgotten and disappears, if it ever existed at all. If the passage from Antwerp cited by Wolitz proves the existence of a cultural taboo against visual art, do not the earlier and later passages disprove the taboo? Sholem Aleichem's novel therefore demonstrates, if novels can be relied on to demonstrate anything about nonfictional reality, that there was no more of a traditional taboo against drawing inscribed in Eastern European Jewish culture than there were taboos against playing children's games, making music, being smart, telling stories, laughing, dancing, or hanging around barnyards. These conclusions regarding a fully embodied Jewish culture would have been self-evident to all critics, were it not for the interference of stubbornly entrenched assumptions proclaiming that "we Jews are not painters . . . we are storytellers."

The conventional wisdom injures Jewish collective memory and impairs critical analysis of Jewish history. Why else in the recent and altogether welcome explosion of scholarship on Spinoza has so little attention been paid to what was noticed in 1705 by one of Spinoza's first biographers, Johann Colerus? According to Colerus, after Spinoza had mastered the

---

46. Aleichem, *Adventures of Mottel*, 295–96; idem, *Letters*, 290; Sholom Aleichem, in *Amerika: Motl Peysi dem hazns un andere mayses* (in Yiddish; New York: Verlag "Freiheit," 1918), 133–34.

47. Aleichem, *Adventures of Mottel*, 174; idem, *Letters*, 216; idem, *Motl Peysi*, 248 [Yiddish].

mechanical arts of glass-making and lens-grinding, "he apply'd himself to drawing, which he learn'd of himself, and he cou'd draw a head very well with ink, or with a coal. I have in my hand a whole book of such draughts, amongst which are some heads of several considerable persons, who were known to him, or who had occasion to visit him."[48] The drawings included a perfectly accurate self-portrait of Spinoza depicted as a fisherman. This precious detail from Spinoza's life should suggest a revision in historiography. Perhaps the detail has failed to inspire even minor corrections of the historical record because Spinoza's portraits have been lost to posterity. Perhaps, too, the detail has been ignored because the visual arts are not considered typical Jewish activities and Spinoza is not considered a typical Jew who might inform our understanding of the status of visual arts in Jewish culture in seventeenth-century Holland.[49]

Spinoza may not belong to the heartland of indigenous Jewish culture, but what shall we say about Isaac Luria's influential disciple Rabbi Hayyim Vital? In both *Sha'ar hagilgulim*, the treatise devoted to the doctrine of transmigration, and *Sha'ar hahezyonot*, the treatise aptly described as a "mystical autobiography," Vital reports that Luria disclosed the cosmic details of Vital's complex genealogy, or metempsychosis. Luria told him "that Cain is the secret [source] of shaping images/drawing (*tziyyur*) and pragmatic performance (*ma'aseh*), while Abel is the Supernal breath of the mouth, which is speech. Therefore, Abel is the source for preachers and orators."[50] Vital drew the proper conclusions: "However, since [my soul derives] from Cain, I am not a speaker or a man of words. I have little eloquence, but I have more ability in shaping images/drawing and pragmatic performance."[51] If this sadly neglected but ambiguous and beguiling passage from

---

48. As cited in Jacob R. Marcus, *The Jew in the Medieval World: A Source Book, 315–1791* (Cincinnati: Hebrew Union College Press, 1999), 384–85. In the most recent and comprehensive biography of Spinoza, this passage is cited but scarcely discussed; see Steven Nadler, *Spinoza: A Life* (New York: Cambridge University Press, 1999), 204. In a recent collection of otherwise splendid studies anchored in vast learning, the visual dimension of Spinoza's life and thought is utterly ignored; see Heidi M. Ravven and Lenn E. Goodman, eds., *Jewish Themes in Spinoza's Philososphy* (Albany: State University of New York Press, 2002).

49. For the current state of knowledge regarding artistic life and patronage among Amsterdam's Jews, see the superb studies of Steven Nadler, *Rembrandt's Jews* (Chicago: University of Chicago Press, 2003); Michael Zell, *Reframing Rembrandt: Jews and the Christian Image in Seventeenth-Century Amsterdam* (Berkeley: University of California Press, 2002), 7–32; and Daniel M. Swetschinski, *Reluctant Cosmopolitans: The Portuguese Jews of Seventeenth-Century Amsterdam* (London: Littmann Library of Jewish Civilization, 2000), 308–10.

50. My colleague Professor Michael Fishbane has graciously reminded me that the technical term *tsiyyur* often denotes the meditational formation of mental imagery and that the term *ma'aseh* might denote the performance of magical or theurgical acts. His remarks do not exclude the possibility that by *tsiyyur* Vital might also be alluding to the actual formation with pen and ink of figures or diagrams on paper or parchment.

51. Hayyim Vital, *Book of Visions* 4.22 (trans. Morris M. Faierstein, *Jewish Mystical Auto-*

the heartland of Jewish spirituality and mysticism cannot incite a desperately needed revision of historiography and Jewish self-identity, what will?

Such a revision appears to be necessary in Kabbalah studies, where the conventional wisdom currently competes for eventual ownership. We have recently been assured by Arthur Green, a particularly astute and rightfully acknowledged authority in the field, that

> the Zohar is a work of sacred fantasy.... It may be said that all theological elaborations [by medieval Jewish, Christian, and Islamic writers], insofar as they are allowed to become pictorial, are fantasy. They depict realities that have not been seen except by the inner eye of those who describe them, or by their sacred sources. In the case of Judaism, prohibitions derived from the second of the Ten Commandments forbade the depiction of such sacred realms in any medium other than words. Perhaps because of this, the literary imagination became extraordinarily rich. All those creative energies that in other contexts might have sought to reify sacred myth in painting, sculpture, manuscript illumination, or stained glass had instead focused on the word, especially on the timeless Jewish project of commentary and exegesis. In this sense the Zohar may be seen as the greatest work of medieval Jewish *iconography*, but one that exists only in the words of the written page, thence to be instilled in the imagination of its devoted students.[52]

The explicit appeal to the Ten Commandments, the stereotypical disqualification of the visual arts, the celebration of textual commentary, the paradigmatic assertion that literature hegemonically sublimates visual energies, and the strained application of the term "iconography" to the Zohar suggest that Arthur Green may have been tailoring the classic text of Jewish mysticism to suit a modern sensibility that prefers the literary to the visual rather than sketching for his readership the contours of Jewish

---

biographies: Book of Visions and Book of Secrets [New York: Paulist, 1999], 176–77). For the parallel source in Hebrew, see Hayyim Vital, "Sha'ar hagilgulim," in *Sidrat kol kitvei ha'ari*, vol. 10 (Jerusalem, 1988), 135 [*Haqdamah* 38:10]. For a masterly exposition of Vital's psychic affinity with Cain, see Lawrence Fine, *Physician of the Soul, Healer of the Cosmos: Isaac Luria and His Kabbalistic Fellowship* (Stanford: Stanford University Press, 2003), 333–41. Alas, even Fine's magisterial biography fails to address the implications of this passage for the history of Jewish aesthetics, both theoretical and practical.

52. Arthur Green, *A Guide to the Zohar* (Stanford: Stanford University Press, 2004), 3–4. See also his introductory comments in *The Zohar: Pritzker Edition*, vol. 1 (translation and commentary by Daniel C. Matt; Stanford: Stanford University Press, 2004), xxxi-xxxii. See also Green's comments regarding the "kabbalists [who] were prevented from displaying their image-laden and richly pictorial conceptions of the Godhead in visual media" in idem, "Shekhinah, Virgin Mary, and the Song of Songs," *AJS Review* 26 (2002): 44–45 n. 172. It is not clear why Green excludes kabbalistic notions of hieroglyphic calligraphy from his consideration of this intriguing issue. For details and bibliographic references regarding kabbalistic hieroglyphics, see n. 53 below.

aesthetics as they appeared in premodern Kabbalah. Other scholarly studies have shown that premodern Kabbalists were as attentive to the actual colors and physical shapes of the Hebrew alphabet as they were attuned to the conceptual meaning of biblical or rabbinic words. Following midrashic precedents, the Kabbalists read letters of the Hebrew alphabet as transparencies, icons, or hieroglyphs conveying pictures of cosmic and divine mysteries.[53]

No need to multiply examples. Evidence, both textual and artifactual, for correcting or overturning the conventional wisdom abounds. Following the exemplary lead of Richard I. Cohen and other cultural historians of Judaism, we can straighten the crooked record.[54] Our minds need not be plagued by credulity and tradition. No longer blinded by the Idols of our Caves and Theaters, Jewish historiography and cultural criticism can recover from the pro-literary and anti-visual malaise it suffered in the nineteenth- and twentieth-century battles for Jewish emancipation, integration, and national renewal. Once upon a time, especially in Protestant settings

---

53. For a readily accessible text in English translation that features reading practices geared toward the iconic or hieroglyphic, see Rabbi Jacob ben Jacob Ha-Kohen, *Explanation of the Letters* (trans. Ronald C. Keiner, *Early Kabbalah* [ed. Joseph Dan; New York: Paulist, 1986], 153–64). For a critical discussion of this text, as well as other examples of similar kabbalistic and Hasidic texts in English translation, see the remarks in Idel, *Absorbing Perfection*, 45–79. For a sample of the Zohar's application of this erotically tinged, iconic reading practice, see Bland, *Artless Jew*, 106–7. For further discussion of the rabbinic and kabbalistic penchant for attending to the physical shape of Hebrew letters, see Joseph Dan, ed., *The Heart and the Fountain: An Anthology of Jewish Mystical Experiences* (New York: Oxford University Press, 2002), 9–15: "The syllables *yehi or* include not only a sound, but also a picture of six letters of the Hebrew alphabet. They include vocalization marks (*nekudot*) and musical signs (*te'amim*). The letters are decorated by little crowns (*tagin*). . . . All we can know is that the totality of the linguistic phenomenon—the sound, the picture, the music, the 'decorations,' . . . and all the other elements combine into the essence of language as a creative—rather than communicative—instrument. . . . Midrashic interpretations may take into account not only the different meanings of the words in different contexts, but also the letters of the alphabet that constitute it, the shape of the letters, their names, their 'crowns,' their numerical value, the shapes and names of the vocalization marks, the shapes and names of the musical signs, and numerous other elements." For a profound study of the visual dimension in kabbalistic Judaism, see Elliot R. Wolfson, *Through a Speculum That Shines: Vision and Imagination in Medieval Jewish Mysticism* (Princeton, NJ: Princeton University Press, 1994). See also Michael Fishbane, *The Exegetical Imagination: On Jewish Thought and Theology* (Cambridge, MA: Harvard University Press, 1998), 13–18. Finally, I am aware of a forthcoming volume of scholarly essays to be edited by Professor Marla Segol (Carleton University) and published by Palgrave that will be devoted to an exploration of the visual diagrams that illustrate and adorn kabbalistic texts and manuscripts.

54. See Richard I. Cohen, *Jewish Icons: Art and Society in Modern Europe* (Berkeley: University of California Press, 1998); and idem, "Urban Visibility and Biblical Visions: Jewish Culture in Western and Central Europe in the Modern Age," in *The Cultures of the Jews: A New History* (ed. David Biale; New York: Schocken, 2002), 731–96. For additional correctives to the hegemonic, pro-literary paradigm, see the references listed above in n. 35.

where the theological principle of *sola scriptura* was diffused and prevailed,[55] it was possible and necessary to argue that Judaism finds its greatest expression in disembodiment, spirituality, and literature. Nowadays, knowing that in Jewish souls flow the spirits of both Cain and Abel, historians can rightfully and forcibly claim that Jewish culture, like all cultures, is neither verbal *or* visual but both verbal *and* visual *and* everything else, as well.

Numerous scholars have already renounced Harold Bloom's highbrow, strictly literary definition of culture and replaced it with the more inclusive definitions of culture articulated by anthropologists. David Biale's remarks are exemplary. Overturning conventional wisdom, Biale summarizes the new style of doing Jewish studies:

> Culture is an elastic term that can be stretched in many different directions.... One way to define culture is as the manifold expressions—written or oral, visual or textual, material or spiritual—with which human beings represent their lived experiences in order to give them meaning. But culture is more than just the literary or aesthetic products of a society. As one witty adage goes: "Culture is how we do things around here." From this point of view, culture is the practice of everyday life. It is what people do, what they *say* about what they do, and, finally, how they understand both of these activities.[56]

The new cultural historians might speak, but will the public and other scholars relinquish what Franz Rosenzweig described as "misgivings" regarding visual art? Will they overcome their inattention to the "practice of everyday life"? Will they cease reiterating the shopworn slogans: "text-centered community" and "We Jews are not painters . . . we are story tellers"? Myths die hard, dogmas are notoriously intractable, and idols

---

55. See the persuasive editorial remarks in Howard Eilberg-Schwartz, ed., *People of the Body: Jews and Judaism from an Embodied Perspective* (Albany: State University of New York Press, 1992), 1–15: "The designation 'People of the Book' is thus one of the visible expressions of a larger modern strategy that attempts to disembody Jews and Judaism in hopes of spiritualizing them.... These feelings have to be understood against the background of European discussions of primitive religion. From the eighteenth century onward, there was a consistent attempt to differentiate primitive and higher forms of religion, a pressing intellectual, moral, and political problem given the discovery of and continuing European encounter with peoples of the Americas, among other people. Unfortunately for Jews, the definition of savage or primitive religion developed as a contrast for Enlightenment views of a 'Religion of Reason' or 'Natural Religion,' which has in turn been influenced by Protestant views of ritual and law as well as European aesthetic tastes that emerged after the breakdown of feudal society. According to these criteria, much of Judaism appeared to fall in the category of primitive."

56. Biale, *Cultures of the Jews*, xvii. Biale's programmatic remarks, as well as the methodological assumptions governing Eilberg-Schwartz's remarks (cited in n. 55 above), point in the direction of cultural studies adumbrated in Raymond Williams, *Keywords: A Vocabulary of Culture and Society* (New York: Oxford University Press, 1983), 87–93.

require iconoclasts with the stature of an Abraham before they give up the ghost. Resistance to the trustbusting of literature's monopoly is formidable.

Perhaps the way to proceed is to tell the story of the story, to recall the dynamics of Jewish emancipation and integration, to describe the tumultuous and fragmentizing European stage for which intellectuals originally composed the romanticizing lines so eloquently rehearsed by Scholem: "everything has become story" or "in the end all that remained of the mystery was the tale."[57] This story begins at the end of the eighteenth century and continues to unfold today. Its protagonists are both Jews and Gentiles. In their predicaments and attempted remedies, the Jews are not alone. Company abounds. As Yosef Hayyim Yerushalmi reminds us, "literature and ideology have been far more decisive [than] modern Jewish historiography" in shaping modern Jewish conceptions of the past. For all the rest of the population, as Richard Rorty reminds us, literature and ideology have played an identical role. They shape conceptions of the past and generate agendas for the future:

> About two hundred years ago, the idea that the truth was made rather than found began to take hold of the imagination of Europe. . . . At about the same time, the Romantic poets were showing what happens when art is thought of no longer as imitation but, rather, as the artist's self-creation. . . . By now these two tendencies have joined forces and have achieved cultural hegemony. For most contemporary intellectuals, questions of ends as opposed to means—questions about how to give a sense to one's own life or that of one's community—are questions for art or politics, or both, rather than for religion, philosophy, or science.[58]

I am suggesting that the story of the apotheosis of the story in Judaism invites us to investigate the parallel and interlocking destinies of Judaism and human imagination in modernity, to trace the transition from Moses Mendelssohn to William Wordsworth and beyond. Judaism suffered seismic upheaval but did not become moribund as a result of emancipation. Much more remained of the living mystery than merely the tale. Caught in the upheavals, many Jews converted to Christianity.[59] The vast majority remained Jews. Many of them were drawn to rational liberalism or religious reform. Like Moses Mendelssohn, they prudishly begrudged the arts

---

57. For a bracing rendition of this story emphasizing the rise of modern English literature as an ideological and secular humanistic response to the rise of the bourgeoisie and the "failure of religion," see Terry Eagleton, *Literary Theory: An Introduction* (Minneapolis: University of Minnesota Press, 1996), 15–26.

58. Richard Rorty, *Contingency, Irony, and Solidarity* (New York: Cambridge University Press, 1989), 3.

59. See Michael A. Meyer, *The Origins of the Modern Jew: Jewish Identity and European Culture in Germany, 1749–1824* (Detroit: Wayne State University Press, 1979), 85–114.

a rightful place in life as long as artists did "not misuse poetry, painting, and sculpture for some ignoble purpose," as long as artists allowed the various "arts [to] show us ethical rules in examples that are fictional and ... beautified."[60] Still others, as described by Yerushalmi, were seized by the "fiercest antagonism to the Jewish past" or gripped by "aching nostalgia for a vanished Jewish past."[61] They turned to literature. They liberated it from its enslavement to edifying ethics and subjugation to ornamental beauty. They concluded that "everything has become story."

Secular and religious alike, Zionist and Diasporan integrationists alike, modern Jews have learned to rely on literature to serve as the common ground that replaces the loss of collective sociological unity, traditional belief in God, or faithful practice of the commandments. This common ground serves to guarantee the coherence and unity of the Jewish people, despite its bewildering contemporary diversity.[62] Even today, as much among the vanguard of new cultural historians as in the soul of Harold Bloom or Moshe Halbertal, the sociopolitical terrors of Jewish disunity or Jewish disappearance from history are kept at bay with fervent belief in texts and storytelling. After conceding that "we might speak of Jewish *cultures* instead of culture in the singular," David Biale, taking refuge in a modified version of the conventional wisdom, reassures his readers that "such a definition would be missing a crucial aspect of Jewish culture: the continuity of both textual and folk traditions throughout Jewish history and throughout the many lands inhabited by Jews. The multiplicity of Jewish cultures always rested on the Bible and ... on the Talmud and other rabbinic literature."[63]

To coin a term for this act of socially constructing reality and identity, it "textifies" Judaism. Intentionally or not, the "textification" of Judaism evades or negates the contentious and potentially divisive implications of geopolitical, nationalistic territorialism. Not unlike the "Orientalists" so astutely analyzed by Edward Said, Jewish intellectuals and scholars who embraced the conventional wisdom produced and transmitted a bookish Judaism drained of discomforting physical artifacts and embodied vitality. Their Judaism "was a textual universe by and large."[64]

So too with regard to human imagination. Developments within Judaism cannot be understood in isolation from developments in general

---

60. Moses Mendelssohn, *Philosophical Writings* (ed. Daniel O. Dahlstrom; New York: Cambridge University Press, 1997), 167.

61. Yerushalmi, *Zakhor*, 97.

62. For a schematic overview of this diversity, see the unflinching exposition by Ezra Mendelsohn, *On Modern Jewish Politics* (New York: Oxford University Press, 1993), 3–36.

63. Biale, *Cultures of the Jews*, xxiv.

64. Edward Said, *Orientalism* (New York: Vintage Books, 1979), 52. See also the entry "textual attitude" in the index for a guide to Said's elaborate and persuasive argument.

society. Just as the Jewish people were not made extinct by emancipation, human imagination and creativity did not die when the scientific revolution, rationalism, and utilitarian positivism created "the discarded image"[65] and caused the "disenchantment of reality."[66] Imagination and creativity evolved. Along with profound developments in the musical and visual arts, poetry and storytelling were transformed. They nevertheless remained as important and vital as ever. As Wordsworth put it, fully aware of the unsettling encroachment of science in daily life, the appropriate business of poetry "is to treat things not as they *are* . . . but as they *seem* to exist in the *senses*, and to the *passions*."[67]

More broadly conceived, to cite Isaiah Berlin, romanticism "bred respect for individuality, for the creative impulse, for the unique, the independent, for freedom to live and act in the light of personal, undictated beliefs and principles, of undistorted emotional needs, for the value of private life, of personal relationships, of the individual conscience, of human rights."[68] The irresistible allure of these romantic ideals partially explains why Scholem recommended Kafka to his students and why so many modern Europeans and modern Jews became and continue to be addicted to storytelling and poetry, even if their addiction entails what Yerushalmi laments as disregard for the discoveries of scientifically critical historiography.

Telling this story of the story, emphasizing its psychological and sociological functions, heightening awareness of its relatively recent and widely shared origin as a response to the pressures of modernity, cautioning against its excesses, historians of Jewish culture might help the public understand that what literature accomplishes for Jewish societies the visual arts also accomplish for Jewish societies, each of the various arts in its own inimitable and irreplaceable way, and each for precisely the same humane and existential reasons. Throughout Jewish history, as in the history of all societies, human beings have not made do and cannot make do without both the literary and the visual arts, and more.

---

65. See C. S. Lewis, *The Discarded Image: An Introduction to Medieval and Renaissance Literature* (New York: Cambridge University Press, 1964), 198–223.

66. See Max Weber, *From Max Weber: Essays in Sociology* (ed. Hans H. Gerth and C. Wright Mills; New York: Oxford University Press, 1958), 51, 139–43, 148, 155, 282, 350, 357.

67. William Wordsworth, "Essay Supplementary to the Preface (1815)," in *The Major Works* (ed. Stephen Gill; New York: Oxford University Press, 1984), 641. For further critical discussion, see Meyer H. Abrams, *The Mirror and the Lamp: Romantic Theory and the Critical Tradition* (New York: Oxford University Press, 1953), 299.

68. Isaiah Berlin, "The Essence of European Romanticism," in *The Power of Ideas* (ed. Henry Hardy; Princeton, NJ: Princeton University Press, 2000), 204.

8

"Reverse Marranism," Translatability, and the Theory and Practice of Secular Jewish Culture in Russian

GABRIELLA SAFRAN

> A nation that has a single language or a single shared tongue and a few related dialects does not have to ponder sociolinguistic theory—it just needs to cultivate its language, to develop new and better forms of it. But when it hasn't been clarified definitively which language is national—whether it's one of three, or maybe all three—then discussion of the mission of the language and the conditions of its correct and fruitful use is inevitable and expedient.
>
> —Ia. Saker, 1910[1]

One of the founding texts of modern Jewish literature has long existed in two languages. In Yiddish, the 1920 play *Der Dybbuk*, by Semen An-sky (Shloyme-Zanvl Rappoport, 1863–1920), was the greatest hit of the Vilna Trupe and the basis for Michal Waszynski's landmark 1937 film. In Haim Nahman Bialik's Hebrew translation, *Hadibbuk* was the signature piece of the Habima Theater, first in Soviet Russia, then in Palestine and Israel. In 2001, the battle for primacy between these versions was complicated by the discovery of a 1915 version of the text in Russian, confirming the evidence that An-sky had written the play in that language first and intended it for a Russian-speaking audience.[2] In a conference volume that Steven J.

I am grateful to the friends and colleagues who helped me think through this article: Zachary Baker, Michael Kahan, Roman Koropeckij, Kenneth Moss, Harsha Ram, and Steven J. Zipperstein.

1. Ia. Saker, "Intelligentsia i 'zhargon.' (Otvet g. Nigeru)," *Evreiskoe obozrenie* 8 (1910): 5.
2. Semen An-skii, "Mezh dvukh mirov (Dibuk)," ed. Vladislav Ivanov, in *Polveka evreiskogo teatra, 1876–1926* (ed. Boris Entin; Moscow: Dom evreiskoi knigi/Evreiskii kul'turnyi tsentr na Nikitskoi, 2003).

Zipperstein and I recently co-edited, we included an English translation of An-sky's Russian play.[3] As we worked with the translator, we found ourselves asking questions about translation philosophy. We both faced a strong urge to re-Yiddishize the play, that is, to bring it closer to the Yiddish final text that we knew. For instance, An-sky's characters speak in Russian about the *tridtsat' shest' pravednikov*, which literally means the "thirty-six righteous ones." Our instinct was to use the most specific and what seemed to us the culturally correct term for this; rather than putting in English "thirty-six righteous ones," we were drawn to *lamedvovniks*. Similarly, some of the characters in the Russian play are *sinagogal'nye zavsegdatai*, meaning people who are always in the synagogue (the Russian term comes from the word "always"). In the Yiddish text of the play, these characters are *batlonim*, and our initial impulse again was to give this same specific and correct term in the English translation, to put *batlans* or *batlonim*. Most thoughtful contemporary translators of Jewish texts would probably share our reaction. In a recent article in *Pakntreger*, the magazine of the Yiddish Book Center, Lawrence Rosenwald called for translating Yiddish writers in a new way, giving "full measure," presenting characters with all their "Jewish competence," and producing translations that are as multilingual as the originals.[4] The Jewish world that the Yiddish writers depict was full of elements that cannot necessarily be smoothly translated into English. Rosenwald calls for including them anyway, avoiding the impulse to make that world seem simpler or more accessible, at the cost of flattening it out or dumbing it down. As a creature of the same world as Rosenwald, I agree with him that a "harder," more foreign-looking translation is often better than a smoother, more anglicized one. To me, non-English words in an English text look beautiful and suggest that I am seeing a truer picture of a distant time or place.

Editing the English translation of the Russian *Dybbuk*, though, forced me to confront and question my own instincts about translation and to reexamine the aesthetic response categorizing Yiddish words such as *lamedvovniks* and *batlans* as authentic, evocative, and beautiful. This play reveals its author's faith in the translatability of Jewish texts and Jewish culture into non-Jewish languages. An-sky, it seemed, believed that Russian was broad enough, tolerant enough, and flexible enough to make room for a satisfying, authentic, modern secular Jewish culture, and he acted on his convictions by writing *The Dybbuk* in Russian and filling it with Jewish

---

3. Semen An-sky, "Between Two Worlds (*The Dybbuk*): A Jewish Dramatic Legend in Four Acts with Prologue and Epilogue," ed. Vladislav Ivanov; trans. Craig Cravens, in *The Worlds of S. An-sky: A Russian Jewish Intellectual at the Turn of the Century* (ed. Gabriella Safran and Steven J. Zipperstein; Stanford: Stanford University Press, 2006).

4. Lawrence Rosenwald, "Four Theses on Translating Yiddish Literature in the 21st Century," *Pakntreger* 38 (2002): 14–20.

cultural specifics, all drawn from Jewish folk and religious culture but all expressed in standard literary Russian. Therefore, we decided in the end that a good translation of his Russian text would be one that maintained this conception of translatability, that avoided Yiddishisms in favor of the most accessible English possible. Instead of *lamedvovniks*, we decided on the English "thirty-six righteous ones," and instead of *batlans*, we put "synagogue regulars." With these decisions, we hoped to give our readers access to the particular concerns of An-sky.

In the decade before the 1917 revolutions, Eastern European Jewish intellectuals like An-sky were fascinated by questions of language. An-sky's friends and colleagues in the Russian empire and beyond it wrote and spoke often about the choice facing the creators of modern secular Jewish culture—writers of novels, newspapers, or plays—among Hebrew, Yiddish, and the local non-Jewish language (Russian, Polish, German, English). One might think that by turning to their debates and to An-sky's own contributions to them, one could find a clear rationale to help answer the questions facing editors of the translation of *The Dybbuk*. This article is an attempt to locate such a rationale. The first part presents a debate from 1910 among An-sky, the literary critic Shmuel Niger, and other Jewish writers about the proper language for modern secular Jewish literature. They argued about whether Jews want to create a modern culture whose texts could be read in non-Jewish languages without translation and could thus represent the Jews to other nations as well as to themselves, or instead to create a culture directed primarily at Jews, with the first aim of affirming their uniqueness. My analysis situates their arguments within the history of theories of translation. The second section complicates their debate with a case study that reveals the tensions around issues of language and translation in An-sky's private life. Though they argued loudly for the value of one language over another for Jews, An-sky, Niger, and their friends lived in constant negotiation among several languages and in seeming contradiction to their expressed principles. Their words, taken as a whole, provide little clear direction for the modern translator, but they offer a window into the intellectual and emotional difficulties of living between languages. As I will argue, each linguistic ideology that An-sky and his friends expressed in print was only a momentary stopping point, one among their many shifting and coexisting attitudes toward their multilingual and multicultural reality.

The *Jewish World* Debate in 1910

The debate about the proper language for a modern Jewish culture, which had been going on in Eastern Europe since the late nineteenth century, heated up in the early twentieth century and especially after the end of the revolutionary period of 1905–1907, when politics seemed to offer less promise and culture emerged in the foreground in the Russian empire. In 1908, Jewish and non-Jewish writers publicly debated the role of Jews in Russian literature and the role of Russian in Jewish literature. The young writer Kornei Chukovsky wrote the first of a series of articles in Jewish and mainstream newspapers about whether Jewish writers could ever find a home in Russian letters.[5] In a related discussion at the Jewish Literary Society of St. Petersburg, An-sky defended a vision of a multilingual Jewish literature, where Hebrew, Yiddish, and Russian held equal positions.[6] Meanwhile, Yiddish writers in specific worked to challenge stereotypes about the inherent stylistic or thematic limitations to literature in that language; young writers in Vilna, including A. Vayter (pen name of Ayzik-Meir Devinishski) and Shmuel Niger, published four issues of *Literarishe Monatsshriften*, a journal meant to showcase highbrow, experimental, and frankly modernist Yiddish work. (Their efforts were met with shock and fascination among older writers such as An-sky, who both criticized the "decadence" of the works published and their inaccessibility to most Jewish readers and tried to help the editors raise funds to ensure the continuation of their journal.)[7]

Particularly strong arguments for the importance of Yiddish for modern Jews were made at the First Yiddish Language Conference, held at the end of August and the beginning of September 1908 in Czernowitz (Chernovtsy) in what is now Ukraine but what was then the far eastern edge of the Austro-Hungarian Empire. The several dozen Jews who attended the conference planned to talk about systematizing Yiddish spelling and grammar, but they ended up spending most of their time talking about how Yiddish, so often dismissed as "not a real language," could get more respect. This meant, among other things, both determining and demonstrating that Yiddish could be used for high-culture functions such as writing poems and serious novels—or, of course, running a scholarly conference. Although historians debate how much the Czernowitz conference actually accomplished, it was the harbinger of further debate about Yiddish and its status for modern Jewish culture.[8]

---

5. See reprints of some of the articles in Evgeniia Ivanova, ed., *Chukovskii i Zhabotinskii: Istoriia vzaimootnoshenii v tekstakh i kommenariiakh* (Moscow: Mosty kul'tury, 2005).

6. See the discussion of An-sky's role in the debates in Il'ia Serman, "Spory 1908 goda o russko-evreiskoi literature i posleoktiabr'skoe desiatiletie," *Cahiers du Monde russe et soviétique* 26 (1985): 167–74.

7. See Kenneth Moss, "Jewish Culture Between Renaissance and Decadence: *Di Literarishe Monatsshriften* and Its Critical Reception," *Jewish Social Studies* 8 (2001): 169–70, 178.

8. On the conference, see Robert D. King, "The Czernowitz Conference in Retrospect," in *Politics of Yiddish: Studies in Language, Literature, and Society* (ed. Dov-Ber Kerler; Winter Studies in Yiddish 4; Walnut Creek: Altamira Press, 1998), 41–49; Emanuel Goldsmith, *Archi-*

Fourteen of the participants in Czernowitz were from the Russian empire, and they included some of the luminaries of Yiddish literature: the Warsaw modernist I. L. Peretz; the talented young prose writer Sholem Asch; Avrom Reyzn, who was already known for his poetry; and the prolific public intellectual Haim Zhitlowsky, who had already moved to New York but was numbered by the participants among the "Russians."[9] For these writers and the other Jews of the empire, the question of the cultural status of Yiddish was complicated by political and sociological factors. Before the 1917 revolutions, most Jews lived in the western provinces that formed the Pale of Jewish Settlement; only some possessed the qualifications that allowed them to move to the imperial capitals, Moscow and St. Petersburg, or elsewhere in the center of the empire. The native language of most Jews was Yiddish; many, especially women who traded in the marketplace, were also fluent in the languages of the Slavic peasants with whom they interacted (Byelorussian, Ukrainian, Polish); and men, particularly elite men, were also educated in the Hebrew and Aramaic of the Talmud and rabbinic literature. Increasingly from the 1860s through 1917, Jews in the Pale strove to educate their children in Russian;[10] at the same time, a growing population of Russian-speaking Jews appeared in the capitals.

Although the imperial authorities, especially after the assassination of Alexander II in 1881 and the ascension of Alexander III, were anxious to regulate and limit any potentially subversive manifestations of non-Russian cultures, the Jews of the empire succeeded in these years in developing secular literature—both books and periodicals—in various languages. Although they permitted the publication of novels and stories in Yiddish, the authorities made it far easier for Jews to publish newspapers and journals in Russian—a language that made their works, from the perspective of the authorities, easy to censor, and that was in addition accessible only to a minority of Jews—or Hebrew, which the authorities knew could be read only by the most educated, rather than Yiddish, the language

---

texts of Yiddishism and the Beginning of the Twentieth Century (Cranbury, N.J.: Associated University Presses, 1976), Max Weinreich, Zalmen Reyzen, and Khayim Broyde, eds., *Di ershte yidishe shprakh-konferents: Barikhtn, dokumentn un opklangen fun der Tshernovitser konferents, 1908* (Vilna: YIVO, 1931); Joshua A. Fishman, *Ideology, Society, and Language: The Odyssey of Nathan Birnbaum* (Ann Arbor: Karoma Publishers, 1987).

9. Joshua A. Fishman, *Yiddish: Turning to Life* (Philadelphia: John Benjamins Publishing Company, 1991), 262. An-sky was tremendously miffed not to have been included in the conference. He read about the conference in the papers and considered going but decided not to, as he wrote Zhitlowsky, "for fear of being in the position of an uninvited guest"; see Letter from Semen An-sky to Haim Zhitlowsky, August 23/September 5, 1908, YIVO Institute for Jewish Research (hereafter YIVO), RG 308 (Zhitlowsky papers), File 72, p. 2.

10. See Steven G. Rappaport, "Jewish Education and Jewish Culture in the Russian Empire, 1880–1914" (Ph.D. diss., Stanford University, 2000).

of the masses.¹¹ Only in 1903 did a daily Yiddish newspaper, *Der Fraynd* (The Friend), begin to come out in Petersburg, and only with the many concessions made during the 1905 revolution were Jews permitted to print more newspapers and to hold public lectures in Russian or Yiddish. The Yiddish theater had been officially illegal since 1883, but the ban was relaxed in 1900 and Yiddish theater flourished in the empire after the 1905 revolution.¹²

The concessions of the years around 1905 obviously spurred Russian Jewish intellectuals to weigh the possibilities offered by the increased opportunities for publication in Yiddish; the Czernowitz conference provided some terms for debate. A year and a half after the Czernowitz conference and the other debates about language, their echoes were again audible in St. Petersburg. In a Russian-language Jewish publication called first *Evreiskii mir* (Jewish World) and then *Evreiskoe obozrenie* (Jewish Review), writers renewed the argument about the proper language for the development of modern secular Jewish culture. The first part of the debate was an explicit continuation of Czernowitz, focusing on Yiddish. Though Hebraists such as Ahad Ha'am had insisted that Hebrew is the only appropriate language for Jewish culture and scorned Jews who wrote instead in Yiddish or Russian, contributors to *Jewish World* argued that Hebrew was accessible only to the Jewish intelligentsia, a small percentage of the people, while Russian and Yiddish both could be truly national languages, in which a writer could speak to the Jews as a whole.¹³ Writing in *Jewish World* in April 1910 under the pseudonym Mathias Acher, the Yiddishist activist Nathan Birnbaum, who had been the chief organizer of the Czernowitz Conference, decried Ahad Ha'am's insistence on Hebrew over Yiddish. He saw such Hebraism as elitist, puritanical, and, in general, out of touch with the Jewish people. Arguing that Hebrew is the only correct language for modern Jewish culture, he insisted, is tantamount to trying to create a nationalism without a nation.¹⁴ In principle, according to Birnbaum, what

---

11. The exceptions were two Yiddish weeklies, *Kol mevaser* (Odessa, 1862–1871) and *Dos Yudishes Folksblat* (Petersburg, 1882–1890).

12. David Fishman, "The Politics of Yiddish in Tsarist Russia," in *From Ancient Israel to Modern Judaism: Intellect in Quest of Understanding: Essays in Honor of Marvin Fox* (ed. Jacob Neusner and Ernest S. Frerichs; 4 vols.; BJS 159, 175–75; Atlanta: Scholars Press, 1989), 4:155–71. Cf. John Klier, "'Exit, Pursued by a Bear': The Ban on Yiddish Theatre in Imperial Russia," in *Yiddish Theatre: New Approaches* (ed. Joel Berkowitz; Oxford: Littman Library of Jewish Civilization, 2003), 159–74.

13. Eremiia N-skii, "K voprosu o iazyke," *Evreiskii Mir* 15/16 (April 15, 1910). One article of Ahad Ha'am to which N-skii et al. were responding was "Riv leshonot" (The Battle of the Languages), *Hashiloakh* (February 1910). See Acher, "K sporu o iazykakh," *Evreiskii Mir* 17 (April 29, 1910): 16 n. 1.

14. Mathias Acher, "K sporu o iazykakh (Vozrazhenie Akhad-Gaamu)," *Evreiskii Mir* 17 (April 29, 1910); idem, "K sporu o iazykakh," *Evreiskii Mir* 18 (May 6, 1910): 11; idem,

makes a work of literature truly national is not language but the fact that it was "created in the shining glow of the wide-awake (*bodrstvuiushchii*) Jewish soul, under the influence of the genuine, living Jewish collective."[15] In practice, this definition would seem to exclude Hebrew, since Birnbaum denied its connection to any genuine Jewish collective.

In July, the debate moved from the well-trodden ground of the battlefield between Hebrew and Yiddish to somewhat newer territory: Yiddish versus Russian. The young literary critic Shmuel Niger jumped into the fray, attacking not only Ahad Ha'am but also those writers for *Jewish World* such as Birnbaum himself. Niger pointed out the irony of the situation: the entire debate about the value of Yiddish was going on not in Yiddish but in Russian, and the defenders of Yiddish were, according to Niger, actually assimilated Jews whose vaunted love for the *mameloshn* was only "platonic" and "sterile."[16] Writing in an urbane, energetic Russian, complete with literary allusions to the classic works of the poet Aleksandr Pushkin, Niger accused his fellow Russian-speaking Yiddishists of being only "sympathizers" with the cause of Yiddish rather than dedicating their full strength to it.[17] He called them products of "reverse Marranism" (*maranstvo*

"Evreiskii iazyk i ego kritik," *Evreiskoe obozrenie* 1 (May 26, 1910); idem, "Evreiskii iazyk i ego kritik," *Evreiskoe obozrenie* 2 (June 3, 1910). The final article ends with the note that Mathias Acher is "N. Birnbaum." Presumably, the series is a Russian translation of Nathan Birnbaum's German article, "Zum Sprachenstreit: Eine Entgegnung an Achad Haam," in *Ausgewählte Schriften zur jüdischen Frage* (2 vols.; Tshernovits: Birnbaum and Kohut, 1910), 2:52–74; cited in Fishman, *Ideology, Society, and Language*, 37. The first eighteen issues of the newspaper version of *Evreiskii Mir* came out more or less weekly from January 8, 1910, until May 6, 1910. Then it was shut down by the censorship, but the editors quickly regrouped, founded a new newspaper under the name *Evreiskoe Obozrenie* (in precisely the same format as *Evreiskii Mir*), and continued to publish series such as Birnbaum's that had been under way. *Evreiskoe Obozrenie* ran from mid-May through August 1910. Starting with the issue of September 10, 1910, the authorities allowed *Evreiskii Mir* to reopen, and it remained in existence until April 30, 1911 (although issue #10 of 1911 was seized by the censors and destroyed). On the history of these publications, see Udo G. Ivask, *Evreiskaia periodicheskaia pechat' v Rossii* (Tallinn: Beilison, 1935), 56–66.

15. Nathan Birnbaum, "Evreiskii iazyk i ego kritik," *Evreiskoe obozrenie* 19 (26 May 1910): 13–14.

16. Shmuel Niger, "O 'sochuvstvuiushchikh'," *Evreiskoe obozrenie* 7 (July 8, 1910): 9. This is ironic, since Birnbaum didn't actually write the article in Russian. He did write it in German, but he was known for his earnest efforts to master Yiddish—which he did not know from childhood—and to use it for public speaking and writing as much as possible. But Niger definitely understood whom he was discussing and saw himself as on Birnbaum's side. He asked An-sky to make sure that Birnbaum saw the issue of *Jewish World* with his article, and An-sky wrote that it would be sent to him; see Letter from Semen An-sky to Shmuel Niger, August 9, 1910, YIVO, RG 360 (Niger Collection), folder 57.

17. The first line of the article contains an allusion to Aleksandr Pushkin's "Klevetnikam Rossii" (To the Slanderers of Russia): "Not long ago the battle about languages was a 'fight among Slavs'" (spor slavian mezhdu soboi); see Niger, "O 'sochuvstvuiushchikh,'" 8.

na iznanku), "because the historical Marranos said that they were Christians but in reality, that is, in the depths of their souls and their cellars, they were Jews, whereas our Marrano intelligentsia makes such a noise and fuss about their nationalism, but in real life they are no less 'goys' than the rest of the assimilated intelligentsia."[18] By coining the term "reverse Marranism," Niger accused these writers of being Jewish on the outside, but Russian on the inside—that is, of having covertly but thoroughly adopted the norms and culture of the dominant group rather than retaining an "authentic" minority culture. His primary concern is not ensuring that the texts of a modern Jewish culture be translatable into a non-Jewish language but rather using an exclusively Jewish language to affirm and maintain difference.

Not surprisingly, other writers for the newspaper rushed to defend the "reverse Marranos." A week later, one of the editors, Ia. Saker, argued that Niger's picture of Russian Jews who betray their roots by writing in Russian rather than Yiddish ignores both reality and history. Russian, he asserted, is the native language of many Jews in the empire, and Jews have already written valuable works in non-Jewish languages, which does not mean that those works are not Jewish: "The work of the contemporary Jewish intelligentsia, which has broken its connection to the language of the people, is a product of the national spirit and structure; without belonging to their nation through language, they have not stopped belonging to it through the other elements of their psyche."[19] That is, a national language is not a necessary quality of national literature: "other elements" of the "psyche" of its writer could make a text indisputably Jewish.

The next contributor to the debate, in September, was An-sky, who was also an editor of the paper. In an article titled "Creative Nationalism and Conversational Nationalism," he accused Yiddishist intellectuals such as Niger of doing little to combat the situation they criticized or to bring assimilating Jews back toward Jewish culture and Yiddish. With their attention to polemics and agitation rather than creative work and the details of education, they were only furthering a "conversational nationalism," shifting attention away from anything of substance and toward a mere "battle of tongues."[20] An-sky criticized Niger for being so in the grip of his ideology that he had become blind to the complexity of life. Instead of unmasking assimilators, An-sky called for thinking about the many educational and economic factors that had created strong connections between Jews and non-Jews, Jews and non-Jewish languages. The Jewish professional

---

18. Ibid., 9.
19. Ia. Saker, "Intelligentsia i 'zhargon.' (Otvet g. Nigeru)," *Evreiskoe obozrenie* 8 (July 16, 1910): 6–7.
20. Semen An-skii, "Natsionalizm tvorcheskii i natsionalizm razgovornyi," *Evreiskii Mir* 19/20 (September 10, 1910): 14.

class, An-sky observed, had been educated through Russian schools and Russian culture, and therefore "they continue to live by means of this culture, both spiritually and materially."²¹ This goes, An-sky insisted, for Yiddishists like Niger too. "We have to have the courage to admit that *all* our intelligentsia *in reality* are 'reverse Marranos,'" An-sky asserted, because "they satisfy all their practical, cultural, and higher intellectual needs not through Jewish culture, but through Russian, Polish, German, and other cultures."²² In order for the Jewish intelligentsia to return to Yiddish, according to An-sky, they would first need to return to Jewish culture, and in order for that to happen, they would need "cultural soil where they could invest their powers and their knowledge."²³ Traditional Jews truly live within a Jewish culture that possesses not only a religion but also its own science and literature, art, festivals and days of mourning, institutions, an educational system, and customs for inside and outside the home. An-sky urged secular Jews to work to create a new Jewish culture that could be equally all-encompassing and compelling, in order to fight "our 'Marranism,' our dividedness and our inconsistency."²⁴

Niger responded to Saker and An-sky in the next issue by taking back some of his earlier arguments and offering a new one. He agreed that if some members of the Russian Jewish intelligentsia had no access at all to Yiddish (or "the jargon"), they should not be asked to use it. But for most of that intelligentsia, he asserted, though they may speak Russian and even think in Russian, that does not mean that their native language is truly Russian.

> For even when they think "in Russian," their "Russian" thoughts often turn out to be translated, *unconsciously* translated, from the "jargon." This "jargon" has a lot of Russian words, maybe more than Yiddish ones, but after all, a language is more than a simple conglomeration of words, a language is something organic, *animate*, and in its spirit, its rhythm, its internal construction, this language is "Yiddish" (*evreiskii*), even if it's a spoiled, distorted "Yiddish." So wouldn't the Russian-Jewish intelligentsia I have in mind act more intelligently, even, if I may say, more beautifully, if, doing violence to neither their own nor another language, they used Yiddish as their own native language, if they used it not only "asleep" but also awake, and did not erect a wall between themselves and their nation.²⁵

In response to Niger's second sally, Saker called for a more serious sociolinguistic study of the reasons behind Jewish linguistic assimilation, and

---

21. Ibid., 16.
22. Ibid., 18.
23. Ibid., 17.
24. Ibid., 18.
25. Shmuel Niger, "Eshche o 'sochuvstvuiushchikh," *Evreiskii Mir* 21 (September 16, 1910): 4–5.

An-sky, in an article titled "Assimilation from the Cradle," called for a new system of education that would provide a real alternative to assimilation.[26] This essay, in which he harshly criticized upper-class Russian Jews who hire Russian peasant women to care for their children and thereby ensure that they will feel more at home with Russian traditions than Jewish ones, provoked a set of attacks on him in *New Times* (*Novoe Vremia*) and other right-wing newspapers.[27] It also marked the end of the debate in *Jewish World*, and the newspaper itself folded seven months later.[28]

While the debate still continued, though, each of the contributors to it reflected in one way or another on age-old philosophical ideas about language and translatability. Translation is based on the conviction that a writer can abstract the meaning of a text from its forms and reproduce that meaning in the necessarily different forms of a different language. One might wonder whether or not this operation is possible at all. The answer depends on how the relationship between thought and language is conceived. On the one hand, universalists, who think that people all think similarly, though in different words, tend to assume that translation is possible. On the other hand, people who think that thought is determined in a sense by the specific words or language in which it is formulated by a specific group of people tend to argue that a text could in principle be untranslatable. Thus, the concepts of translatability and untranslatability bring up questions about whether people from different cultures, with different languages, can ever understand each other. Prevailing ideas about translatability have changed over time. Through the eighteenth century, most of the thinkers who wrote on this question were universalists who assumed translatability. In the early nineteenth century, though, some thinkers— such as the German Romantics—began to suspect that languages and cultures might be incommensurable and thus fundamentally inaccessible to each other, which would suggest that texts can in fact be untranslatable. Since the late twentieth century, philosophers have started to reject the Romantic worldview and to worry that insisting that what is said in one language is fundamentally inaccessible to speakers of another language has uncomfortable political implications, and they have argued instead for translatability as an essential (though perhaps an inaccessible) goal.[29]

---

26. Ia. Saker, "Otvet na predydushchuiu stat'iu," *Evreiskii Mir* 21 (September 16, 1910); Semen An-sky, "Kolybel'naia assimiliatsiia," *Evreiskii Mir* 23/24 (October 7, 1910).

27. *Novoe Vremia*, January 22, 1910, cited in Moyshe Shalit, "Sh. An-ski loyt zayn bukh fun di tsaytungs-oysshnitn," *Fun noentn over* 1 (1937): 232.

28. Ivask, *Evreiskaia periodicheskaia pechat' v Rossii*, 56–66.

29. Raquel de Pedro, "The Translatability of Texts: A Historical Overview," *Meta* 44, no. 4 (1999): 547–59. Although I am following de Pedro in focusing on contemporary translation theory that argued for translatability, some contemporary theorists are more pessimistic than Iser. For some recent contributions to the debate, see Sanford Budick and Wolfgang Iser, eds., *The Translatability of Cultures: Figurations of the Space Between* (Stanford: Stanford University

When they debated the merits of Hebrew and Yiddish, the writers used the language of Romantic nationalism to claim that one language or the other was a more authentic product of "the genuine, living Jewish collective," a truer reflection of "the shining glow of the wide-awake Jewish soul." Once they turned to Russian, they began to use different terms as some of them groped toward a post-Romantic vision of translation and translatability. One example of this kind of contemporary thinking appears in a 1994 essay by the theorist Wolfgang Iser, "On Translatability."[30] He argues for translatability, by which he means gradually coming to understand ideas and images from another culture within their own framework of meaning, rather than just categorizing these things within mental categories provided by one's own culture. He writes: "A foreign culture is not simply subsumed under one's own frame of reference; instead, the very frame is subjected to alterations in order to accommodate what does not fit." This means, according to Iser, that a reader does not imagine that one culture and language is somehow superior to and capable of fully containing another; rather, the reader perceives both his or her own and the foreign language as offering something that can be taken in and understood by the other. Iser associates translatability with comprehension, as opposed to assimilation or appropriation. "Translatability makes us focus on the space between cultures." That is, according to Iser, when a person succeeds in translating something from a foreign language into a native language, the translator inevitably makes adjustments to that native language and to the mental categories it provides. "Translatability ... requires construing a discourse that allows for transposing a foreign culture into one's own. Such a discourse has to negotiate the space between foreignness and familiarity.... For a foreign culture to become comprehensible, a change of attitude toward the familiar one now being penetrated by something other is unavoidable."[31] In Iser's view, cultural translation of this kind is both possible and desirable.

Press, 1996). Within this collection, Sanford Budick exemplifies the very careful phrasing that seems to be in the end an argument for translatability even if *the other* is acknowledged as unknowable: "Whenever we attempt to translate we are pitched into a crisis of alterity. The experience of secondary otherness then emerges from the encounter with untranslatability. Even if we are always defeated by translation, culture as a movement toward shared consciousness may emerge from defeat"; see Sanford Budick, "Crises of Alterity: Cultural Untranslatability and the Experience of Secondary Otherness," in Budick and Iser, *Translatability of Cultures*, 22.

30. Wolfgang Iser, "On Translatability," *Surfaces* 4.307 (1994): 5–13; Wolfgang Iser et al., "Wolfgang Iser's 'On Translatability': Roundtable Discussion," *Surfaces* 6.106 (1996): 5–37. See also Wolfgang Iser, "The Emergence of a Cross-Cultural Discourse," in Budick and Iser, *Translatability of Cultures*, 247–64.

31. Ibid., 5, 6, 9, 11.

The ideas of Iser and his predecessors about translation and translatability offer some vocabulary—a language, if you will, and a set of mental categories—to set the *Jewish World* debate into a wider context. If the modern secular Jewish culture that all of these writers want to create is genuine when it is in Yiddish, but somehow false when it is in Russian, then presumably it cannot be translated from Yiddish to Russian. This is the perspective of Niger. Any attempt to speak Jewish thoughts in Russian seems wrong and ugly to him, indicative of a false, divided ethnic identity that he abhors. This is a Romantic (or perhaps neo-Romantic) view, holding that any given language and national culture are necessarily impenetrable to speakers of another language. To each language its own. Saker, and even more so An-sky, disagree. In defending Jews' use of Russian as well as Yiddish and Hebrew, and in arguing that a culture could be developed in one language and then transferred later to another, An-sky was arguing for translatability, for the ability of Russian to contain and voice Jewish thoughts. In opposition to Niger's idea that to be a Jewish nationalist but think in Russian is dishonorable "false Marranism," An-sky suggested that this multilingual state was the inevitable result of economic and educational factors. Instead of complaining that Russian Jewish intellectuals use Russian, he urged his readers to work with their own "dividedness and inconsistency," regrettable though it might be, and create a modern Jewish culture out of the tools currently available: it seems that the modern culture he envisioned would be both multilingual and translatable. Instead of limiting his definitions of language along ethnic lines (Yiddish or Hebrew for Jews, Russian for Russians), he argued that Jewish artists need to stop arguing about language and get to work writing and otherwise creating a secular Jewish culture that could be as complete and as compelling as the religious culture they had left behind.[32] Language alone, he suggested, is a superficial marker of difference, not enough to ensure that Jews will be able to create and maintain a distinctive modern culture.

An-sky in some ways is anticipating Iser's notion of a kind of translation that creates a space between two cultures and then fills that space with content. The difference between cultures, he suggests, can reside in that space between, where readers of a translation can perceive it and understand it without flattening it out in any way. This is completely different from the Enlightenment belief in cultural universals. Instead, An-sky and Iser both believe that cultural specificity exists and that it can be constructed in an accessible way in any language. For An-sky, the creation of a modern secular Jewish culture ultimately came to mean making such specifics visually as well as verbally accessible, selecting and displaying

---

32. An-skii, "Natsionalizm razgovornyi," 14, 18.

selected elements of Jewish tradition in modern forms such as museums, schools, and plays.[33]

Life and Polemics

Although Niger, An-sky, and their fellow participants in the *Jewish World* debate were able to articulate coherent, even compelling arguments for one stance or another toward the issues raised by living between languages and cultures, their words and behavior in other contexts suggest that it was difficult if not impossible for them to remain consistent. The correspondence and publications of An-sky in particular illustrate the problems he faced in defining himself and his culture as either Russian or Jewish, or in fighting what he had called "our 'Marranism,' our dividedness and our inconsistency."

Even while An-sky attacked Niger in print, he maintained a warm correspondence with him. When *Jewish World* was founded in 1909, An-sky had begun to write to Niger, asking him to submit reviews and literary-critical articles. Writing first in Russian, then for the most part in Yiddish, An-sky expressed his respect for the younger writer's style and judgment of literature. For example, in December 1909, he recruited Niger to review *Anathema*, a play by the popular, scandalous writer Leonid Andreev that was then playing at the New Dramatic Theater in Petersburg (after premiering that October at Konstantin Stanislavsky and Vladimir Nemirovich-Danchenko's Moscow Art Theater). The mystical, Symbolist play with a Jewish setting had provoked debates and disagreements among critics and members of the public. While liberals were divided in their reactions, conservatives saw it as dangerously antireligious. In November and December 1909, scholars gave lectures about the play, and it was performed throughout the provinces until it was abruptly forbidden by a special order of the

---

33. This is different—a bit—from Seth Wolitz's argument that Marranism is a conscious effort by Jewish artists to bring one message to Jews, another to non-Jews. An-sky wants to bring the same message to both groups, at least insofar as he expresses himself in this article. But he, like Wolitz, is in some ways revalorizing Marranism as an existence between languages and cultures. Wolitz writes: "I call it a Marranism . . . the condition in which Jews have existed for centuries in the diaspora: living on two levels, that of the general populace and that of the specifically Jewish. Chagall lived this reality in his art and also in the various worlds in which he moved—worlds that were not fused, but imbricated. Having learned from cubism the power of simultaneity, he adapted its system in art to that of a Marrano living and functioning in two different existences at the same time. His art sends one message to the general public and another to Jews who spoke his language" (see Seth L. Wolitz, "Vitebsk versus Bezalel: A Jewish Kulturkampf in the Plastic Arts," in *The Emergence of Modern Jewish Politics: Bundism and Zionism in Eastern Europe* [ed. Zvi Gitelman; Pittsburgh: University of Pittsburgh Press, 2003], 172).

Ministry of the Interior; the final performance of the play at the Moscow Art Theater was on January 10, 1910.[34] Though other regular contributors to the newspaper had offered to review the play, An-sky wrote to Niger that he would like him to write the review because he was confident that his assessment of this complex, puzzling play would be "original and from a Jewish source."[35]

An-sky sometimes assigned Niger specific topics or suggested Yiddish writers or publications to review and at other times gave him a list of many possible themes or simply asked him to propose a topic. He expressed his confidence not only in Niger's critical judgment but also in his linguistic abilities. "But write something and send it and God will bless you for writing in Russian, since from this motley crew of grave-digging traducers (*khevre-kadishe ibershleper*) from Yiddish into Russian I have already contracted typhus on top of consumption (*tifozne sukhotke*), if not something worse."[36] An-sky insults these poor translators with an untranslatable play on words, replacing the Yiddish term for "translator" (*iberzetser*), literally "one who sets (or carries) over," with *ibershleper*, or "one who awkwardly pulls or drags over." When he expands the expected *khevre* (literally, "comrades," but *khevre iberzetser* would be "those translator fellows," "the usual gang of translators") into *khevre-kadishe* (burial society), An-sky indicates that these translators' incompetence brings them (and perhaps the texts they translate) close to death, a fate that he hints he too fears when he writes that their work has made him ill. By writing to Niger in these terms, An-sky makes a distinction between, on the one hand, old, moribund Jews with poor Russian, and, on the other, himself and Niger, whose mastery of Russian appears connected to their creativity and their vitality. Instead of bemoaning his and Niger's linguistic "dividedness," he celebrates it as a shared source of strength.

The theme of a connection between An-sky and Niger returns in An-sky's letters about the polemic in *Jewish World*. When he decided to attack Niger in print, An-sky wrote to warn him.

> I'm writing a big article now about the national question where there will also be an answer to your article. I may be a bit blunt in it. But I hope you won't be offended: "*Pustilsia v drak, ne zhalei khokhla*" [If you start a fight, you shouldn't be upset about your topknot.] In my article I will pose the question more broadly, and among other things I'll show that you zealots

---

34. Leonid Andreev, *P'esy* (ed. Boris S. Bugrov; Moscow: Sovetskii pisatel', 1991), 657–58.

35. Letter from Semen An-sky to Shmuel Niger, December 27, 1909/January 9, 1910, YIVO, RG 360, folder 57.

36. Letter from Semen An-sky to Shmuel Niger, February 1, 1909, YIVO, RG 360, folder 57. I wish to thank to Zachary Baker for the wording here.

are just as much Marranos on the left side as the "sympathizers," because you also live with foreign cultures.[37]

In the middle of this Yiddish letter, An-sky inserts a Russian saying; he thereby reaffirms the connection between himself and Niger, the perfect mastery of Russian—indeed, the Marranism—that sets them apart from the *khevre-kadishe ibershleper*. The saying he chooses is drawn not from the world of Russian high society but from that of the Cossacks, who are known for the *khokhol*, the topknot produced when they shave all the hair on their head except for a section on top. With this phrase, An-sky simultaneously defends his decision to disagree publicly with his colleague and suggests that the two of them have something in common with Cossacks, the defenders of the Russian empire and the traditional enemies of the Jews. Even while An-sky announces that he will criticize Niger and his fellow Yiddishist "zealots" for their allegiance to non-Jewish cultures, his own phrasing suggests that he also has the urge to rejoice in his and his friend's mastery of non-Jewish vocabulary and behaviors.

After An-sky's article was published, he wrote to Niger about it and again insisted on their similarity. "Although we polemicize in the press, ultimately our ideals and aspirations are just the same. (. . .) I feel immeasurably closer to you than to my co-editor Saker. I would very much like to know the impression my article against you made."[38] Although Niger's answers to An-sky's letters have not been preserved, An-sky's letters to Niger—which continue until the eve of An-sky's death in 1920—testify that the two men remained close. This suggests that Niger responded with at least some enthusiasm to An-sky's letters and to the complex play with Jewish and Russian cultural identities that An-sky carried out in them. It seems that even while in print An-sky and Niger defended opposing views on the question of living within and creating a modern secular Jewish culture—Niger speaking for Yiddish and the primacy of language, An-sky for a mix of languages and the importance of cultural practice over linguistic choices. In reality they both not only lived between two languages and practices but also reveled in their own linguistic skills and the plethora of their cultural options.

Ambivalence about choosing between Russian and Jewish cultures is evident not only in An-sky's correspondence but also in his professional life. A remarkably productive writer and editor, during the same years when he worked at *Jewish World*, An-sky also published in other newspapers and journals and edited other works. Among his clients was *Newspaper*

---

[37]. Letter from Semen An-sky to Shmuel Niger, August 9, 1910, YIVO, RG 360, folder 57.

[38]. Letter from Semen An-sky to Shmuel Niger, October 12, 1910, YIVO, RG 360. folder 57.

for Everyone (*Zhurnal dlia vsekh*), a popular and cheaply produced newspaper meant to be accessible and affordable for Russia's large class of new readers, including peasants and workers with minimal literacy. In 1909, 1910, and 1911, An-sky edited three 128-page, thematically unified collections of Russian and world literature for the popular reader, reprinted from *Newspaper for Everyone* by the publishing house Razum (Reason), titled *Almanac for Everyone* (*Almanakh-Kalendar' dlia vsekh*), and sold for only fifteen kopecks. These publishing ventures reflected ideas about literacy and literature that were prevalent among the Russian intelligentsia and were associated strongly with Lev Tolstoy: educated people have an obligation to work to benefit the peasants, particularly by helping them attain literacy; they must also help protect traditional peasant culture and guard the peasants from "infection" by excessively modern, capitalist inclinations.[39] Tolstoy and his followers had established a publishing house, The Intermediary (Posrednik), to produce cheap editions of selected classical stories for the new reader, and other publishers would eventually follow their lead. The articles in *Newspaper for Everyone* and even more so the reprints in *Almanac for Everyone* spoke for the Tolstoyan virtues of reason, tolerance, modesty, and nonviolence. As a reviewer of one of these volumes noted, "The distinctive feature of these excellent little books is their humane, 'reasonable, good, eternal' content, which is presented in such a generally accessible way that it will be understood by children or by a barely-literate adult reader."[40]

In 1910, An-sky compiled an edition of *Almanac for Everyone* under the title *For God's Truth: The Great Founders of Religion: Fighters for Freedom of Faith and Thought* (*Za pravdu bozhiiu. Velikie osnovateli religii. Bortsy za svobodu very i mysli*).[41] This contained poems, stories, and quotations from various religious and philosophical traditions, with chapters titled, "The Indian sage Buddha," "The Chinese sage Confucius," "The Greek sage Socrates," "Moses, the liberator and the great lawgiver of the Jewish people," "Jesus Christ," "Mohammed," "The martyr for his faith Jan Huss," "The martyr for science Giordano Bruno," and "The martyr for Science Galileo Galilei." The first section, called "Faiths are varied—God is one," contains a collection of short quotations from the Hebrew and Greek Bibles, the Talmud, and Tolstoy himself, all making similar arguments. In Tolstoy's words, "One of the most important commandments that Christ gave to people

---

39. Jeffrey Brooks, *When Russia Learned to Read: Literacy and Popular Literature, 1861–1917* (Princeton, NJ: Princeton University Press, 1985).

40. Iv. Sergeev, "Almanakhi dlia vsekh. Knizhka vos'maia. Arkadii Press. Tsvety Vostoka. Izdatel'stvo Razum. SPB. 1912, str. 128, tsena 15 kop." *Novyi zhurnal dlia vsekh* 12 (December 1912): 133.

41. Semen An-skii, ed., *Za pravdu bozhiiu: Velikie osnovateli religii. Bortsy za svobodu very i mysli* (St. Petersburg: Razum, 1910).

says, 'Do not make distinctions between your own kind and others, because all people are children of a single God.'"[42] Tolstoy's point here directly contradicts An-sky's in "Assimilation from the Cradle." Whereas An-sky had spoken for fighting assimilation and preserving the specificity of Jewish culture—albeit in new secular rather than older religious forms—Tolstoy insists that national or religious differences are fundamentally insignificant and should be forgotten. To return to the debates on translation and translatability that I outlined earlier, Tolstoy is arguing for a universalist view of culture. His statement that different religious forms are all ways of approaching the same God recalls the universalist argument about language that people all think similarly, though they use different words to express themselves. When An-sky designed the *For God's Truth* collection in the spirit of Tolstoy and his universalism, he took a step away from the post-Romantic view of cultural difference that he defended in *Jewish World*, that is, from the argument that such differences are important and that rather than forgetting them one must work to preserve them or construct them consciously anew.

One might argue that An-sky's seeming inconsistency can be attributed to expediency, holding that the articles in *Jewish World*, a publication he himself controlled, reflect his true convictions, whereas he presumably edited the *Almanac for Everyone* on commission and was obligated to support the Tolstoyan views of the publishing house in it. Such an argument, though, would ignore An-sky's deep and long-standing admiration of Tolstoy and his fundamental agreement with Tolstoy's views about art and language. An-sky wrote to Niger that a true "intelligent," in the Russian sense of a politically engaged intellectual, is one who remains close to the folk. "This is the kind of intellectual that Tolstoy is. The real mark of such an intellectual (a real prophet [*nevi haemes*]) is that the folk understands him, follows him, appreciates him."[43] An-sky's words reiterate the skepticism that he expressed consistently about any art forms that are not accessible to all potential viewers or readers. In *What Is Art?*, a book-length essay from the late 1890s, Tolstoy had asserted that art is communication: "Art is a human activity consisting in this, that one man consciously, by means of certain external signs, hands on to others feelings he has lived through, and that other people are infected by these feelings and also experience them."[44] Tolstoy devoted much of the rest of the essay to criticizing "the art of the upper classes" for not effectively communicating feelings: "besides

---

42. Ibid., 5.
43. Letter from Semen An-sky to Shmuel Niger, August 28, 1909, YIVO, RG 360, folder 57.
44. Leo N. Tolstoy, *What Is Art?* (trans. Aylmer Maude; New York: Macmillan, 1985), 51. This is a reprint of the 1898 English translation, which was the first complete and uncensored edition.

... becoming continually more and more exclusive, it became at the same time continually more and more involved, affected, and obscure."⁴⁵ An-sky's comment to Niger suggests that he continued to believe with Tolstoy in the necessity for creative intellectuals to remain comprehensible to non-intellectuals rather than to write in exclusive, involved, affected, or obscure ways.

This ideal might seem difficult to reconcile with An-sky's polemics against assimilation. On the one hand, in urging upper-class Jews, in "Assimilation from the Cradle," to make sure their children were exposed to traditional Jewish culture, he acted on the Tolstoyan inclination to value lower- over higher-class ways, traditional lore over European-style education. On the other hand, by insisting on the need for the Jews of the Russian empire to retain—even reinvent—a particular, exclusively Jewish culture, An-sky speaks for the creation of texts that, from the perspective of the newly literate Russian reader to whom An-sky had devoted many years and pages, would be exclusive, involved, and undeniably obscure. (An-sky had spent much of his twenties in the south of the empire working among miners and peasants, reading to them and observing them; he eventually wrote two books about their attitudes toward literature.⁴⁶) It seems likely that even while in articles such as "Assimilation from the Cradle" he rejected cultural if not linguistic russification and argued for the preservation and recreation of a modern, secular, but exclusively Jewish culture, An-sky simultaneously felt pulled in the opposite direction, toward a broad, inclusive vision of culture and to the idea that one should not make distinctions between one's own kind and others, "because," in the words of Tolstoy, "all people are children of a single God."

The tensions between universalism and particularism and between assimilation and tradition that are so powerful in An-sky's writings in 1910 were apparent also in his private life. In the fall of 1907, he entered into what his friends feared was an ill-considered relationship with Edia (Esther) Glezerman, a much younger woman. He was an ascetic radical in his forties, a peripatetic journalist, and a Jewish cultural activist who had already begun to write in Yiddish and collect Yiddish folklore; she was the daughter of a lamp store owner in Vitebsk, an attractive young woman and a talented pianist who spoke only Russian. Soon after they met and began to correspond, his friends wrote to caution him about what they saw as an ideological mismatch. Vera Zhitlovskaia, the estranged wife of his childhood friend Haim Zhitlowsky, used strong language: "If it would help, I would hold you back until the grave to keep you from marrying that aris-

---

45. Ibid., 76.
46. Semen An-sky, *Ocherki narodnoi literatury* (St. Petersburg: B. M. Vol'fa, 1894); idem, *Narod i kniga* (Moscow: L. A. Stoliar, 1913).

tocratic young lady (baryshnia) . . . but you can't help a madman."[47] When he mentioned his friends' doubts to his intended, she defended herself: "It's not true that I can't deny myself in petty, pathetic matters!" She insisted that she too was a radical of a sort, a visionary who dreamed of a better future:

> I believe that it will be possible to burst out of these cursed chains. If you only knew how I dream about casting off from myself all this filth and becoming completely free from all this petty, everyday, really completely unnecessary and insignificant rubbish of life.

Glezerman wrote to An-sky that these dreams were associated for her with her love for the theater and her ambition to go on the stage.[48]

For An-sky's friends such as Zhitlovskaia, Glezerman was a *baryshnia*, an aristocratic young lady whose pretty speeches about casting off "these cursed chains" should be seen as self-deluding nonsense. They were certain that this spoiled provincial miss could never be a suitable companion for a self-sacrificing radical intellectual such as An-sky. It seems, though, that on some level, An-sky longed precisely for the provincial, middle-class, comfortable lifestyle that he could have with Glezerman. In a draft of an early letter to Glezerman, he wrote of their plans to move together to Vilna and set up housekeeping.

> I'd make a cozy little nest for you, so that everything would be peaceful, joyful, bright for you, so you could rest and give yourself to your music. . . . When we sit at home I'll teach you to play chess. We'll speak French and read Anatole France and [Edmond] Rostand [author of *Cyrano de Bergerac*] in the original. I just haven't decided what color the wallpaper in your room will be . . .[49]

The reading list that An-sky proposes here indicates that when he asserted in the *Jewish World* debate that Russian-Jewish intellectuals "satisfy all their practical, cultural, and higher intellectual needs not through Jewish culture, but through Russian, Polish, German, and other cultures," he was including himself among them. The comfortable life that An-sky reached out for with his marriage to Glezerman implied an orientation toward European—especially French—culture, rather than a return to Jewishness. After the couple moved to Vilna in early 1908, An-sky recognized that his marital life there would seem to contradict the ascetic ideals according to

---

47. Letter from Vera Zhitlovskaia to Semen An-sky, February 2, 1908, Manuscript Division, Vernadsky National Library of Ukraine (hereafter IR NBUV), f. 339 (S. An-sky Collection), N. 782.

48. Edia Glezerman to Semen An-sky, no date, but she uses the formal form of the second person (*vy*), so this must be before their marriage. IR NBUV, f. 339, N. 1268.

49. Letter draft, Edia An-sky to Semen Glezerman, no date, IR NBUV, f. 339, N. 981.

which he had lived earlier, writing with evident irony to his friend and editor, the literary critic Arkady Georgievich Gorenfel'd, "I have rented an apartment and moved from the ranks of the proletariat to those of the petty bourgeoisie."[50]

As An-sky's friends had predicted, the marriage soon foundered and the couple began to argue.[51] An-sky probably could not maintain his professional commitments while living in Vilna, far from the Russian publishing center of St. Petersburg. However, as a loyal Socialist Revolutionary as well as a Jew, he appeared to the Tsarist authorities to pose too great a threat to be granted residence permission for Petersburg (though the police were willing to wink at his habit of spending weeks at a time in the capital, staying on the couch of one friend or another). This seemed hardly a suitable lifestyle for a wife, but when, after two or three months in Vilna, he left Glezerman with her parents in Vitebsk, she was not happy. She hinted that she would like to have a child: "The doctor asked me in detail about our marital life. Then he said that I can't live this way and *I must have a baby*. How do you like that? . . . Oh well, the Devil with all of that!"[52] Her tone indicates that she knows that the doctor's suggestion will not be taken. For the next three years, the couple spent only the summers together, in Finland or Vitebsk; the rest of the year, Glezerman, who had weak lungs, traveled to the Swiss Alps to convalesce. She wrote letters complaining of boredom and loneliness. In March and April 1910, when she insisted on returning to Russia, An-sky responded that he wanted her to be completely well before she came back, and, anyway, he planned to be out of town, giving lectures in Riga, Vitebsk, Kovno, Bialystok, Moscow, and elsewhere, and there was nowhere for her to stay in Petersburg.[53] Ultimately, Glezerman took a lover and returned to her husband in the winter of 1910–11 pregnant. In the spring of 1911, when she suffered a miscarriage (or perhaps arranged an abortion), he accompanied her to the hospital.[54] Glezerman promised to remain faithful but did not, and An-sky finally lost patience, writing to her in August 1911 to ask for a divorce.[55] She asked

---

50. Letter from Semen An-sky to Arkady Georgievich Gorenfel'd, February 4, 1908, St. Petersburg Public Library Manuscript Collection, f. 211, N. 912.

51. Already by April 3, 1908, she was in Vitebsk, writing to him, writing that their life together did not seem that it would "work out" (*ustroitsia*); see IR NBUV, f. 339, N. 1043.

52. Letter from Edia Glezerman to Semen An-sky, April 8, 1908, IR NBUV, f. 339, N. 1047.

53. Letters from Edia Glezerman to Semen An-sky, April 8, 1910/April 16, 1910, IR NBUV, f. 339, NN. 1160–1166. Letter drafts from Semen An-sky to Edia Glezerman, March 16, 1910/March 21, 1910, IR NBUV, f. 339, NN. 969, 970, 982.

54. Letter draft from Semen An-sky to Edia Glezerman, undated, IR NBUV, f. 339, N. 983. In April, An-sky wrote that the pregnancy had ended, suggesting that the cause was Glezerman's tuberculosis. Letter from Semen An-sky to Haim Zhitlowsky, April 11(24), 1911, YIVO, RG 308, folder 72.

55. Letter draft, Semen An-sky to Edia Glezerman, August 22, 1911, IR NBUV, f. 339, NN. 973, 974, 976.

again for forgiveness, but this time he wrote to her that the distance between them had become unbridgeable: "I am sad to see that we speak different languages."[56]

The phrasing is telling, for language had become an increasingly significant point of contention between husband and wife. An-sky had urged Glezerman to work to realize her dreams of becoming an actress. As they both knew, Jewish actors who wanted to go on the Russian stage faced both legal barriers (particularly due to the restrictions on Jews living outside the Pale) and the prejudice of some of their colleagues.[57] The newly legal Yiddish theater, though, offered unparalleled possibilities—if only Glezerman knew Yiddish! She agreed to go to Moscow to study acting, but reacted skeptically at first when her husband proposed that she study Yiddish: "Of course your idea about a Jewish theater is attractive to me too, but where, pray tell, could I learn Yiddish? You could hardly think this possible in Moscow?"[58] Eventually, Glezerman changed her mind. An-sky wrote to Niger in August 1910 that Glezerman had started studying Yiddish after reading Niger's article on it, presumably in *Jewish World*.[59] The next year, in a conciliatory mood after An-sky had asked for the divorce, Glezerman wrote agreeing to become a Yiddish actress and suggesting that she spend three months in a shtetl to master the language.[60] An-sky had agreed to send Glezerman one hundred rubles a month so that she would be able to study and become financially independent. She enrolled in an acting course in Moscow where she studied Russian and European drama. But she did not forget her promise, telling An-sky, "Word of honor, I read in Yiddish every day."[61]

When An-sky and Glezerman negotiated their life together, they found themselves discussing the same cultural and ideological questions that fill An-sky's writings on language and literature. With his frank acknowledgment that as things are now, all the members of the Russian Jewish intelligentsia are addicted to non-Jewish culture, he explains and excuses his own dreams of living in a "bourgeois" home in Vilna with Glezerman, playing chess and reading French. The educational and economic factors that made the Russian-Jewish intelligentsia unable to function in Yiddish,

---

56. Letter draft, Semen An-sky to Edia Glezerman, October 12, 1911, IR NBUV, f. 339, N. 978.

57. Viktoriia Levitina, *Russkii teatr i evrei* (Jerusalem: Biblioteka Aliia, 1988), 151–204.

58. Letter from Edia Glezerman to Semen An-sky, postmark May 1, 1910, IR NBUV, f. 339, N. 1167.

59. Letter from Semen An-sky to Shmuel Niger, August 9, 1910, YIVO, RG 360, folder 57.

60. Letter from Edia Glezerman to Semen An-sky, September 24, 1911, IR NBUV, f. 339, N. 1128.

61. Letter from Edia Glezerman to Semen An-sky, October 24, 1912, IR NBUV, f. 339, N. 1180.

which An-sky described sympathetically in the *Jewish World* articles, had made his wife who she was. His defense of a trilingual modern Jewish culture presents a vision that would allow him to imagine his Russophone wife acting in a Jewish play. The ideal of linguistic and cultural translatability that he defended in "Creative Nationalism and Conversational Nationalism" suggests that both Glezerman and their marriage were redeemable, that the Europeanized Russian Jewish intelligentsia could eventually become producers and consumers of a new Jewish culture that would make sense in their native language, Russian.

But even while An-sky argued for the possibility of creating a modern Jewish culture in Russian, he retained great ambivalence about the language question. We remember that he had written to Niger, the "fanatic" Yiddishist, that he felt closer to him than to his fellow editor, the russophile Saker. An-sky's attempt to reeducate his russophone wife and transform her into a Yiddish actress reveals the fissures between his varied unrealized fantasies—one of a new life as a married member of "the petty bourgeoisie" in Vilna, another of a return to a traditional Jewishness that he associated with the Jewish "proletariat" and its language, Yiddish—and the reality of his peripatetic, solitary, multilingual, and modern urban existence. His second article in the language debate, "Assimilation from the Cradle," in which he argued that upper-class Jews need to bring their children up differently, might be read as emerging from the same impulses that led him to urge Glezerman to learn Yiddish and as a reflection on the educational process that had produced Glezerman, the Russian-speaking *baryshnia*, and an attempt to repair them on paper, if not in reality. The fact that An-sky and Glezerman had no children themselves makes it seem even more that this article provided a kind of compensation for the traditional Jewish family life that he was unable or unwilling to lead. In the same year of 1910, An-sky undertook other projects focusing on the traditional culture of Jewish children, traveling through the northwest parts of the empire—where he and Glezerman both were born—and collecting Yiddish counting rhymes and children's songs, which he eventually published.[62]

By defending the notion, in "Assimilation from the Cradle," that early childhood experiences are crucial for creating an adult producer or consumer of Jewish culture, An-sky took a step back from the ideal of translatability that he had defended in "Creative Nationalism and Conversational Nationalism." If a Jewish text in Russian cannot be fully comprehensible to any Russian speaker, but only to one with the right Jewish upbringing, then An-sky's ideas would seem closer to Romantic nationalism than to Iser's post-Romantic views of language. One could argue that

---

62. Semen An-skii, "Narodnye detskie pesni," *Evreiskaia starina* 3 (1910).

as his marriage with Glezerman fell apart, An-sky moved away from his earlier faith that even Jews as russified as his young wife could participate creatively in the revival of Jewish culture in the Russian empire: he moved toward a narrower vision of that culture, one that would exclude her. An-sky's other work, though, belies this neat trajectory. Like Niger and like Glezerman herself, he was willing to entertain different ideas about language and culture at different points. As we saw, in the year of 1910 alone, he spoke for three different approaches to language and culture: in *For God's Truth*, for a universalist view of culture; in "Assimilation from the Cradle," for a Romantic view; and in "Creative Nationalism and Conversational Nationalism," for a post-Romantic view. Then, as in other years, he seems to have shifted frequently from one vision of modern secular Jewish culture to another and back.

Once An-sky and Glezerman had definitively separated in the fall of 1911, he turned his attention to the organization of an ethnographic expedition through the Jewish Pale of Settlement, an idea he had been contemplating since 1907 if not earlier.[63] The first, trial season of the expedition was in the summer of 1912. Late the next year, An-sky wrote the first draft of what has since become his most famous work, the play *The Dybbuk*. At that point, he finally kept the promise he had made to Glezerman to write the kind of Jewish-themed play in which she could conceivably star. He had suggested repeatedly that she act in one of his short revolutionary plays.[64] In the spring of 1912, seemingly in response to a letter of An-sky's, Glezerman wrote that if he did go ahead and write a full-length play, she was sure the result would be "big and bright." She encouraged him warmly:

> Try it, Semochka. Of course, from the life of the Jewish intelligentsia. . . . But the thing is that there's almost no romance in anything you've written. I think that's crucial for a play. A romance makes a play more lifelike, bright, and complete.[65]

An-sky took Glezerman's suggestion in *The Dybbuk*, which tells the story of a pair of star-crossed lovers, Leah and Khonen, and with his choice to write in Russian, he produced a modern secular Jewish product that could be a vehicle for as assimilated an actress as Glezerman. His decision suggests that whereas he had flirted with more exclusive, Romantic visions of modern Jewish culture, at this point he returned to a post-Romantic faith in translatability.

---

63. On August 30, 1907, his childhood friend Samuil Gurevich wrote that he liked An-sky's idea of traveling to different cities and gathering information about Jewish life; see IR NBUV, f. 339, N. 388.

64. Undated draft of letter from Semen An-sky to Esther Rappoport, IR NBUV, f. 339, N. 980. It appears from his wording that the question has come up before.

65. Letter from Edia Glezerman to Semen An-sky, May 7, 1912, IR NBUV, f. 339, N. 1247.

Although the 1913–14 draft of *The Dybbuk* has never been found, the 1915 version illustrates the ways in which An-sky followed in his own art the principles that he had laid out in "Creative Nationalism and Conversational Nationalism." He worked to create a modern secular Jewish culture by presenting aspects of Jewish reality in Russian, studiously avoiding Yiddish or Hebrew terms, but loading the play with ethnographic specifics. Even more than the familiar, later, Yiddish version, the Russian is a kind of ethnographic museum, a living diorama that seems meant for display at a World's Fair. One can cite innumerable examples of An-sky's attempts to bring the specificity of Jewish culture to the audience of the play. Two that were removed from the Yiddish final version of the play are the dance of the midwife who attended Leah's birth, and the Hasids' singing of a song of Levi Yitzkhak of Berdichev, the "Dudele" (a song that addresses God as "you" — "*du*") in Russian translation. Even more than the later Yiddish version, the Russian is full of legends, folksongs, history, and artifacts of every kind. In spite of the remarkable popularity of the Yiddish *Dybbuk*, critics and theater professionals have always complained about all the ethnographic material that slows down the development of the plot. From a dramatic perspective, the Russian original is far worse, far slower and less stageable than the much-edited Yiddish text. Nonetheless, the Russian text reveals An-sky's dedication to the ideals of cultural translatability that he had defended in *Jewish World* in 1910. Then he had argued that Jewish artists needed to find or create some concrete, translatable bits of culture that can speak of Jewishness in Russian; he suggested that it would be possible to expand the boundaries of the Russian language and culture to include a modern kind of Jewish culture. In his Russian *Dybbuk*, he attempted this task himself.

It is ironic, of course, that this play, which in its original language so clearly illustrates its author's belief in translatability and in the possibility for creating Jewish culture in non-Jewish languages, has become known precisely in those languages defended by An-sky's opponents in the language debate, by the Hebraist Ahad Ha'am and the Yiddishist Niger. Whereas the Russian text speaks of its author's faith in the possibility of creating a modern Jewish culture in a non-Jewish language, the versions we know have come to symbolize two modern secular Jewish cultures created in two specifically Jewish languages. At the same time, though, there is something satisfying and appropriate about the fact that An-sky's play, in its multiple variants, can neither be definitively assigned to a single linguistic canon nor made to speak for a single ideology of Jewish culture. More than any unitary, monolingual text that argues for a single viewpoint, both the play and the multilingual, self-contradictory legacy of its author testify to a signal aspect of the modern Jewish experience, what An-sky called "our 'Marranism,' our dividedness and our inconsistency."

9

Intertextuality, Rabbinic Literature, and the Making of Hebrew Modernism

SHACHAR PINSKER

A melody of *Gemara*
heavy with dreams and yearning
sometimes still rises
unnoticed on our lips
— David Fogel, *Before the Dark Gate*, 1923[1]

Even the most recent Hebrew literature is entangled in the bonds of the Bible ... and from far away, directly or indirectly, it is governed by the greatest tyrant of all — the Talmud, the pasha from across the river.
— Ya'acov Shteinberg, 1917[2]

The Pasha from Across the River

The earliest works of Hebrew modernism were created during the first decades of the twentieth century, mainly in Eastern and Central Europe, before Hebrew became a vernacular in mandatory Palestine. This was a difficult time for Hebrew writers in terms of material means and readership, but also a period of intense experimentation that led to a radical

---

This article is an attempt to summarize many issues I dealt with in my dissertation and that I elaborate on in my forthcoming book about Hebrew modernism. Owing to the nature of this article, I can present an analysis of only a few short examples from the works of writers I discuss here. Nevertheless, I hope the readers can obtain a glimpse into the complexities of Hebrew modernist fiction and its continuities and raptures with Jewish traditional texts. I would like to thank Robert Alter, Chana Kronfeld and Naomi Seidman, and the editors of this volume, Anita Norich and Yaron Eliav, for their advice and support.
1. David Fogel, *Lifnei hasha'ar ha'afel* (Vienna: Mahar, 1923).
2. Ya'acov Shteinberg, *Kol kitvei Ya'acov Shteinberg* (Tel Aviv: Devir, 1957), 289.

change in Hebrew literature. Within a few years, an impressive group of writers, including Uri N. Gnessin, Yosef H. Brenner, Gershon Shofman, Dvora Baron, Hillel Zeitlin, Ya'acov Shteinberg, David Fogel, and the young Shmuel Y. Agnon, came to the forefront of the literary scene, becoming the first wave of what we know as Hebrew modernism.[3]

A number of crucial questions concerning Hebrew modernist fiction remain open: How did modernist Hebrew fiction arise before Hebrew became a vernacular? What poetic and historic shifts enabled its development? How do we understand and evaluate the Hebrew modernist achievement in historical perspective? What are the modernist elements, and what, if anything, is specifically Hebrew or Jewish in this literary project?

These are complex questions for various theoretical and historical reasons. Modernism itself is an elusive term, necessary for our understanding of twentieth-century literature and yet notoriously difficult to define. Modernism is at once a period, a style, and a variety of different literary and artistic movements in locations around the world.[4] Explorations of modernism in "minor" literatures like Hebrew and Yiddish in this period are even more complex, because most generalizations about modernism are based on "major" literatures such as English, French and German.[5] Finally, Hebrew modernism developed within and against the context of emerging nationalism, while European "high" modernism is usually seen in terms of individualized displacement and exile.[6]

Several prominent accounts of Hebrew literary historiography avoid these questions of the development and evaluation of Hebrew modernism and focus instead on what Gershon Shaked, one of the most important historians of modern Hebrew literature in our time, has called "heroic literature," or "a literature against all odds."[7] This common account of Hebrew

---

3. Robert Alter, *The Invention of Hebrew Prose* (Seattle: University of Washington Press, 1988); Dan Miron, *Kivvun orot* (Jerusalem/Tel Aviv: Schocken, 1980).

4. Malcolm Bradbury and James McFarlane, *Modernism 1890–1930* (London/New York: Penguin, 1990).

5. Chana Kronfeld, *On the Margins of Modernism: De-Centering Literary Dynamics* (Berkeley: University of California Press, 1996), 21–34. On "minor literature," see Gilles Deleuze and Félix Gauttari, "What Is Minor Literature," in *Kafka: Towards a Minor Literature* (trans. Dina Pollan; Minneapolis: University of Minnesota Press, 1986); David Lloyd, *Nationalism and Minor Literature: James Clarence Mangan and the Emergence of Irish Cultural Nationalism* (New Historicism 3; Berkeley: University of California Press, 1987).

6. Raymond Williams, *The Politics of Modernism: Against the New Conformists* (London: Verso, 1989), 34; Michael Gluzman, "Modernism and Exile," in *Insider/Outsider: American Jews and Multiculturalism* (ed. David Biale, Michael Galchinsky, and Susannah Heschel; Berkeley: University of California Press, 1997), 231–53.

7. Gershon Shaked, *Hasipporet ha'ivrit 1880–1980*, vol. 1 (Tel Aviv: Hakibbutz Hameuhad, 1977), 31–68. See also the abridged English version in Gershon Shaked, *Modern Hebrew Fiction* (Bloomington: Indiana University Press, 2000). Interestingly, in some places, Shaked does not

literary history is told as a narrative of "progression," a mirror of the national meta-narrative of redemption and territorialization, "negation of exile" and normalization of the Jews as a "nation like all nations." An essential part of this narrative of progression is the struggle against the so-called negative elements that presumably prevented Hebrew from being a vehicle for "normal" modern national literature. Within this teleological scheme, most critics and historians have regarded the role of early Hebrew modernist fiction as pivotal. It was seen as an attempt to "free" Hebrew from the "heavy burden" of classic religious texts, in order to "normalize" its syntax and semantics and to allow it to become a flexible means of literary representation.[8]

In retrospect, writers such as Gnessin, Fogel, Shofman, and Steinberg are being constructed as prototypes for a Hebrew literature that transformed its traditional Jewish cultural language into a secular-national one. In spite of the fact that many of these writers did not identify with the national-Zionist enterprise, or were indifferent toward it, many critics have described them as if they were full participants in the process of "normalization" with complete cohesion between personal, national, and aesthetic self-realization.[9] This portrayal of Hebrew modernism as part of—indeed as a metonym for—the process of normalization through an imitation of European models is one I find quite problematic. In order to explain why, it is necessary to return to the vexing concept of modernism.

Many so-called high European modernists share particular themes, characters, and concerns. The character of the anti-hero, the themes of neurasthenic sensibility, hobbled will, frustrated imagination, and the blurring between reality and fantasy, are the hallmarks of European modernists such as Proust, Musil, Kafka, Gide, Joyce, and Woolf. However, what is both remarkable and revolutionary about modernist fiction at this period is not necessarily the appearance of these themes or characters, but rather a radical new approach to language and narrative.

In many ways, modernist fiction embodies what Richard Sheppard has called "the crisis of language as a means of representation and literary

---

include the fiction produced by the writers of the early twentieth century such as Gnessin, Shofman, Brenner, or Baron as modernist at all, but under the category of "Psychological Realism." In a one chapter of his book, he reserved the term "modernism" to those writers in the 1930s and 1940s whose novels and stories "read like Hebrew versions of German, American, or Russian novels. Jewish elements played no more significant role in the writing" (see Shaked, *Modern Hebrew Fiction*, 113). My approach to Hebrew modernism is different.

8. Yosef Klausner, *Sefat ever safah hayyah* (Krakow: Fischer-Graeber, 1896); Shaked, *Hasipporet ha'ivrit*, 43–48.

9. Simon Halkin, *Modern Hebrew Literature: Trends and Values* (New York: Schocken Books, 1950), 74–110; Shaked, *Hasipporet ha'ivrit*, 478–80; Nurit Govrin, *Telishut vehithadshut* (Tel Aviv: Misrad habitahon, 1985).

expression."[10] Scholars of modernism such as Malcolm Bradbury and James McFarlane characterize this creative crisis as "narrative introversion"—the act of putting the means and modes of art at the center of the work itself, so that "the shock, the violation of expected continuities, the element of de-creation and crisis, are crucial elements of language, style and narrative."[11] Theodor Adorno describes modernist narrative fiction as an act of "negative mimesis." He argues that modernist narratives display a poetics of fragmentation, of nonorganic text in which the negation of synthesis becomes the new compositional principle.[12]

Paradoxically, Hebrew fiction at the turn of the twentieth century became a very apt tool for "negative mimesis," a revision of narrative conventions and fictional language. I would argue that it is precisely the peculiar status of Hebrew as a language that is neither a vernacular, nor entirely a literary "unspoken" tongue, that is at the heart of the matter. In other words, the disadvantage of Hebrew as a nonvernacular language from a realist (or "organic") point of view strangely became an advantage for those Hebrew writers who jumped into the troubling new waters of modernistic poetics in this period. In my view, the *differentia specifica* of early-twentieth-century modernist Hebrew fiction has to do with the fact that it was constructed through, and enabled by, an awareness of Hebrew language as a mode of literary expression in which every lexical, grammatical, and semantic juncture resonates within the echo chamber of Hebrew textual history.

We can examine the particular development of Hebrew fiction in this period through the concept of *Nusah*. The *Nusah*—the formulaic or synthetic style of Hebrew fiction—is associated with Shalom Y. Abramovitz (known as *Mendele mokher sefarim*, Mendele the Book Peddler [1835–1917]). Abramovitz began his career as a Hebrew writer of the Haskalah (Jewish Enlightenment) in the 1860s, but then switched to Yiddish and became the most prominent Yiddish writer of the time. In the 1880s, he started translating his works from Yiddish to Hebrew and began to write Hebrew fiction again after a long break. The result was a new style of Hebrew prose. The literature of the Haskalah relied on biblical strata of Hebrew as its predominant resource; Abramovitz's prose simultaneously employs different historical layers of Hebrew, but the dominant layer is rabbinic.

Let me quote the opening paragraph of the story *Beseter ra'am* ("In the Secret of Thunder"). The story was published in Hebrew in 1886, and is

---

10. Richard Sheppard, "The Crisis of Language," in Bradbury and McFarlane, *Modernism*, 323.

11. Bradbury and McFarlane, *Modernism*, 394–415.

12. Theodore Adorno, *Aesthetic Theory* (trans. C. Lenhardt; International Library of Phenomenology and Moral Sciences; London: Routledge, 1984), 7; Astradur Eysteinsson, *The Concept of Modernism* (Ithaca, NY: Cornell University Press, 1990), 231–53.

considered to be the first story written in the revolutionary Hebrew style that ushered a new period in Hebrew fiction:

אמר מנדיל: זו כסלון העיר, שבה אפתח את סיפורי, חשובה היא ביותר, שכל
תחום־מושבם של היהודים נקרא בשמה. ולא לחינם זכתה לגדולה זו להיות עיר
ואם בישראל; שהרי אין אחד מאנשי מקומנו שלא יתיחס, אם מעט אם הרבה,
לכסלון, ולא תהא לכל הפחות שמינית שבשמינית מסגולותיה העצמיות נרשמת
בו. אם אתם, רבותי, לא נולדתם בעצמכם בכסלון, הריני בטוח, כי הוריכם היו
כסלונים, ואם דם כסלוני אינו נוזל בכל רמ״ח אבריכם ושס״ה גידיכם, על כל
פנים יש לו מקום באחד המקצועות שבמוחכם. נער הייתי וגם זקנתי ולא ראיתי
אחד מאחינו, שמתוך מעשיו והליכותיו ומנהגיו במילי דעלמא ובמילי דשמייא לא
יהא מציץ דבר מה מתכונות כסלוניות. בין הדיוטים ומשכילים, בין עניים
ועשירים, בכולם רשמי כסלון כדרבנות וכמסמרות נטועים.

> Mendele said: The city of Kisalon, in which I will open my story, is very important since the entire Jewish area is named after it. It is not for nothing that the city became as prominent as a mother of all cities. For there is no man among us who lacks a relationship to Kisalon, either great or small, and who does not have inscribed upon him at least a fraction of a fraction of her essential virtues. If you yourselves were not born in Kisalon, gentlemen, I am certain that your parents were Kisaloners; and if Kisalon blood is not flowing in all of your 248 joints and 365 sinews, I am certain that it at least has a place in one corner of your brain. I have been young and now I am old and I have never seen one of our brethren who, in actions, deeds, or customs—in matters of heaven or earth—has no trace of Kisalonic qualities. Whether ignorant or learned, poor or rich, in all of them the marks of Kisalon are as goads and as nails well-fastened.[13]

Without my going into details, it seems clear to me that in this passage most of the idioms, syntax, diction, and word morphology are rabbinic. This is apparent in the structure of syntactical subordination, which was not possible in the biblical style of the Haskalah. There is an extensive use of Aramaic expressions ("in matters of heaven or earth," מילי דעלמא ומילי דשמיא) and other rabbinic idioms, such as the traditional numbering of the body parts, 248 joints and 365 sinews (רמ״ח אברים ושס״ה גידים), or the form of exaggeration שמינית שבשמינית ("fraction of a fraction").

Stylistically, the *Nusah* is characterized by balanced and rhythmic sentences rich with synonyms ("in words, actions and deeds," מעשיו, הליכותיו ומנהגיו; "mother and city in Israel," עיר ואם בישראל), and parallelism ("whether ignorant or learned, poor or rich," בין הדיוטים ומשכילים בין עניים ועשירים). We also see an extensive use of puns and sound patterns. In short,

---

13. Shmuel Y. Abramovitz, "Beseter ra'am," in *Kol kitvei Mendele mokher sefarim* (Tel Aviv: Devir, 1947), 377. English translation is mine.

the *Nusah* style is marked by linguistic wealth, which is also an indication of playfulness and erudition, aesthetic harmony and unity.[14]

The synthetic solution of the *Nusah* was so successful that it immediately became a stylistic model for many writers, from Haim Nahman Bialik to Isaac D. Berkowitz, Shmuel Ben-Zion, Shmuel Y. Agnon (in some of his writing), Haim Hazzaz, and even Israeli writers like Moshe Shamir and Nathan Shaham. The transition from the *Nusah* to what came to be known (belatedly) as "anti-*Nusah*"[15] took many forms. It began during the first years of the twentieth century in stories of Micah Berdichevsky and is probably best exemplified by the modernist writing of Yosef H. Brenner, Uri N. Gnessin and Gershon Shofman. Since some of these writers were preoccupied with evoking process rather than essence, they needed to break with the harmonies and symmetries of Abramovitz's style. They began to write what was, from the point of view of the *Nusah*, "deviant," "distorted," or simply "bad" Hebrew. But ultimately such adjectives are useless, since this new breed of Hebrew prose was a means to realize different artistic goals. Therefore, the distinction between *Nusah* and anti-*Nusah* is important on a stylistic level. However, like many elements in the history of Hebrew literature, it became overloaded with historical and ideological meanings. As we shall see, this obfuscation of the stylistic by the ideological happened almost immediately, as stylistic issues in Jewish literature of the time were never "neutral."

Haim Nahman Bialik, the romantic Hebrew poet who is known as the "national" poet, coined the term *Nusah* in his well-known essay about Abramovitz, "The Creator of the *Nusah*," first published in 1910.[16] Bialik's definition of the *Nusah* in this fascinating essay is both descriptive and normative. For Bialik, the new style is the perfect literary means for a mimetic representation of the Jewish national collective. Clearly, Bialik's construction of the *Nusah* plays on the traditional meaning of the term as a conventional melody for chanting prayers that anyone could follow and emulate. Thus, Bialik understood the *Nusah* as a collective resource that could and should be adapted and transmitted. According to Bialik, Abramovitz "took, drop by drop, whatever he found in the treasure-house of the people's creative spirit and he gave it back, and in a refined form, to the same treasure-house."[17] In a typically romantic fashion, Bialik saw the *Nusah* as expressing "the essence of the national genius," and Abramovitz as "the first national artist in our literature."[18]

---

14. Shaked, *Hasipporet ha'ivrit*, 83–89; Alter, *Invention of Hebrew Prose*, 24–45.

15. Shaked, *Hasipporet ha'ivrit*, 205; Alter, *Invention of Hebrew Prose*, 45–67.

16. Haim Nahman Bialik, "Yotser hanusah," in *Kol kitvei H. N. Bialik* (Tel Aviv: Devir, 1953), 245–46.

17. Haim Nahman Bialik, "Mendele veshloshet hakrakhim," in *Kol kitvei H. N. Bialik*, 242–45.

18. Ibid., 249.

The romantic and national elements in Bialik's perspective clearly constitute his understanding of the rabbinic material itself, especially the haggadah—the nonlegal part of rabbinic literature. This can be seen in his anthology of narratives from rabbinic literature, *Sefer ha'aggadah* (The Book of Legends), which he compiled together with Yehoshua H. Ravnitzki in 1908. In this monumental work, Bialik sought to transform what he describes as the "messy," indiscernible haggadic material buried in the two Talmuds and Midrash into a crystallized "folk literature of the Jews," a well-structured monument that expresses "the spirit of the Nation."[19]

Midrash scholars such as Joseph Heineman, Ephraim E. Urbach, and David Stern have shown that the act of selection and rearrangement of the rabbinic material in the anthology was not without its price.[20] Bialik and Yehoshua H. Ravintzki not only translated all the original Aramaic of the Talmud and Midrash into homogeneous Hebrew (not so different from the *Nusah* style), but they also stripped the narratives of haggadah from their homiletical and exegetical setting, which for Bialik was reminiscent of the stifling environment of the old *Beit Midrash*. However, Bialik did not seem to recognize the loss. On the contrary, he felt that he was not only faithful to the haggadah but was actually "restoring the glory" of these neglected texts.[21]

Similar issues arise in the synthetic style of the *Nusah*. Despite all its stylistic richness, the modes of intertextuality in the *Nusah* style are limited, and create mainly mimetic and ironic effects.[22] Bialik could not see these problems, because for him, both the project of *kinnus* (gathering of haggadic materials) and the creation of a synthetic Hebrew literary style (*Nusah*) were used as central tropes for the "ingathering" of the scattered Jewish people who could recapture their glory by being reassembled in their "palace," the national territory.[23]

---

19. Haim Nahman Bialik, "Hakdama," in *Sefer ha'aggadah* (Tel Aviv: Devir, 1966); idem, "Lekinnusah shel ha'aggadah," in *Kol kitvei H. N. Bialik*, 220–22.

20. Joseph Heineman, "Al darko shel Bialik be'aggadat hazal," *Molad* 17 (1959): 266–74; Ephraim E. Urbach, "Darko shel Bialik be'aggadat hazal," *Molad* 31 (1974): 82–83; David Stern, introduction to *The Book of Legends*, ed. Haim Nahman Bialik and Yehoshua H. Ravnitzki (trans. William G. Braude; New York: Schocken, 1992), xvii–xxii; Mark Kiel, "*Sefer ha'aggadah*: Creating a Classic Anthology for the People and by the People," *Prooftexts* 17 (1997): 177–97.

21. Bialik, "Lekinnusah shel ha'aggada," 222. Around the same time as Bialik's project, Micah Berdichevsky was engaged in a similar yet different task of collecting rabbinic and haggadic materials into several anthologies like *Mimekor yisra'el, Tsfunot va'aggadot, Me'otsar ha'aggadah*. See Dan Ben Amos, introduction to *Mimekor yisra'el: Classical Jewish Folktales* (ed. Micah Berdichevsky; trans. Israel M. Lask; Philadelphia: Jewish Publication Society of America, 1976).

22. See Shachar Pinsker, "Old Wine in New Flasks: Rabbinic Intertexts and the Making of Modernist Hebrew Fiction" (Ph.D. diss., University of California Berkeley, 2001).

23. Bialik, "Lekinnusah shel ha'aggadah," 221; Israel Bartal, "The Ingathering of Traditions," *Prooftexts* 17 (1997): 77–93.

Later critical attempts to describe the history of Hebrew fiction align the stylistic distinction between *Nusah* and the anti-*Nusah* with the common binaries of Jewish/universal, social/psychological and collective/individual.[24] The writings of Bialik and his contemporaries (such as Joseph Klausner and Pinhas Lachover) already contained these dichotomies and paved the way for the framework in which modernist Hebrew fiction is understood even to this day.[25] Thus, the fiction of the so-called anti-*Nusah* writers becomes synonymous with Hebrew literature that is stripped of its distinctive Jewish elements.

This notion of Hebrew modernism as related to the style of the anti-*Nusah* was one of the reasons why many modernist writers were rejected during their lifetime, while in recent decades it has become the very reason for the recanonization of writers such as Gnessin and Fogel. In the state of Israel during the late 1950s and early 1960s arose a new generation, known as *dor hamedinah* (statehood generation), of writers such as Nathan Zach, Amos Oz, and A. B. Yehoshua, as well as critics like Gershon Shaked, Gavriel Moked, and Dan Miron. As the poetics of this statehood generation became the new literary and ideological norm, it has also turned out to be the *telos* of a new Hebrew modernist lineage. In this revised canon, certain modernist writers have been reevaluated and reconstructed as an anachronistic "genesis" of secular Hebrew fiction. These writers are lauded for expressing a quasi-"universal" subjectivity. This construct of "universal subject," trying desperately to erase its own ethnic, religious, and gender identity, becomes in turn the model for the abstract "national citizen" in the Israeli literature of the statehood generation.[26]

This retrospective view of Hebrew modernism is problematic. Within this scheme, many crucial elements in the fiction of Gnessin, Fogel, Shofman, and others are ignored and suppressed.[27] These dichotomies also

---

24. Halkin, *Modern Hebrew Literature*, 344–79; Shaked, *Hasipporet ha'ivrit*, 215; Avner Holtzman, *Hasippur ha'ivri hakatsar bereshit hame'a ha'esrim* (Tel Aviv: Open University, 1993), 79–88; Govrin, *Tlishut vehithadshut*, 26–55.

25. Joseph Klausner, *Yotsrim uvonim*, vol. 2 (Tel Aviv: Devir, 1929), 124–26; Yeruham Fishel Lakhover, *Toldot hasifrut ha'ivrit hahadashah* (Tel Aviv: Devir, 1936–48); Shlomo Zemach, *Masot ureshimot* (Rmat Gan: Masada, 1968), 39–61.

26. Hannan Hever, *Producing the Modern Hebrew Canon: Nation Building and Minority Discourse* (New York: New York University Press, 2002); Hamutal Zamir, "Hanof me'abed et shmo," *Jerusalem Studies in Hebrew Literature* 19 (2003): 219–24. On the "national subject" and the relations between nationalism and literature in general, see Benedict Anderson, *Imagined Communities: Reflections on the Origin and Spread of Nationalism* (London: Verso, 1991); Homi Bhabha, *The Location of Culture* (New York/London: Routledge, 1994), 139–70.

27. The only critic to seriously challenge this view of Hebrew modernism as early as the late 1950s was Baruch Kurzweil; see Baruch Kurzweil, *Sifrutenu hahadashah hemshekh 'o mahpekhah* (Jerusalem: Schocken, 1959); idem, *Bein hazon levein ha'absurdi* (Jerusalem: Schocken, 1966), esp. v–xvi, 333–58.

leave little room for the fiction of a writer such as Dvora Baron, the only canonical Hebrew woman writer in this period. Therefore, paying sustained and careful attention to the intertextual relationship between early modernist Hebrew fiction and rabbinic texts is a necessary step toward a critical reexamination of this corpus.

There Is No Place Without It

The literary work of Uri Nissan Gnessin (born in Starodub, Ukraine, in 1879) and its critical reception epitomize the shifting trends in early-twentieth-century Hebrew literature and culture. During Gnessin's lifetime, critics, readers, and some other writers found his Hebrew style deviant and unacceptable, and his stories and novellas "foreign," "decadent," and "empty of content."[28] However, later, and especially since the early 1960s, critics have begun to direct their attention toward the technical accomplishments of Gnessin's narratives, which they see as akin to a European "stream of consciousness" style.[29] Since then, Gnessin's fiction has been recognized as an important stylistic model for later Hebrew writers such as Ya'acov Shabtai and Amalia Cahana-Karmon. Yet Gnessin's fiction is still considered today to be irrelevant to the major cultural issues that occupied Hebrew literature in the first half of the twentieth century.

One key reason for this paradoxical situation is that Gnessin was considered a "European" modernist whose writing was not related to Jewish language and themes. Gershon Shaked, for example, comes to this conclusion: "The fictional world that Gnessin created is not related to Jews in particular, and the associative infrastructure of his work is not Jewish."[30] Avner Holtzman notes that "more than other writers of his generation, Gnessin removes himself from the horizon of Jewish themes. Rather, his stories reflect the Russian intellectual and mental atmosphere."[31] There is no doubt that Gnessin's fiction was highly receptive to Russian and other European modernist movements of the time,[32] but his way of participating

---

28. See the various remarks on Gnessin in Lily Rattok, ed., *Uri Nissan Gnessin: mivhar ma'amarei bikkoret al yetsirato* (Tel Aviv: Hakibutz Hameuhad, 1977), especially those by Haim Nahman Bialik, Ya'acov Rabinovits, and Shlomo Tsemah.
29. Gershon Shaked, *Lelo Motsa* (Tel Aviv: Hakibutz Hameuhad, 1973), 155–75; Hamutal Bar-Yosef, *Metaforot usemalim biyetsirato shel Gnessin* (Tel Aviv: Hakibutz Hameuhad, 1987); Miron, *Kivvun orot*, 109–209.
30. Shaked, *Hasipporet ha'ivrit*, 424.
31. Holtzman, *Hasippur ha'ivri hakatsar*, 94.
32. Gnessin translated into Hebrew short stories by Anton Chekhov and an essay by the Russian Jewish writer Lev Shestov; from French he translated *Poems in Prose* by Baudelaire, and from German, Obstfelder's short novel *The Cross* and Wasserman's *The Jews from Zurendorf*. On Gnessin and the Russian context, see Itamar Even Zohar, "Gnessin's Dialogue

in this modernist project can be understood only if we pay attention to Gnessin's predicament as a Jewish and Hebrew writer. I maintain that Gnessin's stories and novellas are engaged in an intense intertextual dialogue with rabbinic vocabulary, idioms, expressions, syntax, narrative structures, and themes.

Let me present one short example of what I call Gnessin's intertextual strategy.[33] Following is a key passage in his third novella *Beterem* (Beforehand), published in 1909, in which Uriel Efros, the anti-hero of the novella, contemplates his relationship with his Russian landlady in Kiev. Like most of Gnessin's male protagonists, Uriel is torn between his compulsive attraction to the sexuality of the "other" and his inability to make any significant erotic or emotional contact:

אוריאל הפסיק את טיולו ומידי הביטו אל המטרוניתא שלו, שהייתה כל אותה שעה מוטלת דומם ובפנים של נעלבים ואינם עולבים בנדנדה וכפיה הקטנות אוחזות בסומכות, התנפל אל פינת הסופה הרכה שממולה ומיהר להצית פאפירוסה השד משחת. . . . נו, למה זו יושבת בכאן ופניה ארוכים? את השטויות הללו כבר אינו אוהב. וכי מה הוא נוטל משלה? או שמא הייתה חושבת בתחילה, שנצח יהיה לה מי שיהא שותה את ביצותיה? חה. האריכה פניה משל שממית באה אל גרונה. במטותא, לא בו באשמתו, שפוקה אלווילוויץ׳ שלה, זה האינז׳נית הקצר והמסורבל בבשר, קרחתו הוורודה רטובה לו תמיד וירחים רצופים אינו נמצא בביתו . . . אבל אחר־כך הגישו את ארוחת הבוקר, ואוריאל היה יושב וצוחק דומם לקראת המטרוניתא, שהייתה גם־כן מצחקת לו נוגות, והיה מקבל באהבה את כל מצווה קלה כחמורה שלה. ביצים שלוקות? אדרבה ואדרבה. מה? כוס חלב יש לקינוח? אח, זה יהיה יפה אבל—סופגניות—סופגניות אל מלא רחמים—סופגניות! המנוולות הללו! וכמה דשנות.

> Uriel stopped pacing around and glanced at his *Matronita* (lady), who all that time was lying peacefully, with an expression of everlasting patience (literally, these who are insulting but not insulted) in the rocking chair with her little hands on the chair's arms. He jumped onto the corner of the soft sofa right opposite her and quickly lit his cigarette. To hell with that! Well, why was she sitting here with such a sad face (literally, long face)? He didn't like this kind of nonsense anymore. What was he taking from her? Or maybe she thought that he would sit in here and eat her eggs forever? Ah-Ah—she pulled a face as though a reptile had jumped into her throat. Oh please! Was it really his fault that her man—Poka Eviloviz, the short and stocky engineer, whose pink bald scalp is always damp, isn't

---

and Its Russian Models," *Slavica Hierosolymitana* 7 (1985): 17–36; Anna Petrov Ronell, "Reading Gnessin's Sideways in Its Russian Context," *Journal of Modern Jewish Studies* 3 (2004): 167–82.

33. There is an extensive theoretical literature about intertextuality. For a good introduction to and summery of the field, see Graham Allen, *Intertextuality* (London, Routledge, 2000). See also Jay Clayton and Erich Rothstein, *Influence and Intertextuality in Literary History* (Madison: University of Wisconsin Press, 1991). For a detailed discussion of intertextuality in Hebrew modernism, see Pinsker, "Old Wine in New Flasks."

home for months at a time? . . . But later, they served the breakfast, and Uriel would sit and smile quietly to his *Matronita*, who was also smiling sadly at him, and he would accept with love every one of her commands, lenient or strict. Poached eggs? Of course! A glass of milk for dessert? That would be lovely. But—Oh! God full of mercy—doughnuts! Those damn doughnuts, how greasy they were![34]

In this passage, the narrative switches constantly between what Dorit Cohn calls psycho-narration (the report of the character's thoughts and feeling in the language of the narrator), and narrated monologue (the representation of the inner speech of the character).[35] This combined narrative style, the signature of Gnessin's modernist prose, is enabled through the use of the rabbinic tense *haya* + *poel*: היה יושב, הייתה מצחקת, היה מקבל, which literally translates as "was sitting, was laughing, was receiving." By using this tense, which is found only in Mishnaic and Midrashic Hebrew, Gnessin achieves a sense of habitual, repetitive action that results in blurring both the framework of time and the distinctions between reality and fantasy.[36]

This stylistic device, made possible by Gnessin's reliance on rabbinic syntax, extends from the syntactic to the semantic level and becomes significant in the description of Uriel's relations with the landlady who is also his lover in Kiev. The woman who seduces Uriel is represented in the narrative not in the usual way in Hebrew fiction, using the word "woman" or "foreign woman," but as a *Matronita*. This figure is a distinct character in rabbinic literature, a powerful and highly sexual foreign woman (usually an upper-class Roman or Babylonian woman). In many stories, the *Matronita* seduces a male rabbi and demands a sexual relationship, as in these excerpts from two stories in the Babylonian Talmud and Midrash *Leviticus Rabbah*:

> "Ye mighty in strength that fulfil his word," e.g. R. Zadok. . . . A certain *Matronita* made demands on R. Zadok. He said to her: my heart is faint and I am unable, do you have anything to eat? She answered him: there is unclean (*tame*) food. He retorted: He who commits this may eat this. She then fired the oven and was placing it therein. He ascended and sat in it. She said to him: What is the meaning of this? He said: He who commits the one falls into the other [the fire]. She said: had I known that it is so heinous, I would not have tormented you.

---

34. All the references to Gnessin's stories and other writings are from the 1982 edition of his collected works in Uri N. Gnessin, *Kol kitvei Uri Nissan Gnessin* (ed. Dan Miron and Israel Zmora; Tel Aviv: Hakibutz Hameuchad, 1982). Translations of Gnessin's original works are my own.

35. Dorit Cohn, *Transparent Minds: Narrative Modes for Presenting Consciousness in Fiction* (Princeton, NJ: Princeton University Press, 1978).

36. Alter, *Invention of Hebrew Prose*, 56.

> R. Kahana was selling baskets [in the market], when a certain *Matronita* made demands upon him. He said: I will first adorn myself. He then ascended and hurled himself from the roof towards earth, but Elijah came and caught him. . . . R. Kahana told him: what caused me this, is it not poverty? So he gave him a pocket full of denari. (*b. Qidd.* 40a)

In other cases, the *Matronita* engages in an intellectual/theological dispute with the male rabbi in which sexual overtones permeate the debate and the power struggle between the two:

> A *Matronita* asked R. Yose b. Halafta, in how many days did the Holy One Blessed be He, create His world? He answered: In six days. . . . She asked further: and what has He been doing since that time? He answered: He is joining couples [proclaiming]: A's wife to be allotted to A. A's daughter is allotted to B. She said: This is a thing which I, too, am able to do. See how many male slaves and how many female slaves I have; I can make them consort together. He said: If in your eyes it is an easy task, it is in His eyes as hard a task as the dividing of the Red Sea. He then went away and left her. What did she do? She sent for a thousand male slaves and a thousand female slaves, placed them in rows, and said to them: Male A shall take to wife female B, C shall take D and so on. She let them consort together one night. In the morning, they came to her, one had a head wounded, another an eye taken out. She sent to R. Yose b. Halafta and said to him: Rabbi, your Torah is true, fine and excellent. (*Lev. Rab.* 8:1)

By using the topos of *Matronita* from rabbinic texts, Gnessin invokes a whole cultural framework, which requires the reader to be attuned to the complex emotional, sexual, and cultural position of his protagonist. Mainly, these intertextual patterns mark as culturally problematic the fact that the woman with whom Uriel is involved is a foreign, non-Jewish woman. In addition, they highlight the differences in class and social status. Like the *Matronita* in rabbinic literature, Gnessin's Russian woman is high or upper middle-class, while Uriel is a poor young man from the provinces who seeks a new life in Kiev, like many Jewish male "uprooted" characters in the literature of the period. Moreover, the mixture of attraction and rejection, dependence on and fear of the foreign woman is made more palpable, and more significant, by the intertextual relationship with the *Matronita* so well known by the readers from the rabbinic texts.

When this intertextual framework is established, the readers notice many other rabbinic terms and expressions, such as "those who are insulting but not insulted" (נעלבים ואינם עולבים) (*b. Yoma* 23a), or "accept with love every command, lenient or strict" (מקבל באהבה כל מצווה קלה כחמורה) (*m. Avot* 2:1). These idioms and expressions in Gnessin's texts, which are used to describe Uriel, the woman, and the relations between them, allude to identical or similar expressions in rabbinic texts. It is highly significant that many of these expressions describe the ideal of passivity and gentleness—the "unheroic conduct" of the male rabbi.³⁷ In addition, the passage quoted above makes extensive use of the connection between food and sexuality, which is prevalent in rabbinic discourse.³⁸ Gnessin employs these traditional metaphors and expressions in order to convey the sensation of attraction and repulsion that is central to the mental world of Uriel Efros.³⁹ For sure, there is a radical transformation of meaning in the way Gnessin uses these rabbinic idioms, vocabulary, and themes. The ironic transformation of an expression such as "he accepts with love her every command, lenient or strict," or calling the Russian lover a *Matronita*, when it is applied to this love affair is quite clear. However, the employment of intertextual patterns is far from being only ironic. The transformation carries with it significant layers of meaning from rabbinic literature that are quite important to understanding Gnessin's fiction and the inner world of his characters.

Apart from its importance to understanding the world of this specific novella, the example is paradigmatic of intertextuality in Gnessin's fiction in a few ways: The implied readers can only glean patterns of meaning from the invocation of this rabbinic topos by inference, since the topos in its rabbinic context is mostly absent from the text itself, and the explicit marker of intertextuality is a single word. Furthermore, the meaning is evoked by intertextual relations between Gnessin's text and the accumulation of the various rabbinic sources in which the character of the *Matronita* appears. The intertextual language, thus, does not call attention to itself, but neither does it prevent the associative infrastructure from evoking various complex systems of meaning.⁴⁰

This intertextual strategy has more than one function in Gnessin's modernist fiction. It exemplifies the subtle but powerful way in which this fiction raises issues of ethnic, cultural, and sexual identity. The young Jewish protagonists in Gnessin's fiction are represented as caught between modernity and tradition even after they abandon tradition. At the same time, this linguistic interplay between different discursive systems illustrates the equally modernistic preoccupation with modes of representation and the modernist sense of disintegration of individual subjectivity.

Gnessin expresses the state of ennui of the modern Jewish man, the metaphysical void, as well as the modernist crisis of representation and

---

37. Daniel Boyarin, *Unheroic Conduct: The Rise of Heterosexuality and the Invention of the Jewish Man* (Contraversions 8; Berkeley: University of California Press, 1997).

38. Daniel Boyarin, *Carnal Israel: Reading Sex in Talmudic Culture* (New Historicism 25; Berkeley: University of California Press, 1993); Michael Satlow, *Tasting the Dish: Rabbinic Rhetorics of Sexuality* (Atlanta: Scholars Press, 1995).

39. Miron, *Kivun 'orot*, 176–95.

40. Pinsker, "Old Wine in New Flasks," 15–119; Ziva Ben-Porat, "The Poetics of Allusion," *PTL: A Journal for Descriptive Poetics and Theory of Literature* 1 (1976): 105–28.

the writer's self-consciousness about using fictional language, through a rabbinic/kabbalistic formulation:

יש שאתה נזכר פתאום בארשת פנים חביבים שבלב טוב, בבוקר אחד צוהל של נגוהות, בלילה כחול של מנוחה, כביכול—אבל הלא זה אינו כלום לגבי מה שיש. כלום. ומה שיש, לית אתר פנוי מיניה, חביבי. לית אתר פנוי מיניה.

> Sometimes you suddenly remember the welcoming face of a warm heart, a happy morning of splendor, one blue night of rest, as if to say so—but this is nothing in relation to what there is. Nothing! And what there is— there is no place without it, my friend. There is no place without it.[41]

As in the previous example, the patterns of meaning in this intertextual moment are manifold. Besides the activation of the "original" meaning in the alluded text, there is a radical displacement of meaning. In this example, Gnessin's text employs the Aramaic expression לית אתר פנוי מיניה ("there is no place without it"), which is used in rabbinic, kabbalistic and Hasidic texts to describe the *Shekinah*—the immanent presence of God, to describe the existential and psychological void and lack of coherence.[42]

What remains powerful in Gnessin's textual world, however, is the echo chamber of Hebrew language. In Gnessin's fiction, the statement "there is no place without it" can be also read as a meta-poetic statement. It articulates the sense of inability to escape the "prison house" of language in general, and the multilayered history of Hebrew language in particular. Therefore, just as Gnessin's fiction constructs a modernist subjectivity, it also uses elements from the Jewish textual world in order to represent it.

Uri Nissan Gnessin was a pioneer of Hebrew early modernism. In the stories and novellas that he wrote during the first decade of the twentieth century, he created a refined style of Hebrew narrative that was as revolutionary and innovative as any of the modernist European authors who wrote in French, German, or Russian. This literary innovator is the same young man who was barely out of the yeshiva in the small town of Puchep, where his father was the Hasidic Lubavitch rabbi. Gnessin's education equipped him with a language that was a relic of the old world of traditional Judaism (which he seemingly left behind) but at the same time could also express quite aptly the rupture and complexities of modernist subjectivity. Gnessin was indifferent to any Zionist or national activity, but he was highly committed to Hebrew and to the exploration of the dilemmas of modern Jewish culture. In order to understand the outstanding achievement of Gnessin, and the emergence of Hebrew modernism in this period,

---

41. Gnessin, *Kol kitvei*, 215.
42. Dan Miron, *Hahim be'appo shel hanetsah* (Jerusalem: Mosad Bialik, 1997), 387.

we must reckon with the fact that Gnessin's fiction simultaneously marks a radical break with Jewish textual tradition and forms another fascinating and challenging chapter in the very tradition it repudiates.

What Remained of the Melody of Gemara?

It is possible to trace similar, though not identical, dynamics in the work of the poet and prose writer David Fogel. Fogel was born in 1891 in Podolia. In 1912, he immigrated to Vienna, and later to Paris, where he continued writing Hebrew poetry and fiction until his death in 1944. This was at a time when the center of Hebrew literature and culture was gradually shifting to Mandatory Palestine. Even more often than Gnessin, Fogel was perceived by many readers and critics as the Hebrew modernist writer most remote from Jewish language or themes.

The history of the literary reception of Fogel's work has already been written and analyzed more than once.[43] For my purposes, it is important to note that during his lifetime, Fogel's fiction and poetry were rejected, usually with a mixture of misapprehension and shock.[44] In the 1960s, though, his poetry became a model for statehood generation poets like Nathan Zach and Dan Pagis.[45] In the last two decades, Fogel has also been rediscovered as a writer of prose fiction. However, this recent "rediscovery" of Fogel's fiction is, yet again, part of an ideological and poetic struggle, this time to advance Hebrew fiction that is understood to be "universal" rather than "particular" or "Jewish." Note the following analysis of Fogel's Hebrew style by Shaked written in 1986 and reflecting the prevailing attitude during the period in which Fogel's fiction was republished and attracted much attention:

> Fogel's secular language has liberated itself from the norms of literary Hebrew, the burden of its cultural accumulation and the yoke of its

---

43. Michael Gluzman, "The Politics of Simplicity in Fogel's Poetry," *Prooftexts* 13 (1994): 15–20; Chana Kronfled, "Fogel and Modernism: A Liminal Moment in Hebrew Literary History," *Prooftexts* 13 (1994): 45–63; Dan Miron, "Ahavah hatluyah badavar," in *Adderet levinyamin* (ed. Ziva Ben-Porat; Tel Aviv: Hakibbutz Hameuhad, 1999), 29–95.

44. Early criticism of Fogel's poetry was published by Ya'acov Rabinovitz (1922), Avraham Shlonsky (1922), Yehudah Lavi (1923), David A. Friedmann (1923), Ben-Zion Katz (1927), Baruch Katzenelson (1930), Isaac Norman (1932). Early responses to Fogel's novel and novellas include Avraham Broydes, "On the Novel Hayyei nissu'im," *Davar* 25, no. 2 (1930); H. Yatsiv, "Hayyei nissu'im," *Davar* 6, no. 7 (1930); Moshe Shlanger, "'Al hayyei nissu'im," *Ktuvim* 29, no. 5 (1930).

45. Nathan Zach, "About a Forgotten Poet" (in Hebrew), *Masa* (August 23, 1954); idem, *Zeman veritmus etsel Bergson uvashirah hamodernit* (Tel Aviv: Alef, 1966); Dan Pagis, introduction to *Kol hashirim*, by David Fogel (Tel Aviv: Hakibutz Hameuhad, 1966): 14–70.

symbolic meaning. I wish to emphasize that the language is one clear sign of Fogel's having cut himself off the mainstream of Jewish tradition.[46]

How accurate is this perception of Fogel as the Hebrew modernist most remote from Jewish language, who fashions a "secular language" that has freed itself from the "burden" of the cultural accumulation of meaning?

Fogel's novel *Hayyei nissu'im* (Married Life) is an interesting case.[47] The novel takes place in Vienna between the two world wars. It recounts the troubled relations between the young Jewish intellectual Rudolf Gurdweill and his Viennese wife Thea Von-Takow. The notion that *Hayyei nissu'im* is an "Austrian-Viennese novel that *happened* to be written in Hebrew"[48] is so common that it has hardly ever been challenged. According to Menahem Perri, the editor and critic who was instrumental in rediscovering Fogel's prose in the 1980s, and Shaked, who helped put his work into historical and literary perspective, Fogel "was powerfully influenced by the decadent atmosphere of Vienna, the writings of Otto Weininger, and other Viennese writers such as Arthur Schnitzler, Beer-Hoffman, Stefan Zweig and Herman Bahr."[49]

It is a mistake, however, to see *Hayyei nissu'im* as an imitation of a decadent Viennese literature whose Hebrew is coincidental.[50] There is no doubt that Fogel was part of the Jewish Viennese cultural milieu and was highly attuned to all the literary and cultural developments during the years he lived and worked there. Moreover, the plot of the novel indeed employs many of the concerns, motifs, and even clichés of the Viennese decadent novel. But the fact that Fogel employs Hebrew as a language of fictional representation is the crucial twist of the novel and its most interesting aspect. The appropriation of the decadent novel is made possible precisely by highlighting Hebrew as a "literary" nonvernacular language, which is not the language of the fictional universe. By using Hebrew this way, Fogel

---

46. Gershon Shaked, "A Viennese Author Who Wrote in Hebrew," *Modern Hebrew Literature* 11 (1986): 20–27; idem, afterword to *Hayyei nissu'im*, by David Fogel (Tel Aviv: Hakibutz Hameuhad, 1986), 335–44.

47. David Fogel, *Hayyei nissu'im* (Tel Aviv: Mitzpeh, 1929–30).

48. Shaked, "Viennese Author"; Menahem Perri, Afterword to *Haye nisu'im*, by David Fogel; Yair Mazor, *Lo al hashir levado* (Tel Aviv: University Press, 1986); Hamutal Bar-Yosef, "Life of Love and Marriage in Vienna" (in Hebrew), *Yediot Aharonot* (May 15, 1987); Ariel Hirshfeld, "Lethal Love" (in Hebrew), *Koteret Rashit* 207 (1986); Aharon Komem, "The Drama of Guilt and Innocence" (in Hebrew), *Maariv* (May 15, 1987).

49. Shaked, "Viennese Author," 21–22; Perri, "Introduction." On decadent literature, see Mario Praz, *The Romantic Agony* (New York: Meridian Books, 1956); Jacques Le Rider, *Modernism and the Crises of Identity: Culture and Society in Fin-de-Siècle Vienna* (New York: Continuum, 1993).

50. To the best of my knowledge, the first critic to state that this conception is misguided was Yoram Bronovsky, "The Woman, the Vampire, the Man, the Rabbit" (in Hebrew), *Ha'aretz* (June 12, 1987).

creates a mimetic dissonance that thematizes the modernist preoccupation with language, representation, and subjectivity, and literally houses these themes within the novel itself.

Because of the nature of my discussion here, it is impossible to engage in a comprehensive analysis of the novel. However, one paradigmatic example can help to demonstrate the intertextual strategies that are common in this novel:

ריח חריף ונעים של עור מעובד ושל צבעי אריג טריים נדף מן המחסנים הפתוחים. הורגשה מסביב עבודה מרובה, עבודה חשאית ומאומצת, ובגורדוויל נתעוררה תשוקה לגשת ולסייע לפועלים לטעון את הארגזים, לתמוך ביד ובכתף ולנצח כוח-ההתנגדותו של המטען. אותו רגע ראה את עצמו כמנודח, כמוצא מכלל המסייעים לקיומו של עולם. ככל אלו שאינם מסוגלים לעבודה גסה מפאת העדר הכוחות הגופניים, ראה דווקא בזו את הדרך לסיפוקו השלם של האדם. גורדוויל נתייצב מרחוק והביט בקנאה אל הפועלים. לא, עם הללו ודאי שלא יכול היה להתחרות! שלח מבט מזלזל בגופו הצנום והקטן, שנדמה לו כעשוי רק עצבים ומוח לבד, וניתק ממקומו. לא הספיק לעבור צעדים מועטים והנה נדמה לו שקוראים בשמו.

> A pungent, pleasant smell of leather and freshly dyed fabric wafted out of the open warehouse doors. All around there was a sense of industrious labor, furtive and strenuous labor, and Gurdweill felt an urge to go up to the workers and help them load the carts, to lend a hand and shoulder and overcome the resistance of the heavy load. At that moment, he saw himself as exiled, excluded from being among people who are helping to sustain the world. Like all those who are unfit for physical [lit., gross] labor because of lack of bodily strength, he considered that to be the only way for a person to achieve a full satisfaction. Gurdweill stood at a distance and watched the workers with envy. No, of course he could not compete with men like these! He cast a derisive glance at his own skinny and small body, which seemed to him to be made of nerves and brain alone, and he detached himself and moved away. He hardly walked a few steps when he thought he heard someone calling his name.[51]

This passage is a good example of Fogel's distinct modernist Hebrew style, oscillating between impressionist and expressionist modes of narration.[52] It begins with sensory impressions, the smell of the fabrics and leather and the sight of workers loading the carts. These impressions prompt Gurdweill's urge to join the workers, but here the inner consciousness of his shrunken body takes over. In this process, Gurdweill is defined as a subject through and against the "other," the Viennese workers around him.

---

51. Fogel, *Hayyei nissu'im*, 18. The quotations from the novel are taken from the original publication (1929–30) and not from the mixed version that was published in 1986. Translation is mine.

52. Kronfeld, "Fogel and Modernism," 45–46.

He senses himself as an absence, and his body as a mental fragment made only of *brain and nerves*. In the theoretical framework of Judith Butler, we could say that Gurdweill's inertia in spite of his desire mirrors his inability to form subjectivity free from the implicated gaze of the "other."[53]

But the process of the shattering of the experience of the "self" is not merely about an abstract, universal construct. The Hebrew language that Fogel uses is what indicates the relations between subjectivity, desire, and cultural identity. For example, Gurdweill's sense of being different from the Viennese workers is articulated by verbs and expressions that have many echoes in the Jewish textual tradition, such as "being in exile" (מנודח), and "excluded" (מוצא מן הכלל), which literally means "taken out of the collective"). The Hebrew word מנודח is based on a biblical verb form found only in Isa 8:22. The rare passive participle form is a modernist *portmanteau* of two different roots: דחה (reject) and נדה (excommunicate). This combination of verbs was possible because of the extensive use of the form נדה, which in rabbinic texts means both to reject and to be wayward (as in the "wayward city"), and the verb נדה, which is used in the sense of excommunication.[54] In Fogel's hands, these words designate a kind of internal punishment for the temptation posed by the "other."

The expression "taken out of the collective" creates a similar pattern of meaning. The notion of *klal*, or *klal yisra'el* in rabbinic texts designates an inclusive national/ethnic collective. In this passage, the group of Viennese workers is constructed as the collective of those who sustain the world (כלל המסייעים לקיומו של עולם). This expression highlights the surprising ways in which traditional concepts and language are employed in Fogel's prose, in a manner that Walter Benjamin has elsewhere called "against the grain."[55]

In rabbinic texts, the few righteous people who are fully engaged in Torah study are referred to as those who sustain the world—מסייעים לקיומו של עולם. For example, tractate *Shabbat* in the Babylonian Talmud includes the following statement (119b): אין העולם מתקיים אלא בשביל הבל תינוקות של בית רבן ("The world endures only for the sake of the breath of school children"). Likewise, earlier in the same tractate (114a), is the following remark: בנאים אלו תלמידי חכמים שעוסקים בבנינו של עולם כל ימיהם ("*Banna'im* [builders], these are scholars, who are engaged all their days in the upbuilding of the world").

---

53. See Judith Butler, *The Psychic Life of Power: Theories of Subjection* (Stanford: Stanford University Press, 1997), 2–11.

54. *B. Sanh.* 50a; *t. Qidd.* 4:8; *t. Sanh.* 14:1. On the word מנודה as excommunicated, see *Avot R. Nat.* 1:1; *b. Eruv.* 100b; *t. Meg.* 1:2.

55. Walter Benjamin, "Theses on the Philosophy of History," in *Illuminations* (ed. Hannah Arendt; trans. Harry Zohn; New York: Schocken, 1968).

Similarly, the mixture of desire and disdain for the physical, manual labor that Gurdweill cannot perform is represented in the Hebrew narrative as "crude labor" (עבודה גסה), which the character sees as necessary to achieve full satisfaction. This crude labor counters the implicit traditional Jewish notion of intellectual satisfaction and productivity whose masculine model is the Torah scholar and its later incarnation, the *mentsch*.

These intertextual patterns signal the simultaneous multiplicity of cultural systems that inform the narrator's discourse. Throughout, the novel uses perceptions not only common in anti-Semitic discourse but also prevalent in some Zionist-national writings of the era: the view of the diasporic Jew as an unproductive *luftmentsch*, alternatively characterized as "decadent," "feminine," or "homosexual."[56] Such attitudes are boldly juxtaposed with the traditional Jewish valorization of spiritual and intellectual work. A crucial aspect of Fogel's modernism is that these conflicting systems are evoked without an attempt to create cohesion or integration.[57]

These intertextual patterns make us realize that Fogel was *not* an outsider who cut himself off from the Hebrew and Jewish tradition. For Gnessin and Fogel, as well as other writers who insisted on writing Hebrew fiction in Eastern and Central Europe, outside the context of the national territorialization of Hebrew in Palestine, the attempt to forge a modernist subjectivity unveils the surprising force of this language as a medium for modernist narrative as well as for a profound examination of cultural identity.[58] In many ways, Fogel's modernist critique of subjectivity and his critique of the human condition must be understood as specifically Jewish. One important way is his use of the Hebrew language, and his unique modernist Hebrew style. In its continuing dialogue with the Jewish textual tradition, Fogel's fictional work tells us as much about Hebrew modernism as about the complexity of modern Jewish identity.

A *Heder* of Her Own

It is clear, I hope, that the nature of modernist Hebrew fiction and the intertextual engagement with rabbinic texts has important cultural and ideological implications. This is especially true for writers such as Gnessin and Fogel as well as for Shofman and other writers in this period, for whom

---

56. Boyarin, *Unheroic Conduct*, 51–72; David Biale, *Eros and the Jews* (New York: Basic Books, 1992), 149–76; Michael Gluzman, "The Longing for Heterosexuality: Zionism and Sexuality in *Altneuland*" (in Hebrew), *Te'oryah uvikkoret* 11 (1997): 145–62.

57. Eric Zakim, "Between Fragment and Authority in David Fogel's Representation of Subjectivity," *Prooftexts* 13 (1994): 103–24.

58. Robert Alter, *Hebrew and Modernity* (Bloomington: Indiana University Press, 1994), 62–74.

the very existence of their Hebrew text becomes a kind of portable homeland. Against the process of the territorialization of Hebrew language and literature, they created Hebrew fictional worlds in the multilingual environment of Kiev, Vilna, Warsaw, Vienna, Berlin, London, and Paris. In this context, their act of reimagination and reappropriation of traditional Jewish texts is also a form of cultural resistance. They point to a zone of freedom that is always beyond reference—that is, beyond the hermetic cohesion between nationality, language, territory, and ethnic identity.[59]

However, it would be wrong to limit my discussion to Hebrew modernists in Eastern and Central Europe. There were other writers in this period who immigrated to Palestine but resisted the ideological imperative to write about the newly created Jewish national-Zionist collective or about the individual and representative national subject.[60] One of these writers is Dvora Baron, who chose to continue writing about Eastern European towns and *shtetls* both before and after her immigration in 1910.

Baron was also the only recognized woman writer in a time when Hebrew literature was the nearly exclusive domain of men. For these and other reasons, the critical reception of her work is fraught with contradictions. While many were enthusiastic about the appearance of a woman writer, very few took her writing seriously on its own terms.[61] Because Baron does not fit neatly into the dichotomies of *Nusah* and anti-*Nusah*, social and psychological, Jewish and universal, she is typically left outside the Hebrew modernist map.[62]

Any reader of Baron's fiction would notice that she employs many biblical, talmudic, and midrashic texts in her stories. Nurit Govrin, one of the most important scholars of Baron's work and her biographer, even describes her stories as "born out of the verse."[63] Govrin's assumption is that Baron's stories represent a conceptual system in which a verse is exemplified or illustrated by a narrative, and the narrator is parallel to a traditional preacher. This critical assumption seems to reinforce the standard reading of Baron as a traditionalist, nonmodernist writer who is telling autobiographical tales about her childhood's *shtetl* and documenting its milieu. In this context, Baron's employment of midrashic language and techniques is read as compatible with the represented world of the *shtetl* and its presumed "static" mode of representation.[64]

---

59. Hever, *Modern Hebrew Canon*, 37–44.
60. Ibid.; Kronfeld, *Margins of Modernism*, 1–17.
61. Naomi Seidman, *Marriage Made in Heaven: The Sexual Politics of Hebrew and Yiddish* (Berkeley: University of California Press, 1997), 67–92; Orly Lubin, "Tidbits from Nechama's Kitchen: Alternative Nationalism in Dvora Baron's Fiction" (in Hebrew), *Te'oryah uvikkoret* 7 (1995): 159–76.
62. Shaked, *Hasipporet ha'ivrit*, 452–66; Miron, *Kivvun orot*, 378–94.
63. Nurit Govrin, *Hamahatsit harishonah* (Jerusalem: Mosad Bialik, 1988), 128.
64. See, e.g., the essays about Baron and her fiction by Ya'acov Fikhman (1932), Pinhas

In fact, Baron's stories are a fascinating case of modernist fiction in disguise: her fiction was not recognized as modernist until very recently because of the traditional camouflage it wears, both in narrative style and subject matter. But looking deeper, we see that Baron makes sophisticated and occasionally subversive use of the exegetical and narrative aspects of Midrash, homilies, and other traditional genres. It is precisely the use of the conventions of these genres and texts that creates Baron's modernist fiction and enables her to engage in a cultural critique of the national body, and especially of the place of women within it.[65]

One brief example of Baron's intertextual strategy can be seen in the short story *Genizah* ("The Book Burial"). The story appeared in two different versions. It was published for the first time in 1908, when Baron lived and wrote in Mariampol, Lithuania, and in a different version in 1922 in Palestine in the literary supplement of the paper *The Young Laborer*.[66] I have elaborated elsewhere on the differences and similarities between these two versions. Here it is important to stress that despite the radical differences between the two versions, both are based on themes of burial and renewal, death and revival, all rooted in the traditional concept of *genizah*. According to Jewish law, *genizah* is the act of burying scriptural and other sacred books that become worn, so as not to desecrate the name of God and the sacred writings (called in Yiddish *shemes*, "names").[67] The ritual also indicates that the study of Torah may be renewed and continued. On a symbolic level, the book is given a burial just like a person, which points to the revival of the books and all that they stand for.[68] However, by activating intertextual patterns of meaning, Baron's story calls attention not just to the symbolism of the *genizah* but also to the gaps between the symbolic meaning and sociohistorical reality.

For example, the story recounts a struggle of the female narrator to place her mother's *tekhineh* within the ritual of the *genizah*. The *tekhineh,*

Lahover (1934), Avraham Kariv (1939), which appear in the collection edited by Ada Pagis, *Dvora Baron: Mivhar ma'amarei bikkoret al yetsiratah* (Tel Aviv: Hakibutz Hameuhad, 1974). See also Sheila Jelen and Shachar Pinsker, introduction to *Hebrew, Gender and Modernity: Critical Responses to Dvora Baron's Fiction* (Bethesda: University Press of Marlyland, 2006).

65. Seidman, *Marriage Made in Heaven*; Lubin, "Tidbits."

66. The early version (1909) appears in Dvora Baron, *Parshiyot mukdamot* (Jerusalem: Mosad Bialik, 1988). The late version (1922) appears in Dvora Baron, *Parshiyot* (Jerusalem: Mosad Bialik, 1968). For an analysis of the difference between the two versions, see Shachar Pinsker, "Unraveling the Yarn: Intertextuality and Cultural Critique in Dvora Baron's Fiction," *Nashim* 11 (2006): 244–79.

67. See "Genizah," *Encyclopedia talmudit* 5:232–9 (in Hebrew).

68. "Raba also said: A scroll of the law which is worn out may be buried beside a *talmid hakham*" (b. Meg. 26a). See also Yehezkel Feinhandler, *Sefer ginzei hakodesh* (Jerusalem: Kiryat Sefer, 2002). I would like to thank the writer Haim Be'er who directed my attention to this book and discussed with me the issue of *genizah* and its historical and cultural significance in Ashkenazic Jewish culture.

which functions throughout the story as a metonym for women and femininity, is a genre of personal prayers composed for women and sometimes by women.[69] Iris Parush claims that the religious and cultural act of reading *tekhineh* is characterized by a strong connection to concrete experience and the mundane sphere.[70] Thus, the appearance of the *tekhineh* within the *genizah*, among the canonical and "masculine" sacred books, is perceived within the fictional universe of this story as a subversion of the cultural, social, and symbolic order.

The narrator reports about the sermon of her father the Rabbi, who speaks in front of the open grave full of books:

הרי גם הקבר הפתוח, המלא כולו ספרים. אבא עומד סמוך לקבר הוא מדבר;
קולו רועד "רבותיי:. . . היום הרי אנחנו. . . גונזים את ספר התורה שלנו. . . את כל
תשמישי הקדושה הללו. . . אלא, רבותיי, אל תהיו סבורים שלנצח יהיו כל אלה
גנוזים כאן. . . הנה יום יבוא ובא גואלנו. . . וכאן זוקף אבא את ידו פעם כלפי קבר
זה ופעם כלפי קבר אחר. אז. . . אז. . . נצא מכאן. . . ואתנו. . . ואתנו ניקח את
ספרנו אלה.

Here too is the open grave, filled to the top with books. Father is standing right by the grave. He speaks, his voice tremulous: "Friends, today we bury our Torah scroll . . . these torn prayer shawls, these holy books . . . do not imagine for a moment that they will stay buried forever. . . . For surely the day will come . . . when our Redeemer arrives (and here Father gestures toward one grave and then another) and then . . . and then . . . we will take our leave of this place, and with us . . . we will carry these books along with us too.[71]

The promise of revival that the rabbi makes in his speech prompts the narrator to describe her own imaginary version of his vision:

הריני רואה: המשיח—בוא בא! הרי הוא רוכב על סוסתו הצחורה כשהוא תוקע
בשופרו תקיעה ארוכה, תקיעה גדולה: טרו-טרו-טרו. . . ורעש גדול ייעור פתאום
בכל בתי הקברות. שלדים מתנועעים, עצמות מזדעזעות, מקשקשות, מתקרבות
אלו אל אלו, ועלה עליהם בשר, וקרם עליהם עור. הרי ערב-רב של מתים חיים.
כולם עטופים לבנים והכל פניהם כלפי מזרח. הנה גם אבא שלי, פניו נוהרים,
עיניו נוצצות, ספר תורה חבוק לו אל ליבו, והוא מנשקו ומחבקו. כשהוא קורא:
רבותיי. . . הכל קחו. . . הכל!. . . את הספרים הבלים. . . את כל הדפים הכמושים
רבותיי, את התורה שלנו. . . הנה עוברת גם אמא שלי: כמה כפופה היא אמא! כמה
שרויים הם פניה בדאגה. היא סופקת את כפיה, ובקול נמוך נמוך היא נאנחת

---

69. Chava Weissler, "The Religion of Traditional Ashkenazic Women," *AJS Review* 12 (1987): 73–94.

70. Iris Parush, *Nashim kor'ot* (Tel Aviv: Am-Oved, 2000), 70–71; Shmuel Niger, *Der pinkes* (Vilna: Kletskin, 1913), 138–85.

71. Baron, *Parshiyyot mukdamot*, 152. English translation is based on Naomi Seidman's translation in Dvora Baron, *The First Day and Other Stories* (Berkeley: University of California Press, 2001).

The Making of Hebrew Modernism 223

וטוענת: היכן היא "תחינתי"!... ליבי מתחלחל בקרבי ומוחי מתבלבל, בקשי הריני דוחקת את עצמי לבין ההמון ורצה-הביתה. דקירה עזה הריני חשה בתוך צלעי השמאלית, נשימותי נעשות תכופות מרגע לרגע, פני מזיעים, תלתלי ראשי מתנפנפים באויר—ואני רצה. הנה היא "התחינה". בקרן זוית היא מונחת, עליה פזורים, וכתמיה הצהובים בולטים כל-כך... אני חוטפת אותה וחוזרת אל בית הקברות. וכאן—הרי אבא עומד עדיין, פניו חיוורים, עיניו רטובות הן ושפתיו נעות. והרי אני סמוכה לקבר הפתוח: "טזזזז.... ככה מתלחשים עלי התחינה כשהם נוגעים בספרים הבלים שבתוך הקבר. ונדמה לי שספרים בלים אלה גוערים ומטיחים כלפי תחינה עלובה זו דברים קשים: ס-מ-ר-ט-ו-ט הלאה מכאן.

And a picture unfolds before my mind's eye. I see the Messiah, he's really come! Here he sits astride his snow-white mare, blowing a long blast on his shofar, a long blast, toot-toot-toooooot. And a great commotion breaks out in all the graveyards. Skeletons stagger about, dry bones rattling and shaking; and the bones come together, bone to bone, and the sinews and the flesh grow upon them and join together, and the skin comes together to cover them up. A throng of the living-dead; shrouded in white and all facing east.... Here is my father, too; his face radiant, his eyes sparkling, the Torah scroll pressed to his heart and he kisses and embraces it, embraces and kisses it, calling out: "Friends! Take it all, all of it... all the torn books, all the crumbling pages.... Friends, our Torah, our Torah!" Along comes my mother, too; how stooped her back is! Her face is drawn with worry. She wrings her hands and softly sighs and pleads: "Has anyone seen... my book of supplications? Where is my *tekhineh* collection? Where did it disappear to?" My heart quakes, my brain reels in confusion. I force my way through the crowd and run home. I feel a stitch in my left side, I'm panting, dripping sweat, my curls blowing wildly in the wind, but I keep running. Here's her *tekhineh*. It's lying in the corner, its pages have come loose, it's covered with yellowish stains.... I grab it and race back to the graveyard. My father is still standing there, face pale, eyes teary and lips moving. And now I'm the one who's right by the open grave. "Sh-sh-sh-sh!!!!" The pages of the *tekhineh* rustle as they touch the other worn books in the grave. And it seems to me that those torn holy books reproach the poor wretched *tekhineh*. "Filthy r-r-r-a-g! Get out of here!"[72]

On a textual level, this picture is based on the prophecy of the "dry bones" from Ezekiel 37, mixed with a pastiche of several descriptions of messianic time in Midrash and the Talmud.[73] This point in the narrative, where Baron activates several classic Jewish texts, is also the point where the modernist element takes over and becomes salient and the realist framework of the story is ruptured. Baron employs here a technique of surrealist modernism,

---

72. Baron, *Parshiyyot mukdamot*, 153–54.
73. *B. Sanh.* 90–92; *Gen. Rab.* 28; *Lev. Rab.* 27. See also Yehuda Even Shmuel, *Midreshei ge'ullah* (Jerusalem: Mosad Bialik, 1954).

manipulating subcanonical genres such as gothic tales, and mixing them with rabbinic texts.

What we find in this imaginary vision is that the promise of redemption and revival, evoked by the father-rabbi in such a "natural" conventional way, becomes much more complex and less utopian when seen through the fictional perspective of the female narrator. This critical intervention is not just, as Govrin has argued, about "the secondary place of women in traditional Jewish society."[74] In 1908, when the story was written, the concepts of redemption and revival were anything but abstract and mythological. They were loaded concepts, fraught with ideological meanings within the context of the Zionist-national revival movement. Thus, Baron signals to the readers that even in the utopian-national future, the place of the feminine and exilic *tekhineh* is endangered. Because of the symbolic logic of the *genizah*, if the *tekhineh* is not brought to a proper burial, it will not be redeemed.

In order to bring the *tekhineh* to the burial, the narrator must actively intervene; but because of the lack of closure in the story, it is never clear whether this action succeeds or fails. Baron thus highlights the question mark that hovers around the place of women—as well as both Yiddish and traditional Eastern European Jewish culture—within the newly created Hebrew-national culture: Will they also get a proper burial? Will they be revived, or remain erased and forgotten, even in the utopian national future? Will they become models for modern Hebrew and Jewish literary and cultural expression?

Reading Baron with attention to both her modernist tendencies and her intertextual strategies makes it clear that her turn to the world of the *shtetl*, as well as to the traditional forms of midrash, sermons, and *tekhinehs*, is *not* (as some critics have suggested) a forced move to the margins assigned to her by the patriarchal establishment.[75] It is an active choice that enables her to create modernist Hebrew fiction and at the same time challenge modern Hebrew culture from within.

Baron's case causes us once again to realize the peculiar situation of Hebrew literature in the first decades of the twentieth century. Unlike other national literatures, in which a woman writer needed "a room of her own," in Hebrew literature at this time the potential female writer needed not just a room (*heder*) but also a *heyder* of her own—an intensive Jewish textual education that enabled her to produce modern Hebrew texts. Baron had access to this textual universe, and she certainly had the temperament and talent to deal with it in a creative way. Her resulting intertextual

---

74. Govrin, *Hamahatsit harishonah*, 159.
75. Lily Rattok, *Haqol ha'aher: sipporet nashim be'ivrit* (Tel Aviv: Hakibbutz Hameuhad, 1994), 261–350.

engagement with traditional Jewish texts is original, modernistic, and also deeply critical.

Epilogue

> The Rabbis said: "There are no two prophets who prophesy in the same style"—and they spoke well. For where there is no individuality, where there is no new and original vision of the world, which finds its own proper idioms, there is no style.
>
> —David Fogel, 1931[76]

One of the main paradoxes of Hebrew modernism, expressed so poignantly by Fogel in a 1931 lecture he gave to an audience of Jewish women in Poland, is the fact that it forges a new subjectivity using a dialogical language, "populated" with multiple "voices" from Jewish tradition. Essential to this paradox is the sense of a radical break: of individuality, originality, and marginality, which are in and of themselves made possible by the complex engagement of Hebrew language with the Jewish textual past.

The very fact that Fogel explicitly uses a rabbinic phrase—"There are no two prophets who prophesy in the same style"—in order to articulate his modernist poetics captures this paradox quite well and is yet another example of modernist intertextual strategy which I have attempted to uncover. Fogel indicates to the reader that he is quoting a familiar rabbinic saying. However (in a manner that is actually close to Baron's intertextual practice), he quotes only part of it and leaves out important information.[77] The phrase he cites is taken from a discussion of the nature of prophecy in the Babylonian Talmud:

> אמר רבי יצחק: סגנון אחד עולה לכמה נביאים, ואין שני נביאים מתנבאין בסגנון אחד.

> Rabbi Yitskhak said: One sign [signon][78] comes to a few prophets, yet there are no two prophets who prophesy in the same style. (b. Sanh. 89a)

The context here is significant. The rabbis are attempting to establish a way to distinguish between a false and a true prophet, and the question of

---

76. David Fogel, "Lashon vesignon besifrutenu hatse'ira," Siman kri'a 3–4 (1974): 387–91.
77. See Pinsker, "Old Wine in New Flasks," 228.
78. The word signon is derived from the Greek and the Latin signum, the main meaning of which is "sign." But signon in Rabbinic Hebrew can also designate individual style, and this is how it is used in modern Hebrew. Rabbi Yitskhak's dictum plays on these two meanings.

the nature of prophetic language and style arises: Can one distinguish between false and true prophets based on their style and language? One dominant rabbinic tradition holds that the biblical prophets composed (or uttered) words that are "not theirs" but rather a representation of "someone else's" (in this case a radical "other"—God himself). And yet, according to Rabbi Yitskhak, each prophet has a singular style, which can be identified despite the similar concepts and words expressed in it, and despite the fact that the "origin" of them all is the same divine source.

Fogel's use of the rabbinic phrase in the context of his lecture is paradoxical in itself. Rejecting the poetic and ideological system of the *Nusah*, he articulates an alternative one by quoting a rabbinic phrase. Drawing on the logic of the rabbinic text, Fogel claims that no two Hebrew writers should write in the same style, even though they all draw on the same language and same "sources" of textual history.[79] From this perspective, Bialik's notion of the *Nusah* as something that can be collectively transmitted and emulated for purposes of literary representation of the nation is an absurdity within Fogel's modernist poetics.

At the same time, by using this phrase, Fogel appropriates and problematizes the romantic-national idea of the Hebrew writer as a modern prophet—a singular genius who is also "watching the house of Israel" (הצופה לבית ישראל). In his lecture, Fogel rejects this role, so prevalent in Hebrew literature and culture at the turn of the twentieth century. Instead, Fogel uses the perfect phrase that will enable him to rework the trope of the "writer as a prophet," in order to forge a radically different modernist poetics.

The very fact that the defamiliarization of the trope of "the writer as a prophet" is performed through an intertextual strategy—a modernist mutual activation of meaning by evoking a rabbinic text—exhibits Fogel's commitment to Hebrew as a "Jewish language." While simultaneously denaturalizing the nationalist, romantic, and mimetic conceptualization of Hebrew language and literature, Fogel embraces the multilayered Hebrew as a means of modernist literary expression.

No less important is Fogel's alternative historical mapping of the Hebrew literature of his period in the same lecture. He vehemently rejects "the masters of language," the writers "of prattle devoid of . . . a trace of individuality," but singles out Gnessin, Baron, Shofman, and Brenner (thus connecting himself with them) as writers whose "individuality" is the mark of "their style."[80]

As different as they may be from each other in personality, in their poetics, and in the different years and locations in which they were active,

---

79. Notice that even in order to create the analogy between the author and the prophet, Fogel uses a very common talmudic phrase, "they spoke well."

80. Fogel, "Language and Style," 390.

there are certain elements common to Gnessin, Baron, and Fogel that enable us to understand in better ways the special characteristics of Hebrew modernism. One important element is the awareness and appropriation of various poetic and ideological norms by juxtaposing different systems of discourse. Their intertextual practices are an essential part of this strategy. Employing intertextual strategies enables each writer to uncover both the conventionality and points of disjunction within various systems of discourse. They rely on the "literariness" of Hebrew and its strong dialogical-intertextual nature in order to *denaturalize* the national ideological system and its attempt to transform the "many" voices of textual Jewish history into "one"—a singular, monological "Jewish tradition." As I have attempted to show, this denaturalization is an act of literary and cultural resistance to various projects of literary and ideological integration.

It becomes clear that ideas expressed in rabbinic texts can be aptly used as expressions of radically different and even conflicting systems of discourse and belief. Such systems include gender and sexuality in the urban world of Central Europe in 1920s, and the Eastern European Jewish *shtetl* of the nineteenth century. We can find side by side ideological concepts of romantic national awakening together with the traditional Jewish affirmation of diasporic life. Each one of these writers challenges attempts to "translate" and to create a smooth transformation of rabbinic texts into a new secular national culture, be it by the effort to turn rabbinic haggadah into a folk literature, or by the foregrounding of messianic and apocalyptic elements giving them secular-nationalist interpretation.

As their intertextual practices demonstrate, Gnessin, Fogel, and Baron do not ignore the existence of folkloric or national elements in rabbinic literature. On the contrary, Fogel and Gnessin's employment of rabbinic language in order to "represent" the language of their narrators and characters uncovers the fact that "folkloric" styles can indeed be found in the rabbinic corpus.[81] The appearance of rabbinic language in the nationalist discourse of characters like Jenia and Fridin in Gnessin's story *Jenya*,[82] or Shalom-Noah in Baron's story *Gilgulim*,[83] affirms the fact that messianic and apocalyptic elements are indeed a part of rabbinic literature. However, their modernist intertextual strategies and their poetics of juxtaposition also reveal rabbinic texts as being multifaceted and dialogic. At their most basic, what all three writers expose is the use and abuse of the Jewish textual tra-

---

81. See Gnessin's story *Ktatah*, in which he uses rabbinic language and themes in order to represent market characters like Kopey Bandit (Gnessin, *Kol kitvei*, 487–98), or characters like the shoemaker Verubicheck in Fogel's novel. For a more detailed analysis, see Pinsker, "Old Wine in New Flasks," 89–106.

82. Gnessin, *Kol kitvei*, 7–43; and see Pinsker, "Old Wine in New Flasks," 49–65.

83. Baron, *Parshiyyot*, 383–411; and see Pinsker, "Unraveling the Yarn," 262–79.

dition. Because these writers lived and worked in a period of major cultural and ideological change, this exposure results in a powerful, unsettling critique—if we are ready to see it.

As I have pointed out, all three writers were considered marginal both during and in the first generation after their lifetimes, but in the last decades they have become belated prototypes for poetics and ideologies that are very different from their own. Thus, Gnessin and Fogel came to be the purported origin of secular national Israeli literature. Baron, on the other hand, is even now outside the new modernist canon. Instead, she has been imagined as a model of a feminist writer who criticizes the traditional Eastern European Jewish world by "exposing its unjust treatment of women." Alternatively, she is inadequately construed as the woman writer who withdrew into a confined corner because of patriarchal hegemony. I believe that this historical constriction must be seriously reconsidered. By focusing on various modes of intertextual dialogue with traditional Jewish literature, we can attain a better, more nuanced understanding of the outstanding project of Hebrew modernist fiction.

10

Brooklyn Am Rhein?

The German Sources of Jewish American Literature

JULIAN LEVINSON

The recent publication of Cynthia Ozick's novel *Heir to the Glimmering World*, which features an eccentric, exiled, and stubbornly devoted Jewish scholar from Berlin, suggests that the time may be ripe to reflect on the place of German Jewish culture in the Jewish American literary imagination. Ozick's fascination with the figure of the scholarly German Jew (she calls him "densely, irrevocably German")[1] brings to mind two additional recent novels: Allegra Goodman's *Kaaterskill Falls*, which examines the fate of an Orthodox community in Washington Heights, modeled on the Breuer community from prewar Frankfurt;[2] and Arthur A. Cohen's *An Admirable Woman*, which describes the travails of a German Jewish intellectual, modeled unambiguously on Hannah Arendt.[3] The German Jewish figures in these books are marked by a predilection for abstract philosophizing coupled with a peculiar intransigence of spirit. Largely absent from these characters are the familiar traits, sensibilities, and forms of self-expression that Jewish American writers from Delmore Schwartz through Philip Roth have taught us to associate with Eastern European Jews and their American offspring: these German Jews are scholars, clinging tenaciously to the Truth; not shlemiels, using their wits to navigate their way through the modern world. And while these novels focus on Germans as part of a broader agenda of addressing the Holocaust, I would propose that they are also meditations on the significance and viability of an alternate form of Jewishness, associated with prewar German Jews and their particular ways of

---

1. Cynthia Ozick, *Heir to the Glimmering World* (New York: Houghton, Mifflin, 2004), 4.
2. Allegra Goodman, *Kaaterskill Falls* (New York: Dial Press, 1998).
3. Arthur A. Cohen, *An Admirable Woman* (Boston: D. R. Godine, 1983).

engaging with the world. What can be gained by exploring this German connection? How might our overall picture of Jewish American literature be sharpened through recognizing and illuminating its dialogue with German Jewish culture? In the spirit of the higher criticism, that famous invention of nineteenth-century German philology, let us consider this a tiny adventure in modern source criticism—specifically, an inquiry into how Jewish American writers have made use of the "G" source.

Ancestral Worlds

When most critics have set out to define the characteristic tonalities and narrative strategies of Jewish American literature (read English-language texts by American Jews), they have often turned their gaze toward Yiddish—either Yiddish literature or the Yiddish language itself. In studies dating back to the 1970s, Irving Howe, Ruth Wisse, and Sanford Pinsker have traced the reemergence of the "shlemiel," or saintly fool, a stock figure from Yiddish tradition, in English writings by Nathanael West, Saul Bellow, Bernard Malamud, and others.[4] In a more recent elaboration of this argument, Janet Hadda proposes that the "soul of Ashkenaz" has transmigrated from Yiddish literature to Jewish American literature, leaving its imprint on recent work by writers such as Steve Stern, Allen Hoffman, and Pearl Abraham. Hadda claims that "[t]he issues they raise in their Anglophone voices are precisely those with which earlier Yiddish writers were grappling before the Shoah."[5] Shifting the emphasis from content to form, Robert Alter finds evidence in Philip Roth's writing of "the discursive strategies of the Yiddish-speaking ancestral world," which he cites as the sine qua non of "the Jewish voice."[6] And Hana Wirth-Nesher has called attention to the ways in which the offspring of Yiddish-speaking immigrants have forged their own voices in English, by inscribing "traces of immigrant speech into their writing, by retaining an 'accent' of ethnicity."[7] In all of these different arguments, we are invited to imagine something like a literary family tree, rooted in Eastern Europe and branching out (with more or less success) into America.

---

4. See Irving Howe, *World of Our Fathers* (New York: Harcourt, 1976); esp. Ruth Wisse, *The Schlemiel as Modern Hero* (Chicago: University of Chicago Press, 1971); Sanford Pinsker, *The Schlemiel as Metaphor: Studies in Yiddish and American Jewish Fiction* (Carbondale: Southern Illinois University Press, 1971).

5. Janet Hadda, "Imagining Yiddish: A Future for the Soul of Ashkenaz," *Pakn Trager* 41 (2003): 19.

6. Robert Alter, "The Jewish Voice," *Commentary Magazine* 100 (1995): 43.

7. Hana Wirth-Nesher, "Traces of the Past: Multilingual Jewish American Writing," in *The Cambridge Companion to Jewish American Literature* (ed. Michael P. Kramer and Hana Wirth-Nesher; Cambridge/New York: Cambridge University Press, 2003), 114.

The emphasis on the Yiddish roots of Jewish American writing is not, of course, without warrant. It makes sense sociologically—the majority of American Jews trace their own roots to the Yiddish-speaking East—and it goes some distance toward illuminating the distinctive cast of many Jewish American texts, many of which are indeed infused with immigrant accents and populated by stock figures from Yiddish literature. Moreover, it has the merit of providing at least one stable criterion for establishing the "Jewishness" of a text written in a non-Jewish language: what makes a Jewish American text "Jewish" is the way it recalls the Eastern European past. The usefulness of such a criterion should not be underestimated, especially as the effort to define a canon of modern Jewish literature has become increasingly relevant to American Jewish self-definition. Witness, for example, the proliferation of Jewish literary anthologies, Jewish book clubs, and Jewish reading series, not to mention the landmark project of the National Yiddish Book Center to name to "100 greatest works of modern Jewish literature." Yet this emphasis on Yiddish has limitations. Most clearly, it tends to collapse the category of "Jewish" into that of "Yiddish," reifying the specific arrangements and cultural styles of Eastern European Jewish life (generally nineteenth-century Jewish life) as authentic Jewishness. As dynamic and vibrant as this culture unquestionably was, when seen in the context of the long dureé of Jewish life, its specific expressions must be finally seen as only one among any number of possible "Jewish" cultural formations.

Furthermore, this emphasis on Yiddish origins tends to reinforce the tendency to plot the history of Jewish literature as a narrative of inevitable, mournful decline. As Jewish American writers grow more and more distant from what Alter names the "Yiddish-speaking ancestral world," their very connection to Jewishness must become attenuated. Thus, Howe notes in the same breath that the Yiddish culture of immigrant Jews is fading and that "American Jewish fiction has probably moved past its high point."[8] And, as though it required no explanation, Alter concludes that "Roth's language of course cannot have the historical range of Mendele's."[9] The view that surfaces, in short, is of Jewishness as an ever more diffuse identity, dependent for its survival on a specific ethnic heritage and a specific set of communal structures with weakened traction in America.

How does such a view transform when we read Jewish American writers not only as heirs of Yiddish writers but also as participants in a dialogue with German Jewish culture? If the "Y" source might be said to inflect English-language writing through its accents and tonalities, what about the "G" source? As a preliminary consideration, we must acknowledge that, generally speaking, the conditions of Jewish life in German-speaking

---

8. Irving Howe, ed., *Jewish-American Stories* (New York: New American Library, 1977), 16.
9. Alter, "Jewish Voice," 44.

regions of Europe (particularly from the period of the Emancipation through the Weimar era and particularly in urban areas) militated against the formation of the same kind of "thick" Jewishness that we find among Eastern European Jews. Even without subscribing to the fantasy that Eastern European Jews inhabited entirely insular communities, barely touched by the gentile world, we can say that Jewish communal structures maintained a greater degree of autonomy in the East than they did in the West. Indeed, the language, rituals, and even "sensibility" of modern German Jews could, and in many cases did, become unmoored from traditional Jewish sources, so much so that it was possible for a German-born Reform rabbi named Bernhard Felsenthal to write in 1890, after immigrating to America: "Racially, I am a Jew. But spiritually I am a German, for my inner life has been profoundly influenced by Schiller, Goethe, Kant, and other intellectual giants."[10]

But while such a sentiment confirms one of the received views of German Jewry as devoted above all to asssimilationism, we must also consider the more *productive* aspects of this encounter between Jews and German culture. Here I am following the work of Ismar Schorsch, who has described the dynamic, ongoing struggles of German Jewish philosophers, historians, and theologians to "accommodate consciously an ancient, non-Western religion to the inescapable consequence of a radically new legal status without destroying its sense of integrity and continuity."[11] Indeed, from Samson Raphael Hirsch's *Nineteen Letters on Judaism* through Heinrich Graetz's eleven-volume *History of the Jews* through Martin Buber and Franz Rosenzweig's Bible translation and adult education projects in the 1920s, a common effort might be discerned to reformulate and defend Judaism in the face of (and in the language of) the surrounding Christian majority.[12] A common approach in the work of these extremely varied figures (and many more besides) involves the effort to distill an "essence of

---

10. Quoted in Stephen J. Whitfield, "Declarations of Independence: American Jewish Culture in the Twentieth Century," in *Cultures of the Jews*, vol. 3, *Modern Encounters* (ed. David Biale; New York: Schocken, 2002), 381–82.

11. Ismar Schorsch, *From Text to Context: The Turn to History in Modern Judaism* (Hanover, NH: Brandeis University Press, 1994), 256. In addition to Schorsch, another historian whose work lies behind my reflections in this essay is Michael Brenner, whose work on the "Jewish Renaissance" in Weimar Germany emphasizes the creative dimension of German Jewish culture; see Michael Brenner, *The Renaissance of Jewish Culture in Weimar Germany* (New Haven: Yale University Press, 1996). These works provide an important corrective to the received view of prewar German Jews as craven assimilationists.

12. Samson Raphael Hirsch, *Neunzehn Briefe über Judentum* (Altona: J. F. Hammerich, 1836); in English, *Nineteen Letters on Judaism* (trans. Bernard Drachman; New York: P. Feldheim, 1960). Heinrich Graetz, *Geschichte der Juden von den ältesten Zeiten bis auf die Gegenwart: aus den Quellen neu bearbeitet* (11 vols.; Leipzig: O. Leiner, 1853–76); in English, *History of the Jews* (trans. Bella Löwy; 6 vols.; Philadelphia: Jewish Publication Society of America, 1946).

Judaism"—a distinctive set of tenets or propositions that sets Judaism apart from other worldviews. As we will see, this project of distilling an essence of Judaism—often linked to an underlying "Jewish Idea"—will speak directly to the needs of Jewish literary artists in America in several generations, who confront mutatis mutandis a similar set of challenges.

Recovering the Jewish Soul

One way to track the relevance of German Jewish culture for Jewish American writers is to consider the important role played in their education (*Bildung*?) by Heinrich Graetz, parts of whose history were available in English as early as 1867. If history has become "the faith of fallen Jews" (in Yosef Hayim Yerushalmi's formulation),[13] we might say that it was precisely this ersatz faith that inspired Jewish writers from Emma Lazarus to Cynthia Ozick, both of whom have identified Graetz as a decisive influence. Lazarus began versifying under the star of her mentor Ralph Waldo Emerson only to fashion herself as a forcefully partisan Jewish poet when a wave of pogroms swept through Russia in the 1880s. In order to raise the Jewish consciousness of her co-religionists, she published a number of poems and essays in journals such as the *American Hebrew* and the *Jewish Messenger* impugning anti-Semitism and celebrating the heroism of Jews who have defended their "Golden Truth" throughout history and amidst the most brutal kinds of oppression. Among these "Jewish" works were a parable adapted from the Talmud and transcribed into blank verse ("The Birth of Man"); a long narrative poem based on a fifteenth-century epistle from a loyal Jew to his former master, who became a bishop after conversion ("An Epistle from Joshua Ibn Vives of Allorqui"); a verse tragedy about the martyrdom of the medieval Jews of Nordhausen ("The Dance to Death"); and a host of poems about Jewish figures from Bar Kokhba to Rashi. In such works, Lazarus creates a series of exemplary characters, archetypal Jewish heroes whose inner fortitude and devotion are proffered as a model for contemporary Jews.

Nearly all of her material, as well as her overall conception of Jewish history, comes directly from Graetz, whom she read under the tutelage of a Reform rabbi who arrived from Posen to serve as pulpit rabbi for New York's Temple Emanuel. Referring to Graetz, Lazarus later wrote that she was "firmly convinced ... of the truth of the axiom that a study of Jewish history is all that is necessary to make a patriot of an intelligent Jew."[14]

---

13. Yosef Hayim Yerushalmi, *Zakhor: Jewish History and Jewish Memory* (Seattle: University of Washington Press, 1982), 84.

14. Emma Lazarus, *An Epistle to the Hebrews* (ed. Morris U. Schappes; New York: Jewish Historical Society of New York, 1987), 8.

What made Graetz so serviceable for Lazarus was his construal of Judaism through the broadly Romantic vocabulary with which she was already familiar. There is, from this perspective, an underlying "Jewish Soul," which reveals itself most clearly at moments of crisis. For Graetz, following the original theorists of the *Wissenshaft des Judentums*, Judaism could be reduced to a single idea, one that in Hegelian fashion is brought to "maturity" and revealed through the processes of history. "If we survey Judaism in its broad outlines," Graetz wrote in 1849, "and if we remove the husk from the grain—the productive ideas from the gross facts—we would come upon the original vital impulses that are implicit in the very idea of Judaism."[15] For Graetz, this idea of Judaism was first expressed as a protest against paganism: "It is precisely to negate [the idea of paganism] . . . that constitutes Judaism's predestined vocation: to show the paucity of truth in paganism and its harmful effects on social morality."[16] Jewish history becomes from Graetz's perspective a continuous battle between worldviews in which Judaism figures at once as endangered minority and as challenger.[17] The "outer life" of Judaism is a history of suffering at the hands of an intolerant majority (the pagan world slips into Christendom in his narrative), while the "inner history" is a history of scholarship, pious devotion, and the sheer refusal to capitulate.

Interestingly, Graetz was also a devoted champion of Heinrich Heine, a pioneering Jewish writer in a non-Jewish language and also one of Lazarus's favorite poets (she published a book of Heine translations in 1882). In his writings on Heine, Graetz may have provided Lazarus with a means of conceptualizing her own work as part of a recognizably Jewish tradition. Graetz looked to Heine first and foremost as the consummate Jewish opponent of Christendom, as somebody whose veins were "imbued with true Jewish spirit," in spite of his apostasy. Heine's renunciation of Judaism was not true apostasy, Graetz proposed, but rather like the covert acts of "combatants who, appropriating the enemy's uniform and colors, can all the more easily strike and annihilate him."[18] With this portrait of Heine as combative Jewish poet, "hiding out" in the German language,

---

15. Heinrich Graetz, "Constructions of Jewish History," in *Ideas of Jewish History* (ed. Michael Meyer; Detroit: Wayne State University Press, 1988), 221–22.

16. Ibid., 222.

17. Graetz himself played a key role in the struggles of German Jews against the new waves of anti-semitism that appeared in late-nineteenth-century Germany. During the very years that Lazarus was reading his history, he was engaged in heated disputes with the historian Heinrich von Treitschke over the alleged anti-Christian sentiments in his work See Susannah Heschel, "Jewish Studies as Counter History," In *Insider/Outsider: American Jews and Multiculturalism* (ed. David Biale, Michael Galchinsky, and Susannah Heschel; Berkeley: University of California Press, 1998): 107.

18. Graetz, *History of the Jews*, 5:536.

Graetz interestingly anticipates various contemporary theories that link minority writing to complex and subversive forms of mimicry and underhanded critique.[19] For Lazarus, a newly self-aware American Jew writing in English, this overall notion must have been empowering indeed. Graetz's view of the Jew as defiant Other to Christendom, assailing its pieties from within, is indeed a guiding premise for a number of Lazarus's poems—from "The Crowing of the Red Cock," in which she impugns the "long role of Christian guilt" throughout the centuries to "The Guardian of the Red Disk," a dramatic monologue from the perspective of a Christian anti-semite, whose hypocrisy is plainly revealed for all to see.[20] Thus, Lazarus, in her explicitly Jewish poems, collected in a volume called *Songs of a Semite*, employs a set of tropes traceable to Graetz.[21] As she followed his lead, she opened a space for subversive Jewish self-expression within American literature.

Ludwig Lewisohn, arguably the most influential Jewish literary artist of the 1920s, also found a way of conceptualizing Jewishness by reading German Jews. Born in Berlin, Lewisohn came to America in 1890 at the age of eight, settling with his family in Charleston, South Carolina. The early trajectory of his life seemed destined to lead him toward total assimilation: by his early adolescence he considered himself a Christian and a Southern-gentleman-in-the-making.[22] Like Lazarus, however, he journeyed from the distant margins of Jewish cultural life into its center, and by the mid-1920s he had become a self-appointed spokesman to an American Jewish community he perceived as spiritually ailing and psychologically self-deluded. His message—which he hammered home in diverse works including the autobiography *Up Stream*, a volume of reportage entitled *Israel*, and the novel *The Island Within*—was that assimilation crippled the Jewish soul, that it was a false promise extended by the intractably anti-semitic modern nation state.[23] He sought to rouse American Jews to recover and reassert their Jewishness, which he associated not so much with any particular set of practices or rituals, but with an inherently moral stance and tendency to

---

19. See, e.g., Gilles Deleuze and Felix Guattari, *Kafka: Toward a Minor Literature* (trans. Terry Cochran; Minneapolis: University of Minnesota Press, 1986); Henry Louis Gates, *The Signifying Monkey: A Theory of African-American Literary Criticism* (Oxford/New York: Oxford University Press, 1989).

20. *Emma Lazarus: Selected Poems and Other Writings* (ed. Greg Eiselein; Orchard Park, NY: Broadview Press, 2004).

21. Emma Lazarus, *Songs of a Semite* (New York: Office of "The American Hebrew," 1882).

22. See Ralph Melnick, *The Life and Work of Ludwig Lewisohn* (2 vols.; Detroit: Wayne State University Press, 1998).

23. Ludwig Lewisohn, *Up Stream: An American Chronicle* (New York: Boni and Liveright, 1922); idem, *Israel* (New York: Boni and Liveright, 1925); idem, *The Island Within* (New York: Harper & Brothers, 1928; repr., Syracuse: Syracuse University Press, 1997).

defy the status quo (hence the image of moving "up stream" becomes the title of his autobiograhy). As he explains in his final book, *The American Jew: Character and Destiny*, Jews are destined to meet the resistance of the "pagan world" for the "single moral and metaphysical reason that [they] by their very existence have issued to the world the challenge of righteousness."[24]

Lewisohn developed his understanding of Jewish difference in the first place by reading Jewishness through German Romantic concepts like the "national spirit" and "the soul of the folk," traceable to thinkers like Johann Gottfried Herder. His views developed further through his reading of Freudian psychoanalysis and Zionism, which he considered two pillars of a single Jewish protest against assimilation. He writes:

> [It is not] without its special and high significance that Vienna, where Jewish assimilation has produced its richest fruits, is also the city whence arose with Theodor Herzl the movement of political Zionism and with Sigmund Freud that science of analytical psychology which city whence arose with, though applicable to all men, is first of all an effort on the part of the Jewish people to heal itself of the maladies of the soul contracted in the assimilatory process.[25]

Vienna is for Lewisohn a laboratory for the experiment of Jewish assimilation, and the results demonstrate its impossibility. Psychoanalysis, according to this reading, is indeed the "Jewish science," closely allied to Zionism insofar as it returns assimilated Jews to their abiding, though repressed, Jewishness. Both psychoanalysis and Zionism are also deeply moral cultural projects, in Lewisohn's view: if Jews issue in their very existence "the challenge of righteousness," the lifting of barriers to Jewish self-expression necessarily strengthens the forces of justice. The struggle to liberate the "inner Jew" thus has broad social and political implications for the world at large.

Lewisohn's novel *The Island Within*, widely considered his most successful fictional work, represents his effort to imagine this "Viennese" motif of Jewish return within the context of American life. The narrative traces a gradual attenuation of Jewish faith and identity through four successive generations. The first breach comes in 1840 in Vilna, where the patriarch Mendel is lured by the early stirrings of the Haskalah; his son Efraim takes a further step, moving with his wife to the Prussian city of Insterburg to seek his fortune as a brandy distiller; and his son, Jacob, makes what appears to be the final gesture of assimilation, emigrating to America,

---

24. Ludwig Lewisohn, *The American Jew: Character and Destiny* (New York: Farrar Straus, 1950), 168.

25. Ludwig Lewisohn, *Mid-Stream* (New York: Boni and Liveright, 1929), 123.

where he prospers as the owner of a department store. The hero of the fourth generation, Arthur Levy, has married a Gentile "new woman" of the 1920s and become a successful New York psychologist. As if drawn by an unconscious need to understand his lost Jewishness, he gravitates toward the new field of Freudian psychoanalysis. In a moment of insight, he discovers the key to his patients' (and his own) psychic maladies in their desperate efforts to hide from their Jewishness: "Flight from experience. . . . Yes, the mechanism of the Jewish anti-Jewish complex was precisely analogous to the mechanism of insanity. . . . He felt this urge toward flight himself, flight away from a reality that had no inner meaning, from a burden that seemed irrational."[26] Levy sees no option for himself but to reconstitute his past, a resolution that leads him to Graetz's *History of the Jews*. In Graetz, Levy perceives "gleams of a dim grandeur," and when he encounters a long lost relative, Reb Hacohen, he suddenly gains access to the lost world of Jewish tradition. Hacohen, it turns out, needs a psychiatrist for an American commission to investigate anti-Jewish violence in Rumania. He enlists Levy, who, once again like Lazarus, seizes the opportunity to return to "his people" via philanthropic labor. In the novel's final passage, we read of Levy's newfound certainty that "the sky curved over him like a tent against the outer darkness and that the earth which his foot trod was his natural habitation and his home."[27] He has been saved from the turmoil of psychic alienation, having found refuge, like the Israelites in the desert, in the security of a "tent."

Writing in different genres and in the face of different challenges (the Russian pogroms in one case, the rise of American nativism in the 1920s in the other), Lazarus and Lewisohn both center their work on the notion of an indelible Jewish soul. Their specific formulations of this notion (which, after all, can be found variously articulated throughout the history of Judaism) draw upon German Jewish models, specifically the work of Graetz. In the period after World War II, this dialogue between Jewish American writers and their German predecessors continues, even as the patently Romantic formulations of Lazarus and Lewisohn will be displaced by other emphases.

The Postwar Theological Imagination

The period after World War II has been commonly associated with the rise of a new generation of Jewish writers (Saul Bellow, Alfred Kazin, Isaac Rosenfeld, Bernard Malamud, Grace Paley, Philip Roth, etc.), whose

---

26. Lewisohn, *Island Within*, 141.
27. Ibid., 266.

particular combination of vitality, critical acumen, and angst has often been attributed to their precarious position between the Yiddish-speaking immigrant past and an American present to which they were only partly reconciled. The sensibilities of these writers have been linked to the broader tradition of "Yiddishkayt," associated with the socialist and humanist traditions of Eastern European Jewry. But alongside these figures and making their mark somewhat later (in the 1960s, say, rather than the 1950s), there emerged another group of writers of a somewhat different cast of mind, for whom Judaism as a religion had remained or had become once again a live issue. Among these writers we might include Arthur A. Cohen, Cynthia Ozick, and Chaim Potok, each of whom introduces an unambiguously *religious* dimension into Jewish American writing. The "Jewish" dimension of their writing, to put it another way, cannot be adduced from the "voice" they use or from their overall ethos, so much as from the concrete ideas they propound and defend. And while the difference between Bellow-Malamud-Roth and Cohen-Ozick-Potok might be simply chalked up to a difference between secular and religious worldviews, we might refine this view and distinguish them according to the different Jewish traditions they engage with, the difference sources for their writing. Once again, we may be able to discern a difference here between a "Y" source and a "G" source.

Let us begin with Arthur A. Cohen, a brilliant and largely underappreciated figure who was at once theologian, art critic, novelist, anthologist, and a writer of intricate, aphoristic essays of Judaism. After a first book on Martin Buber, Cohen wrote *The Natural and the Supernatural Jew*, an ambitious theological study placing German Jewish thinkers from Mendelssohn to Franz Rosenzweig alongside American Jewish thinkers from Mordecai Kaplan to Will Herberg. Cohen's central project here is to reconcile the existentialist emphasis on human freedom with the traditional Jewish emphasis on the authority of revelation and tradition. His guiding thesis involves the distinction between the "natural Jew," grounded in an empirical, historical situation, and a "supernatural Jew," who "exercises his freedom to intend Transcendence."[28] Every Jew, Cohen proposes, contains both aspects, though the "natural" Jew might forget his "supernatural" vocation, which is his true role in history. Where Lewisohn faults assimilated Jews for *repressing* their indelible Jewish selves, Cohen warns against *forgetting* what links the Jew to eternity: "the natural Jew, enmeshed in the historical, cannot help but despair."[29] The vocabulary has shifted from psychoanalysis to existentialism, but what has remained is the notion of an abiding Jewishness that stands in need of being recovered.

---

28. Arthus A. Cohen, *The Natural and Supernatural Jew* (New York: Pantheon Books, 1962), 6.
29. Ibid., 313.

For Cohen the key figure in Jewish thought was Rosenzweig, the one-time student of Hegelian philosophy who famously recommitted himself to Judaism in 1913 on the verge of conversion. In 1967 Cohen wrote: "I regard Rosenzweig as a personal model, moreover as an appropriate model for contemporary Jewry. The question of Judaism was raised by him as a fresh problem, as an almost unheard of, improbable claimant to human attention."[30] In his essay "Franz Rosenzweig's The Star of Redemption: An Inquiry into its Psychological Origins," first published in 1972, Cohen speculates on how the dialectic between the natural and supernatural Jewishness played itself out in Rosenzweig's lived experience growing up in a highly assimilated family in Cassel, Germany. A key role, Cohen argues, was played by Rosenzweig's uncle Adam, a mysterious Orthodox Jew who lived with the Rosenzweig family. Uncle Adam, Cohen speculates, was "a witness to a reality remembered, lived but untransmitted.... Uncle Adam was the immediacy of the Jewish world."[31] This formulation points to a tension pervading Cohen's own work: the Jewish world is present but enigmatic, a possible form of allegiance without any rationale or structure of transmission. When Franz first departed for school in 1893, this uncle seized him in both arms, shook him violently and said emphatically "my boy you are going among people for the first time today; remember as long as you live that you are a Jew." Cohen speculates that this must have been a formative experience for Rosenzweig, the first time anyone suggested to him the invisible gulf dividing Jews and Gentiles in German society.

Rosenzweig's delineation of the messianic dimension of Judaism in *The Star of Redemption* impresses itself deeply on Cohen's complex novel *In the Days of Simon Stern*, a key text in American Holocaust literature. Written from the perspective of a blind, oracular narrator named Nathan, it recounts the emergence of a possible Messiah during the 1940s in New York. The messianic figure Simon Stern (whose name is a translation of Simon Bar Kokhba, while also evoking Rosenzweig's "Star") receives news of the death camps and determines that "now is the time to begin the work of redemption."[32] He travels to Europe and retrieves a group of Holocaust survivors, a saving remnant whom he houses in a version of Solomon's Temple, rebuilt on Manhattan's Lower East Side. The messianic project self-destructs, however, as if in confirmation of the wisdom behind the rabbinic injunction against "forcing the end." Nevertheless, the novel's narrator assures us that the possibility of redemption remains ever-present. The character of Simon Stern, Cohen suggests, is a *failed* Messiah, not a *false*

---

30. David Stern and Paul Mendes-Flohr, eds., *An Arthur A. Cohen Reader* (Detroit: Wayne State University Press, 1998), 143.

31. Ibid, 16.

32. Arthur A. Cohen, *In the Days of Simon Stern* (New York: Random House, 1973), 86.

one, meaning that what was missed was in fact an entirely real possibility. The novel is thus at once playful and profoundly serious in its declaration of faith in Judaism's redemptive mission. Inspired by Rosenzweig's formulation of the messianic idea (and drawing also on Gershom Scholem's work on Shabbtai Zevi), Cohen sets out to construct what he calls a "messianic epic"—a novel based on the premise that human history remains open to the incursion of the divine.

Cohen's close friend and associate Cynthia Ozick has similarly sought to develop a form of narrative discourse centered on a central "Jewish Idea." If for Cohen the Jew is fundamentally a witness to the fact that the world is unredeemed (and still awaits a redeemer), for Ozick, the Jew is above all a witness to the dangers of idolatry. "The single most useful, and possibly the most usefully succinct, description of a Jew—as defined theologically, can be rendered negatively: a Jew is someone who shuns idols."[33] By idolatry, she means in particular something she variously names "the religion of Art" or "aesthetic paganism."

In her much-discussed essay "Towards a New Yiddish" (1971), in the course of an extended rant against Jewish New Leftists, Ozick offers Allen Ginsberg as an example of a Jewish writer who subscribes to fundamentally un-Jewish ideas. In particular, Ginsberg is guilty of seeking through art the "mystical unknowingness of 'psychedelic consciousness.'"[34] The literary text, in Ginsberg's hand, becomes a portal out of history, into ecstasy, and, crucially, away from any possible covenant with God. "When man is turned into a piece of god," she writes, "he is freed from any covenant with God."[35] Authentically Jewish writers, by contrast, bear witness in their work to the reality of the covenant. Their work issues not from the drive toward mystery but from what she calls the "reciprocal moral imagination." It must bear witness to history, to what can happen and what has happened, to the function of individual agency, and finally the possibility of *teshuvah*, which she glosses as a narrative moment, a "turning." It should be noted, however, that most of her own works focus not so much on such turnings as on the failures of individual Jews to achieve them. Consider the protagonists of *The Cannibal Galaxy* and *The Messiah of Stockholm*,[36] who appear to be marked out for great things and who seem to be embarked on a path toward higher truths, but who end up psychically shriveled, victims of their ultimate blindness. Ozick's narratives tend to be cautionary tales, pointing toward the Jewish Idea through its negation.

---

33. Cynthia Ozick, *Art and Ardor* (New York: Knopf, 1983), 186.
34. Ibid, 163.
35. Ibid.
36. Cynthia Ozick, *The Cannibal Galaxy* (New York: Knopf, 1983); eadem, *The Messiah of Stockholm* (New York: Knopf, 1987).

Whereas Cohen borrows his Jewish Idea from Rosenzweig, Ozick has suggested that it is Leo Baeck's essay "Romantic Religion" that stands behind her conception of Judaism. As she told one interviewer, Baeck's essay, "which I read at twenty-five, seemed to decode the universe for me."[37] Baeck defines a "romantic religion" as one in which "tense feelings supply the content, a romantic religion seeks its goals in the now mythical, now mystical visions of the imagination."[38] Such a religion is entirely distinct from Judaism, which Baeck calls a "classical religion," structuring behavior in accordance with law. Baeck's definitions in this essay—indeed, the very terminology—move into Ozick's essay, specifically in her attack on Ginsberg and his new left colleagues. Moreover, Baeck's polemic against Romanticism will resurface throughout Ozick's fiction. In her story "The Pagan Rabbi," for example, the promising rabbinical student is called a "closeted romantic," and we watch as he is seduced and destroyed by the rhapsodizing, mystical impulse associated with "romantic religion." Even though Ozick's fictions have often been associated with the "magical realist" vein running through I. B. Singer and Bernard Malamud, we can see that her overall conception of Judaism, which informs all of her work, employs the theological categories animating the tradition running through Herman Cohen and Baeck.

My contention here, once again, is that when we hear these Jewish American writers grappling with the notion of a single "Jewish Idea"—and trying to construct a "Jewish" literary discourse around this "Idea"—we have begun to tread upon German territory. The very notion that a culture might be distilled into an "Idea," and that this Idea would exist in a state of conflict with the Ideas of other peoples, is in large measure a legacy of German Romanticism, and even when we hear, as in the case of Baeck, an explicit polemic against Romanticism, this basic conception of culture remains in place. Baeck's signature theological work was, after all, called "The Essence of Judaism." One of the great projects of German Jewish thought, from the period of civic emancipation through the rise of the Third Reich, was to explain and justify the continued existence of Judaism by appealing to some sort of essence, whether tied to the Idea of monotheism or that of the possibility of redemption. It is not surprising, then, to find Rosenzweig behind Cohen's formulations and Baeck behind Ozick's.

A final word should be added here about Chaim Potok, one of the best-selling Jewish American novelists of all time and yet someone whose sensibility veers sharply away from that of Bellow, Malamud, or Philip Roth.

---

37. Joseph Lowin, *Cynthia Ozick* (Boston: Twayne, 1988), 16.
38. Leo Baeck, "Romantic Religion," in *Judaism and Christianity* (trans. Walter Kaufmann; Philadelphia: Jewish Publication Society of America, 1958), 108.

In terms of "voice" or literary style, Potok's greatest debt is owed to Ernest Hemingway.[39] At the same time, it is arguably possible to learn more about Judaism—its sacred texts, theological positions, and different forms of expression—from Potok than from any other Jewish American novelist. What Potok presents in his novels, indeed, is not only what he experienced from his youth in Brooklyn, but everything he learned on his way to becoming ordained as a rabbi from the Jewish Theological Seminary of America. "I went to JTS," he has explained, "not to become a rabbi, but to become an educated Western Jew, not an Eastern European Jew, a Western Jew in the sense of a deep scientific knowledge in traditional texts."[40]

Potok's overall conception of Judaism and Jewish history reflects the very same premises we saw in the work of Heinrich Graetz. Like Graetz, Potok views Jewish history as the scene of ongoing conflict with surrounding cultures and divergent worldviews. "We are a people with a long history of cultural warfare," Potok explained to an interviewer. "Four thousand years of culture wars. The first was with the culture of the river civilizations in the Near East. . . . We were then involved in a culture war with Greek and Roman paganism . . . [then with] Christianity and for a period of time, with Islam. . . . We are now involved in a fourth culture war and that is with secular humanism."[41] This idea of conflict, vividly manifest in the famous baseball scene that introduces *The Chosen*,[42] is also related to growth (the Graetzian view is, after all, linked to Hegel). Thus, Potok's great theme is the way Judaism endures and transforms through interaction with the outside culture through one of its defining expressions: in *The Chosen* the conflict is with Freudian psychoanalysis; in *My Name Is Asher Lev*, it is with visual art; and in *In the Beginning* it is with the higher criticism of the Bible.[43] In each case, the conflict of worldviews issues in a transformed, but nonetheless vital, form of Judaism.

Most illuminating for our purposes is Potok's decision to name the warring Yeshivas in *The Promise* after two of the giants of German Jewish thought.[44] Reuven Malter attends the Samson Raphael Hirsch Yeshiva, where he studies Talmud with a staunchly Orthodox Holocaust survivor. But he learns about text criticism, the notion that different editions of the Talmud must be brought to bear on its interpretation, at the Zechariah

---

39. This observation was compellingly made by Potok's fellow writer and associate Hugh Nissenson in a memorial lecture given at the University of Pennsylvania.
40. Daniel Walden, ed., *Conversations with Chaim Potok* (Jackson: University of Mississippi Press, 2001), 175.
41. Ibid., 9.
42. Chaim Potok, *The Chosen* (New York: Simon & Schuster, 1967).
43. Chaim Potok, *My Name Is Asher Lev* (New York: Knopf, 1972); idem, *In the Beginning* (New York: Knopf, 1975).
44. Chaim Potok, *The Promise* (New York: Knopf, 1969).

Frankel Seminary, where he studies in spite of his professor's protestations.[45] What the novel restages here is the debate between Hirsch, the father of neo-Orthodoxy, and Frankel, whose notion of a "Historical Judaism" marks the beginnings of what would become Conservative Judaism. Reuven ultimately embraces the historical method of Frankel, even as he resolves to teach in the graduate school named for Hirsch. Conservative Judaism is valorized by the text, even as homage is paid to the rigors of the Orthodox.

One key question remains to be asked: What happens when Potok (or any of the other figures we have considered) imports these German Jewish theological quandaries to America? How does the conflict between Hirsch and Frankel restaged in *The Promise* transform when it is restaged in a narrative that takes place in postwar Brooklyn? My suggestion is that there remains a distinctly *American* dimension to these German-inspired writers. It comes through in the implicit idea within their work that the "cultural warfare" between Jewish and non-Jewish cultures, or between different tendencies within Judaism itself, might also be read as a symbol for the growth of the individual—any individual, Jewish or not. If all of these writers seem to be inspired by a "promise," it is not only the promise offered to Abraham by God in Genesis ("I will make of thee a great nation"). It is also, implicitly, a promise offered by America that individual selfhood can be crafted and won. And so insofar as America exists as a tacit frame of reference for these writers, it offers hope that the struggles of German Jews to define and sustain themselves as Jews might now reach a new kind of fruition. The Jewish Idea, formulated in Germany, may be further developed in America, or at least that is what these writers seem to suggest.

Conclusion

A little over forty years ago the esteemed Bible scholar Samuel Sandmel once expressed a certain impatience with a tendency he found in biblical criticism.

> I confess to becoming weary of a typical Ph.D. exercise: the discovery of sources alleged to exist in documents. Stated absurdly, the premise behind such studies, now that biblical scholarship is at least 160 years old, seems to be that nobody ever wrote anything: he only copied sources. . . . What Philo tells he got from the rabbis; what Jesus taught, he got from the rabbis; what Paul taught, he got from the rabbis or the Wisdom of Solomon.[46]

---

45. For a discussion of Frankel and "historical" Judaism, see Schorsch, *From Text to Context*, 253–65.
46. Samuel Sandmel, "The Haggada Within Scripture," *JBL* 80 (1961): 108.

My proposal here is that when it comes to the study of Jewish American literature, precisely the opposite is true, namely, that we might benefit from just such an emphasis on "sources." As we have seen, the story of influence traced through Yiddish reads as a story of dwindling inheritance. Writers from the second or third generation after immigration might still hold onto enough of the "world of their fathers" to inscribe its traces in their work; but eventually the legacy will run dry. On the other hand, if we emphasize "sources" we can see that Jewish writers in one cultural situation might self-consciously apprentice themselves to other Jewish cultures that experienced similar challenges. The responses developed by one set of Jewish thinkers and writers might then be adapted, refined, and reapplied. This model of Jewish cultural production can help us work against the tendency to imagine a historical trajectory marked by inevitable decline.

What our group of Jewish American writers develops from German Jewish sources is the notion of a Jewishness associated primarily with ideas (ethical monotheism, exile, anti-idolatry, etc.) rather than with ethnic styles. Their writing styles reveal little of the overall feeling or "voice" of "Yiddishkayt," instead, their texts explicitly argue in favor of a set of ideas defined as Jewish. This German-American connection should not be particularly surprising, of course. Having confronted the challenge of reconceptualizing Jewishness in the face of a Protestant majority in a non-Jewish language, German thinkers from Graetz to Rosenzweig generated a storehouse of images and rhetorical forms that could be borrowed and adapted by Jewish literary writers facing similar challenges in America. When the historian Michael Meyer concluded his study of German Jewish thought, *The Origins of the Modern Jew*, he proposed that the American Jew of his day was engaged in the same quest for Jewish self-definition that Mendelssohn and his successors had engaged in. "It remains to be seen," he added, "whether [the American Jew] will be able to draw significant content from the Jewish tradition to shape a uniquely Jewish identity."[47] What he may not have realized and what our tiny adventure in source criticism suggests is that one of the "Jewish traditions" that Jewish American writers have drawn on is precisely the one contained in—or, rather, constituted by—the writings of German Jewish thinkers from Hirsch to Graetz to Baeck to Rosenzweig.

---

47. Michael A. Meyer, *The Origins of the Modern Jew: Jewish Identity and European Culture in Germany, 1749–1824* (Detroit: Wayne State University Press, 1967), 182.

11

Diaspora and Translation

The Migrations of Jewish Meaning

NAOMI SEIDMAN

After surviving the Warsaw Ghetto and the camp at Vittel, my father was in France when the Second World War ended. Oddly enough, he had been raised in a Hasidic household wealthy enough to have had a French governess; he also studied French history in Warsaw in the 1930s in the course of his Ph.D. work. His French was thus nearly as good as his Yiddish (though his accent was so thick that my father joked that he spoke Yiddish in five languages), uniquely suiting to serve as an unofficial liaison between the French authorities and the refugee community pouring into Paris after the war. One morning not long after Liberation, my father was called to the train station, where the police were holding a group of Jewish refugees who had managed to cross three or four borders without any documents. The scene in the station was chaotic, the refugees were upset and exhausted, and my father asked the police if he could speak with the group. *"Yidn, hot nisht keyn moyre. Di politsei zenen avade goyen, aber zey zenen nisht natsim—gornisht shlekht vet geshen."* Don't be afraid, he reassured them. While the French were certainly *goyim*, they weren't Nazis; nothing bad would happen to them. My father explained to the group that he would keep track of where they were taken and the Jewish community of Paris would arrange for their release as soon as possible.

One of the police officers, curious about my father's rapid-fire Yiddish exchange with the crowd, asked him what he had said to calm them. Thinking fast, and thinking in French, my father "translated" his Yiddish words for the policemen: "I quoted to them the words of a great Frenchman: 'Every free man has two homelands—his own, and France.' I assured them that they, who had suffered so much, had arrived at a safe haven, the birthplace of human liberty." As my father told it, the *gendarmes* wiped away patriotic tears at his speech.

I begin with a translation story, rather than with theoretical considerations, to make the point that translation is usefully understood through the lens of narrative, which insists on the relevance of the cultural, material, and political conditions of its production. But is this indeed a translation narrative? Without assuming that this story is exemplary of Jewish translation, I would like to suggest that it opens a number of approaches to that question. In arguing that it is "a basic fact of [Yiddish] that it has a differentiation language," Max Weinreich has provided us with the tools to analyze my father's words to the refugees: Ashkenazic Jewishness, Weinreich writes, "was not 'general' German life plus a number of specific supplementary traits, but a distinct sphere of life, a culture system."[1] The psychic separation of Jews from non-Jews expressed itself in many linguistic features, most manifestly in that category of vocabulary called *lehavdl loshn*: "there are words applied to Jews (or even neutrally, when no differentiation is intended), and these have a parallel series that has to begin with a derogatory connotation or one of disgust." Chief in this parallel series is the word *goy*, its derivations, and its semantic relatives—*shkotzim, shikses*, and so on. My father, then, in using the word *goyim*, was invoking the entire culture system Weinreich describes, one that sharply distinguishes between the realm that is "ours" and the realm that belongs to "them."

Weinreich appends to his discussion of this *lehavdl loshn* a remark of some relevance to my father's story:

> Since the rise of the secular sector the function of the differentiation language became even more variable, more dependent on the situation and the linguistic context. All in all, among very large segments of the community the entire category of differentiation language is now no longer in vogue, except for special purposes of stylization.[2]

A person capable of producing the French speech I have quoted here was certainly also capable of drawing upon a neutral vocabulary for referring to non-Jews—Weinreich mentions *nit-yidn* as a nonderogatory alternative; no doubt, my father took advantage of these alternatives in other contexts. It is significant, then, that in speaking to the refugee group, he *chose* the traditional *lehavdl loshn* rather than a neutralized secular code. Weinreich's suggestion that a secularized or modern Jew might take recourse to Yiddish's *lehavdl loshn* for purposes of stylization is not entirely illuminating here; nor does the story give us reason to suppose that my father particularly meant to denigrate the French policemen. Any disparagement

---

1. Max Weinreich, *The History of the Yiddish Language* (trans. Shlomo Nobel; Chicago: University of Chicago Press, 1973), 185.
2. Ibid., 195.

implied by his language must have been secondary to his main purpose, which was to reassure the group of refugees that his intentions toward them were entirely friendly. If my father mobilized the differentiation resources of Yiddish, it was to signal to the group that he was a real Jew, one of "us" rather than a neutral player on the deracinated urban field. My father's words were thus a speech act, *doing* something with words rather than merely communicating information. Indeed, the performative quality of his Yiddish speech transcends the word to which I have directed attention. Beyond the content of what he was saying, beyond the choice of the word *goyim*, and before the vocative, "*Yidn*," my father's Galicianer Yiddish was itself performing his Jewish affiliations, announcing where he came from and where his sympathies could be assumed to lie. Speaking Yiddish has been described as the construction of a portable Yiddishland, and my father could be said to be clearing a shared Jewish space—indeed, given the dialectical variation within Yiddish speakers, *constructing* a shared space—within the public arena of the European metropolis. Yiddish, in such speech acts, has a meta-value, signifying in itself—in its distinctive sounds rather than in its communicable content; it is a discourse, we might say, in addition to being a language. The implications for translation of such an understanding of language are ominous: if the very use of Yiddish is a form of signification, if the sound and intonations of the language have pride of place in the act of communication, then the usual techniques of translation—focused as they are on the transmission of "content"—can hardly begin to operate.

The untranslatability of languages, insofar as they are ethnic codes, does not, however, entirely exhaust the meaning of the translation narrative I am presenting here. My father's Yiddish speech is not simply difficult or impossible to translate into other languages; he clearly didn't *want* to translate it, whether or not he could have. My father's translation performance, his refusal to translate, must be understood in the context of the scene at the train station: he spoke in the presence of the very embodiment of state authority (a state that, in the not too distant past, had collaborated in anti-Semitic activity), the French police. Against the "merely" semiotic differentiation enacted by Yiddish we must range the political power of the French state apparatus to differentiate between refugees and citizens, foreign aliens and new immigrants. It is within this power structure that my father's Yiddish remarks must be calibrated. From this point of view, these remarks belong to what James C. Scott calls the "hidden transcript," the secret communication of a subjugated group, in contrast to the public transcript, that is, the official histories as the record of what can be said in the presence of power. Scott argues that "slaves, serfs, untouchables, the colonized and the subjugated ordinarily dare not contest the terms of their subordination openly. Behind the scenes, though, they are likely to create and defend a social space in which offstage dissent to the official transcript of power relations may be voiced."[3]

In the case we are discussing here, my father's words to his fellow refugees are delivered not "behind the scenes" but rather in very earshot of the authorities. As in other examples Scott cites, the hidden Jewish transcript here involves a direct, nonobsequious evaluation of the power structure on which the survival of the subjugated group depends. It is in the very nature of such communication that it not enter the public arena—French, in this case. Although Weinreich never states this explicitly, *lehavdl loshn* could be construed as necessarily such a hidden transcript, available to the Yiddish-speaking community if only for letting off steam, but never to be uttered before non-Jews who might understand it; the presence of Hebrew elements in *lehavdl loshn—beys hatifle* (slightly changing the vocalization of the Hebrew phrase *beys hatfile*, house of prayer, to mean house of folly) for church, *oyso ha'ish* (literally, that man) for Jesus, is further evidence that the language of differentiation was intended to be concealed. Mistranslation, then, is the crucial device that allows this transcript to remain hidden. My father's signaling of his Jewish affiliation in the Yiddish words, and his open evaluation of the dangers to the refugee group posed by their arrest by the French police, can hardly be separated from his refusal to render this speech transparent in translating it into French.

And what of my father's French remarks? In speaking French to the police, my father was also performing, signaling a different set of affiliations: he was a foreigner, that much could hardly be denied, but an educated foreigner, whose knowledge of French extended to French history and who respected the ideals on which modern French society was based. This performance, unlike the Yiddish, built a bridge across ethnic lines, both in my father's very use of a language that was not his and in the words he spoke, that subtly recommended compassionate behavior by reminding the police, in flattering ways, of the ideals of French Enlightenment rhetoric. It is tempting to read my father's French remarks as a mere cover for the authentic speech he addressed to his fellow Jews, but I think that would negate the insight that his Yiddish remarks were *also* strategically chosen, and ultimately for the same ends as the French speech. Moreover, my father's French was as unintelligible to the Yiddish speakers he addressed as his Yiddish was to the French speakers. They may also have been untranslatable into Yiddish. The words he chose to express the role of France in bringing democracy to the world were precisely those that would have the least resonance in the experience of Yiddish speakers: what could the sentence "Every free man has two homelands—his own, and France" possibly mean to someone who lacked even a single homeland?

---

3. James C. Scott, *Domination and the Arts of Resistance: Hidden Transcripts* (New Haven: Yale University Press, 1990), xi.

The gap my father exposed as he concealed between Yiddish and French, and between French and Yiddish, is no ordinary translation gap among others. What is inexpressible or irrelevant in Yiddish are the very philosophical and political grounds for translation as universal communication. As Tejaswini Niranjana writes, "Translation has traditionally been viewed by literary critics in the West (at least since the Renaissance) as the noble task of bridging the gap between peoples, as the quintessential humanistic enterprise."[4] Aleida Assmann similarly views the modern impulse toward translation as emerging from the eighteenth-century "enlightened philosophers who invented universalistic concepts like 'natural law,' 'common notions,' 'lumen naturale,' or 'reason.'"[5] In suggesting by his translation performance that this universalist discourse was, in fact, properly French, my father implicitly exposed a chasm at the heart of the very enterprise of translation. Jewish experience serves here as the limit case for the dream of the mutual transparency of cultures in the light of humanism and reason. Indeed, Jewish languages have historically played that role: Austria's 1781 Edict of Tolerance reversed the Jewish Regulations (*Judenordnungen*) and granted Jews "completely free choice of all non-civic branches of commerce . . . and wholesale trade" on the condition that they refrain from using Hebrew or Yiddish in the commercial sphere. As Article 15 proclaims: "Considering the numerous openings in trades and manifold contacts with Christians resulting therefrom, the care for maintaining common confidence requires that the Hebrew and the so called Jewish writing of Hebrew intermixed with German . . . shall be abolished."[6] Toleration to Jews might be granted, but the edict suggests that as long as the relationship between Jews and non-Jews continued to lack "common confidence," Jewish languages could not be welcomed into the family of European languages as equals—or to put it into translation terms, as "linguistic equivalents."

There is of course a third level of linguistic performance implicit in this story, that of its retelling as a translation narrative in which both languages are rendered visible—either in Yiddish version, as my father initially related the story, or in its later (partially) English version, as I am rendering it here. These rewritings, or retranslations, belong to a number of genres: they serve as autobiographical allegory, stories that represent identity as split, multiple, or shifting. They are also trickster tales, boasting of the

---

4. Tejaswini Niranjana, *Siting Translation: History, Post-Structuralism, and the Colonial Context* (Berkeley/Los Angeles/Oxford: University of California Press, 1992), 47.

5. Aleida Assman, "The Curse and Blessing of Babel; or, Looking Back on Universalisms," in *The Translatatibility of Cultures: Figurations of the Space Between* (ed. Sanford Budick and Wolfgang Iser; Stanford: Stanford University Press, 1996), 95.

6. Joseph II, "Edict of Tolerance," in *Jewish Emancipation: A Selection of Documents by R. Mahler* (ed. and trans. Raphael Mahler; New York: American Jewish Committee, 1941), 19.

successful manipulation of a power with more official authority and fewer linguistic gifts at its disposal. In its boasting, my father's story draws the listener in on the joke, allowing her to share the narrator's privileged position above the monolingual dupes in the story. It must surely have been part of my father's pleasure in telling the story that he could now share with his family both sides of who he was as he could not have in the train station; it was certainly part of my pleasure in hearing it to feel superior to the adults — policemen! — on the platform. As a boast, we may fairly be skeptical of its faithfulness — did my father really call the French policemen *goyim*? Did he use the word Nazis, which they might have been able to pick out of the rush of Yiddish words? The medieval Jewish–Christian disputations in Paris, we might recall, produced two separate linguistic records, in Latin and in Hebrew, each declaring victory for its own side.[7] The Hebrew account, in particular, is full of devastating and witty Jewish ripostes to the Christian disputants that would no doubt have spelled death to any disputant who had actually dared to utter them.[8] In the safety of one's own language, and over one's own dining room table, history itself is translated as it is rewritten.

I have postponed asking the question of whether my father's story can be taken as illustrative of certain principles of Jewish translation — indeed, whether it counts as a translation narrative at all. Weinreich helps make the case that Yiddish discourse is centrally constituted by its capacities for differentiation — that is, by what might be seen as its untranslatablity. But such differentiation language, Weinreich implies, also characterizes Talmudic Aramaic, from which the Yiddish usage of *goy* derives (in the Bible, *goy* simply means nation). In *The Periodic Table*, Primo Levi describes (and translates) a similar code for discussing, for instance, the realm of Christianity in his own Jewish dialect of Italian. As Levi writes,

> In this case, the originally Hebraic form is corrupted much more profoundly [than in the case of codes used in commercial settings], and this for two reasons: in the first place, secrecy was rigorously necessary here because their comprehension by Gentiles could have entailed the danger of being charged with sacrilege; in the second place, the distortion in this case acquires the precise aim of denying, obliterating the sacral content of the word, and thus divesting it of all supernatural value.... *A-issá* is the Madonna (simply, that is, "the woman"). Completely cryptic and indecipherable — and that has to be foreseen — is the term *Odo*, with which, when it was absolutely unavoidable, one alluded to Christ, lowering one's voice

---

7. Thibaut de Sezanne, ed., *Extractiones de Talmut* (Paris, 1242); in English, see Hyam Maccoby, ed. and trans., *Judaism on Trial: Jewish-Christian Disputation in the Middle Ages* (Rutherford, NJ: Fairleigh Dickinson University Press, 1982).

8. Jehiel of Paris, "Vikuah Rabbenu Yehiel mepariz," in *Otsar vikukhim* (ed. Judah D. Eisenstein; New York: Hebrew Publishing Company, 1922), 81–86.

and looking around with circumspection; it is best to speak of Christ as little as possible because the myth of the God-killing people dies hard.⁹

This identification of Jewish languages with a hidden transcript is not absolute, even in Weinreich's generalizing terms: In a striking translation performance, Weinreich uses Tertullian's injunction that "Christians may live together with non-Christians, but it is not allowed to die together with them," precisely to illustrate Jewish cultural separatism: "Jews could not separate themselves from Christians, nor did they always think very much about this possibility; but they fought shy of Christianity with might and main. 'You have chosen us from amidst all the nations,' to paraphrase Tertullian's formulation. Jews lived among Gentiles, but not with them."¹⁰ Even in discussing Jewish cultural distinctiveness, Weinreich demonstrates the permeability of linguistic and religious borders. Translation, as that liminal cultural space, both exposes and unsettles the notion of cultural difference.

The resistance to translation, as Weinreich implies, may in fact be a widespread phenomenon, an unavoidable by-product of cultural identity in its differentiating mode. George Steiner suggests as much in *After Babel*, denying the commonsense notion that the function of language is primarily to communicate. Arguing that "mature speech begins in shared secrecy," Steiner hypothesizes the following narrative for the genesis of language:

> In the beginning the word was largely a pass-word, granting admission to a nucleus of like speakers. 'Linguistic exogamy' comes later, under compulsion of hostile or collaborative contact with other small groups. We speak first to ourselves, then to those nearest us in kinship and locale. We turn only gradually to the outsider.¹¹

Whatever one makes of this as a history of the development of language, Steiner provides a useful corrective to the assumptions that cultures inevitably aspire to be translated and that translators aim to be accurate. Such an aim, universalist in its trajectory, is itself far from universal. It does, however, exist within Jewish culture, just as there are many instances of non-Jewish resistance to translation. The Jewish-Hellenistic philosopher Philo, for instance, writes of his satisfaction that the Septuagint provided access to the Torah in the Greek tongue, so that "those admirable, and incomparable, and most desirable laws were made known to all people."

---

9. Primo Levi, *The Periodic Table* (trans. Raymond Rosenthal; London: Abacus Books, 1986), 11.
10. Weinreich, *History of the Yiddish Language*, 185.
11. George Steiner, *After Babel: Aspects of Language and Translation* (3rd ed.; Oxford/New York: Oxford University Press, 1998), 242.

Philo goes on to hope that if the reputation of the Jews continues to grow, "every nation, abandoning all their own individual customs, and utterly disregarding their national laws, would change and come over to the honour of such a people only."[12] And although I have suggested that my father's enlightenment speech was paradoxically untranslatable into Yiddish, I am reminded that he did translate it for the benefit, although perhaps not for the enlightenment, of his family. Evidence that Yiddish is perfectly capable of rendering a universalist, if not universal, message is very nearly coextensive with the history of modern Yiddish literature.

Nevertheless, I would argue that this story stands well within the mainstream of Jewish translation discourse, even if does not pinpoint its essential nature. If rabbinic literature has a foundational narrative of Jewish translation, it would have to be the talmudic account—itself a reworking of earlier Hellenistic and patristic accounts, Philo's included—of the translation under Ptolemy of the Bible into Greek, an event of world-altering dimensions both within and outside the Jewish community: Philo as well as the church fathers viewed this event as the providential beginning of God's communication with all of humankind; at least some rabbis, by contrast, viewed it as a cosmic catastrophe, writing that "on the day the Bible was first translated into Greek, the world went dark for three days" (*Massektot ketannot soferim* 7). The rabbinic sense of the consequences of this translation draw upon midrashic conceptions of language as having a world-creating, and thus inevitably also a world-destroying, force—the speech-act to end all speech-acts. The account of the translation itself, related in *b. Megillah* 9a and elsewhere, is marked, less cosmically, by an ambivalence about the translation project, which is viewed as forced upon an unwilling group of Jewish elders:

> King Ptolemy assembled seventy-two elders and placed them in seventy-two rooms, without telling them why he had brought them together, and he went in to each of them in turn and said to them: "Translate for me the Torah of Moses your Teacher." God put an idea in each of their hearts and they all agreed on the same idea and they wrote out for him "God created in the beginning," and "Let me make man in the image and form," etc. (*b. Meg.* 9a)[13]

In the continuation of this passage, the Talmud lists another dozen or so passages that the Jewish elders rendered strategically, rather than in the most straightforward way, in order to avoid theological or political misunderstandings (for instance, translating "Let us make man," in God's

---

12. Philo, *Mos.* 2.43–44 (trans. Charles D. Yonge, *The Works of Philo* [Peabody, MA: Hendrickson, 1993], 494).

13. All unattributed translations are my own.

speech in Genesis 1:26 as "Let me make man," to avoid the implication that God is a plural noun). It might be more accurate to say, in fact, that it was not misunderstandings of the Bible that the translators were avoiding but rather its understanding, which is reserved for Jews alone. *Megillah* tells us, then, that the first Greek translation of the Bible is, with God's miraculous intervention, not a perfect translation—as Philo and the fathers view it—but rather a perfect mistranslation, in which the rabbis come up with the same mistranslations despite being in separate cells.[14] God himself is invested in, indeed is a full participant in, the privacy of Jewish discourse, at least at thirteen strategic translation cruxes in the Hebrew Bible. The world, with Ptolemy's guidance, has the Bible, but it does not exactly have the Torah, and for Jews that has made all the difference.

The notion that not only the integrity of Jewish culture but also Jewish political survival somehow depends on strategic mistranslation continues to our own day: in the 1998 film *Life Is Beautiful*, Guido, the Italian-Jewish protagonist, mistranslates a concentration camp guard's German orders for the sake of his young son, who is hiding among the inmates; in this case, the mistranslation prevents a murderous discourse from entering a Jewish realm rather than safeguarding Jewish secrets. In these three narratives, my father's, the Talmud's, and the scenario played out in *Life Is Beautiful*, secrecy, linguistic opacity, double-talk and mistranslation are linked with the integrity of the borders of the Jewish community in the face of external threat. In his essay "On Translating Homer," Matthew Arnold writes: "Probably [all] would agree that the 'translator's first duty is to be faithful'; but the question at issue is, in what faithfulness consists."[15] Fidelity, in the sort of translation conducted under the watchful eye but uncomprehending ear of an Egyptian king, an SS guard, or even a benign *gendarme*, means faithfulness to one's embattled community rather than to any abstract ideal of linguistic equivalence.

In focusing on translation performances that are shaped by asymmetrical relations between cultures rather than essentially symmetrical relations between languages, I am indebted to the work of postcolonial translation studies. This subfield is often said to begin with the groundbreaking publication of Tejaswini Niranjana's *Siting Translation: History, Post-Structuralism and the Colonial Context*. Exploring the Indian translational arena, Niranjana argues that translation cannot be understood outside of the trajectories of capitalism, Christian missionary movements, and

---

14. Referring to this story of the miraculous mistranslation of the Bible, my father would joke that the real miracle would have been if seventy-two rabbis sitting in the *same* room had produced a single version.

15. Matthew Arnold, *On Translating Homer* (London: Smith, Elder, 1896), quoted in Willis Barnstone, *The Poetics of Translation: History, Theory, Practice* (New Haven: Yale University Press, 1993), 41

European imperialism: A close reading of colonialist texts encourages us to recognize that translation "comes into being overdetermined by religious, racial, sexual, and economic discourses."[16] In particular, Niranjana is interested in "the question of the historical complicity in the growth and expansion of European colonialism in the nineteenth and twentieth centuries of those interested in translating non-Western texts (for example, missionaries engaged in spreading Christianity) and those involved in the study of 'man.'"[17] That such colonialist discourses are also operative in the heart of Europe, and long before the nineteenth century, is evident from a footnote in Niranjana's text, in which she warns us that "We must not forget . . . that the concept of the humanistic enterprise is enabled by the repression of heterogeneity *within* the 'West.' Imperialism allows the West to conceive of the other as *outside* it, to constitute itself as a unified subject."[18] If Niranjana is right about the utility of the repression of the heterogeneity within the West precisely to the humanistic enterprise of translation, then Jews become paradoxically central to Western translation in the suppression of their difference. Jews are refigured in this conception not only as untranslatable figures—we might say, unconvertible to Christianity—but also as the very site of untranslatability.

This formulation, however, does not exhaust the position of Jews in Western translation. Jews are the target of Christian missionary hopes, but they are also the source of Christian genetic anxieties stemming from the historical reliance of the church on the texts, and indeed on the translations, of a rival religious group. Alongside the colonized status of Jews in Christian Europe we must also set a variety of other relationships, including, in the case of Hellenistic Alexandria, a Jewish approach to translation that bears a distinct resemblance to the model of universal translatability of which Niranjana is so skeptical. In developing an approach to Jewish translation, or to translation in general, it might be worthwhile to lay out the material, cultural, and discursive conditions of translation Niranjana rightfully insists on and allow them to determine the shape of the story, whether as a narrative of negotiating power imbalances or as a dream of bridging human differences—or, as in the case of my father's story, as both at the same time. Such an approach would insist that translation stories are not merely epiphenomena to the true stuff of translation, the relationship between source and target texts, methods of achieving equivalence, obstacles to achieving equivalence, etc. The narrative approach to translation, as I implied at the beginning of this essay, would insist rather that translation cannot be separated from the circumstances of its production, that it

---

16. Niranjana, *Siting Translation*, 21.
17. Ibid., 47–48.
18. Ibid., 47 n. 1 (emphasis original).

in fact represents an unfolding of those conditions. Translation more particularly appears as a negotiation of an unavoidably asymmetrical *double-situatedness*. As such, it both complicates and is informed by issues of identity. Because translation is necessarily also a political negotiation, it appears not strictly as a linguistic exercise but also in a variety of relational modes: translation not only as colonialist, imperialist, or missionary appropriation but also translation as risk, as assimilation, as treason, as dislocation, as survival. There are no absolutely neutral borders between languages, and certainly not between Jewish and non-Jewish languages; traversing these borders, then, must involve the translator and the translated culture in the vicissitudes of history itself. Jewish translation is the history of Jewish border crossings, from the island of Pharos in Ptolemaic Alexandria (if not earlier) to the passport-less refugees in post-Liberation Paris.

Once one takes translation as a form of movement (as etymological understandings of translation in fact do), then the Yiddish-French translation comes into focus as a translation whose truth resides in the story it tells, rather than in the "accuracy" of its linguistic transfer. My father's translation can provide us with a personal map of a particular set of intellectual influences (that is, his Hasidic upbringing and his doctorate in French history), as well as a more general strategy for the series of border crossings my father made alongside his fellow refugees (from postwar eastern or Central Europe, through Paris, to the United States). In this reading, what my father said in Yiddish and what he said in French are equally true, equally faithful to who he was, and equally illuminating of a journey he (and his first Yiddish audience) took, first in post-Liberation Paris and then again in his subsequent retellings of this story and indeed in my own.

Translation narratives, then, are temporal narratives, drawing our attention to the fact that translations unfold within time, paralleling and as part of our mortal lives. In an otherwise famously difficult essay on translation, Walter Benjamin makes this much absolutely clear: translations are part of the life of an original text, or rather of its "afterlife." Benjamin writes: "In its afterlife—which could not be called that if it were not a transformation and a renewal of something living—the original undergoes a change."[19] The original changes not because of any necessary loss, or deliberate concealment, but rather because it participates in the movement that is the necessary correlative of a text being alive. If we call this movement, in the case of Jews and their texts, diaspora, and resist as Benjamin does the rhetoric of loss, then Jewish culture emerges as a continual translation and transformation, in different languages and at different moments in time.

---

19. Walter Benjamin, "The Task of the Translator," in *Illuminations* (ed. Hannah Arendt; trans. Harry Zohn; New York: Schocken, 1969), 71.

The notion of translation as transformation steers clear of the assumption that translation must proceed through a strict equivalence, a fidelity to original sources, if it is not to risk their absolute betrayal; transformation assumes rather that translation, as André Lafevere argues, is one mode of "rewriting."[20] Jewish literature is everywhere a phenomenon of this sort of self-translation. And once one realizes that translation unsettles the distinction between Jewish and non-Jewish languages, such a process of self-transformation overflows the borders of Jewish life itself. Christianity, in a sense, is the product of just such an overflow.

The notion of translation as a dimension of diaspora, and thus, of Jewish history, might be illustrated by a characteristically intertextual passage in Sholem Aleichem's *Tevye der Milkhiger*. In this chapter, *Lekh lekho*, Tevye relates the story of his expulsion from his hometown through a translation, a rewriting, of the Genesis story of God's telling Abraham to leave his hometown. Tevye begins his sad story by asking Sholem Aleichem which *parsha* he's reading this week: "*Vayikra? Bey mir get eyn ander sedre: di sedre lekh-lekho*" (Vayikra? I'm on a different portion entirely—on *Lekh lekho* or Get out).[21] In linking his story to the third portion of Genesis, and to the practice of reading through the Pentateuch on a yearly cycle, Tevye suggests that his life, and perhaps all of Jewish life, is a repetition of what has already been written in the Torah. But Tevye goes on to translate the Hebrew words of the Genesis portion into Yiddish, that is, to give the *taytsh*—which means both the meaning and the Yiddish rendering—in a bitter mimicry of traditional Jewish pedagogical techniques.[22] But Tevye's *taytsh* is far from a literal one:

> *Lekh lekho—hot men mir gezugt—do zolst aroysgeyn, Tevye, meartsekho—fun deyn land, umemoyladitkho—un fun dayn dorf, vu du bist geboyrn un upgelebt ale deyne yorn, el ha'arets asher ar'ekho—vuhin di oygen veln dikh trogn!*[23]

> *Lekh lekho*—they said—get out, Tevye, *me'artsekho*—of your country, *umemoyladitkho*—and of your village, where you were born and grew up and lived your entire life, *el ha'arets asher ar'ekho*—to wherever your eyes carry you!

Even within the purely Jewish discursive space of a Yiddish conversation between Sholem Aleichem and Tevye the Dairyman, there are multiple

---

20. The term is elaborated in André Lafevere, *Translation, Rewriting and the Manipulation of Literary Fame* (New York/London: Routledge, 1992).
21. Sholem Aleichem, *Gantz Tevye der milkhiger* (New York: Morgen-Freyheit, 1937), 200.
22. In my elementary school, this portion was the first one taught to beginning students, though Tevye, as a boy, would probably have been introduced to the Pentateuch through the portion of *Vayikra*, precisely the one he rejects as the correct portion in his exchange with Sholem Aleichem! I want to thank Anita Norich for pointing this out.
23. Aleichem, *Gantz Tevye*, 200.

modes of translation at play. It would be fair to say that the meaning of Tevye's remarks emerges from the gaps between his Hebrew sources and Yiddish "translations," just as my father's story, told and retold in Yiddish and English, derives its significance from the space *between* its discursive moments. Homi Bhaba has characterized the site of translation as central rather than peripheral to cultural creativity: "it is in the 'inter'—the cutting edge of translation and negotiation, the *in-between* space—that carries the burden of the meaning of culture."[24] Translation, navigating between repetition and difference, mimesis and parody, well describes the movement that connects the traditional Jew with a biblical source text while registering the disparities between the exalted biblical world and its belated and fallen counterpart. In translating the providential order of God to Abraham into a harsh Czarist decree, Tevye suggests both that the Bible is his eternal guidebook and that this guidebook must point in new and unforeseen directions. Tevye's words here are both translation and mistranslation, and the notion of equivalence can hardly account for the resonances between source and target texts—the fact that Tevye translates God's showing Abraham the land he must go to into his own having to go where his eyes carry him. Tevye's translation insists that his own situation cannot be read outside its biblical source text, and that the biblical text must be reread in the light of his own situation: only an attention to the in-between space can tell this Jewish story. Thus Tevye's expansive, we might say midrashic, reading of *memoyladitkho*, enables us to see, in the light of Tevye's expulsion from Anatevka, the pathos of God's decree to Abraham; if Tevye implies that the czar acts like a God, he also suggests that God acts something like a czar. In the simultaneity and dissonance that connect and divide the lives of the patriarchs and their namesakes in the Pale of Settlement, a narrative emerges of the Jewish attachments to texts and displacements from homelands—that is, of Jewish history. Jewish literature and culture are the afterlives not only of the Bible (itself, of course, a translation), but also of our own continual translations and retranslations of ourselves, from Ur to Cana'an, Alexandria to Anatevka, Paris to New York and Berkeley.

---

24. Homi Bhaba, *The Location of Culture* (New York/London: Routledge, 1994), 38.

AUTHORS' BIOGRAPHICAL INFORMATION

Kalman P. Bland is Professor of Religion and Jewish Studies at Duke University, a medievalist focused on Jewish intellectual history. His publications include *The Artless Jew: Medieval and Modern Affirmations and Denials of the Visual*.

Gabrielle Boccaccini is Professor of Second Temple Judaism and Christian Origins at the University of Michigan. He is the author of many books and articles on the intellectual history of ancient Judaism. Among the recent books he has edited are *The Origins of Enochic Judaism* (2002), *Enoch and Qumran Origins* (2004), and *The Early Enoch Literature* (forthcoming).

Yaron Eliav is the Jean and Samuel Frankel Associate Professor for Rabbinic Literature and Jewish History in Late Antiquity at the University of Michigan. His most recent book is *God's Mountain: The Temple Mount in Time, Place, and Memory* (2005).

Martha Himmelfarb is Professor of Religion at Princeton University. Her most recent book is *A Kingdom of Priests: Ancestry and Merit in Ancient Judaism* (2006).

Julian Levinson is the Samuel Shetzer Associate Professor for American Jewish Studies at the University of Michigan. He has published articles on Jewish American literature, Yiddish poetry, and representations of the Holocaust in film and literature. His forthcoming book is entitled *Exiles on Main Street: Jewish American Writers and American Literary Culture*.

Dan Miron, a scholar in the fields of Hebrew and Yiddish literary studies, has published about forty books and monographs. He is currently the holder of the Leonard Kaye chair for Hebrew and Comparative Literature at Columbia University.

Anita Norich is Professor of English and Judaic Studies at the University of Michigan. She is the author of *Discovering Exile: Yiddish and Jewish Amer-*

ican Culture during the Holocaust (forthcoming), *The Homeless Imagination in the Fiction of Israel Joshua Singer* (1991) and co-editor of *Gender and Text in Modern Hebrew and Yiddish Literatures* (1992).

Michael Satlow is Associate Professor of Early Judaism at Brown University. He is the author of *Creating Judaism: History, Tradition, Practice* (2006) and *Jewish Marriage in Antiquity* (2001), and has written extensively on issues of gender, sexuality, and marriage among Jews in antiquity.

Shachar Pinsker is Assistant Professor of Hebrew Literature and Culture at the University of Michigan. He recently co-edited (with Sheila Jelen) the book *Hebrew, Gender, and Modernity: Critical Responses to Dvora Baron's Fiction* (2007). His forthcoming book is *The Making of Modernist Hebrew Fiction: 1900–1930*.

Moshe Rosman teaches Jewish history at Bar-Ilan University in Israel. His most recent book is *How Jewish Is Jewish History?* (2007).

David Ruderman is Joseph Meyerhoff Professor of Modern Jewish History and Ella Darivoff Director of the Center for Advanced Judaic Studies, University of Pennsylvania. His latest book is *Connecting the Covenants: Judaism and the Search for Christian Identity in Eighteenth-Century England* (2007).

Gabriella Safran is Associate Professor of Slavic Languages and Literatures at Stanford University. She is the author of *Rewriting the Jew: Assimilation Narratives in the Russian Empire* (2000) and the co-editor with Steven Zipperstein of *The Worlds of S. An-sky: A Russian Jewish Intellectual at the Turn of the Century* (2006).

Naomi Seidman is Koret Professor of Jewish Culture at the Graduate Theological Union in Berkeley. Her first book, *A Marriage Made in Heaven: The Sexual Politics of Hebrew and Yiddish*, appeared in 1997, and her second, *Faithful Renderings: Jewish-Christian Difference and the Politics of Translation*, in 2006.